Other Lives

MW00803534

Other Lives

Mind and World in Indian Buddhism

SONAM KACHRU

Columbia University Press

New York

Published with the support of
The Ludo and Rosane Rocher Foundation

Columbia University Press wishes to express its appreciation
for assistance given by the Office of the Associate Dean for Arts and Humanities
of the University of Virginia in the publication of this book.

Columbia University Press
Publishers Since 1893
New York   Chichester, West Sussex
cup.columbia.edu
Copyright © 2021 Columbia University Press
All rights reserved

Library of Congress Cataloging-in-Publication Data
Names: Kachru, Sonam, author.
Title: Other lives : mind and world in Indian Buddhism / Sonam Kachru.
Description: New York : Columbia University Press, 2021. |
Includes bibliographical references and index.
Identifiers: LCCN 2020054758 (print) | LCCN 2020054759 (ebook) |
ISBN 9780231200004 (hardback) | ISBN 9780231200011 (trade paperback) |
ISBN 9780231553384 (ebook)
Subjects: LCSH: Dreams—Religious aspects—Buddhism. | Sleep—Religious aspects—
Buddhism. | Consciousness—Religious aspects—Buddhism. | Vasubandhu—
Criticism and interpretation.
Classification: LCC BQ4570.D73 K33 2021 (print) | LCC BQ4570.D73 (ebook) |
DDC 294.3/442—dc23
LC record available at https://lccn.loc.gov/2020054758
LC ebook record available at https://lccn.loc.gov/2020054759

Cover design: Lisa Hamm
Cover image: Detail from the *Gaki-zoshi* (*Scroll of the Hungry Ghosts*),
handscroll, color on paper, 26.8 × 138.4 cm. Late Heian period (late twelfth
century). National Treasure, AK 229. Kyoto National Museum.

FOR JANE,

JANMĀNTARE 'PI NIDHANE
'PY ANUCINTAYĀMI

The main cause of a philosophical disease—is a one-sided diet: one nourishes one's thinking with only one kind of example.

—Ludwig Wittgenstein, *Philosophical Investigations*

It was like the case of a man who has dozed off in his daytime in the midst of a large group of people and while asleep sees a celestial city with beautiful mansions appearing there in his dream, and sees the whole summit of the polar mountain, with groves and gardens, with innumerable nymphs all around, innumerable godlings living there, and various celestial flowers scattered about, and sees wish-fulfilling trees providing various celestial garments, jewel ornaments, and flower garlands, and sees musical trees producing all kinds of sweet celestial sounds, and many kinds of forms of pleasure and diversion, and hears the sweet sounds of the music and singing of the heavenly nymphs, and perceives himself as being there, seeing the adornment of the celestial arrays all over the place. The group of people who are there in the same place do not see this, are not aware of it, do not observe it, because it is the vision of the man in his dream, not the vision of the group of people in the same place. In the same way the enlightening beings . . . by unhindered contemplation of all the spheres of knowledge of enlightening beings saw the inconceivable power and mastery of the Buddha.

—"Entry into the Realm of Reality," in *The Flower Ornament Scripture*
(translated by Thomas Cleary)

CONTENTS

ACKNOWLEDGMENTS

I think often of what Apollonius said to Euxenus. Before committing my thoughts to paper, I too should have liked "to practice silence for a long time, reading more," particularly as I've come to feel all too well the truth of the (Chinese) Buddhist saying that I've picked up from Michael Nylan, "Open your mouth and you've made a mistake" (*kaikou biancou*). Where I haven't, I owe it to others.

My principal debt remains to my advisors at the University of Chicago: Daniel A. Arnold, Steven Collins, and Matthew K. Kapstein. Though no longer with us, Steve has been a keenly felt presence throughout the making of this book, and beyond. I no longer always feel as if he is reading over my shoulder. Instead, I like to think that some of the time I have been speaking with him.

My debts to Wendy Doniger are too many to list. I'll say just this: during the defense of my qualifying paper, she asked me whether I really meant to call *The Twenty Verses* enigmatic and if so, why. This book, born in that conversation, offers a belated and inarticulate answer.

Acknowledgments make me anxious. I can't bear thinking that I've left anyone out. I here list those who over the years have helped shape my thoughts as far as this manuscript is concerned, whether through correspondence or conversation, criticism or encouragement. I ask forbearance of those I have inadvertently omitted. I thank Michael Allen, Dan Arnold, Eyal Aviv, Jordan Bridges, Arindam Chakrabarti, Collett Cox, Lorraine Daston, Jonardon Ganeri, Jay Garfield, Jennifer Geddes, David Germano, Aaron Glasser, Charles Goodman, Phyllis Granoff, Janet Gyatso, Maria Heim, Kapil Kachru, Birgit Kellner, Jowita Kramer, Emily Lawson, Dan Lusthaus, James McNee, Karin Meyers, Shankar Nair, John Nemec, Andrew Ollett, Cat Prueitt, Chakravarthi

Ram-Prasad, Andy Rotman, Robert Sharf, Michael Sheehy, Mark Siderits, Susanna Siegel, Sean M. Smith, Evan Thompson, Davey Tomlinson, Roy Tzohar, Anand Venkatkrishnan, Devin Zuckerman.

Kurtis Schaeffer and David Germano conspired to get me to part with an embarrassingly untidy first draft. I am grateful to them, as I am to Wendy Lochner: she believed in this project from the start and has worked wonders to see it through to print. My sincere thanks as well to the many reviewers who endured a manuscript bereft of insight and grace and whose criticisms have helped to make it better.

I am mindful of the extraordinary skill and effort that Adriana Cloud, Zachary Friedman, Lowell Frye, Lisa Hamm, Leslie Kriesel, and the rest of the staff at Columbia University Press have brought to bear on my manuscript. They have my sincere gratitude.

I have accrued personal intellectual debts. Jane Mikkelson's pathbreaking work on philosophy in the first person and imaginative experiments in early modern South Asia and Europe have been a continual source of inspiration and edification. They have served as a model for my own work. Richard Nance practically wrote an essay's worth of painstakingly detailed, philologically informed, and philosophically imaginative criticism on a first draft. Bryce Huebner, as outrageously supportive as he is incisive, has been unswervingly generous with his time and his reflections for years. His thoughts have shaped some of my own. Lastly, in the past two years I have been fortunate enough to have the opportunity to think about and to teach philosophy with Zachary Irving. This has changed my intellectual life here.

During the run-up to this manuscript, I was fortunate enough to be a part of three reading groups that have left their mark on this work. Bryce Huebner and Eyal Aviv invited me to join weekly sessions devoted to Xuanzang's *Ch'eng Wei-Shih Lun*. I thank them, as well as Jay Garfield, Sean Joyce, Genevieve Hayman, James McNee, Roy Tzohar, and Tadeusz Zawidzki, for an experience that has been a lasting source of inspiration, edification, and delight. At the University of Virginia, I thank Inger Kuin, Andrej Petrovic, Ivana Petrovic, Karl Shuve, and Janet Spittler for conversions on ancient religion and philosophy without borders; and my thanks to Andrew Ollett, Sarah Pierce Taylor, and

Anand Venkatkrishnan for the invitation to think and read with them over the summer of 2020. These conversations have sustained me during a difficult time.

The Department of Religious Studies at the University of Virginia is an especially collegial place to work. I thank the staff, my colleagues, and their students for all they have done to make it so.

Publication of this book was made possible with the help of grants from The Ludo and Rosane Rocher Foundation and the office of the associate dean for arts and humanities at UVA, Alison Levine. I am grateful to them for their support, and for the Arts, Humanities, and Social Sciences Grant and UVA Summer Research Award in 2019 and 2020, which made completion of this work feasible.

I was fortunate enough to have Emily Lawson, an outstanding poet and philosopher, prepare the index for this volume. My thanks for her insights, her hard work, and her patience.

The cover image is a detail from the Gaki-zoshi, the late twelfth-century scroll of the hungry ghosts (*gaki*) housed at the Kyoto National Museum. I have many people to thank for help with acquiring the image and necessary permissions. My thanks to Satoko Sakaguchi of the Kyoto National Museum, and to Ananya Chakravarti, Toshihiro Higuchi, Lisa Kochinski, Ariana Maki, Tori Montrose, and Dorothy C. Wong for all their help.

In the end, it took a family to turn a manuscript into this book. I don't know how to thank them. Especially A., who has promised not to tell me if it's just too terribly boring. This is their book, our first.

Other Lives

INTRODUCTION

Human experience is not confined to waking life. Do experiences in dreams matter? Many maintain that humans are not the only living beings who have experiences. Does nonhuman experience matter? The Buddhist philosopher Vasubandhu of Peshawar, who flourished in the late fourth and early fifth centuries of the Common Era, appears to have thought so. In a work called *The Twenty Verses*, the only unimaginative thing about which is its name, he effectively argued that we cannot understand the relationship of mind and world without taking into account contexts of experience that go beyond those that many philosophers, working at different times and in different traditions, have deemed normative: the waking experience of human individuals.

Buddhist philosophy can suggest a way to connect the fact that we enjoy experiences when dreaming and the experiences of other life-forms. For they each, Buddhists supposed, provide us with contexts of possible experience to which we are connected. We dream and wake, and then fall asleep and dream again. Buddhist philosophy, furthermore, teaches that we live now as one life-form, then another: most of us shall experience another way of being minded, and we have all experienced other ways of being minded in the past.

By "ways of being minded" I mean to gesture at ways in which creatures can be oriented at the world in thought, given different ways of thinking, perceiving, feeling, attending, and so on.[1] In the next chapter I will entitle myself to this way of talking with the help of Buddhist vocabularies of frames of mind. But we may use the phrase informally for now to say this: Buddhist accounts are committed to the thought that we do not live our entire life waking, nor are human beings unique for being minded. We exemplify a distinct way of being minded in dreams, and other lives exemplify other minds, to use this latter phrase in Peter Godfrey-Smith's sense of creatures who, even though only distantly connected to us, nevertheless exhibit forms of mindedness comparable to and yet unlike our own.[2]

Here's why this matters. By beginning his work with an appeal to other human contexts of experience (like dreaming) and other life-forms and their environments important to Buddhist cosmology (such as the lives of hungry ghosts and beings in hell, more about which below), Vasubandhu effectively reminds his interlocutors that Buddhists must believe that other lives and other minds ought to influence the way we describe what being minded involves. He also takes it that doing so has consequences. Thinking with such alternating contexts of possible experience, to put it impressionistically for now, has the consequence that the concepts of "mind" and "world" can be shown to be peculiarly entangled.

The view in rough outline goes as follows. Some of Vasubandhu's interlocutors believed that perception is paradigmatic of what it means to be minded; and perception, they appear to suggest, is a context in which mind and world, two separable things, come into some variety of relation. From the vantage point Vasubandhu would have us occupy in *The Twenty Verses*, however, this is to start the story too late. Perception, he will attempt to show his interlocutors, is the culmination of a story which involves the twinning of beings and their environments. To exhibit mindedness just is to be the kind of being that it befits one's history of action to be; and this, it turns out, comes down to saying that to exhibit mindedness is to be the kind of being that is fitted to the environment one's actions have contributed to making. We don't always see it, but in perception we are being put in touch with history, the history of what we have made of the world and what we have made of ourselves. Or, that's what Vasubandhu would have his interlocutors acknowledge as the central thrust of their own tradition.

As it turns out, it is a revisionary view, and, as such, challenging.[3] So too is Vasubandhu's way of encouraging us to make the necessary revisions. Just how challenging will become clearer in this introduction as well as throughout this book, but it can be somewhat comforting to know that the difficulty is not our own.

This book takes up Vasubandhu's challenge to think with perspective-diversifying contexts for two reasons. I wish, firstly, to recover Vasubandhu's account of mindedness; not to defend it, mind you—merely to understand it. Secondly, and relatedly, I wish to recover Vasubandhu's conceptual toolkit. I want to know not only what he thought, but also how. That means, at the very least, that I wish to understand his vocabulary and his concerns better.

Unfortunately, this results in a bit of a tension: while seeking to contribute to a *history* of philosophy, because of its interest in concepts and norms governing explanation and description, this book tilts rather far toward an interest in the abstract. The paragraphs have the distressing feel of tedium in places, which is a shame because, to speak more grandly, and more tendentiously, I wish to evoke what it was like to think with his conceptual tools about the world to which he took himself to be responsible in thought.

Speaking of Vasubandhu's contemporary, Buddhaghosa, Maria Heim says that "he approaches scripture with a literary, even poetic, sensibility, alert to the special qualities of the Buddha's speech whereby it conveys something infinite within its limited forms."[4] I have come to believe that there is an aesthetic component to the norms governing successful description and analysis in Vasubandhu's work as well, one that may be made precise with the help of a vocabulary that straddles the norms of reasoning in scholastic Buddhism and the norms governing aesthetic appreciation in Sanskrit literary culture. Though I won't really address this issue explicitly till the conclusion of the book, I provide clues to that end in the conclusions to chapters 5, 6, and 7, resting on evocation for the most part until the very end. But there is an experiential texture to thinking in another time and place and while environed in a particular scriptural tradition, and I have tried to evoke a taste of Vasubandhu's intellectual world even in the driest of paragraphs.

Here, in this introduction, I will explain what I am explicitly after in this book and how to use it. I'll begin by showing my reader around *The Twenty Verses*, after which I'll introduce the perspective-defying examples and what I call Vasubandhu's "interesting thesis" about mindedness.

THE TWENTY VERSES

This book does not offer an introduction to Vasubandhu. Nor does it seek to offer a high-relief picture of what we know of his life or oeuvre; it will not quarry for sources for his views.[5] Instead, I will focus on one work in particular, the so-called *Twenty Verses*, by which title I shall here mean the twenty-two (or, as is more likely, the twenty-one) verses as well as the prose commentary in which the verses are embedded. In fact, for the most part I'll be focusing on only parts of it: the part from the beginning that takes up dreams and the experiences of nonhuman life-forms in other worlds; and the part at the end where Vasubandhu appeals to dreaming once again, this time as a metaphor and model for what understanding consists in. Relatedly, I should caution the reader that my unmarked use of "Buddhism" and "Buddhist" does not aim at generality; I seek, instead, to center myself within the intellectual world of Buddhist thought as presented in *The Twenty Verses* and related works (more about which below), expressing also thereby the sometimes contested perspectives that Vasubandhu and his interlocutors bring to bear on that world.

I have included a translation of this short but endlessly engaging work in the appendix. Even as this book is not written as a commentary to the entirety of *The Twenty Verses*, the translation is not intended as a crib to the original. Keeping in mind the availability of many translations of this work aimed at specialists, as well as philologically and philosophically rich commentaries, I have offered my own (hopefully) user-friendly translation as an aid for readers unfamiliar with Indian Buddhist philosophy who wish to contextualize the use I have made of *The Twenty Verses* in this book. As my citations to *The Twenty Verses* refer to my own translation,[6] readers are advised to consult the appendix for a brief statement of the principles that have guided the translation and its presentation.

Here's an overview of Vasubandhu's *Twenty Verses*. Beginning with a rather humdrum example of error in the prose introduction, it quickly goes on in verses 3 and 4 to invite us to think through the case of experience in virtual environments, in dreams, and in the hellish environments of life-forms quite distinct from our own. At the other end of the work, in verses 19 and 20, Vasubandhu introduces the topic of dying and madness, inviting us to think through what it means to be alive by appealing to narratives of possession and mental power.

It is helpful to think of the text as being framed by consideration of possibilities enshrined in Buddhist cosmology and narrative that may require revision of some part of the common-sense commitments of Vasubandhu's interlocutors and those of his readers, then and now. In verse 21 Vasubandhu claims that we do not so much as know our own minds, an argument that brings this extraordinary work to a close.

In the intervening verses, Vasubandhu's work involves us in a consideration of phenomena at two extremities of scale. He considers the constitution of living environments and the beings who populate them in verses 4 through 7; and in verses 11 through 15 he considers the internal structure of matter, focusing on the very idea of indivisible atoms and the constitution of the familiarly scaled objects we take ourselves to perceive.

What is Vasubandhu after? In *The Twenty Verses*, Vasubandhu commits himself to defending a particular view as the Buddha's own. The view he ascribes to the Buddha is one that would have the Buddha council a restriction. When describing factors related to the full range of possible states sentient beings may enjoy, Vasubandhu understands the Buddha to recommend that we drop talk of the objects the experiences appear to be about, and which some believe serve as causes for these experiences.

I will offer a more precise characterization of this in chapter 1 when I discuss some features of Vasubandhu's technical vocabulary in more detail. For now, we may put things in the following way: Vasubandhu believes the Buddha's considered view to have been that we ought to speak of the full range of ways of being minded—all possible ways of being directed at the world in experience—*without* invoking objects as causes of content, without referring to anything, in fact, that goes beyond experience.

THE EXAMPLES: A CONCEPTUAL LABORATORY

Vasubandhu wishes to defend the intelligibility of restricting ourselves to talk of experiences while dropping reference to objects as causes of experience. He also wishes to defend taking it that this is what the Buddha meant to teach us as his considered view. The latter is an ambitious goal. I briefly discuss why in the appendix, where I also discuss what Vasubandhu thought one had to do in order to try to ascribe a view to the Buddha. My goal for the book is much more modest. I wish to understand the view of mindedness Vasubandhu develops to help us make sense of the Buddha's restriction.

To do this, it is helpful to orient oneself by briefly considering the prima facie difficulty that Vasubandhu's interlocutor appears to have with the restriction. We will discuss the interlocutor's puzzlement in detail in chapter 3. What follows is a schematic outline intended to introduce the examples that Vasubandhu adduces to help us begin taking the measure of his proposal.

The difficulty is this: How can one so much as describe episodes of experience without invoking any objects to serve as their cause? You are now reading one sentence. Now another. If you can sort your experiences, perhaps this has something to do with the sentences on the page or on the screen. That is, perhaps it is the objects that serve as the causes of our experience that give shape to experience, allowing us to identify, sort, or otherwise structure them.

The interlocutor has something like the following picture in mind. There is a link between what an experience is about and the factors that explain or render intelligible my experience. For example, in some cases I understand having an experience of X—when and where I do—because it is typically caused by X, which as an object, a concrete particular occupying a place at a particular time. The idea of an object will have to get a bit more refined, something I will discuss in chapter 1. Take it, for now, that we are speaking of sensory experiences of physical things, with medium-sized things playing the role of paradigmatic objects. With such examples in mind, the interlocutor also appeals to the distinction between private and shared experiences. Perhaps that difference is only to be understood with reference to the distinction between virtual and real objects, real objects being those one might meet with in space? What of another distinction, the distinction between the way in which some experiences orient us to successful interactions with things and others don't? One can be moved to brush away what one thinks is an insect only to realize that it is a floater in one's retina. Doesn't the distinction require us to make reference to the nature and place of the objects in the two cases? For a large class of experiences, if I experience X as soliciting physical interaction in some particular way, such interaction is successful only if X is an object in a place where it can exemplify the properties my experience suggests it has and on which my interaction will depend.

To sum up the interlocutor's worry: Were we to make no reference to objects in our description of episodes of experience, we would render experience unintelligible or inexplicable. We wouldn't be able to say that my experience was "of" anything. The examples Vasubandhu initially evokes in response to this are intended to motivate the possibility of describing experience without reference to objects. The examples create a laboratory of sorts. Discussing the ethical relevance of Buddhist narratives, Amber Carpenter speaks of their being laboratories insofar as "multiple narratives are just so many experiments run on us, the audience, where we are able to test and expand our powers of moral discernment and judgment."[7] Vasubandhu's examples, I believe, function in an analogous way. They test the vocabulary we are likely to rely on when describing experiences and they test our judgments with respect to which experiences deserve to count as paradigmatic.

Most basically, we must expand our intuitions. I like to think of the examples as the first step in the long task that is decentering our reliance on our collective and (so-called) normal frame—the human waking experience. The examples will attempt to show us that the typically unmarked view from the perspective of a normal human individual is not truly a "view from nowhere": the view from normal is not a view from nowhere; nor is the view from the waking life of humans such a view.[8] If the examples are successful, they will elicit from us a recognition of much that goes unexamined in our reports of experience, including our untested belief that we are in possession of anything like the norm for possible experience on the basis of the distinctions we bring to bear on our human case alone. Our categories have been contoured to fit descriptions of a small part of the full range of human experience. What if this is an insufficient basis for the language we shall need to describe the full range of *possible* sentient experience?

Take the examples in at a glance. We first meet with an ordinary individual human being, but one afflicted with some sensory impairment. We then meet with a dreamer, one with the ability to experience complex environments in dreams, and therein, the all too human experience of sexual gratification; in-between, we are also introduced to a community of beings whose world seems to be part of our own, but only in the way a nightmarish reflection in a mirror in a room may also be said to be "in" the room. And finally, we are to consider beings in hell, and the beings they believe to be the source of their pain: the guards in hell tasked with inflicting pain on beings suffering there. No one example is identical to another; no example is cursory. And with each, what we are being asked to consider becomes a little more complex.

Our first example shows us a person suffering from some type of damage to their sensory capacities, like cataracts, and thus suffering from a rich variety of presented content that cannot be provided a concrete correlate from among existent items in a physically described visual field of view.[9]

Our waking life presents us with examples of experienced content that seem to be richer than an account in terms of objects can provide. The contents of hallucination, or the fine meshing that can result from ophthalmia, or—to take an all too relevant example for me—the scotoma associated with a migraine, are not "in" a room in the way that an object is thought to be. Are they "in" the visual field in the way that objects as contents are? Is my experience of them, or my experience involving them, any less concrete for these contents not deriving from something in a room in the way that objects are? We can spend a lifetime on getting our vocabulary clearer with just such examples, but the second example presents us with something more involved: the case of a dreamer capable of enjoying sexual gratification without a partner in the real world, but in a world seemingly as spatiotemporally coherent as the one we encounter in waking experience. Dreams do not only involve virtual content but virtual environments. Are my experiences of virtual content "in" a virtual environment? And is the virtual environment "in" the world in the way that objects are supposed to be?

Vasubandhu goes on to introduce us to something far more complicated—the case of the nightmarish looking-glass world of the *preta* of Buddhist cosmology, communities of beings with whom we can share our spatiotemporal world, but seemingly not our experience of our shared environment.[10] The name *preta* simply means "the departed" in Sanskrit. It once referred to the unlucky dead who did not receive the ritual attention needed for them to become ancestors.[11] It is often now translated from Buddhist texts with an eye on the Chinese translation of the word as "hungry-ghost" (餓鬼). I will use the latter translation, by now more common and more evocative.

The waking experience of hungry ghosts is a collective nightmare. As Vasubandhu says, "all hungry ghosts, and not just one alone, see a river filled with pus. . . . along with a river filled with pus they also see the river filled with urine, feces, and so on, and see the river guarded by beings holding staffs and swords."[12] As for being in hell, which Vasubandhu introduces next, that means physical and psychological pain. As Vasubandhu says in his magisterial work *The Cutting Edge of Buddhist Thought*:[13] "Beings in hell invariably suffer from mental disruption. For their vital parts are unceasingly hurt over and over by several different kinds of torments, and they are at the mercy of [or, are struck by] painful sensations. They cannot, in the first place, so much as attend to themselves in thought, much less think of what ought to be done and not done."[14]

We are all prone to error and we are creatures that periodically dream. But except for short stretches in which we are, or imagine ourselves to be, in altered circumstances, we—those of us who have leisure to write and read books like this—are not at the present time privy to being in the world as a hungry ghost must be. Nor are we in hell. Not really. We do not have misery, frustration, pain and the inability to be oriented in thought as the norm for our experience.

With these examples we are dealing with life-forms different from ours and not simply a redescription of possible human existential misery, though the experience of it can, to different degrees, be made real for us in philosophy, ritual, narrative, or through contemplative exercises.[15] This points to a distinction in the kinds of examples with which we are dealing (and it is not the only distinction). To see what I mean, let us try and allow the examples to develop in the sequence in which they are offered, moving from simple episodic experiences to rather more complex cases.

Even a cursory look suggests that there is such a sequence to be discerned. We move from a person suffering from a disease of the eyes to people enjoying sexual gratification in dreams. But waking up from a dream is not anything like being able, from one moment to another, to determine that some particular item or way of having items presented to us in perceptual experience is distorting or virtual. To capture the differences and the development in the examples, it is helpful to have them laid out in a stilted, formal and schematic way, with an eye to what is involved in describing the contents of the experience. Doing so has the added benefit of telegraphing the shape Vasubandhu's interesting thesis will take, which any interpretation of his interesting thesis must respect.

Consider the first case of someone beset with visual distortions on account of some ocular impairment. This example tracks an individual, one who is abnormal with respect to the species to which they belong: "An individual S can have experience of some X, though no X is present as an object to serve as the cause of his or her experiencing X." The resulting experience is in a way global—we are speaking of an impairment that affects all subsequent experiences for that individual. Given the focus on an individual, the case is nevertheless interesting for suggesting a range of cases where (a) content constitutive of our experiential field of presentation at a time contains more in it than is produced by objects we are in causal contact with, and (b) that it may not be immediately apparent from an inspection of the phenomenal evidence of any single event which items in the field are merely phenomenal, and which derive from objects.

But we are explicitly dealing with non-normal conditions, by appealing to the experience of subjects who do not satisfy the definition of perceptual acquaintance as knowledge in a normative sense. Such definitions typically restrict the concept of perceptual acquaintance only to all normal, healthy perceivers. But this in turn suggests that we must clarify what is involved in speaking of a norm for a community of beings. We must do so not merely by aggregating them as individuals but by thinking of them collectively in terms of the type of beings they are.

The next example Vasubandhu introduces gets us closer to this, by being more involved than the example of sensory impairment that effects individuals. This is suggested by the fact that instead of selecting an example from among one group of subjects of a particular type, namely those with some ocular disease (and thus not counted as normal perceivers), we point out a class of experiences that affect all members of a given species, for some significant time: "All members of a class S of subjects, under certain possible conditions that obtain for all members of the class, periodically experience a range of nonshared content for a length of time, when no corresponding objects as causes of content obtain." That is, all subjects dream for some significant part of their lives. To grant this is not only to grant that we possess a notion of a virtual experiential environment that is richer than the notion of an object as cause of content might allow. We do have that, as we shall see when we follow Vasubandhu's talk of dream environments in chapter 3. But we are also shown the need to speak of a temporally extended sequence in such an environment. We do have not only one aberrant individual, but normal individuals of a group. Crucially, any individual, for some stretch of time, will have experiences *like* this.

As with the example from impairment, here too it is possible to know that the phenomenological content does not have corresponding objects as causes, but the way in which this is known is crucially different. It requires "waking up." I propose here that we see that "waking up" is not like determining that the item curiously floating in front of this keyboard is not a bit of dirt on the screen, or just in front, but a scotoma. Waking up is not (despite the predilection of some epistemologists to say this) to see that our beliefs about one episodic experience will not survive waking up. It is that an entirely different range of experiences seems to be available. This can be shown in another way. Consider that it is not one or another item that is in question. There is no one item I could point to in a dream and say I am dreaming. It is, rather, a global situation, affecting the entire content of the temporal duration of experience, and called into question as such upon waking.

So, "waking up" is not like determining an item is not present as an object. It is, rather, to have one context of possible experience take the place of another. The next example may be described as a generalization of what a collective context of possible experience might look like. It is possible to think that "all members of a class R of subjects, distinct from humans, by virtue of being members of type R, experience individually a range of shared content for a length of time, when no corresponding objects as causes of the kind of content members of R have available to them can be specified." These examples model, firstly, the range of content and affective states available to individuals, and, secondly, the possibility of individual beings of the same life-form enjoying similar content and possibilities for action under equivalent conditions. This is far from the example of the individual with cataracts we began with, and even richer than the case of dreaming. Importantly, this account requires that one's description of mental phenomena go beyond the resources available to any single subject restricting themselves to the phenomenal deliverances of their own mind. On the basis of the schematic presentation of the way the examples develop, I would like to say that Vasubandhu is tacitly attempting to delineate a very particular notion.

If pressed to distinguish the case of the person suffering from a cataract from the example of a community of beings, I should like to say that the latter involves a notion of an entire context of possible experience of content, while the former does not (a context of possible experience being that which determines the kind of content and possibilities of action available for a certain kind of form of life). In addition, this suggests dreaming and waking as different frames for the organization and intelligibility of our experience, though neither of them is capable of sufficiently embracing the totality of human life, much less the totality of another life-form.

Characterizing content may be far more complex than the simple-minded insistence on objects might allow for. Let us take the example of how complicated the description of the experience of a hungry ghost can get. In some narratives, the experience of frustration on the part of the hungry ghosts with respect to the kind of content available seems to involve some measure of dependence on the human phenomenological experience of objects and possibilities of action as a norm. To get the phenomenology of their experience right—by definition—seems to involve that descriptions of their experience be parasitic on descriptions of the human experience of the same spatiotemporal environment.[16] Going beyond the formulation above, understanding hungry ghosts additionally requires that we see how "all members of a class R of subjects, distinct from humans, by virtue of being members of type R, experience individually a range of shared content for a length of time, whereas all human subjects under the same conditions experience the contrary." That is, the content a hungry ghost enjoys is intrinsically comparative. It's entailed in the description of them and what they experience. To adapt a phrase from Locke, hungry ghosts enjoy "inverted [human] content":[17] "To be a hungry ghost is to experience ~X upon reaching location A, when initially poised to see and desire X in A, where human beings would also see and desire X in A."[18] This "inversion" of content concerns the transformation of content of one moral and aesthetic type into its moral and aesthetic contrary. A mango seen from a distance by a hungry ghost will turn to ashes or to feces in its mouth. This inversion, moreover, only extends to perceptual content and not evaluations. A hungry ghost evaluates things and experiences much as we do. That is what I mean by their situation being intrinsically comparative.

But this suggests that the situation, for want of a better word, is normatively far richer than my first gloss concedes. The entanglement of human and hungry ghost experiences is psychologically significant, given the possibility of rebirth and the fact that their lot can be ours. And the entanglement is morally significant. One becomes a hungry ghost because of acting in a certain way and exhibiting a certain range of vices, the true nature of which the horror of the hungry ghost case reveals. But if a hungry ghost's condition, including the norms that govern the range of content they have available to them to experience, befits the severity of what they have done in the past, and interacts with the norms that govern the human case so, one might well ask: What does the presence or absence of an object have to do with any of this? In fact, we ought to ask: Just what kind of descriptions do Buddhists have recourse to when describing possible experiential contexts for sentience?

The answer, as one might have suspected by now, will have to invoke karma—accounts of action and their consequences. Vasubandhu's last example takes up the perspective of beings in hell and directs our attention to Buddhist accounts of the role of action in the making of such collective environments. This book follows his lead. If we are to understand Buddhist accounts of having and being in a world, Vasubandhu suggests, we will need to think as Buddhists have when they have thought about sentient beings cosmologically, which is to say, in terms of their being life-forms, or, indeed, even worlds. That's a way of putting things that keeps an eye on Buddhist terminology that I shall explain in chapter 3, where I take up the tools we shall need to see the central lesson of thinking of life-forms and their environments.

Part of the central lesson lies in this: we cannot describe something as a context for experience without making reference to the kind of being for whom such an experience would be available, and whose nature is expressed by such an experience in that context. We must, that is, think of beings, environments, and the range of possible experiences as entangled together.[19] The rest of the lesson involves seeing how this connection is secured by the history of action.

DREAMS ON ONE SIDE, DEMONS ON THE OTHER

The title of this section is inspired by Emerson's once writing that what is "strange in our life" is that all our life is accompanied by "dreams on one side & by the animals on the other."[20] If we understand "animals" to include nonhuman life-forms and ways of being minded, this is a fair way of characterizing my approach to Vasubandhu's examples. As I shall interpret them in this book, they are intended to orient us to the need to think cosmologically of what accompanies our waking life. We need to consider that dreams and waking, although they involve distinct phenomena, form alternative and alternating contexts for experience; and we shall need to widen our sense of the nonhuman life that forms for Vasubandhu the non-ignorable differences with which the possibilities of our life are inseparably bound up.

They are inseparably bound up with us through causal links that obtain between us and other life-forms in the past, present and future, and therefore they are also conceptually relevant to making sense of our current experience, as I'll try and show in chapter 4 with the help of some conceptual machinery Buddhist scholastics developed to think with Buddhist cosmology. But the examples have not always been read that way. Thought to be "exotic" by some, the examples of other life-forms have proved embarrassing to a number of modern interpreters of Vasubandhu's thought.[21] Such interpreters have either restricted themselves to dreams as a more epistemologically "respectable" example to think with, thus centering the private experience of individuals, or they have opted for developing merely abstract possibilities to take the place of Vasubandhu's cosmological examples.[22] I think such attempts to adapt Vasubandhu's views uncritically to modern sensibilities fatally distort Vasubandhu's conceptual goals.[23] Vasubandhu's other worlds do not derive from mere stories that may not even correspond to a possible world; nor are they merely "might have beens with which we are not causally continuous," to borrow Nelson Goodman's trenchant characterization of possible worlds.[24] Descriptions of these worlds were treated by Vasubandhu and his interlocutors as having the status of natural historical reports, which is why they were held to be good to think with and to explore, with the help of thought experiments, as I try to show in chapters 4, 5, and 6.

It is important to note that it is not only moderns who have chosen not to focus on Vasubandhu's cosmological examples. Indian philosophers such as Śabara, Bhāviveka, Kumārila Bhaṭṭa, Uddyotakara, and Śaṅkara, to name a few among those we shall meet in chapter 2, have also favored an approach to Vasubandhu that directly or indirectly offsets the importance of cosmology. They do this not out of modern sensibilities, but in accordance with the norms of an epistemic culture that came into prominence after Vasubandhu with the cultivation in South Asia of epistemology. Coming into view in the sixth century CE, this was to become a multigenerational endeavor in which claims made by individuals belonging to different traditions were taken account of and debated using a public vocabulary (generations in the making) and public criteria of reasoning, free from commitments couched in specific vocabularies associated with the scriptures of any one tradition.

Here's how to get the measure of such an enterprise. Think of an idealized rational actor—in Sanskrit, an actor who resorts to evaluation before acting, the *prekṣāvat*, one who wants to know how to maximize the chances of success in activity. Such an actor possesses a complement of logical tools and relies on experiences and epistemic criteria when making decisions. Now, define what is reasonable as what makes sense for this ideal-type subject to believe and to do in order to maximize their success.[25] Additionally, consider that it is only worth defending claims that are couched claims to which such a rational actor is entitled when restricted to evidence and reasons defined and assessed in public terms.[26] There could be no place within such an epistemic culture for the comparatively tradition-specific vocabulary and values that Buddhist cosmology involves, nor for the distinct norms of success that might govern description or explanation in a strictly Buddhist scriptural context. At the close of chapter 6 I briefly consider a clue Vasubandhu may have left us regarding the latter, insofar as I consider the kind of norms by which Vasubandhu's own practice might be assessed.

Of course, this is a caricature of history. But it will allow us to note the following: some modern philosophers who do not share in the presuppositions of premodern Buddhist philosophy and some premodern Indian philosophers who, however otherwise sympathetic to Vasubadhu's background commitments, restricted themselves to the norms of epistemology as a public epistemic culture, could converge on this much—when interpreting Vasubandhu, they focused only on the examples from dreaming and error, assuming that in their reconstructions of Vasubandhu they could preserve the sense of Vasubandhu's conclusions, even when they disjoined them from his arguments and examples.

I think that this has been a mistake. I follow here instead Wittgenstein's insight: "If you want to know what is proved, look at the proof."[27] Wittgenstein was speaking of mathematical proof. And in that context, he believed that the result gets its meaning from the demonstration. It is also useful to generalize this as a historiographical maxim to guide our study of Vasubandhu's cosmological arguments. In chapter 2, I try to show that the quasi-solipsistic individual that results from the arguments from dreaming that have been reconstructed for Vasubandhu, a creature insulated from its natural and social worlds, is about as contrary to the spirit of Vasubandhu's arguments as it is possible to be. And in chapter 3 I present a very different way of understanding the arguments from dreaming, emphasizing there Vasubandhu's interest in virtual environments in which experience and interaction are possible and salient, a conception that anticipates the full-scale model of an environment he will find in Buddhist cosmological conceptions of life-forms and their worlds. In chapters 4, 5, and 6, I will consider the shape an account of perceptual content might have to take as suggested by the actual explanatory mechanisms responsible for the generation of beings and their environments.

To aid in our study of this, I provide in chapter 4 an overview of some of the technical vocabulary Vasubandhu could rely on when thinking about life within the parameters of Buddhist cosmology. And in chapter 5 I consider issues that arise when Buddhists attempted to describe the constitution of living beings and their environments, while reconstructing Vasubandhu's reliance on processes responsible for structuring experience over time. My goal is to provide a paradigm of thought within which we might situate Vasubandhu's use of hell as an example of a thought experiment, one tasked with illustrating the complex issues that arise when describing and explaining an environment of experience and points of tension within the received Buddhist paradigm. I follow Vasubandhu's thought experiment in chapter 6.

My book is dedicated to the proposition that Vasubandhu wishes for us to travel farther and farther away from a certain constricted conception of ourselves. To focus only on the experiences of individual humans while taking such experiences at face value imparts a centripetal thrust that centers our own selves. I take the analytic thrust of *The Twenty Verses*, instead, to be centrifugal: to follow Vasubandhu is to place oneself within a cosmological framework that destabilizes familiar descriptions of oneself. The Buddhist philosopher working in the epistemic culture of Indian epistemology I described above will take Vasubandhu to have asked: What do we know on the basis of experience? I have found it useful to consider a different question: What kinds of creature are we? And what difference does it make for us to describe ourselves as the kind of being who dreams and is reborn as a different life-form?

Li Zhi, a philosopher and writer who flourished in sixteenth-century China can offer us a feel for what generalizing our sense of alternative and alternating contexts of possible experience might mean. At the end of his life, this man of letters reconsidered the self-assurance with which he used to think about the salience of cosmology to descriptions of ourselves. Writing a preface to an anthology of ghost stories in 1598, "Unstringing the Bow," he says: "When people reach the point at which in daylight they do not see humans and in darkness they do not see ghosts, then 'a single thread runs through' darkness, daylight, people, and ghosts."[28]

Li Zhi was once sure that humans and ghosts were as distinct as our dreaming and waking lives. Now our diurnal life, divided into dreaming and waking parts, is paired with a possibly alternating pair, human and nonhuman. It is not self-evident what it will mean for our sense of ourselves to think that there is a "single" and unifying thread between these alternating contexts of possible experience. Talk of a single thread, as Jennifer Eichman reminds us, is an allusion to Confucius's saying that "a single thread runs through history."[29] In Vasubandhu's case, the single and unifying thread is provided for by Buddhist cosmological commitments to continuity (without identity) across lifetimes. I introduce this single thread in the guise of what I shall call the cosmological individual in chapter 4, though it is useful to see that Vasubandhu found the shape of the account he would offer in *The Twenty Verses* somewhere else, and perhaps a hint of what it might mean to appeal to a wider context of salience, in accounts of what it is for us to be persons.

THE SHAPE OF VASUBANDHU'S INTERESTING THESIS

I'd like to now place before the reader the logical shape of Vasubandhu's thesis, first in terms of its appeal to wider contexts of salience for explaining experience insofar as we are persons, and then, in the next section, by considering an appeal to the category of life as a structure of non-negligible variation.

Heidegger once wrote that "if idealism emphasizes that Being and Reality are only 'in the consciousness,' this expresses an understanding of the fact that Being cannot be explained through entities," to which he added, "yet [this] fact . . . does not absolve us from inquiring into the Being of consciousness, of the *res cogitans* itself."[30] One must not, that is, treat the mind as just another item in the world—as the sort of thing that could stand in relation to other items in the world. For another thing, one must not think of the world as an inventory of objects. Jointly, this gives us a picture on which we are not to treat our having things in view, and as being available to view, as having to do with their causal influence of one sort of thing (say, physical objects) on another sort of thing, say minds.

The introduction of *The Twenty Verses* does claim that all the Buddha wished to have us keep in view through his teaching can be understood as restricted to talk of experience as involving presentations of content; it also claims that such presentations of content can—and indeed should—be described without invoking objects as causes of content. Let us set aside whether or not saying this much makes Vasubandhu an idealist, a concern I believe has played an outsized role in constraining our reading of Vasubandhu's work.[31] For my purposes, the more interesting question is whether Vasubandhu "absolved" himself, to use Heidegger's phrase, from thinking through what it means to speak of mindedness in the absence of objects.

What I will call Vasubandhu's interesting thesis, most clearly on display in verse 9 of *The Twenty Verses* and in his comments thereon, indicates that he does not. I will discuss it here because it is a handy way for us to get our first glimpse of the form of the concepts we shall explore throughout this book.

In verse 9, Vasubandhu offers us an account of what the Buddha meant by speaking of twin conditions for the occurrence of episodes of awareness. Vasubandhu thereby offers us a thesis concerning *the meaning* of our concepts of experience, awareness, and mind, one that revises a particular picture that relies on objects to make sense of them. It is helpful to offer a schematic sense of the picture we are meant to offset. Consider experiences of hue, or smell, and so on. A common way of describing the occurrence of such episodes—enshrined in the Buddhist theoretical vocabularies Vasubandhu was familiar with—is to speak of their having twin conditions. In the case of a visual experience, such conditions will include some sensible occasion (like colors) and the functioning of a visual capacity capable of registering sensory contact with the relevant sensible occasions. To treat these conditions as things is to treat them, first and foremost, as separable items, capable of being characterized independently of one another and thus counted independently. Treating the conditions this way gives us three different items: the twin conditions, and an awareness event. Here's the picture: experience is paradigmatically a relation that presents to us as content some of the elements involved in a more basic relation, that between objects of experience and capacities for experience, paradigmatically (though not exclusively) sensory occasions and sensory capacities.[32]

Vasubandhu's interesting thesis would have us recast all of this. He says, for example, that the Buddha meant something quite different from separable things when speaking of twin conditions for an experiential event: "A conscious mental event possessing some specific manifest content, such as some particular hue, for example, comes into being on account of a seed or dispositional power attaining the end of a directed process of change.[33] The Blessed One spoke of these two—the dispositional power and the manifest content—as being, respectively, the two conditions for perceptual experience called the eye and hue, to continue with our example of visual experience."[34]

This revises the above picture almost point for point. We no longer have three separable things. Count them. There is only one: a process of which a conscious experience is a terminal part. Instead of speaking of what is manifest in experience (a manifestation of some X at which I am directed at in experience), we are directed to speak of the manifestation of something entirely different: a power, associated with us in the past as a disposition, that has changed us in certain ways over time to result in our having an experience later. This, to put it mildly, can seem to be quite a bizarre or at least baroque way to describe what I have in view in experience.

This book will help the reader understand the view better and why it had to be expressed this way. It will help to think of it by looking at what Vasubandhu has said in terms of what I would call the form of the description he has adopted. Elsewhere, Vasubandhu favors talk of dispositions and manifestation in contexts where one discusses latent features of mental life, such as, say, dispositions to anger. Take the following questions: What is it for a person to be angry? What does is it mean to be a sensual person?

To ask this, Vasubandhu's analysis intimates, requires speaking of not just an instance of a categorical property—an occurrence of anger, or an instance of indulging a sensory experience—but of something distinct in kind, *a propensity for* the occurrence of anger, or sensory indulgence. Thus, characterized as propensities, speaking of properties tells us something about the people who have them, something of their personality, of the kinds of experiences they have had and the kinds of experiences they are likely to have, and the way in which experiences are likely to mark them. But what are we saying of persons when we speak of them thusly? What kind of thing is it the presence of which would make such statements about them true?

Vasubandhu's answer involves taking it that we are speaking of a dispositional power on the part of a psychological continuum constituting persons, such that, when presented with the right conditions, the continuum will manifest certain kinds of occurrent experiences based on prior experience. The basic idea is that experiential events don't spin free of context: think, for example, of persons as changing contexts for experiences—experiences occur in contexts effected by the trajectory of past experiences, and seeding—and so shaping—the trajectory of future experiences.[35] We are creatures who bear our past within us. We cannot understand our responsiveness to what there is without understanding the ways in which we are poised to experience what there is, in the present, by the past.

I shall argue that Vasubandhu, in *The Twenty Verses*, effectively generalizes the lessons of this account. We are being asked to replace the idea of an object as something that comes into view for us in experience by the idea of the manifestation of what we have been conditioned to be able to have in view. The latter, unlike the former, is not separable from the kinds of beings we are. When considering mindedness more generally, then, Vasubandhu is asking us to allow our explanations to move among the same logical categories he had developed in order to answer questions like "What is it for a person to be angry?" or "How do we remember?" or, more fundamentally, "What is it to be a person?"

I'll have more to say about the form this imposes on Vasubandhu's descriptions at the close of chapter 4, where I will discuss Vasubandhu's commitments to habituation to action as a source for the structuring of contexts of experiences, be they persons or worlds. Generalized, the lesson comes to this: when describing what comes into view for us, and how, we have to consider the wider context provided by the kinds of beings we are. But Vasubandhu's account will require of us to forego describing ourselves in terms of psychological or forensic categories alone; in *The Twenty Verses*, we must consider ourselves to be not only persons but also living beings.

BEING MORE-AND-LESS THAN HUMAN

In this book I am more interested in the conceptual shape of the explanations Vasubandhu is offering than I am in any consideration of the metaphysical picture he will ultimately need if is to be entitled to the form of description and explanation he prefers. I want to understand his basic gesture, his appeal to his fellow Buddhist scholastics that they ought to contextualize talk of perception within the wider framework afforded by Buddhist accounts of life, action, and the constitution of environments—topics typically insulated in the essays and discussions of Buddhist philosophy of that period (and later) from debates concerning perceptual experience. I wish to understand what Vasubandhu's recontextualization involved. To do so, we have to recover the conceptual vocabulary used by Buddhists to think about life as a structured space of variation.

There is a parallel one might draw to motivate the effort. In an epigram to his notebook M, Darwin once recorded a striking thought: "Plato says in *Phaedo* that our 'imaginary ideas' arise from the preexistence of the soul, are not derivable from experience. Read 'monkeys' for preexistence."[36] Set aside for now the distraction that it is Darwin's materialism that would have struck a late nineteenth-century reader as being radical, even as it is that Vasubandhu's apparent mentalism might strike a reader as being remarkable in our time. Instead, focus on this: Darwin is noticing that we need contexts wider than individuals and individual lifetimes if we are at all successfully to describe mindedness. Plato saw as much, though Darwin maintains that the right sort of context has *a very different conceptual shape* than does the notion of a soul and it ought to be looked for in a very different place than where metaphysics has traditionally looked for it.

What Darwin saw was that we need a context of variation and continuity across vast times genealogically linked through descent. Vasubandhu's interesting thesis recognizes something similar. He did not have available to him natural history as practiced by Darwin, of course. But I will argue that he did find something of comparable conceptual power (in one important sense) in Buddhist cosmology.

Life, as understood in Buddhist cosmology, provides for a space of variation and set of relations constraining how individual beings may develop over time, expressing now one life-form, now another. It also provides a dynamic account of how living beings come to occupy the environments that they do, even as they act to make environments over time. I wish to recover this way of thinking to help a reader begin thinking about things as Vasubandhu did.

One of the most basic ways in which this way of thinking oriented Vasubandhu has to do with what I call thinking of ourselves as being more-and-less than human.

As we shall see in chapter 5 onwards, Vasubandhu suggests that when thinking about the mind, we should allow for two things. Firstly, in applying the concept of mind to an individual, we must be sensitive to an individual's expressing some form of mindedness appropriate to a life-form, capturing the characteristic possibilities and capacities tied to certain life-forms that are realized in certain environments. And secondly, we should allow that no one life-form can exhaust what it means to possess a mind: at least, we must allow that there are what we called above "other minds." We must use a *more-and-less than human* conception of mind, even as we think about minds with some specificity. This allows for a distinctive kind of generality that it is useful to become comfortable thinking with as one explores Vasubandhu's ideas in this book.[37]

Such generality invites the question: Did Vasubandhu believe there to be forms of experience in principle available to us that are not, for that, causally connected to us as a part of the structure of rebirth and that are not, properly speaking, a part of life understood as above? The answers to this are linked to the answer to other questions: Does acquiring the picture of life as a structure for possible forms of mindedness make any difference to our experience? Does a human being change by thinking of themselves as more-and-less than human?

Though not discussed at length in *The Twenty Verses*, such issues are brought up at the close of Vasubandhu's companion work, *The Thirty Verses*. In chapter 7, I turn to Vasubandhu's appeal to the metaphor of dreams in *The Twenty Verses* as a structure of understanding; I end that chapter with a consideration of his invocation of talk of reality in *The Thirty Verses* to suggest a way of thinking about what is possible for us to experience, particularly when we allow that some radical break with life as a structure of experience is possible.

I shall there make the following clearer: internalizing the kind of revisionary view of mind that Vasubandhu presents can change the possibilities for experience we now have available to us. Thus, it may turn out that what I will here (for the most part) present as theoretical exercises was also intended as part of a variety of contemplative exercises. I will discuss this in chapter 7, where I shall explore Vasubandhu's sense of the limitations of any conceptualization of mind and the limits of our theoretical vocabularies given the reality of unactualized possibilities for experience—the forms of experience not yet actualized in the collective life-forms recognized in Buddhist cosmology.

I will also briefly touch on the limitations of any book that seeks, as I have done, to center its concerns in Vasubandhu's arguments concerning the lives of hungry ghosts or beings in hell, or any of the lives catalogued, charted, and entertained in Buddhist cosmology and narrative. For these other life-forms that serve as concrete possibilities for us in Buddhist theory are not the only variety of other life that can matter to a Buddhist philosopher. The lives of others we shall consider in this book are concrete possibilities for us given rebirth, and the account stresses the presence of our past within us. But at the end of the day, the lives that matter must also include the unactualized possibilities, all the varieties of felicity that might yet be and that living beings have yet to make real for themselves. Talk of karma has us look back. After internalizing the lessons karma has to teach us, I suspect Vasubandhu would have us face the other direction.

1

PRESENTATION, OBJECTS, REPRESENTATIONS

Vasubandhu's interesting thesis has to do with how things come into view for us.[1] In the introduction I spoke loosely about experiences, or episodes involving the presentation of content. Vasubandhu's way of speaking of concrete episodes in which things come into view for us involves talk of *vijñapti*s, meaning instances involving presentation of content at which we are directed and (however sometimes indiscernibly so) conscious. He also claims that his interesting thesis is incompatible with taking it that the content involved in such episodes, whether or not it appears to involve objects, is actually derived from objects.[2] I have been using the word "object" to translate Vasubandhu's use of the word *artha*. But I have not yet offered a precise characterization of objects. Nor, for that matter, of *vijñapti*. We need a better handle on both.

This chapter is offered as a way of tuning our instruments, so to speak. Steven Collins liked to say to me in conversation that translating philosophy can be as difficult as translating lyric poetry, a view he ascribed to Roland Barthes.[3] It is a view with which I have increasingly come to agree. I wish to explain my choice of translations and to be as transparent as possible as to the consequences of my choices. As with all translation, I do not believe that there are absolutely right or wrong choices; much will depend on audience, context, and purpose.

In the chapters to follow, I shall use the word "object" in a (distressingly) generalized sense to track what I think is behind Vasubandhu's use of *artha* (and later in the text, *viṣaya*). I shall use it to name any putative item in the world (whether physical or mental, in the case of *artha*) that might be recruited to play a causal role in a story tracking the source of content in experiences, and which is thought to possess a nature, linked to the causal powers invoked by us to explain an experience, independently of the experiences with which it is related. I shall avoid using the word "representation" as an equivalent for what Vasubandhu means by *vijñapti*, preferring to speak instead of episodes involving the presentation of content.

A reader who can live with these choices is welcome to skip this brief chapter and to turn to the next, where we shall take up reconstructions of Vasubandhu's supposed argument from dreaming.

PRESENTATIONS OF CONTENT

In *The Twenty Verses*, talk of *vijñapti* is presented as a way to speak of the mental as a univocal category: "'Thought' [*citta*], 'mind' [*manas*], 'awareness' [*vijñāna*], and 'presentation of content' [*vijñapti*] are coextensional synonyms . . . 'thought' is used so as to include all mental functions."[4]

There are contexts where one can lean on usage and etymology to suggest different shades of meaning for each of the words above, even if, as some maintain, they refer to one and the same sort of thing at the end of the day. Thus, using *manas*, one might stress broadly cognitive capacities, rather than a generalized quality of directed awareness shared by sensory and cognitive awareness, which one can use *vijñāna* to mean.[5] And explaining the morphological shape of the word *citta*, Vasubandhu introduces another dimension, leaning on a common explanation among Buddhist scholastics of the word in terms of the root *ci-*, which means to pile up, to heap, to collect, instead of citing the root *cit-*, "to think." It is helpful not to dismiss this as false etymology. Think of it, instead, as an explanation that refocuses our attention on how the word might be used. Leaning on the etymology Vasubandhu has provided on the basis of "to pile up," one can see that the word *citta* might be used as a normative conception of the mental—that which serves as the basis of action, or that which bears the influence of past actions—and which serves thus as the root factor tracked by ethical concepts such as *being skillful* or *unskillful*.[6]

So, Buddhist philosophers are aware that we can speak of the mental in diverse ways. And some would consider providing different referents for these words, maintaining that there are different sorts of mental processes that deserve to be listed as the referents for the different functions and the different kinds of content it is possible to mean when speaking of mind.[7] But for the purposes of this discussion, we may unify the mental by foregoing ontological questions and concerning ourselves only with what is at issue in having content and engaging content in a very general sense.

To understand Vasubandhu's expansive gesture to comprehend talk of mind and mental functions, it is useful to describe what he has in mind with the help of the following verbal device. Vasubandhu's talk of mental events, let us say, invokes a mental frame.

To speak of a mental frame is a way of describing the occurrence of content and the ways in which it is engaged.[8] The basic presentation of content on the part of a mental event (*citta*) supports the occurrence of mental functions (*caitta/caitasika*) that, because of their ways of engaging the content presented by the mental event, serve to further specify the kind of content made available, and thus serve to individuate its psychological, moral, and causal profile.[9]

Mental frames serve as the basis of all ways of being minded. To facilitate reference to the mental frame as a whole, I suggest taking it that Vasubandhu has treated *vijñapti* along the lines of a determinable expression, the determinates of which would specify the exact place and nature of the function with respect to the mental frame, whether it counted, for example, as instances of thoughts, sensory awareness, feelings, memory, attention, or more complicated kinds of mental functions yet. One can enter into debate, as Buddhists did, with respect to which functions are necessary entailments for having content and which are contingent. (More about this in chapter 4.) But all beings exhibit a mental frame with some basic mental functions filling out the content available to them. The life of all beings, then, involves *vijñapti*.

Speaking etymologically, and keeping in mind its use as a count noun, in the context particularly of Buddhist philosophy of mind, a *vijñapti* is an instance of—or that through the occurrence of which there is—"a making known," for a *vi-jñapti* is a "causing something (in particular) to be known." Despite the verb *jñā-*, though, it is perhaps better to use a softer verb than "to know" in this context, given the precise valences this verb may enjoy in classical Indian and contemporary epistemology. We might try "to become aware of" when speaking generically, allowing specific cases to determine the precise valence awareness acquires in each case.

Vijñapti is usually used by Vasubandhu (and not only Vasubandhu) to gloss that which characterizes an event of awareness *as* an instance of awareness. Technically, it serves to name the criterial function characterizing awareness events.[10] But if there is no metaphysical difference between the function and that which it serves to characterize (as Vasubandhu believes there is not), then *vijñapti* can also serve to name the event that counts as an instance of a conscious or experiential event.

Despite the way I phrased things in the introduction, *vijñapti* and "experience" are not strictly synonyms. Vasubandhu uses the mental function known as affect (*vedanā*)—defined as involving "experience" (*anubhava*)—to entitle himself to speak of the experiential (and qualitative) properties involved in content-carrying mental events.[11] The mind, if understood *only* in terms of the criterion provided by the presentation of content at which we are directed (*prativijñapti*), would not in the absence of *vedanā* be strictly *synonymous* with what (anglophone) philosophers today, after Ned Block, mean by phenomenal consciousness, or "experience: the phenomenally conscious aspect of a state [defined by being] what it is like to be in that state."[12] The issues here are delicate. For the purposes of this book, as every instance of a mental frame entails affect, the relevant distinction between the intentional presentation of content and experience *cannot* be a thesis to the effect that experience and information encoded in representations are strictly *separable*, however much it might matter that there is an analytic distinction to be made. For our purposes, when zooming out of the details of the mental frame, we may treat "presentations of content" and "experience" as overlapping ways of speaking of the same thing.

But there is one catch. The term *vijñapti* functions as a count noun—not unlike our phrase "mental event," but not in a way that would have us restrict our description of a mental event to a description of content from the resources of a single experiencing subject. We are not best served by *identifying* mental events with experiencings, as if to say, the only things that are true of a mental event are those that are available in such experiences as these *vijñaptis* sustain. They enjoy, for Vasubandhu, also nonexperiential being.[13]

This is one reason to eschew certain translations, notwithstanding the rather striking initial resonance between the thesis we are concerned with here and certain formulations of philosophers in the late nineteenth and early twentieth centuries, as, for example, those of F. C. S. Schiller, who said that "the whole world in which we live is experience and built up out of *nothing else than* experience."[14] If this sounds an awful lot like Vasubandhu's opening remarks that in some sense our description of the full range of phenomena taught by the Buddha comes down to being *vijñapti*, this is precisely why one must resist the urge to render Vasubandhu's statements in these terms. Vasubandhu did not mean his restriction to mental events to imply, as Bradley put it, that "to be real is to fall within sentience."[15] There is no pressure to equate the semantic force of "existence" and "reality" with "being perceived."[16]

What is most basically at issue in talk of presentative function is not really consciousness, or experiential properties, but events involving what we today call "aboutness." Consider that what is distinctive of conscious events is typically characterized by glosses such as the following: it is that which has some X as an intentional object (*tad-ālambanatā*), or with some engagement of content (*tad-ākāratā*), or, as Vasubandhu prefers to say in *The Twenty Verses*, that which has some specific manifest content (*tad-ābhāsa*).

If one can use *vijñapti* to signal the directedness of content in awareness, the term does not prejudge answers to a battery of questions entailed by the underdetermined notion of being directed at content. Shall we think of "being directed" or "aboutness" as a real relation? A quasi relation? Is the phenomenological fact of being directed at an object—or, perhaps, the causal function that is "making something known in an act of experience"—a function of the causal influence of a freestanding object?

Unlike *vijñapti*, talk of "representations," for some time now the most common translation of *vijñapti*, does seem to me to prejudge answers to these questions.[17] I'll get to my reservations below. First, we need to address the question of the apparent relation presentations of content have with the objects they can seem to be about, as well as the nature of objects.

OBJECTS

The word "object" is promiscuous in Anglophone philosophy. In some contexts, this book, the letter "e" on the keyboard of my last laptop, and my daughter's favorite crayon might compose an object. In other contexts, it means more familiar things. Like crayons, though not so much the letter "e" on my keyboard.

The word *artha* is also promiscuous, though it comes by its promiscuity honestly. Firstly, it enjoys a slightly different sense in different theoretical contexts, where it can come to be used oriented by different topics. Thus, in the context of linguistics, as Vasubandhu knew, *artha* can mean "referent," whereas in philosophy of action it means "the purpose for which one acts." In the context of theories of perception it means something more like object, though in a sense to be clarified.[18]

It is also promiscuous for another reason that invites an analogy with the behavior of the word "object" in contemporary Anglophone philosophy. Depending on one's background metaphysical commitments, what counts as a generic notion of an object might be very different. Thus, one might begin with a pot or a jar as an object. But if there are no such part-possessing complex items in one's ontology, perhaps it will have to be something else that serves as a generic object. Something like a volume of color, for example, or an instance of flavor—something we would not ordinarily find natural to call an object.

I will offer an account of my use of the word "object" to track Vasubandhu's use of *artha*, which will help us see why very different things we, as well as Buddhist philosophers, would keep apart in some theoretical contexts can and should fall within one category in another discursive context. The upshot of my discussion will be that the phrase "intentional object" is a nonstarter, a point that, in turn, will set us up for the discussion of representation.

But I'd like to motivate my generic use of "object" by considering why, to begin with, it might *not* be a good choice to cover the paradigmatic cases a Buddhist philosopher might wish the word *artha* to comprehend. A. S. Barwich has recently argued that our sense of objecthood in connection with perceptual experience has far too long been bound up with talk of visual experience. Our paradigmatic case of objects is provided by things that we see. But it is not obvious that any notion of visual objecthood generalizes for other senses. It is not obvious for us and it would not have been obvious for the Buddhist philosophers with whom Vasubandhu was in conversation.[19]

We ought to be wary of fixing our notion of an object by taking as our standard what we pre-theoretically take ourselves to see, for doing so involves making a mistake in terms of assumptions about scale, mereological complexity, and what I will call modal invariance.

According to Buddhist philosophers, the word *artha* can be used paradigmatically to pick out whatever serves as the physical scope for the functioning of senses, a notion for which the term *viṣaya* is typically used in intratheoretic Buddhist discussions.[20] Such use must do justice to what can serve as the scope for all senses. As far as Vasubandhu understands the use of this category, the paradigmatic kinds of items (*artha*) recruited to explain perception are typically instances of sensible properties—colors, rough edges, sharp noises, acrid smells, and so on—understood as concrete particulars in their own right, taking up space—filling it, in fact—and, by virtue of this, being capable of causally interacting with physical sensory capacities and thus generating content in experiences. But different sensory modalities may feature different kinds of inputs that perform the above functions in very different ways. And all of them, Buddhist philosophers take it, involve causal actants quite different from the kind of things we pre-theoretically take ourselves to be acquainted with in vision and the commonsense idea of objects (as property possessors) we enshrine in talk of pots and tables and persons and trees.

Firstly, sensory occasions are scaled very differently than the medium-sized objects we see. True, Buddhists sometimes speak of "gross" physical inputs; but what they mean by "gross," though debated, is not what we mean by "medium-sized objects" on any proposed interpretation of "grossness" that they provide. They are speaking of small-scale phenomena. They mean either something that resists co-occupation and is therefore extended, however small the scale; or something that satisfies the threshold of perceptibility and can thus show up in perception at all.[21] Neither of these tracks our conventional sense of medium-sized objects like pots or persons.

This leads to the second point. The mereologically complex (part-possessing) objects that we take ourselves to see—those possessing depth and exhibiting the kind of structure that can sustain the perception of figure and ground—are not explanatorily basic; rather, they must be explained by appeal to far less structured or even mereologically simple inputs.

Which brings me to the third problem. Talk of objects, particularly when grounded in a notion of visual objects, can promote a notion of (modal) invariance and methodological uniformity that may not be appropriate. Take the notion of mereological structure. Just how much structure is necessary for something (or a collection of somethings) to serve as occasions for a sensory system? It turns out that there might not be an answer that can generalize across the sensory modalities.[22] But if a Buddhist scholastic answer will need to be determined by context and type of sensory system in question, this counts against thinking that there is only one notion of objecthood.

One charming example of modal invariance in connection with objects is provided in the *Questions of King Milinda*. The king proposes an example to his Buddhist interlocutor. Imagine the self as a knower in a body as a person in a house: the self can sense through the senses as this person might look through the windows they choose to look through, seeing the same object now through one then through another window. The king gives the example of his manservant who walks in and out and may be glimpsed through successive windows.[23] But the occasions of sensory experience, the Buddhist monk Nāgasena replies, and here most Buddhists would agree, are simply not like this. They are too tightly individuated to the senses and proper to them. So too are the metacriteria Buddhists developed to classify and organize the sensibles. If we inspect the list of possible sensory particulars and their classification, it is unclear whether there is any single form, model, or set of criteria determining what a sensory particular in general, independent of any particular sensory system, must be like. What does a cloud, a sound produced by the contact of a hand on the skin of a drumhead, or the coarse feel of gravel or something acrid have in common? How would Buddhist scholastics answer this in ancient and medieval South Asia?

The matter deserves further historical study, but we can say this much: what we want for the sense of an *artha* is something both less and more finely characterized than what the word "object" might mean in current philosophical usage.[24] We should not take it to be a formal notion, as in the contemporary conception of unrestricted mereological fusion (on which any items, anywhere, can be taken to compose an object), nor do we want to include *only* what J. L. Austin derisively called medium-sized specimens of dry goods. Our concept must be elastic enough to allow for hues or the visual texture of fog, pools of water, tangy smells, rough surfaces, patches of darkness. And yet, the trouble is that the concept is not only restricted to the way in which Buddhists use it in intratheoretic debates. So, on the evidence of *The Twenty Verses* alone, we cannot only mean sensible occasions. We must also include animals (such as bees) and environments (mountains) and also mental events, as when I think about something I have experienced in the past, while excluding (as we shall see) any virtual bees, or merely apparent environments.

How shall we characterize such a collection?

INTENTIONAL OBJECTS AND BEYOND

Consider the distinction made between two ways of speaking of the role of a sensory particular in Buddhist scholasticism. One may describe a concrete particular as a *viṣaya* or as an *ālambana*; which is to say, one may describe it as the scope for the functioning of a physical sense on the one hand, and as it is taken up as an intentional object on the other. The distinction is made clearer in a brief definition offered by Vasubandhu in his *The Cutting Edge of Buddhist Thought*: "What, then, is the distinction between a *viṣaya* and an *ālambana*? A *viṣaya* is that, given which, and with respect to which, there is the characteristic causal activity [of the sensory capacities]; that which is grasped, or taken up in perception by a mental event or a mental factor dependent (for its content) on a mental event, is an *ālambana*."[25] This distinction, as I shall here interpret it, can give us a clue for a generalized notion of object that will be useful to us going forward.

For Vasubandhu, to describe an item as an intentional object alone—as what is taken up by thought—is to make no reference to its prior causal role in generating content. To speak of a particular, however, is to presume that such a characterization is possible, as does reference to an object-field for the sensory capacities, for example.[26] What this means may be captured by one of Vasubandhu's arguments to show that it is part of the very idea of an *ālambana* that it does not entail the existence of what is had as content.

We join with Vasubandhu at a moment in *The Cutting Edge of Buddhist Thought* where he proposes a view that we can be related to intentional objects in the absence of real objects. In other words, there can be nonexistent items present to thought. In my translation, I have rendered *ālambana* as "content." The passage begins with the incredulity of Vasubandhu's interlocutors:

> —We hold that even things past and future can serve as content. But if they do not exist, how can they be content?

—We reply as follows: they exist in the way that they are taken up as content. And if one should ask, "How are they taken up as content?" we would reply thus. They are taken up as something past and as something future, respectively. For it is in fact not the case that a person enjoying the experiential memory of some X that is past, whether an instance of hue or a feeling, perceives that "X presently exists"; rather, that person perceives that "X existed." In fact, one remembers something past as it was experienced when it was present, and the future is grasped by thought as it will be when present. One has the concept of something presently occurrent to thought if and only if it exists exactly in the way that it is taken up. It is thus established that thought can occur even with content that does not exist.[27]

The content of memory is experienced as having a temporal aspect. We experience something that we once experienced *as* past, that is, as no longer obtaining—this is part of what makes the content of experiential memory what it is. Our characterization of the phenomenological content of my episode of experiential memory requires the aspectual shape with which I experience the object, and this in turn means that thought in memory does not reach some object in the past directly, but rather, as Vasubandhu would be inclined to stress, *the prior experience* of that object. In speaking of conditions for the occurrence of experiential memory, we may reach back in the past only as far as the occurrence of the experience of the object that might at some subsequent time, given certain conditions, be recollected.

To claim, however, that all phenomenological content licenses an inference to the existence of an object that we experience would mean that there was some kind of occurrent relation between an existing object and the experiential event, and that in turn could mean one or both of two things: that something we now recollect existed in the past or that the object we now recollect experiencing presently exists. Let us grant Vasubandhu's interlocutor here that if we count some occurrence as an episode of experiential memory of an object, then there was some prior time when one was in experiential contact with some object. (Vasubandhu will, in fact, take issue with this in *The Twenty Verses.*)[28] How does such a supposition help explain the content as presented by the experiential memory? Is there some curious kind of relation holding directly between the past object and the current recollection?

If there was, shouldn't that mean that I experience the thing directly again, seeing it now as it was, not crucially under the description of "being past" but instead "as present"? And, Vasubandhu argues, if we say that there is some relation between my current recollection of my experience of something as past and that thing as it presently exists, we would not be able to explain what I have in view. To take an example, consider the case of recollecting the experience of something like a slice of chocolate cake, seen and smelt (though sadly not eaten) twenty-five years ago. Surely the physical description of what, if anything, remains of that slice of chocolate cake is not anything like the thing I have in view as the slice of chocolate cake in my recollection. On the model Vasubandhu and his interlocutors share, the sensible occasion—described in terms of what it is composed of—succumbs to eventual dispersal into constituent atoms: there would be, after a certain time, nothing left to be related at the time of the occurrence of recollection. But then the description of that sensible occasion as it now would be, a description required if we are to treat that sensible occasion as a presently operative cause, offers us no purchase on what is recollected as it is taken up in experience.

The problem Vasubandhu has identified can help us provide a general characterization of the notion of object at issue. To call something an object is to describe a particular in a certain way, or so I shall here understand the use made of *artha*, on the model of a generalization of the explanation of *viṣaya*.

The lesson is that we should not confuse the description of something as content—even when it involves an object—with a description appealing to that something as an object. And the criterion for being an object in the relevant sense is this: something is playing the role of an object when it is recruited into casual relations and when it is defined as independent of us.[29] More carefully, an object in a generalized sense is any item, depending on one's metaphysical intuitions, that is recruited in causal explanations in general, and, in particular, to explain the fact that one seems to be able to intend things in experience and believe that this has something to do with the thing one has in view in experience.

Whether that turns out to be more like a happening, or something composed of stuff, or a part-possessing whole—or even whether a mental event could play the role—depends on the particular metaphysical tradition in question. What matters for the generic use of *artha*, I believe, is that the powers something is ascribed as an object are properties or capacities that typify it as independent of the event of mind with which it comes to be related.[30]

When Vasubandhu eschews objects in connection with presentation of content, this is what is being denied. The way in which something comes into view cannot be looked for in separable causes. But what of relations that are not instances of causality narrowly construed? What of thinking of presentations of content as involving a quasi relation between an awareness event and something like an intentional object? Tellingly, Vasubandhu does not make use of the term *ālambana* in *The Twenty Verses*. I think this is insightful on his part and consistent with the claim I shall reconstruct as his own. Vasubandhu's guiding idea in getting rid of objects also involves getting rid of *any structure that might suggest a contingent and relational conception of how things come into view.* Presentations of content do not consist in a present relation between two types of things in a given event.

If we do not mean to count two items when speaking of a mental event and its internal object, I suggest we simply drop talk of internal objects as misleading and follow Vasubandhu's example, speaking instead of manifest content with some phenomenological shape, the experience of which is suggestive of real relations between distinct particulars that ultimately do not obtain as experienced.

AGAINST REPRESENTATIONS

I said above that translators sometimes favor talk of representations in connection with *vijñapti*. I think this is a mistake. I will not be able to convince everyone, but, at the very least, I hope to entitle myself to avoiding talk of representations.

The basic reason for my hesitation has to do with my desire to eschew anything suggestive of relations between awareness and some variety of a countably separate item. And representations, typically, involve an appeal to something like a relation between separable items.[31] But it is perhaps better to try to get a working feel for the metaconceptual problems that wait for us should we attempt to identify the theoretical function of *vijñapti* in

Vasubandhu's work and representations in either early modern or modern Anglophone philosophy.

In the bulk of philosophical literature from early modern times until very recently, mental features, states, properties, or events are described as representations when we wish to highlight a certain way in which they function: as making some X known. That seems promising enough to render them candidates for translating what a *vijñapti* is and does. But to call something a representation in the early modern period feels not so much like a first-order description of the fact of being aware of something; rather, it is part of a theoretical attempt to describe being aware in a way that suggests a mechanism by which one is aware. That is, to name something a representation can be explanatory in a way that speaking of what comes into view through episodes of presentation is not.[32] At least not on its own.

This holds true, I believe, whether or not we favor what (confusingly enough) is called a presentation view of representation in early modern thought. Broadly speaking, there are two ways of speaking of representations, as presentations and as surrogates.[33] On the presentation view, a representation of X is something that presents X as it appears to us but in a particular way. Of the number of things in view, there is only X, but X as presented to us in a certain way. On the surrogate view, a representation of X is a something, Y, located in the mind and which stands in for X and so directs the mind to X. There is, thus, one more thing in addition of X of which to keep track in our description.

Both forms of representation are varieties of relation that bring something into view. The ways in which they might do so are many, depending on mechanisms featuring resemblance, causation, or more abstract relations yet. If one was not already impressed by the difference between the explanatory ambition of "representation" and *vijñapti*, it should be noted that speaking of such mechanisms in connection with Vasubandhu introduces three further problems.

Talk of representations as relations to objects involves a picture that we might have entertained *had* Vasubandhu maintained talk of *viṣaya* and *ālambana*, talk of objects and ways in which the mind comes to be related to objects. Secondly, speaking of mechanisms will complicate a straightforward gloss on Vasubandhu's commitments to phenomenology; thirdly, it will obscure the hints he has offered as to the causal mechanism he believes actually underwrites the availability of content.

Consider what Vasubandhu in *The Twenty Verses* has to say of the things that hungry ghosts experience. He says that "insofar as these beings are constituted by a process involving the ripening of morally equivalent actions, *all* hungry ghosts, and not just one alone, see a river filled with pus."[34] What hungry ghosts see, insofar as they are hungry ghosts, is not a representation of pus. As far as the ghosts are concerned, they see pus. We may describe it otherwise because we don't think there is any pus to be seen in that way. That way of putting things leaves open that humans might perhaps believe that *there is something* that the hungry ghosts are seeing but which they are misrepresenting as pus. Or, perhaps, it is that the hungry ghosts are imagining content where there is none. Either way, what the hungry ghosts think they see directly we must describe in other terms. But here is the point: the language of *vijñapti* is employed in such a way as to be available to the hungry ghosts to use of their own case. They may say that they enjoy episodes involving the presentation of content and mean that they are in an environment in which there just is, as seems to be manifest, "a river filled with pus [along with such things as] urine, feces, and so on, and see the river guarded by beings holding staffs and swords."[35] To call these "representations" gets their phenomenology wrong.

Moreover, I do not even believe that "representation" quite works as a second-order category in this instance. It makes the wrong second-order move as far as Vasubandhu is concerned. Vasubandhu does have available to him a way to redescribe an episode of awareness as *vikalpa* or construction, as when one determines that its content is not had as a result of the influence of an object, being derived, instead, because of a process by which content is constructed or imagined. I'll discuss such redescription in more detail in chapter 7. For now, let us ask: If we describe the pus that is presented to a hungry ghost as an instance of constructed content, should we redescribe the presentation as a representation? Do we get the mechanism by which content is presented correctly?

There are two ways in which we might try to preserve talk of representation for Vasubandhu here. Perhaps we mean to say, firstly, that the hungry ghosts are experiencing something that is recasting what there is in the hungry ghosts' environment as pus. Or, we mean to say, on behalf of Vasubandhu, that the pus *represents* the actions (*karma*) that they have done and for which what is presented to them in experience is a variety of befitting consequence.

Take the first case, on which we would have the pus serve as a representation of some input that is there. This preserves the structure of an object serving as input and a representation as medium and as output. This will soon run into a problem. It renders opaque just what Vasubandhu's denial of objects amounts to, if it is not a denial of there being any causal role *of that sort* in the generation of content. And it sounds a whole lot like the way in which Vasubandhu's interlocutor is inclined to speak about things.[36]

Vasubandhu's use of "manifest content" presented by episodes of presentation allows him to keep the naïve phenomenology of our perceptual reports. We enjoy presentations of content that (appear to) put us in touch with a manifest world of objects, environments, and things, without epistemic intermediaries of any kind. The causal machinery responsible for this constitutes the manifest scene and is, as it were, invisible "within it." And the causal story is fairly distinctive: it is, Vasubandhu says, "insofar as these beings are constituted by a process involving the ripening of morally equivalent actions, [that] *all* hungry ghosts, and not just one alone, see a river filled with pus."[37]

Now consider saying that what the hungry ghosts see represents their karma. This is an interesting thing to say.[38] But were we to speak like this, we would be talking about the manifest content of a *vijñapti* representing something in the past, something like the disposition for a being to become a hungry ghost and to see things that it befits a hungry ghost (or someone destined to become a hungry ghost) to see. One might claim Vasubandhu invokes this in verse 9 when he speaks of "a mental event . . . [eventuating] based on a corresponding dispositional power, or seed, proper to it," and having that as its manifest content.[39] But if we wish to capture this by speaking of "representation," then we would be using the word "representation" to overlap not with Vasubandhu's use of *vijñapti* but with his use of the relation between manifest content and the relevant dispositions. This is not typically something that proponents of talk of "representation" in connection with Vasubandhu have in mind.

A TRANSLATOR'S DILEMMA

It will be objected that there is a perfectly simple sense available for us to use today: representations are things that carry information about other things.[40] What can play the role is plastic, be it systems of states, events, or processes, and our identification of what counts as a representation can be divorced from the explanatory concerns that dominated the use of this term in the early modern period.[41] They are the basic units of cognitive science, serving as those items that cognitive processes manipulate. Can we not agree, when discussing Vasubandhu's commitment to a mental frame in translation, that we may set up an intertheoretic analogy—*vijñapti*s are to Buddhist scholasticism what representations are to cognitive science: basic content-bearing units that higher-order processes manipulate?[42]

If one wishes to use "representations" in such a careful way, gloves on, so to speak, with sensitivity to the problems above, then I can squint my way past my reservations with the word. But I would like to offer one last set of cautionary remarks. The idea of representation used in this way is just not easy to control when offered as a translational medium.

I will develop the problem as a translator's dilemma. The dilemma takes the form of problems resulting from thinking of the kinds of notions of representation that could have been intelligible to Vasubandhu. I'll run the argument through with the help of Robert Brandom's distinction between premodern and modern (and early modern) concepts of representation, beginning with Brandom's sketch of the premodern view: "Premodern (originally Greek) theories understood the relations between appearance and reality in terms of *resemblance*. Resemblance, paradigmatically one of the relations between a picture and what it pictures, is a matter of sharing properties. A portrait resembles the one portrayed insofar as it shares with its object properties of color and shape . . . the thought behind the resemblance model is that appearance is veridical insofar as it resembles the reality it is an appearance of."[43] Vasubandhu did have available to him the model of resemblances, having used it to gloss how to think of the occurrence of mental events with content in a work that likely antecedes *The Twenty Verses*: "Just as one says that an effect, by virtue of conforming to its cause—insofar as it exhibits a resemblance [to its cause]—occurs even though the effect does not do anything, just so one says that awareness is aware on account of coming into being resembling [its cause], although it does not do anything whatsoever. What, then, is the likeness? Its having the phenomenological profile of some particular."[44] Vasubandhu has here offered a carefully worded description that commits to very little.[45] We know that there is some account to be had of why the event has the "shape" that it does, its seeming to be "of" something in a way conformed to what serves as its cause.

This statement of what it is that makes an event of awareness an event of awareness seems to incline to an account that would make what comes into view for us be a function of separable causes linked by some shared property in resemblance. But Vasubandhu's formulation does not require us to settle on an object as the separable cause, just because reference to intentional content does not privilege any particular account of what is serving as cause; nor does it settle what sort of causes we shall need to invoke. He wants to make the process passive, and not the achievement of a subject or instrument. Otherwise this brief statement says little. It is not inconsistent with a number of possible views, offering us thereby a model that may be satisfied in very different ways. A representationalist, as I have described one above, one whom Vasubandhu could have found intelligible, would model it with a combination of proximate objects, causes, and likenesses. But notably Vasubandhu chooses not to speak like this in *The Twenty Verses.*

On the other hand, were we to move from speaking of resemblance to speaking of our distinctively modern "metaconcept" of representation, I think the extended concept that would result would have been quite out of Vasubandhu's ken. Consider, for example, the possibility of saying that what is manifest to me in my experience is a representation of my environment in the sense that *the structure* of my qualitative experiences encodes information concerning distal features of our environment. The notion of describing manifest experience as a description-dependent construction (*vikalpa*), though plenty abstract and potentially counterintuitive, does not involve the idea of treating mental episodes as the outputs of an information-encoding and information-retrieving suite of processes. There is a crucial intellectual ingredient missing.

In Brandom's story (based on ideas derived from John Haugeland), what is missing is the mathematization of physical phenomena. Galileo, for example, could have periods of time appear as the lengths of line and accelerations as the area of triangles. The notion of resemblance and shared properties is of no help in understanding the relationship between mathematized appearances and the reality of which it is ostensibly an appearance. Instead of thinking of sharing properties in common, we must think with a notion of global isomorphism of two models of information:

> Descartes came up with the more abstract semantic metaconcept of *representation* required to make sense of these scientific achievements—and of

> his own. The particular case he generalized form to get a new model of the relations between appearance and reality (mind and world) is the relationship he discovered between algebra and geometry. For he discovered how to deploy algebra as a massively productive and effective appearance of what (following Galileo) he still took to be an essentially geometric reality. . . . he saw that what made algebraic understanding of geometric figures possible was a global isomorphism between the whole system of algebraic symbols and the constructions possible with geometric figures.[46]

I don't know how else to put it except to say that (to the best of my knowledge) there is nothing like the notion of an isomorphic model in Vasubandhu; nor, then, is there any trace of the abstract mathematical notion of information typically involved in contemporary talk of representations or any version of manipulations of content understood as information. I cannot therefore control for distortions that may result when translating Vasubandhu's words concerning concrete, conscious—however dimly so—presentations of content with the help of such metaconcepts.

So, here's the dilemma: the sense of representation as resemblance, a sense that would have been intelligible to Vasubandhu, does not appear to have been ultimately satisfying to him. On the other hand, the sense of representation he does not appear to have considered (or left behind) rests on an abstract conception of information that might have been entirely unintelligible to him. The overarching issue, then, is that it is possible Vasubandhu would either have rejected or simply not understood what we mean by representation.

To avoid this labyrinth, I've chosen to steer clear of suggesting any intertheoretic identities between contemporary cognitive science and Vasubandhu's thought.

2

HOW NOT TO USE DREAMS

The waking have one common world, but the sleeping turn aside each into a world of their own.

—HERACLITUS[1]

Reading the first of Descartes's *Meditations*, Hobbes was unimpressed, believing that "the difficulty in distinguishing the waking state from dreams is a matter of common observation."[2] As old as philosophy itself, dreams, philosophically speaking, were not news.

But Hobbes was thinking of the simplest possible thing one might mean by dream arguments. To get a feel for this, ask yourself, "How do you *know* that you are not right now dreaming?"[3] Confucius suggested the question to Yan Hui in *The Book of Zhuangzi*;[4] Socrates asked this of Theaetetus.[5] Narrowly understood, such arguments seek criteria that can distinguish dreaming from waking experiences. More narrowly, they seek to identify criteria that are or can be made available to the experiencer as part of the experience.

Though a long-credentialed concern in ancient Greek as well as Chinese skepticism, any story of arguments made with the help of dreaming does not end here.[6] For philosophers have been concerned not only to tell whether one is actually asleep. Socrates, for example, went on to ask: How does one know that what we experience in dreams is any less true? René Descartes found this to be the compelling question. Don't ask, "Am I dreaming?" The question, instead, is this: "What if dreaming and waking are epistemically equivalent contexts?"[7]

We may think, and can even reason in dreams, the same as in waking; and waking life is not always necessarily as vivid as some experiences in dreams can be. What is most basically at issue, then, is our reliance on waking sensory experience as paradigmatic of knowledge and the possible limitations of such reliance. What if an emphasis on experience, thought by many to be the surest way to underscore the presence of the world, actually confines us to a virtual existence inside our own minds?[8]

For many interpreters, Vasubandhu offered us something worth calling an argument from dreams. But for the most part, such accounts have Vasubandhu not using dreams to test the wisdom of any unswerving reliance on sensory experience as a criterion for knowing. Instead, such reconstructions would have him exploit the limitations of experience in the following ways: "Experience in dreams can suggest that we have no evidence in waking experience sufficient to take us beyond the presentation of objects in experience to knowledge of the existence of extra-mental objects."[9] Or, sometimes the reconstructed argument is thought to entitle a conclusion: "Dreams do not give evidence of extra-mental objects; but they do give evidence of our being related to something else in experience, something like phenomenal objects."[10] Sometimes, the conclusions are not so much skeptical as dogmatically directed, as involving the further claim that "one has reason to suppose that there are no (extra-mental) objects, because we can show that our situation is the same as that of being in a dream or some state indistinguishable from one in which we are presented with nonexistent objects."[11] Whichever route one takes, these reconstructed arguments from dreaming constrain the sense of Vasubandhu's proposal, though some will do it more dramatically and more directly than others. I am less interested in the conclusions to which these different patterns of arguments tend than I am in the wisdom of attributing to Vasubandhu any naïve reliance on experience as paradigmatic of knowledge. I am, in other words, invested in making more perspicuous the stance that these reconstructed arguments maintain, a stance the reasoner must take up if the arguments are to reach their respective conclusions.

In what follows, I shall use these reconstructions of Vasubandhu's argument to help us spot the battery of presuppositions they can, in certain contexts, all seem to share. My goal is diagnostic. I want to show why it is important that we do not ascribe to Vasubandhu the wrong argument from dreaming.

WHAT DO YOU MEAN, *THE WRONG ARGUMENT FROM DREAMING*?

It used to be maintained that the first verse of *The Twenty Verses* opened with an argument. The argument was thought to go as follows:

> This is really nothing but the presentation of content,
> on account of the presentation of objects that do not exist (1a–b)—
> Just as is in the case of a person with cataracts
> seeing nonexistent meshes of fine hair and the like (1c–d).[12]

The prominence given to this may be due, however, to a later rearrangement into verse of what was once an introductory prose clarification of Vasubandhu's thesis. The clarification is better read as follows: "Just this episode of awareness arises, having an object as its manifest content. Just in the way there is the visual experience of nonactual hair or double moons on the part of those suffering from ocular disease, but there is no actual object whatsoever."[13] Perhaps, then, the emphatic appearance of an argument was not Vasubandhu's intent.

But let us assume, counterfactually, that Vasubandhu could have made an argument for his claim here based on a variety of experience. What sort of an argument would it be? And what kinds of experiences would he have chosen to make his claim? Using dream experiences, I will reconstruct an argument exploiting Vasubandhu's use of a demonstrative, tacitly inviting one to reflect on what it is like to inhabit one's experience first-personally. I will then offer a second argument, one that classical South Asian philosophers reconstructed for Vasubandhu and that was offered in the form of an *anumāna*, a particular kind of epistemic argumentative form.

Both arguments, I attempt to show, will have the effect of situating one entirely within the phenomenal character of experience, disposing one to treat episodes of experience as interpretively independent and complete contexts. By having us inhabit experience as a variety of inner space, they constrain what Vasubandhu can mean by restricting us to talk of presentations of content in the absence of objects. They do so, moreover, in ways that seem to go against the spirit of his thesis.

SPEAKING FIRST-PERSONALLY

Note the use of the demonstrative "this" (*idaṃ*) in what looked like Vasubandhu's thesis above: "This is really nothing but the presentation of content." It is a feature that survives in the prose introduction that scholars tell us is closer to what Vasubandhu intended to say: "Just this episode of awareness arises, having an object as its manifest content."[14]

There are things Vasubandhu has said about the use of a demonstrative that can help us understand the way in which a counterfactual argument might proceed. But first, notice how the use of the demonstrative underscores the phenomenological counterintuitiveness of his claim. Vasubandhu at one point in *The Twenty Verses* (in his comments on 10bcd) does claim that "*this* is just an instance of the presentation of content, having as its manifest content phenomena such as hues, and the like; but no corresponding phenomenon *defined* independently as being a hue, and so on, exists."[15] To use "this" in this way is to gesture at what is present to an experiencing subject. To introduce talk of defining criteria is to invite us to consider the difference between, on the one hand, a description that underscores *how* things are manifest to and, on the other hand, a description that tells us *what* is manifest to us.[16] For example, Vasubandhu's interlocutor takes it as a possible description of my experience of something blue that there is something involved in my experience the definition of which would go beyond something's seeming to be blue, describing it as something possessed of extramental criteria. This is what the restriction in speaking of there being "*just* presentation of content" denies. This is important. The argument we reconstruct for Vasubandhu ought not to peddle banalities. And to use the demonstrative as we are now doing does not, as it goes against what Vasubandhu elsewhere considers to be the conventional way of parsing its use.

In general, the use of a demonstrative of proximity like "this" in Sanskrit is understood as situating one in a (potentially implicit) first-person stance, bringing what is referred to within the present mental horizon of a speaker.[17] But elsewhere, Vasubandhu acknowledges on the basis of everyday idiom that the referent of such a demonstrative (as well as indexicals like "here") must nevertheless be understood in terms of what is evident in the world around us.[18] If I say "this" in describing what I am seeing, the tendency, according to custom, would be to understand that I am gesturing not to the experience alone nor to the experience primarily; rather, my principal and paradigmatic reference would remain what was presented in experience, understood as a variety of things or stuff in the world.

We can make the point stronger. We might hold, in fact, that the degree to which something mental counts as ostensible and as a suitable referent for a demonstrative is the degree to which it involves objects among its conditions. Even setting aside the stronger point, it is at least clear that Vasubandhu did not think his restriction obvious, given his acknowledgment of the conventions governing the use of demonstratives. Vasubandhu's restriction must be justified by any reconstructed argument. Vasubandhu suggests that when we say "this," we should overlook the object and attend to the mental event manifesting content: an event that may allow us to speak of a locus of phenomenal presence, the field of presentation as a whole. How does one move from the conventional use of the demonstrative to this tendentious use? What could justify this?

It is not a question, surely, of whether we *could* claim to use "this" to gesture at the visual field as a whole and not simply pick out the object seen.[19] In our reconstructed argument, Vasubandhu would need to say that there does not exist anything that could have the necessary criterion to distinguish it from the event of experiencing.[20]

And this is where the example of dreams might enter.

To generate a counterfactual first-person argument, let us "move toward" the claim by asking: "Is this that I am now experiencing a part of a dream or waking experience?" Imagine, that is, transposing what Vasubandhu has said in his opening statement into first-person speech, guided by the use of the demonstrative: "This, all this, anything I take in, should not be described as involving anything beyond the event of something appearing to me. I must not allow myself to infer anything beyond this, what is presently presented in my experience. Why? Because *this* might be a dream. For a dream would be structurally indistinguishable from what I am now experiencing." Of course, Vasubandhu does not say any of this. But perhaps we can suppose that he meant to *intimate* such a reception of his argument, and we might motivate such a supposition by appealing to his illustration of a dream environment. We can allow ourselves to feel our way into the possibility that we might be dreaming right now, and to sustain that feeling, by reading Vasubandhu's subsequent remarks and taking the following point: experience in dreams can show us that even the experience of environmentally embedded content need not intimate that we are awake. We might come to think the following: dropping objects from our characterization of episodes of presentation of content need not make a phenomenological difference—there need be no experienced difference between a world in which our experiences are caused by objects and one in which they are not. If that is true, then perhaps we had better restrict our descriptions to what our evidence is capable of supporting: we have evidence of presentations of content, but not of objects as causes of such content.

If successful, this argument has moved us into a context where the resources of first-person experience are to be relied upon as a guide to the description and understanding of experience. We do not need to say that the resources of first-person experience—how things seem to me first-personally to be—are shown by this argument to be adequate to the reality of experience. I described the experience above as if it involved events, structured in terms of subject and object. Is that how experiences really are? I am not sure that this argument forces me to consider that experiences enjoy merely experiential being in a way that would leave me no room to distinguish between appearance and reality.[21] But it does seem as if it inclines me in that direction. The argument seems to suggest that what we need to know of the experience we can know by resting within the evidence of first-person experience. Whatever I need to know will be based on some categorical feature(s) manifest to me in experience that can be interpreted on the basis of that experience.

This could promote a reading of Vasubandhu's denial of objects that is committed to methodological individualism and internalism with respect to the mind. Methodological individualism is the belief that it is possible to individuate the contents of mental events on the basis of a solitary subject. Internalism makes the claim that we can individuate the contents of a mental event without reference to facts not disclosed within the phenomenal resources of a first-person perspective. Even more basically, such an argument would sustain what Irad Kimhi has called epistemological separatism, the attitude that maintains that "the content of a perceptual episode is individuated by its sensory appearance qualities. So, the intrinsic properties of a perceptual state are the phenomenal properties which a subject experiences as a result of a direct sensory contact with the object."[22] Jointly, individualism, internalism, and separatism are the consequences of uncritically treating first-person experience as paradigmatic of what we may claim to know. They contrive to treat experience as an interpretively independent and complete context—treating mind, as it were, as what I shall call inner space.[23]

But it is not at all clear to me that Vasubandhu thinks of mind as inner space. In fact, I will present the case that Vasubandhu uses dreams to intimate that experiential events might not be entirely captured by descriptions restricted to what is made manifest by such experiences. They possess more than experiential being. Which is important, as it will be the causal characterizations of events that will show us how to revise our sense of what experience involves, a sense typically based on what is manifest to us in experience.

Let me step back for a moment. A reader should note that Vasubandhu is disinterested in claiming that there is no experiential criterion to distinguish waking experiences and dreams. Later in *The Twenty Verses* he makes the distinction with the help of the Buddhist scholastic concept of torpor (*middha*): "Since, thought in sleep and dreams is afflicted and overcome by torpor . . . the consequences of what is done by those asleep and those awake are not equivalent" (18cd).[24] It seems here his interlocutor acknowledges as a truism that the differential success in the cases of actions attempted by dreamers and those who are awake requires a finer-grained account of these as different kinds of experiential states with different sources for them. Importantly, Vasubandhu agrees. He just doesn't believe that objects are the only source for the phenomenal and functional properties of experience, believing there to be other factors that may contribute to the texture of experience—factors such as the degree of metacognitive control one can exert in and with respect to one's experience. Or, so he understands torpor: "What is *middha*? It is the contraction of thought, whose subsequent functioning is not autonomous."[25] (The sense of lack of autonomy with respect to function has to do with the inability to keep intentional content in view, according to Sthiramati.)[26]

Whether or not Vasubandhu is successful in securing a distinction, or whether he has the conceptual and epistemic resources even to try, is another matter. What matters is that there will be cases where we shall have phenomenal experiences whose causal contexts (and hence final interpretation) will not always be evident from within the context of experience alone. Or, so Vasubandhu believes, which is why he can believe (as we shall see later) that we do not, just by virtue of having experiences, know our own minds.

All told, then, Vasubandhu seems to want to call into question the authority of how things seem to us first-personally to be. No experience on its own provides a context of interpretation for itself, particularly not when restricted to categorical phenomenal features manifest in experience. In fact, this is the point of his appeal to the metaphor of dreams and waking: we do not know a context C until we, as it were, wake up from it and reinterpret it in light of a new evidentiary context. But more about this in chapter 7.

AGAINST THE COMPLETENESS OF EXPERIENCE

The *metaphor* of dreaming used by Vasubandhu at the end of *The Twenty Verses* challenges the conclusion of reconstructed arguments from the possibility that we are literally dreaming now, challenging any reason to construe any one context of experience as an independent and complete evidentiary context. The modern-dress version shows us how a reconstructed argument from dreams works in the other direction, nudging us into a certain way of regarding the authority of experience. Fortunately, it is exegetically forced, a problem that also besets premodern reconstructions of arguments for Vasubandhu made on the basis of dreams.

It is tempting to believe that the mischief involved in the suggestion of mind as inner space has to do with the explicitly first-person cast of the argument. What I will try to show now with the help of the premodern reconstructions is that this is not the case. The problem really has to do with the nature of dreams when used as an example in a certain way, whether or not the argument is actually couched in the first person. The problem derives from allowing dreams to serve as a model for what experience as such consists in. When we do that, the fact of being environed first-personally potentially comes along for the ride.

I would like to preface our discussion of the premodern reconstruction of Vasubandhu by considering a distinction between using an example to illustrate a claim via an analogy and using an example as a model in a formal epistemic argument. To argue for a distinction between an illustration and an argument has precedent. Consider how the (influential) *Mahāyānasaṃgraha* introduces a clarification of the thesis to which Vasubandhu commits himself in *The Twenty Verses*: "These mental events have been described as nothing but mental events, given the absence of objects. What is an example of this? Examples are to be had in such cases as dreaming. For in dreams, being nothing but consciousness in the absence of objects, various things appear—physical forms, sounds, smells, tastes, haptic content, dwellings, forests, open spaces, mountains and so on."[27] Despite the appearance of an argument, dreams here function as a clarification via an analogy. It helps us see what it might mean to make the claim that we should restrict ourselves to episodes involving the presentation of content alone. Dreaming here is not unique; the passage goes on to list other examples that might be included, such as cases of illusions through magic, hallucination, and optical illusions on account of sensory impairments. But dreams are considered to be especially helpful to illustrate the intelligibility of the idea on offer.

Crucially, the *Mahāyānasaṃgraha* recognizes that there is a further question: How can we know that any such analogy holds? Do we "wake up" from our waking life as we wake up from dreams? Short of an experience suitably describable as waking up, the *Mahāyānasaṃgraha* contends, it is only on the basis of scriptural precedent and arguments that one can even consider the analogy to be a meaningful one.[28] I would recommend taking it that the *Mahāyānasaṃgraha* is invested in a hermeneutic concern: Can we learn to bring ourselves under a certain kind of description? To that end, note two features of the situation. We are dealing with a partial likeness: there are ways in which the analogy might hold, and other ways in which it might not. And the use of the illustration entails a pedagogical program, one involving further instruction and argument. Taking it, instead, that dreams may actually serve as an explanatory model for experience tout court need involve neither of these two features.[29]

There is wisdom in a hermeneutic approach to the use of an analogy to dreaming. Phenomenological experience, based on introspection alone, may not allow us to admit such a redescription of our waking lives. And a hermeneutic orientation to experience (employing a metaphorical structure of dreaming) can undercut the suggestion we shall see the epistemological argument make through its appeal to literal (and not metaphorical) dreams as a model and evidentiary example (and not an analogy).

BACK TO INNER SPACE

Were we to follow some philosophers in thinking that Vasubandhu is offering an independent epistemic argument in his introduction, we must think that Vasubandhu believes he has already provided us with a reason to believe that objects do not exist. Or, we must think that he has given us reason to conclude that the deliverances of our perceptual experience could not be related to objects. But that would imply that he begins his work with a howler.[30]

The howler is this: it is surely not enough to say that since "*some* events present phenomenal content that can be determined to be without corresponding objects," therefore "all mental events present phenomenal content without corresponding objects." We can spot the fallacy easily enough when it is put like this. What if we phrase things using the language of inferences from signs or classical South Asian epistemic argument, the *anumāna*?

To provide an epistemological argument from signs (*anumāna*), we need a site (P), a target feature we wish to establish (S), and a reason (H), a candidate feature that can warrant or establish S. The inference, then, is this:

> P has/is S, because it has/is H.

Crucially, we are to see this on the basis of an evidentiary example. This is another site that exemplifies both H and S. The example fixes the relevant nature of the target site for the purposes of the argument and serves, in essence, as a miniature model of it.

Does Vasubandhu's introduction present us with a valid argument from signs based on a well-chosen exemplum?

Take the Buddhist philosopher Bhāviveka's reconstruction of an argument from dreaming: "[We] observe that consciousness arises even without objects [*artha*] such as form, because it arises with the image [*ābhāsa*] of such [objects], just as the cognition of material form arises in a dream."[31] This is just as fallacious as the howler we considered above, as Bhāviveka goes on to demonstrate to his own satisfaction. Consider the unmotivated example, as the Nyāya philosopher Vātsyāyana did. There is no reason to think that our waking experiences are relevantly like dreams in any global way. Indeed, the very reason dreams can support the sense of the example works against them, given that it is only on waking that we come to discern this peculiarity of dream experiences. We do not wake up from our waking experiences.[32]

Anyone wishing to reconstruct a formal epistemic argument from signs on behalf of Vasubandhu must ask themselves what gives us a reason to suppose that, for anything like the general class of experiences we enjoy in normal waking life, our presentations of content do not feature objects. Philosophers did rise to the occasion and address the confusion of scope (as in our way of putting the point with the help of generality), and the unsuitability of the example. They provided epistemically valid arguments that allow us to speak of an argument from dreaming. What we'll see now is that these reconstructions also lead to a model of mind as inner space, a fact that has to do with the way in which the example of dreaming is pressed into service as a model for mind.

Uddyotakara offers a particularly ingenious attempt to reconstruct a formal epistemic argument from Vasubandhu's introduction. The argument exploits a rule that would not permit the inference to employ or make reference to any feature or site whose interpretation (or status) is in dispute.

Thus, we may reinterpret Vasubandhu's howler. Take it, instead, that what he is doing in the opening is putting a certain class of features out of play by demanding that they be the topic in dispute. Thus, the class of "external objects" and "experiences that purport to present evidence of them" are ruled out of bounds. They cannot be appealed to as premises in a debate.

Thus motivated, one can then begin with a logical reconstruction of the reason in Vasubandhu's opening statement. Begin by taking the thought

> *some appearings involve the presentation of nonexistent objects*

to mean what Uddyotakara translates it to mean:

> *all experiences that we can agree upon*, as in dreams, *involve the appearance of the sort of items (H) that do not exist (S).*

The point is to generate a relationship between "appearance" and "nonexistence" in which evidence of appearance can be used as evidence for the nonexistence of what appears.

If left at that, one would have to think that militant skepticism is the only view we can creditably reconstruct Vasubandhu as having endorsed. But one can employ a kind of jujitsu to make this a stronger argument than the skeptic's use of it would recommend. One would need to say that the only evidence we have for fixing the nature of the mental is provided by the class of "all appearings insofar as they are noncontroversially judged to be correlated with nonexistent objects."

Which brings us to an argument intimately related to a reconstruction of Vasubandhu we owe to the Mīmāṃsā philosophical tradition. This argument requires of us a way to fix that what is *essential* to appearings is not external objects, but, in fact, the nonexistence of intentional objects.[33] To do this, however, we need to pull off the trick of finding just the right type of experience as an example that can show what is necessary and sufficient to grasp the very idea of experience. Thus, one finds added to Vasubandhu's claims an important premise—that the case of dreaming shows us what is *essential* and *sufficient* to acquire the very idea of experience:[34]

1. The mental is univocal: all mental events, insofar as they are mental, share in one nature.
2. Experiences in dreams are mental events.
3. What it is to be a mental event is indicated by the nature of its content—and dreams show us what this kind of object is: namely, that it is intrinsically a nonexistent object.
4. We must believe, on the basis of this, that this shows us the intrinsic nature of all mental events, including *perforce* waking cognitions: all mental events must involve nonexistent objects.
5. Otherwise, it would involve us with two entirely separable types of mental events if we allowed, contrary to univocity of the mental (in [1]), some tokens of the type "mental event" to involve a relation with existent objects.[35]

The use of this reconstruction was influential not only with respect to the history of interpretations of Vasubandhu in medieval South Asia but also with respect to contemporary formulations of Vasubandhu's argument, such as that offered by B. K. Matilal.[36] It has the following consequence: we must claim that Vasubandhu did not want to articulate a difference between waking and dreaming. It also would suggest that he had no way in which he *could* do so—even if he should have wanted to.[37] For it puts us back into the stance into which my reconstructed, first-person argument moved us—that of experiencing mind as a variety of inner space, crediting experiential contexts as complete and possessed of un-revisable authority.

THE TROUBLE WITH INNER SPACE

Śaṅkara saw the implications of this variety of argument reconstructed on behalf of Vasubandhu. Situating oneself like this, restricting oneself to this way of bringing one's life under a description, one would not even have the resources to generate the contrastive concept of "externality" (as in "external objects") that such an argument would ostensibly have to use in order to frame its conclusion.[38] Situating oneself in inner space does not only change the claims to which one may assent. It changes the conditions for what is available to one to assent to, and the meaningfulness of so doing.

I think that Śaṅkara was right about the implications of such an argument from dreaming with respect to the stance it recommends, but that we are incorrect in supposing that all authors who invoke dreaming, like Vasubandhu, subscribe to the reconstructed argument that Śaṅkara had in his sights. What's nevertheless relevant is that Śaṅkara helps us see how insulating our lives within inner space has consequences. And it is helpful to know just what these consequences are if we are to attribute to Vasubandhu such a reconstruction on his behalf.

Here's what Śaṅkara sees so clearly: the reconstructed argument from dreaming moves us into a mode of description that jettisons any reference to epistemic, metaphysical, and hermeneutic contexts wider than my current experience. I'd take it further: a subject, described with the resources of inner space, would lose all meaning and collective framing, losing thereby anything that could serve as constraints on its experience, whether in terms of its being an embodied being, a social being, a part of collective history, or, as a natural being, a member of a species.[39] Perhaps inarticulate, such a subject would be devoid of dispositions, trajectories, or any latency. And as the epigraph from Heraclitus suggests, a subject whose essence is disclosed in dreams is a subject that has become a world unto itself.

That a subject can make (and not only find) a world in dreams is an old thought in South Asia.[40] But was such a world ever taken by Vasubandhu to be sufficient? There are different moments in the history of philosophy in South Asia when, in different ways, experiments with the narrative and conceptual intelligibility of mind as inner space and virtual subjectivity became prominent. Vasubandhu, I think, would not wish for us to count him as part of such a visionary company.[41] Not at this stage of the argument, at any rate. And not at such cost.

ARGUMENTS FROM DREAMS AND ARGUMENTS FROM ILLUSION

It will take the rest of this book to argue for that, but we can suggest how to make the point by trying the following thought experiment: What would Vasubandhu have made of the arguments reconstructed for him and the conception of mind as inner space that results?

There is actually a way to try to answer that question. Though not often invoked in contemporary reconstructions, there is an argument we have reason to believe Vasubandhu had *available* to him, and so one that he could have used had he been so inclined. The argument, like some contemporary reconstructions of Vasubandhu's arguments on the basis of dreams and error, belongs to the family that philosophers today call "arguments from illusion."[42]

As J. L. Austin summarizes the role played by such arguments in the work of neo-empiricists such as A. J. Ayer, "The argument from illusion [Ayer's term] is intended primarily to persuade us that, in certain exceptional, abnormal situations, what we perceive—directly anyway—is a sense-datum; but then there comes a second stage, in which we are to be brought to agree that what we (directly) perceive is always a sense-datum, even in the normal, unexceptional case."[43] We can generalize this picture by dropping talk of "sense-data" specifically and speaking, instead, of any variety of inner accusative—or locative, or gerundive in Sanskrit—any item capable of entering into a relation (perhaps only a quasi relation) with the events for which they serve as content.

As Austin notes, for proponents of arguments from illusions, conflicting appearances may include different appearances to different observers, or different appearances to the same observer in different conditions.[44] The characterization also holds true for the arguments from illusion in the *Mahāyanasaṃgraha* that were available to Vasubandhu.

I have claimed that Vasubandhu follows the same strategy as the *Mahāyānasaṃgraha*: exemplification for the sake of clarification precedes a direct argument for the view, and a direct argument for his view requires that we show much more than we might be able to elicit from the example of dreaming, given that we have no experience analogous to "waking up." But there is one crucial difference between Vasubandhu and the authors of the *Mahāyānasaṃgraha*: the latter introduces several of the same examples that Vasubandhu does, but not to exemplify the thesis. They are made to demonstrate, instead, an incoherence with respect to the concept of an object by using an argument from illusion: "How can the nonexistence of objects be understood? As the Blessed One has said: 'A bodhisattva . . . comprehends the fact that all mental events are objectless by (1) By the awareness of conflicting cognitions with respect to a single object, as with the various cognitions on the part of hungry ghosts, beasts, men and gods.'"[45] This is the first of four rather different types of argument, the remainder of which need not detain us here.

What matters to us now is that Sthiramati, perhaps seeking to align Vasubandhu more closely with the *Mahāyānasaṃgraha*, not only thinks this argument available to Vasubandhu but uses it to reconstruct Vasubandhu's claims. As a possible reconstruction of the logical function of Vasubandhu's examples, it deserves to be taken seriously, if only diagnostically, because it will make explicit one premise from which Vasubandhu, elsewhere, unequivocally distances himself from.

In his commentary on Vasubandhu's *The Thirty Verses*, Sthiramati believed he had to offer Vasubandhu a master argument in order to show not only that episodes involving the presentation of content could not have content due to the influence of objects, but that the very idea of objects serving as causes of our content involves some degree of incoherence. Sthiramati is commenting on verse 17a–b, where Vasubandhu outlines a reason for claiming that thinking of mental events as instances of construction (*vikalpa*), as opposed to representations of extra-mental causes of content, allows him to make the following point: "This mental process is a process of conceptual construction; whatever has been conceptually constructed does not, by that token, exist. Therefore, all this is just presentation of content."[46] While this does look like an argument, it does not yet have a justification of its premise: that mental process is a process of conceptual construction. It is this premise for which Sthiramati attempts to provide an argument in his commentary on using a version of an argument from illusion.[47]

The argument Sthiramati offered may be reconstructed for him as involving two arguments spun out with the following important premise: one and the same mechanism must be able to explain the generation of content in illusions and veridical cognitions alike. On the basis of this premise, Sthiramati offers two arguments, the first of which runs as follows:

> But how can it be shown to be true that the content of mental events does not exist? For the following reason: some X with Y as its cause occurs only (a) given all causal conditions are satisfied and (b) when there is no factor counteracting Y. An awareness event can occur even when its objects do not exist, as, for example, in cases such as illusions, a city of celestial musicians, dreams, ophthalmia, and so on. And were the occurrence of an awareness event to be bound up with the object (as its cause), no awareness of such things as illusion could arise, on account of its object not being present. Therefore, an awareness event occurs on account of the ceasing of a prior mental event of the same type, and not from an external object, given the occurrence of the awareness event even in its absence.[48]

The argument trades on a suitably restrictive sense of the relation between a cause and an effect, such that if some X is claimed to be an effect of some cause Y, then, all things being equal, X should always and only come to be when Y is present. But on this supposition, we cannot make sense of objects as causes of content, because it is part of the concept of error, or our concept of such experiences as dreaming, that we enjoy experiences without objects as causes. According to the premise, this should incline us to see another explanation for the appearance of content for putatively successful instances of cognition as well.

Sthiramati's second argument runs as follows: "Even when the object does not vary, perceiving subjects have cognitions which mutually conflict. And it does not make sense to predicate a manifold and inconsistent nature of something singular. Therefore, the following should be accepted: on account of having a nature that is the result of projection, the intentional object of thought [*vikalpa*] does not exist."[49] This is as neat an encapsulation of an argument from conflicting appearances as one might find anywhere. To motivate it in Sthiramati's hand, we need to point out that the concept of "cause" is linked to the concept of "existence." Only existent items can serve as causes. But to be existent, for many Buddhist philosophers, also requires possessing a metaphysically simple identity. However, Sthiramati thinks that claiming that the content of our cognitions is caused by objects would saddle us with attributing to the putative cause a nonsimple or even contradictory nature in such cases where perceivers report conflicting content with respect to a single cause.

Sthiramati does not specify which cases of conflicting content he has in mind. But we can easily recruit here two varieties of cases. We have already met with the use of cosmology in the *Mahāyānasaṃgraha* in this connection. There is also a longstanding example of another kind: "On seeing a beautiful young woman enter a room, a son experiences respect, a glutton avarice, some jealousy, and an ascetic who has spent a lot of time learning to experience the intrinsic impurity of beautiful things, disgust; while another type of sage might experience compassion for the woman."[50] This gives us a psychological basis for sufficient variation to make the point. Whether or not it really makes sense to treat differences in character as differences in lifeforms will occupy me in the conclusion. For now, we can at least say that Sthiramati's argument is clearly a descendent of a long generation of arguments from illusion.

Sthiramati's appeal to the principle that a single mechanism must be able to explain all manner of experiences, along with the Mīmāṃsā argument from dreaming we considered above, shows us something else about the more general argument from illusions. What is at stake is the identification of something that can serve as the common core of all mental occurrences, what it is to be minded. Because we have given no alternative model of cause other than objects (or inner surrogates for objects), Sthiramati's argument would suggest that either objects cause content or that all the relevant properties constitutive of experience are internal to what is manifest by experience, which could incline to a variety of inner space, though here we are not invited to inhabit it quite so directly as we are in the Mīmāṃsā reconstruction.[51]

Sthiramati believes that we may use the above arguments to argue for Vasubandhu's views. But the question remains: If Vasubandhu had such arguments available to him, why did he not use them in the form that Sthiramati reconstructed for him?

WHAT'S SO DIFFERENT ABOUT VASUBANDHU?

Should it matter that he did not use them? It should. There are two problems with the kind of approach adopted by Sthiramati, problems we would do well to consider when interpreting Vasubandhu. It is not only the case that Vasubandhu did *not* offer any such argument; one can also show that Vasubandhu did not seem to place much stock in arguments from conflicting appearances. In one case where Vasubandhu considers an argument from conflicting appearances—a recognizable instance of attempting to argue from the case of an illusion to the nonexistence of a phenomenon—it is unclear what, if anything, we are meant to take away.[52] And in another, the one that will concern us here, he explicitly takes issue with one of the argument's central premises.

The context for the second case is provided by Vasubandhu's arguments to the effect that the Buddha did not mean to deny that there was such a thing as pleasure; instead, Vasubandhu maintains, the Buddha was invested in claiming that pleasure qua pleasure is dissatisfying. But Vasubandhu is faced with an argument based on a premise not unlike Sthiramati's. His interlocutors maintain that if pleasure is to be a genuine variety of feeling and an independent variety of appraisal of things in the world, then whatever causes it in one person must unfailingly cause it in everyone. (Sthiramati, you will recall, maintained that if some X is claimed to be an effect of some cause Y, then, all things being equal, X should always and only come to be when Y is present.) Vasubandhu's reply is instructive:

> With respect to the argument from the fact that there are no invariant causes of pleasure, we respond that this demonstrates a lack of understanding of causes. For a given object is alternatively the cause of pleasure or pain depending on its basis, the experiencing subject. The object alone is not a cause. If an object serves as the cause of pleasure in connection with a body in a certain state, it will remain a cause of pleasure when that body is in that state again.[53]

Vasubandhu is not impressed with attempts to show that causes that do not generate identical effects in different subjects at all times cannot be causes: far from disclosing something inherently absurd in the notion of an object as cause of content, such arguments exhibit the failure to acknowledge that objects interact with subjects in complex ways, thereby yielding up different occasions to different types of beings in different contexts. It is by virtue of being related to beings with complex characteristics that objects can dispose beings to feel and appraise differently.

If Vasubandhu believes *this* and believes that causal explanations may rely on relational features, it is hard to see why he would credit any such ambitious argument from conflicting appearances available in Buddhist literature, given that the central lesson of such arguments (as Étienne Lamotte pointed out) is something that anyone comfortable with the idea of relational causes can count on to support their own view: the fact that we cannot recruit an object in an explanation of what is experienced without making reference to the type of subject whose experiences the explanation seeks to keep in view.[54]

Which brings us to the point at issue: the value of Sthiramati's reconstructions lies in their showing us the potential cost in any attempt to run together cases of illusion and the possibility of differently constituted communities of beings and their conflicting phenomenological experiences. Sthiramati's reconstructed arguments from illusion stop where Vasubandhu might very well have us begin, with the insight that specifying a cause of experience might have to make reference to the complex variety of dispositional bases associated with perceiving subjects. "The object alone is not a cause," we saw Vasubandhu say above to his interlocutor in *The Cutting Edge of Buddhist Thought.* If one believes that objects are insufficient, then two things follow: We cannot use them in good faith to motivate arguments from illusion. And, more importantly, we are left to reconsider the shape an explanation must take if it is to capture how things come into view for us. If the explanation begins to shift from objects, it may require, for example, complex structuring principles that link objects to subjects of certain kinds. And that might begin to require an account that goes beyond the categorical properties available to us within inner space. At least, reliance on dispositions may well go against the core of epistemic separatism, on which, as Kimhi notes, the qualities of appearances are presumed to be separable in the following sense: such phenomenal qualities that a subject may experience in any instance are independent (and graspable as such, independently) of the content of any experience they had earlier, or will have earlier.[55] The whole thrust of Vasubandhu's account inclines to showing us that this is just not so.

Where does that leave us for now? It is one thing to show that there is a continuity between dreaming and waking insofar as they enjoy nonpresent objects in some sense. But it is entirely another thing to claim that the idea of dreaming or the idea of illusion shows us what we need in order to fix the sense of our concept of mind.

J. L. Austin's criticized arguments from illusion precisely because they presuppose a concept of mind to begin with.[56] Had Vasubandhu been able to see the reconstructions offered for his view, I suspect he would have said the same thing. His careful and piecemeal deployment of examples in what I have called his laboratory of experience at the beginning of *The Twenty Verses* seem to be designed to offset what reconstructions of Vasubandhu suggest: that the case of dreams or illusions could give us a norm for the mental or a world.[57] There is no one type of experience that can serve as the norm for another model of mindedness. Nothing but *another world* can give Vasubandhu a model for having experience as if in a world.

What of dreams? As we'll see next, Vasubandhu's interest in them, distinct from the skeptical arguments we have reconstructed on his behalf, might suggest why dreaming need not be stale news after all.

3

THE PLACE OF DREAMS

The sage will be the same asleep or awake.

—"EXCERPTS FROM THE LIFE OF EPICURUS"[1]

This chapter develops a new account of Vasubandhu's concern with dreams. On my account Vasubandhu is concerned with what I will call "the place of dreaming." We shall ask questions like these: How shall we talk about what happens in dreams? And what implications does the continuity of dreaming and waking experiences hold for the kinds of beings we are? This, I hope you'll agree, is quite distinct from the variety of arguments from dreams that have been reconstructed for him by modern and premodern interpreters.

Granted, my concern is one that is easily mistaken for a skeptic's use of dreams. Consider one way in which this can happen. Epicurus, as Diogenes Laertius has it, said that "the mental images of madmen and dream images are realities, since they activate the mind, whereas the nonexistent does not thus activate it."[2] As the twinning of madmen and dreamers here suggests, this is indeed in the neighborhood of the classical skeptic's concern. And it is true that one can quite easily fold this issue of the "reality" of dream occurrences into the traditional skeptical use of dreaming. All one has to do is to link this statement to a causal account of the origin of images. Thus used, Epicurus's saying becomes an argument to the effect that, since a similar causal story accounts for representations in perception and the occurrence of images, we ought to see that one and the same story might govern sleep cognition and waking.[3] Therefore, we cannot be sure of what we encounter in waking perceptions.

But this possible use of Epicurus's saying should not blind us to the arguably more basic question: Just what sorts of things are dreams? In other words, what is their place among the various odds and ends that make up the furniture of the world as determined by one's fundamental metaphysical commitments? We're trying to get clear on how we are to describe dreams, their occurrence, the phenomenology associated with them, and their salience.

Epicurus's saying shows us how easy it is to conflate very different types of questions concerning dreams. It is only very recently in Anglophone philosophy that there has even been anything like a concerted and coordinated effort to generate the geography of concepts we shall need in order to do justice to the rich phenomenology that sleeping, waking, and everything within and between these states entails.[4] Vasubandhu, as I read him, is using his laboratory of examples to contribute something important to our vocabulary and our sense of ourselves: we are beings who enjoy experiences in virtual environments, and this fact about us can matter. I will offer here a reconstruction that will get us to see what it might mean to inhabit a virtual environment, why experiences therein might be salient for us, and why such salience matters to our appreciation of the account Vasubandhu is developing in *The Twenty Verses*.

THE CONTEXT FOR VASUBANDHU'S ARGUMENTS FROM DREAMING

The first context for the use of dreams is this: at the beginning of *The Twenty Verses*, Vasubandhu is challenged by an interlocutor to understand the intelligibility of experience in the absence of objects. In other words, to understand an experience of X as a variety of concrete happening we must understand two things: that the experience is what it is because of its being of X, and that it occurs at all because of X. It is X's constitutive and explanatory role that shows why certain other features necessary to describing some experiences might hold. It is the nature of X, for example, that will determine how the experience, as effect, will occur: whether as something situated in space and time (or not), whether privately or publicly, and whether as causally functional or not.[5]

For example, when I drink something that appears to be water and everything goes as it should, one wants to say that I quench my thirst *because* there is water in the glass. This function of water (whether involved in every instance of my acquaintance with water or not) is part of what is involved in an experience of water being an experience *of* water. An absence of liquid, or another liquid, will function differently, and constrain a very different sequence of events to occur. We cannot bring any mental event under an intelligible description as an event with such-and-such content and as one that exhibits such-and-such range of possible functions without reference to objects.

Importantly, it is the interlocutor who offers Vasubandhu the initial invocation of virtuality and who draws a contrast with waking experience:

> Fine hairs, for example, appear only to those who suffer from an ocular disease, but not to others. Why is it that the function of hair, or bees, for example, is not discharged by the hair and the bees and other things seen by those who have such an ocular disease, whereas it is not the case that such functions are not discharged by their real counterparts in other contexts? Why is it that the food, drink, clothes, poison, weapons, among other things seen in a dream do not have the causal efficacy to satisfy, respectively, hunger, thirst, and so on, that their counterparts outside of a dream do?[6]

The interlocutor speaks of what is *experienced* in dreaming and applies to it a contrastive structure:

In a dreaming context, I see A and A* does not behave like A in a waking context.*

The interlocutor thus introduces talk of a virtual object, a virtual object being describable as being "as if X but not X."

Thus, take the example of bees. If I dream of myself walking in a garden, I will see virtual bees in the garden, not bees. (We are, of course, using the interlocutor's way of putting things now.) Bees live in the world. Virtual bees can live in my mind, among other virtual spaces. Or, consider a sexual partner. A person is one sort of thing. The virtual being in a possible dream, another. What I have access to when I dream of a person is neither that person, nor a person, however alike one might be to the other. And that can matter.

The interlocutor wants to say that, absent objects, Vasubandhu has only virtual objects. And one can't make sense of experiences of virtual objects. The interlocutor wishes to see this as entailing unreality and unintelligibility of experience as we know it. But why? It cannot be because a virtual X is not the same thing as an X. That is given. He wants to say something important is missing. The argument, instead, might be this:

A virtual X cannot be met with in space, so it can support no immersion and it cannot be interacted with as an X, nor function as an X; therefore a virtual X is not only not a real X, but not *as real as* X in the following two senses: it is not an element that can take its place as belonging to a list of type of things with which we interact in this world. It has no place, no distinctive causal powers, and thus cannot matter.

In what follows, I will piece together an argument that will reject this anti-realism about the possibility of virtual experience. It will reject virtual anti-realism by advancing slowly to make two points about immersion and inter-action: we'll make the case about immersion with the help of Vasubandhu's point about seeing particulars, and we'll consider a wide-angled approach with the help of the implications of an analogy to wet dreams, an analogy that will help us make the case for interaction. Jointly, they will allow Vasubandhu to claim that we do enjoy experiences in virtual environments and that, as we shall see, such experience can often be salient.[7]

SEEING VIRTUAL CONTENT

Vasubandhu's first point is made as follows: "First of all, how is it that in a dream, even in the absence of a correlated object, particular things—whether bees, gardens, women, men, or what have you—are seen only in particular places, and not everywhere, and seen in these particular places only at particular times, not at all times? From this it follows that one can have spatiotemporal constraints on experience even in the absence of objects."[8] Vasubandhu preserves his interlocutor's use of the verb "to see" (using verbs formed from the root *dṛṣ-*). But he adds to this an emphasis that was missing in the way his interlocutor framed the point. We *see* items *as* embedded in a spatiotemporal frame. That is not entailed by the interlocutor's way of framing the notion of virtual content. We need to revise the interlocutor's structure of virtual experience at least to say,

In a dreaming context, I see A (at such-and-such place at a time) . . .*

There are two parts to this sentence. We see something in a *situated* way as part of a course of experience; and *we see* such things. The interlocutor uses the verb, but perhaps does not there reflect on what his use might mean. It is a contested verb to have used, then and now.

There are all too many reasons for philosophers to question the use of verbs like "see" in a strict sense to describe experience in dreaming. For one thing, it has been maintained that we may not experience anything in dreaming.[9] And if one grants that one is experiencing, shall we describe it as presenting as, but failing to be, an experience of the kind we enjoy in wakeful moments? That might be what "seeing" would imply. Which amounts to claiming for dreaming the status of a kind of hallucination. But it is not obvious that we are, as it were, hallucinating in dreams. Then again, it is not any more obvious that we are imagining when dreaming. This is the problem: Just what is the right verb to describe what is going on in dream experiencing? How active or otherwise shall we construe it as being? And how continuous will any type of function we pick to describe dreaming be with its waking counterpart? How continuous are perceiving X, imagining X, hallucinating X, anyway?[10]

These questions may emerge in several languages and at different times. If Vasubandhu and his interlocutor agree to use "to see" in connection with dreaming, this might mean something. Just what that something is is not, admittedly, all that easy to describe, but one of the questions at stake in this discussion has to do with the continuity of presentative function of mental episodes across different kinds of conscious contexts of experience. It is fair to say, then, that to use the language of "seeing" is to subscribe to the thought that we are in the neighborhood of experience in dreams. And it is also to suggest something about the quality of what I will call perceptual presence in dreams.

"Seeing" (*darśana*) is a word that can slide from sensory to epistemic senses. At the other end of *The Twenty Verses* (17ab), someone tries to say that "seeing" is used in such a way as to entail that somewhere in the process we have been in contact with sensory objects.[11] Indeed, some Buddhist philosophers claim, by way of appeals to established convention, that "to see" something entails a distinctive variety of sensory rather than cognitive awareness, one enabled by sensory contact.[12] But in addition to the phenomenological presence associated with sensory experience, it can also point in the direction of an epistemic achievement that is only metaphorically and not literally connected to sensation. As in chapter 8 of *The Cutting Edge of Buddhist Thought*, Vasubandhu reports of the epistemic achievements of the path of self-cultivation, given that they involve perceptual acquaintance, that "knowing" in the relevant sense just is "seeing."[13]

To say that one can see in dreams suggests that we can pry apart the sense of perceptual presence and its epistemic weight. To see in dreams is not to know; perhaps it is only to be poised as if one were in waking contact with something, though Vasubandhu does not describe dream experience as hallucination (or hallucination-like) explicitly.

We can say this much at least: Vasubandhu is stating that there is no such restriction to the sense of perceptual presence. And experience of such presence (overlapping in some ways with such presence in waking contexts) may be generated in a number of contexts, not only in strictly sensory experience. Part of the experience of such presence is an immersive feel in a spatiotemporal environment in which one is situated along with what one sees.

SEEING AND EXPERIENCING

Perhaps I am being too quick with the word "experience." Seeing, one might complain, need not entail experiencing.

In order to indicate more of the phenomenology of dreaming that is intimated by immersion, cues may be sought from a wider background than is strictly appealed to in *The Twenty Verses*. In a review of the function of the analogy of dreams, Masaaki Hattori reports that, among various uses, the example is used particularly in Yogācāra literature in order to describe the possibility of something worth calling "experience" (*anubhava*) in the absence of external causes of content.[14] The idea is to show us something richer than what is captured in speaking of enjoying presentation of nonexistent objects. The point is to suggest that we *respond* to nonexistent objects when presented with them, as in dreams.

This richer concept is highlighted by words like *anubhava*, *upabhoga*, or the even more technical *vedanā*, meaning hedonic tone and appraisal.[15] It is not intentionality alone (that is, our having something in view), but *vedanā*—our experiential responses to content disclosed by episodes of awareness—that is often taken to be analogous to experiences in a dream.

A little terminological housekeeping is called for. Vasubandhu defines affect as a *threefold experience* (*trividhānubhava*).[16] He further enumerates what experience here means in terms of three possible modes of responsiveness to content: (1) where one wishes to remain or be united with some X; (2) where one wishes to be separated from X; and (3) where one's response does not consist in being disposed to either unite or separate from X.[17]

Vasubandhu's use of *vedanā* shows us why it is the presence of affect that takes us beyond the simple registering of the presence of content and toward the distinctive form of engagement that involves action-guiding appraisal.[18] "Experience" (*anubhava*) is a richer word in Sanskrit than "presentation of content" (*vijñapti*): talk of *anubhava* can entail the use of first-person qualitative descriptions to capture what undergoing this kind of mental event involves.[19] And this richer sense, which straddles pre-theoretical and theoretical ways of speaking, is reserved on the part of Vasubandhu and philosophers in his scholastic tradition for descriptions involving *vedanā*.

To be willing to speak of dreams in connection with affect and experience suggests that dreaming can involve:

(a) responsiveness to content, at least seeming to involve affordances and solicitations to action; and
(b) qualitative experiential texture associated with responsiveness to content.

What difference does this make? It is one thing to claim that I can have intentional content, something that is present to apprehension that does not exist—say, the scotoma during a migraine. But this seems to be different than saying that I can have an experience of—or a coherent, temporally extended, dynamic, appraisal-involving, and action-soliciting engagement with—nonexistent things.

Let's say that we have technology that is capable of reproducing the "content" of the dream onto a screen as the subject dreaming the dream sleeps. Consider the difference between this person experiencing their dream and watching a film in which the content of their dream is reproduced.[20] I would maintain that there *is* a difference between merely *seeing* the content projected and dreaming the dream. The way the content is *had*—the way it solicits and responds to our changing responses—is part of what is comprehended by speaking of "experience" here: in a phrase, the dream is experienced by the dreamer, while the projected dream, one could maintain, is merely seen.

To link dreaming and experience as the metaphorology of Yogācāra Buddhism does, and as the arguments of Vasubandhu may invite us to do, is *not* like saying that to dream may be analogized to watching a movie. I think that Vasubandhu wants to say that dreaming is less like watching a movie, or reading a book, and more like stepping into one. It's immersive. It puts you in it, so to speak—into the experienced presence of what is manifest. And the presence or absence of objects does not seem to have much of anything to do with either characterizing or explaining this, as far as Vasubandhu is concerned.

DESCRIBING EXPERIENCES

One further aspect of what I am calling a more robust notion of experience thus elicited may be seen by Sthiramati's comments on *vedanā* in his commentary to Vasubandhu's *On the Five Heaps*.[21] This is a point that will allow us to connect the language of experiences with a concern with the spatiotemporality of experiences in dreams.

To see the point Sthiramati wishes to make, we may develop the idea that experience goes beyond the notion of the presentation of content. Awareness, insofar as it involves apprehension per se (*upalabdhimātra*), is not construed by Buddhist philosophers as involving any reference to spatial properties. The point Sthiramati thinks is interesting about *vedanā* is that we frame our experienced feelings as if they were spatiotemporal. Not only can I say that in pain I am aware of my hand—but I can say that there is an instance of *vedanā*, a feeling, *in my hand*.[22]

The point, however, is *not* to say that such experiences are *truly* spatially situated—as are, for instance, items that are counted as material. An item counts as material because its characteristic properties depend on its ability to resist co-occupation in space. We are not trying to explain the reason for our linguistic practice, or our phenomenological reports, which seems to slide full-blown experiences closer to the nature of spatially situated things. Instead, in this discussion we are given to understand that enjoying such experiences involves a tacit construal of them being events in a spatiotemporal frame, whatever the ultimate explanation of such a linguistic fact may be. For one thing, Buddhist philosophers accord to *vedanā* the status of a mental function; also, we might see here a recognition that the kind of spatiality we credit to such phenomenal content is not reducible to physical space. As some contemporary philosophers have argued, the "in" in phenomenal judgments does not enjoy transitivity with the "in" of physical location. To use an example I picked up from others in school, imagine having a pain in your hand, and then putting your hand in the oven. It would be odd to say that the pain is in the oven.

So too, with properties. I experience (as I typically do) a pain in my head. I walk quickly while I have a headache and at some ascertainable speed. It would be odd to assign my headache the same speed, or any trajectory through space and time. Given how they highlight the curious status of the spatial and phenomenal content of *vedanā*, I think Sthiramati and Vasubandhu would agree.

The point we need to make on analogy with affect is this: to claim that dreams are like experiences is to say that we possess, by virtue of having these occurrences—even in the absence of present objects as causes of content—the disposition to credit the content, and the experiences of such content, as occurring in a spatiotemporal framework that is not, however, commensurable with a spatiotemporal frame of physical things.

Perhaps the right thing to say on behalf of Vasubandhu is not only that we experience immersion in a virtual space in dreams, but that experience itself entails some such notion as virtual space.

DREAMS AND INTERACTION

Thus far, by clarifying an analogy in the available literature, the above line of argument leaves us with the phenomenological intuition that experiences *do* occur in dreams and our experiences are immersive.

Should we credit such experiences with concreteness? The analogy to feeling is indicative. Vasubandhu's first example of dreaming may be after something more fundamental: if dreams involve experiences, can such experiences be said to *be* or to *involve* events? Instances of *vedanā* are causal. They have effects and are situated in causal chains. What of dream experiences?

Consider the contrasting sentence the interlocutor provided, now revised to reflect Vasubandhu's qualification about spatiotemporal constraints: "In a dreaming context, I see A* as being in place X at time Y, but A* does not behave as does A in a waking context." Spatiotemporal occurrence is insufficient to get us to speak of the concreteness of virtual objects, even if we are comfortable with speaking of virtual structures and contexts for experience. We need to see a virtual object as falling into a causal nexus. The interlocutor associates concreteness with objects, to which Vasubandhu's response is brief: "Take the example of a wet dream, defined by the emission of semen in the absence of sexual intercourse."[23]

If an experience of a virtual object can be a cause, then it can be described as an event; and it is if an event, then we can speak of it as being bound up with other events in a manner indicative of supporting a causal function. The language of events and causation—and thus, of concreteness—may apply across physical and virtual spaces.

Take the possibility of experiential environments that are distinct in kind from our experience of public objects to be a form of virtual realism avant la lettre. With digital experiences in mind, David Chalmers has suggested thinking of virtual realism as a contemporary package of views holding that: (1) Virtual objects really exist; (2) events in virtual reality (such as taking a walk through a virtual environment) really take place; (3) experiences in virtual reality are nonillusory; and (4) virtual experiences are as valuable as nonvirtual experiences.

To apply this to Vasubandhu, we will have to modify the third view to say that "experiences in virtual reality can be nonillusory," or at least that subjects of virtual experiences do not necessarily possess the best interpretation of them, the one under which they are nonillusory; and we will have to modify the fourth to say that "virtual experiences can be as salient as nonvirtual experiences." But once we do, I think Vasubandhu can quite safely be read as having offered us a premodern version of this package of views.[24]

OF INTERACTION AND VIRTUAL OBJECTS

The experience of a virtual environment can be misunderstood. It will be misunderstood if it suggests homogeneity of experiential contexts, or that dreams as a virtual environment is the model, rather than the indication of a model, of the account we shall need to explain having things in view. Let me intimate this with the help of the Buddhist philosopher Śubhagupta (who flourished in the eighth century CE).

Śubhagupta recognized that there are two claims here.[25] First, there is the claim that virtual content can involve the discharge of causal functioning, which allows it to satisfy desires. Then there is the possible claim that virtual content can be action guiding and recruited to factor into explanations that credit the satisfaction of desires as an instance of successful practical action on the part of a rational agent.

Śubhagupta accepts that Vasubandhu's example shows the former but denies that it supports the latter.[26] This is an important point. Interaction in dreams cannot be a model for action in waking life. Nor do I believe that Vasubandhu wishes to claim that it can. (There is, firstly, a problem with metacognitive control, as we discussed in the last chapter in connection with torpor. And secondly, the scope for deception in dream experience is too great for it to serve as a normative model for epistemic and practical success.)

Vasubandhu's claim is not that there is no distinction between dream and waking contexts. For now, he only seeks to show that virtual objects can be experienced and interacted with. And even if the point is meant to indicate that we ought to treat waking experiences as if they trafficked with virtual content, this is not to say that virtual objects in dream are the same as the contents we interact with on waking. There is a distinction to be drawn between dreaming and waking contexts, a distinction that is internal to the use of the example.

This has the air of an admission. One thing that might give a reader pause is the belief that something has gone wrong in Vasubandhu's example and in my discussion of it thus far. The example of a wet dream seems to presuppose a distinction between, on the one hand, dreaming and waking, and, on the other hand, between the mind and the body. Isn't that the force of appealing to effects of a wet dream, the "real effects," one wants to stress, premised on the availability of a context of an entirely different kind than the dream?

We presume the example works because, in principle, there is or can be evidence of a wet dream beyond the dream. Some physiological changes that occur during the dream can, in some cases, become evident upon waking. That's one way in which we come to know that the consequences of the event in the dream need not be confined to the dream. We might also say the same for nonphysical evidence, such as we possess when we remember the dream upon awakening. Either way, the force of the example requires not being limited to one context alone. But doesn't any appeal to virtual realism because of wet dreams here defeat itself, since it is based on a pairwise distinction it is supposed to undermine?

Vasubandhu, I would argue, is *not* guilty of the philosophical equivalent of a mixed metaphor or of thereby begging the question. This would only be the case were we committed to the thought that Vasubandhu uses the example of dreaming to call into question the distinction between waking and dreaming *entirely*. Once more, that is not the claim on offer. What he wants us to take away, rather, is this: whatever else the distinction between waking and dreaming might consist in, it cannot consist in there being two entirely insulated realms, any more than it can consist in there being (ultimately) only one realm. If we reply that they do seem to be phenomenologically insulated from one another, this might just be the point: causal continuity constitutive of mental continuity need not entail phenomenological continuity, and vice versa.

Making the point about the causal continuity of contexts of experience this way does entail the limitation of phenomenological experience in one context alone. But this is not a criticism of Vasubandhu's point, being merely inconsistent with certain interpretations of Vasubandhu. In fact, I believe that the limitation of experience in any one context is a part of what he wishes to show us.

Imagine running through the following argument:

(a) Virtual counterparts of objects do not involve the presence of objects they are like.
(b) Only objects, and not virtual counterparts, have causal powers.
(c) We can experience virtual counterparts in some contexts to have powers objects have, even where objects are absent.[27]

Something here must give. I believe this is what Vasubandhu would suggest: there is a source of causal power, but it should not be located where experience in a virtual environment suggests it should be located. We are primed by the structure of experience, in dreams no less than in waking, to experience in terms of objects related to a subject of experience. But we should not look for causes of our experience in some putative virtual object. There might be a more complicated account on which there is some causal process that can explain the way in which virtual content is brought into being in a manner consistent with one's desires, an account that will also show us how it can seem to be that the virtual content manages to satisfy desire. But we must not expect that we will necessarily be able to anticipate the shape of such an account just on the basis of what is manifest to us in experience.[28]

Vasubandhu's brand of virtual realism helps call into question the wisdom of looking to objects for explaining experience; and it helps shift the explanatory direction away from manifest contents to some causal process not necessarily evident within experience.

THE PLACE OF DREAMING

My account thus far has used the idea of virtual realism to tell a story that can say why Vasubandhu may have been invested in dreams at the beginning of *The Twenty Verses*. It is a different story from the one that he is usually credited with. I grant that my account will seem unusual. In defense of it, I think it will help to consider Vasubandhu's argument (as I have reconstructed it) in a global context. On my view, it is making sense of the place of experience in a virtual environment that is at issue. What that means is that dreams show us we have a potential problem making sense of a continuous description of the alternating contexts our experience appears to involve.

This has been seen to be the thrust of appeals to wet dreams in other places and other times. At the age of twenty-three, Leibniz wrote about "the spontaneous ejection of semen without any contact in sleep; in wakers it is expelled only when they are strongly agitated, but in sleep the spirits are moved internally by a strong imagination alone and without any rubbing of the members."[29] Leibniz will make two points with the help of the example, the first of which, the importance of crediting some experiences to the role of imagination rather than sensory contact, was also made by Shahrastānī, who, writing in the twelfth century, saw something similar in the example: "The imagination has a remarkable ability to influence both the movements of bodies and the behavior of souls. Is not the pollution in sleep an effect of the imagination within the body?"[30] Interestingly enough, Shahrastānī is here providing an argument to his readers to motivate them to take meditation in Indian traditions seriously—meditation here being construed as an exercise of the imagination with the capacity to impress upon the physical world. The larger context of Shahrastānī's discussion of nocturnal emission is even more apposite to the topic at hand. To credit the imagination with causal powers is to argue for the place of thought in a sensible world. Shahrastānī's use of this example illustrates what I mean by a concern with the place of dreaming. To ask for the "place" of experience, or virtuality, or mind in the world is to ask the following: How are we to allow our descriptions of mind as causally efficacious to hook up, as it were, with descriptions that locate causal efficacy in physical concrete particulars? In other words, how do we coherently situate what is mental within spatiotemporal causal chains?

Consider here a point Matthew Kapstein raises in connection with Vasubandhu's way of speaking of persons in *Against Selves*: "I think that Vasubandhu . . . damages his own case from the very outset by relying rather heavily on examples of characteristically *spatio*-temporal continua—for instance, a moving fire, a lamp-light, and a growing plant. What is never made completely clear is just what it is that these examples are supposed to reveal about the unity of a continuum that is only partially physical, and which at times may be completely non-physical."[31] Kapstein's point is well taken. We can even supplement it with Vasubandhu's explicit commitments elsewhere that state that spatiotemporal continuity is essential to the kind of continuity subjects exhibit.[32] I raise the issue not to introduce a metaphysical problem; I just want to make sure that we take away the right analytic lesson from the example of wet dreams.

As Leibniz, potentially, did not. Nothing within a dream experience, Leibniz went on to note, could tell us whether something was a dream or not. Only the coherence of some putative stretch of experience with other experiences, linked together in terms of causal antecedents and effects, could show us how to group things together as episodes of waking or dreaming. Leibniz was not troubled by the implications of this. Shahrastānī may or may not have been, but in directing our attention to the example of wet dreams the way he did, he also directed our attention to the different sorts of causes that may be involved in different contexts of experience. Examples like wet dreams, he effectively reminded us, serve to bring continuity into focus as an issue, raising thereby, however implicitly, the following questions: When linking dreaming and waking experiences in a single causal story, what are we doing? What manner of account will we need whether we sharpen the divide between consciousness in sleep and in waking states or blur the boundaries between them? And for what manner of subject will such accounts be salient?

DREAMS AND THE SALIENCE OF VIRTUAL ENVIRONMENTS

The kind of virtual realism I have been reconstructing for Vasubandhu makes the claim that there are virtual environments in which we may become immersed for a time. We can also summarize the above discussion of the place of dreams this way. Vasubandhu's virtual realism also claims that these virtual environments are salient. By speaking of the salience of virtual environments, I mean, firstly, to indicate that virtual environments are not causally isolated from experience in contexts that matter to us. Experience therein can lastingly change us. Secondly, experiences in virtual environments can be indicative of the kind of beings we are. Jointly, virtual environments are not ignorable stages of our lives.

I will use the example of wet dreams to show what it means to speak of the salience of Vasubandhu's virtual realism, and the implications this can hold for the account he is going to offer in the rest of *The Twenty Verses*, answering thereby at least some of the questions we raised above.

Let us take a high-relief view of the terrain. Speaking of the philosophical traditions of Europe, Catherine Wilson maintains that "the alleged ontological distinction between the real world and the fictional world is frequently held to extend to an emotional and moral insulation,"[33] separating one sphere of our lives from another. This is broadly the view against which virtual realism sets itself. In doing so, we must counter a particular way of weighing the distinction between virtual and nonvirtual contexts of experience. And we must counter the insulation of what is experienced in disparate contexts.

It won't do to think in terms of unwieldy contraries, such as European and non-European traditions. Philosophers in the ancient Mediterranean pursued various approaches to the distinction between dreaming and waking and have put this distinction to a variety of uses, as have philosophers in South Asia and China. Such diversity also holds true of the ways that philosophers might push back against the insulation of dreaming and waking as normatively salient contexts. Thus, I do not wish to be misunderstood. Let's not even pretend to consider being exhaustive. There are simply far too many ways in which dreams came to matter to ancient philosophers.

But we can try to be indicative. E. R. Dodds once suggested that there were two reasons for the persistence of dreaming in the life and work of (European) philosophers of antiquity. The first reason had to do with the historical intuition that "dreams . . . are related to man's inmost life";[34] and the second, which he took to be the simpler to understand, had to do with dreams being (in some sense) other worlds. Dreams extend the stage of our lives, presenting a world in which it is possible to meet with the dead and the gods. This extension of our stage of possible experiences, far from being considered less real in the ancient world, would have reality flow *from* dreams.[35]

Of course, it is not always easy to keep such emphases apart. A person's secret life—where they go, or the range of experience available to them, when invisible to an outside observer, as when they are asleep—may be treated as involving another world: "Wherever he may travel in his dream," says Ajātaśatru to Gārgi of the person who rests in the space within the heart in the *Bṛhadāraṇyaka Upaniṣad* (2.1.18), "those regions become his worlds."[36] The place to which one journeys when asleep may be treated as a cosmological realm, a third realm "between this world and the other world," to use Yājñavalkya's language: a vantage point onto the layout of this world and the next, and a world the person remakes with "materials from the entire world" taken apart and put back together "in that place [where] this person becomes his own light."[37] Students in the early *Upaniṣads* (as well as students of the *Upaniṣads*) have long looked for clues to the secrets of being a self in the different horizons of experience made available by different stages of sleep. In some Buddhist works, dreams are similarly important, serving as sites of modal significance: in them we may come face-to-face with other worlds, where what we wish for, imagine, or fervently believe is actualized: in dreams we may make real what has long remained only a possibility in our world.[38]

Of course, dreams have long been category-blurring sites of significance. In our case, I will restrict our attention by asking only the following question: What do dreams as a virtual environment say about who one is? Though other dimensions to the growing salience of dreams in Buddhist philosophy, ritual, and contemplative cultures can be found,[39] inspired by Catherine Wilson's concerns, I would like to suggest that if we want to understand what rendering less absolute the distinction between dreaming and waking may have implied for one's sense of the possibility and salience of mental continuity, a good place to start is by situating Vasubandhu's example of wet dreams within the long history of Buddhist concerns with monastic rules.

There are two very different ways to think about beings like us. We can see this by insulating our waking experiences from things that are done and that happen in a dream.[40] That way, we can speak about ourselves as persons (understood as a forensic category restricted to waking experience).

Consider the difference between inadvertent and deliberate emission of semen. That is, consider the difference between having a wet dream and masturbating. To masturbate is to act. Centering the account in the example of male masturbation, there are, on the account of the Pāli works devoted to monastic discipline (*Vinaya*), at least three factors that go into making masturbation a complete act: intent, exertion, and successful completion through ejaculation.[41] These three factors must be present if an event is to count as a censorable breach of monastic discipline.

This suggests a putative insulation of some stretches of our mental life from other stretches. We may experience virtual sex in dreams, but we cannot be described as having acted or as having been responsible for what transpires in a dream. What kind of insulation is it? Unlike the insulation Catherine Wilson is responding to, this is not based on the distinction between falsity and truth. The insulation is not metaphysical and invariant, but practical and contextual. In some forensic literature, there is awareness that what we do in waking contexts of experience can influence what happens in sleep. Take the following scenario: a monk goes to bed with an impassioned mind and prepares to ejaculate in his sleep by holding his penis in his hand or placing it between his clenched thighs.[42] This is considered to be equivalent to overt action. Yet, in ordinary circumstances, emission because of a sexual encounter in a dream, despite being an overt consequence of events in sleep—even if some of these events were to be credited as varieties of (non-overt) action—is not.[43]

How we bundle together different stretches of our lives can vary, depending on the criteria we use. While the forensic insulation of persons into waking and dreaming contexts is standard, there is also a tendency in Buddhist discourse to resist forensic insulation—or at least to question the helpfulness of the forensic distinction for thinking of what is involved in psychological continuity per se. Particularly when considering an individual as the site of ethical transformation. For dreams, particularly wet dreams, have proved relevant to determining the degree to which one has successfully internalized the supererogatory norms and regimens of self-control that constitute the Buddhist path to freedom.

Consider the story maintained in the Sarvāstivāda tradition of Mahādeva's first thesis (of five) that led to a rupture in the Buddhist monastic community.[44] The first of these theses reportedly concerned the possibility that those who have achieved the normative ideals of Buddhist self-cultivation—the worthy ones, or *arhat*s—could undergo sexual experiences in sleep. If they could be susceptible to the influence of external agents, such as demons, the thought went, this might indicate a failing with respect to the ideal-typical form of ethical subjectivity. The ethical significance of dream experiences consists in recognizing that the causal description of what happens in a dream—its conditions of possibility, and its consequences—are not to be insulated from our account of the range of factors constitutive of being kinds of beings. In other words, what we are like is revealed to us no less in our sleep than it is in our waking life.[45]

There is a practical way to make this point. One can believe, as Epicurus did, that the true mark of a sage is the extension of control to all possible contexts of one's life, whether asleep or awake. To think this is to appreciate the distinction between dreaming and waking, while recognizing that someone is not exhaustively describable in terms derived from either context, waking or dreaming, alone. This idea is suggested by philosophers in the Mahāsaṃghika tradition when they take up the contested points related to Mahādeva: "The Buddha has neither sleep nor dream."[46] This is said to deny the possibility that the Buddha, like the perfected *human* beings (the *arhats*), could still be susceptible to nocturnal emissions. Instead of sleeping, a Buddha is said to be ever in a state of concentrated attention (*samādhi*); and he does not dream because "dreams are invoked by such things as intending-to-act [*cetanā*], categorization [*saṃjñā*], or desire [*kāma*]."[47] Dreaming and waking, then, are pairwise possibilities that are inseparably linked, together constituting the possibilities associated with our creaturely form of life.

The ethical concern with the full range of possible experience offers us a hint as to the kind of description of individuals we will need in the rest of the book. We need to be alert to the possibility that there does not exist any *single context* for possible experience that allows us to get the measure of an individual. Instead, we must entertain an idea that is structurally richer: that we are creatures of *multiple contexts* of possible experience, connected yet disparate. The point is subtle in allowing for a distinction between waking and dreaming, while stressing continuity and their equal weight as experiential contexts.

The point is too subtle, perhaps. Sometimes, what I am calling here the salience of virtual environments can be lost through flat-footed metaphysical interpretation of utterances concerning the relationship between the contexts of waking and dreaming. I have in mind the kind of metaphysical interpretation one might (incautiously) think one finds in the *Larger Prajñāpāramitā* when it says that "the state of dreaming and the state of being awake, all that is not two nor divided."[48] This sounds like it says that there are no real grounds for distinguishing between dreams and waking experience. But its own subsequent narrative of a dreaming being seems to suggest more delicate concerns having to do with the salience of one's quality of mind, which can remain invariant across dreaming and waking contexts.[49] This quality of mind can be looked for both when one is asleep (in the quality of one's dreams, perhaps) and when awake (in the quality of one's attention).

In some contexts, as when assigning praise and blame in forensic matters, we will not need to bring the full scope of a human life under a description. In others, as when assessing the ethical shape of a life, we might. As Steven Collins reports, Buddhist formulations of ways of being ethically laudable in connection with abstention from sex would have one have nothing to do with sex "even in dreams," to say nothing of while awake.[50] What of the context with which *The Twenty Verses* is concerned? That of determining what explanations of having the world in view are to look like?

I would claim that this background for the differently calibrated salience of wet dreams in forensic contexts—as distinct from practices of self—in Buddhist discourses is relevant for understanding claims for the continuity of events for experiences in dreaming and waking. Vasubandhu's example of dreaming elicits this with a simple yet satisfying question: What if the account of having content in view needs to take its bearings from accounts of being an ethically appraisable type of being rather than from categories developed to account for the deliberate and conscious life of individuals as picked out by an investment in the issue of forensic responsibility?

THE LESSON OF DREAMING

Writing of the desert fathers of the early Christian community (beginning around the third century CE), Peter Brown discusses the "perfect purity of heart" granted by God to select saints in these terms: "They had been freed from sexual fantasies in dreams associated with nocturnal emissions . . . The sexuality of the emission created a disjunction between [the monk's] public, daylight self and a last oasis of incommunicable privatized experience."[51] The lesson of dreaming, particularly wet dreams, concerns the nature of the disjunction between our private and public selves. If we do enjoy experiences in private, virtual environments, and if such experiences are salient to us, then we might neither be best described nor completely described by appeal to any one type of context alone. What shall we make of the disjunction? In practices of self, whether in Buddhist South Asia or in the Christian world of North Africa and the greater Mediterranean, persons tried different ways of experimenting with such fissures with different implications for the possible alterations of consciousness that can result therefrom. To try to not overlook either context in one's theory of mindedness is no less consequential.

Contexts for possible experience are distinguished from one another by their having distinct sorts of content and forms of mindedness available in them; at the same time, they can be causally continuous. What happens in one context can influence what happens in another, though this might not be available to us when we restrict ourselves to what is available to us to experience in any one context alone. At least this is the suggestion I find in Vasubandhu's use of dreaming

Perhaps this is beginning to sound as if I am describing the experience of dreaming (and implicitly, that of waking up) almost as if to fall asleep is equivalent to coming to be a different type of being through rebirth. I have been influenced by an analogy that Vasubandhu (among others) knew, in which the transition from one lifetime to another in rebirth is thought of as being analogous to waking up after a long sleep.[52] The analogy has implications.

Confucius took the lesson of dream experiences in a virtual environment to be this: it shows us that what we call "I" is mysterious.[53] If there are virtual environments, what of the subjects who are immersed in experiences of them? If Anglophone philosophy has only just begun developing a sustained interest in the link between nonwaking experiences and subjectivity, Buddhist philosophers working generations after Vasubandhu did not shy away from the implications of the analogy. Thinking of rebirth in new contexts for possible experience in connection with dream experiences suggests something of the nature of the kind of subjects we might be. Thus, Prajñākaragupta advanced the notion of "the body in a dream," a phrase he used to underscore the reality of the *virtual subjects* who are immersed in dream experiences, as well as their dream interactions and patterns of identification therein.[54] Virtual subjects in a dream act, feel, and even cause changes in the bodies of the subjects they wake to find themselves being again.[55] Prajñākaragupta uses the idea of virtual subjects to flesh out the analogy of rebirth into possible contexts for experience and dreaming this way: my body in this life is to the body in another life what my body in waking experience is to the body I experience, identify with, and use when asleep.

Vasubandhu might be interested in telegraphing an adjacent point. Dreams, I argued on his behalf, suggest a variety of virtual realism: there are virtual environments to experience and interact with, and the experiences of virtual subjects therein are salient to us. They are salient to us because of being causally connected to what we experience in other contexts, and because of being indicative of the kind of beings we are. We are not shown to be the kind of creatures we are in any one context alone.

But this suggests something of the kind of creatures we are. Consider generalizing the lessons of dreaming and waking as the analogy to rebirth suggests. What if we ought to think of ourselves as consisting in *many* types of subjects, each in a different context of possible experience, all of them causally connected to one another, though bounded off from one another by the limitations of experience in each context? Dreams may be only one of many other virtual contexts with which our lives are bound up. I think this is what Vasubandhu's arguments from dreaming are intended to intimate, thereby giving us our first glimpse in *The Twenty Verses* of the *cosmological individuals* we are and the virtual environments we might inhabit.

What we will need to appreciate is twofold. While dreams are individual virtual environments, there might be collective virtual environments. And we might be creatures who span several virtual environments, collective and individual, over vast spans of time. In the rest of this book, we shall consider more fully what that means.

4

COSMOLOGY FOR PHILOSOPHERS

He reflected on what would have been the continuous flow of his life in the future, a constant uninterrupted cycle of births in hell realms and the realm of hungry ghosts.

—*THE STORY OF DHARMARUCI*[1]

Breathing is habit. Life is habit. Or rather life is a succession of habits, since the individual is a succession of individuals.

—SAMUEL BECKETT[2]

Dreams can only take Vasubandhu so far. To get to where Vasubandhu wishes to lead us in the rest of *The Twenty Verses*, we must follow his more capacious use of alternating contexts of possible experience. We need to think about life, and we need to think about it cosmologically.

"Cosmology" is not an obvious word to use. For one thing, it does not mean the study of "the continuous flow of life," to borrow a phrase from my epigraph, which is what we shall be talking about here. And if one defines "world" as a maximally inclusive whole containing every region of space-time, then my talk on behalf of Buddhist cosmologists of "worlds" will not make sense; nor, perhaps, will talk of virtual, disembodied life-forms fit comfortably.

I shall use the word "world" in its schematic sense to mean a given region of being rather than an encompassing whole.[3] I shall use the word as an equivalent to *loka* in Sanskrit, which, as we shall see below, Buddhists used to speak of life-forms (and the possibilities of experience associated with different life-forms) in addition to meaning our shared physical context.[4] To study worlds in these senses, as we shall see, has to do with framing ourselves in a certain way, mindful of the salience of possibilities, given that variation and continuity across contexts of variation are basic to life as some Buddhists understood it.

Particularly, I will ask the reader to use the word "cosmology" to track what in Vasubandhu's *The Cutting Edge of Buddhist Thought* may be treated as three distinct yet overlapping issues:

(a) What phenomena, and what kind of relations among these, structure variation across different life-forms and within a single form of life? Vasubandhu thinks of this as the study of constraints on mindedness,[5] and he takes this to be undertaken in chapter 2 of *The Cutting Edge of Buddhist Thought* by the study of relations. We shall consider it briefly in the section under structures of variation below;

(b) What forms of life are there, and in which environments are the possibilities associated with these forms of life actually realized? This is what the study of worlds examines; it is discussed in chapter 3 of *The Cutting Edge of Buddhist Thought*;

(c) How do we understand what is involved in moving from one structure of possible experience, from one life-form, to another? As we shall see, this is effectively to ask how action structures movement across contexts of experience. Vasubandhu addresses this in part of chapter 3 and in parts of chapter 4 of *The Cutting Edge of Buddhist Thought*. We will consider it below when we take up the issue of (what I shall call) cosmological description.

In what follows, I restrict my attention to worlds that are linked to life-forms and that are causally continuous with one another. In particular, I shall not, then, consider what Mahāyāna Buddhists knew as Buddha fields: coherent sets of possible experiences made available for an experiencing subject of sufficient mental agility by an advanced being.[6] These were used by Buddhist philosophers as possible worlds to test modal intuitions about what is and what is not possible to conceive, as some tell us explicitly.[7] Our concern shall lie, instead, with concrete possibilities, the worlds of rebirth—those of animals, gods (sometimes titans), hungry ghosts, hell, and humans. Though such worlds have proven no less good to think with. With reference to cosmology as here narrowly defined, Buddhists have used it to explore what sentience and sapience can involve, using the structure of possible experience as sources for scripting imaginative experiments with and enactments of possible experience as different life-forms;[8] and as conceptual and contemplative tools in pursuit of self-understanding[9] and self-fashioning.[10]

In this chapter my interests are much more circumscribed and fairly abstract. Most basically, we must explore the issues raised above—(a) through (c)—to get a feel for how the categories of mind and life are conceptually related. Thus equipped, we may use cosmology to indicate how we may find our first true sense of the direction Vasubandhu's arguments will take in *The Twenty Verses*. We will conclude with a brief diagnostic reading of the way in which he describes the example of the hungry ghosts to help a reader spot its dependence on cosmological thought.

VARIATION AND DIVERSITY

In this chapter, as well as the next, we will need to think about variation. Today, as Mark Ridley reminds us, the terms "individual variability" and the modern "variation"

> are used in a nontemporal sense, to refer to the various forms that exist within a species. The human species in this sense shows variation with respect to size, personality, skin colour, and so on. In colloquial language, this is often called diversity, and words derived from the verb "vary" often refer to change over time. Biologists, however, have come to use "variation" to refer to inter-individual differences at any one time, and they tend to use "diversity" to refer to the difference between species. "Biological diversity" refers to the full array of life, from microbes to coral reefs to tropical forests.[11]

While it is difficult not to let contemporary concerns dominate the resonance of these materials, the Buddhist cosmological picture that will emerge is distinctive. We must neither prejudge connections or the false-friend-like overtones of these words (such as "diversity"), nor allow the genuine overlap of concern not to come through. Therefore, I shall use the terms "variation" and "variability" as referring to the full array of life.

I mean by this to indicate, on the one hand, the differences that pertain to individuals within a species and across species (for which one might use the word *bheda* in Sanskrit, though not exclusively);[12] and I also mean to include the diversity of possible objects that characterizes environments, correlated with life-forms (for which one might use the word *vaicitrya*, though not exclusively).[13]

To think about living beings, we must recognize variation as constitutive. There is no one type of living being that exhausts what life involves. There is no one life-form that can serve as the norm for all life, nor one parameter associated with one life-form that we may use as the norm in our descriptions of other life-forms. We need many parameters, anchored in many different life-forms, to grasp life conceptually.

But we must not confuse the cosmological picture we are describing here with contemporary notions of variation and diversity. For example, on Darwin's view there is a sense on which the notion of a species is blurred, not definite, and "open"—given that there is no end to diversity and variation over time and at a time. The effect is that "when you look carefully, you find that variation within a species blurs into differences between species."[14]

There is no corresponding notion, I think, in Vasubandhu's cosmology. It is important to note that life-forms as possibilities *do not vary* over time. Rather, it is *individuals* who, over time, come to express one from a few of the fixed number of possibilities, again and again.

Variation and diversity, furthermore, might be ambiguous values. The human case for Buddhists is certainly diverse and various, forming a contrast with the uniform pleasures (or tedium, in some cases) of heaven. But such variety in the human case (as we shall see in the next chapter) is thought to be a result of our morally diverse natures, our being capable of both good and bad. This is not necessarily a good thing, though the range of possible human experiences and capacities allow humans to experience and to respond to suffering far more readily than other life-forms.

Meanwhile, cosmogonic stories of how beings come to take diverse forms—diverse physical shapes and psychological identities—suggest that the generation of diversity is infelicitous.[15] And while some Buddhist utopias—the lands of felicity—can foreground the variegation of sensible textures and materials available to be experienced there, their backgrounds are often conceived of as flatlands—as flat "as the palm of a hand"—without mountains or gorges or topographic variation of any kind. The idea, perhaps, being that any variation, even so much as "up" and "down," is too much of a concession to inequality.[16]

Thus primed to possibly false overtones, it is nevertheless helpful to say that cosmology is a study of variation and that we must grasp the variability exhibited by life in all its possibilities if we are to understand ours. To think about this with Buddhists, we are going to need a conceptual tool that has largely gone overlooked. We must understand the idea of factors that determine what it is to be a sentient being, and, thereby, we must understand what "determining" something consists in. To do this, we shall need a variety of constitutive relation expressive of *ādhipatya* in Sanskrit, typically translated as "dominance," "influence," or "determination," the last of which points us in the right direction.[17]

SENTIENCE AS A SPACE OF VARIATION

Let's begin simply. I implied that it won't work to try and describe sentient beings in terms of one factor alone, say consciousness. It certainly wasn't enough for Buddhist philosophers. To grasp what it means to be sentient, they thought of sentient beings as constituted of determinable features, the different possible determinates of which vary across different possible contexts of experience. Thus, a student of Buddhist systematic thought picking up chapter 2 of *The Cutting Edge of Buddhist Thought* would learn to think of sentient beings in terms of twenty-two features responsible for the phenomenological, biological, and ethical shape of sentient lives. These features included the different possible bases for their forms of sensible experience, their possible classifications (as male or female), their different possible lifespans, their possibilities for ethical cultivation, and so on.[18]

Cosmology, then, involves the study of this space of possibilities and its conceptual implications, not least for the vocabulary we use to bring ourselves under a description. In being encouraged to analyze the constitution of beings in this way, one is interested, moreover, in what determines what is possible and impossible for beings. Life, thus understood, requires a special toolkit. For example, consider that being male or being female may represent distinct ways in which beings might be thought to be constituted. Now consider the distinction between being female or male, on the one hand, and the possession of sex organs on the other.

By the fifth century CE, Buddhist as well as Jaina intellectuals had the intellectual resources, in the words of Leonard Zwilling and Michael Sweet, for "disentangling sex, sexuality, and gender."[19] Jaina philosophers could distinguish biological sex (*dravyaliṅga*), marked by primary and secondary sexual characteristics, from psychological features having to do with what we would call gender (*bhāvaliṅga*).[20] Buddhists could too, distinguishing, for example, between sexual organs (*liṅga*), the inferred physical features responsible for sexual differentiation (*indriya*), and gender, or *being* male or female (*puṃsatva/strītva*, or *puṃsa-bhāva/strī-bhāva*), expressed not only (or not even principally) in the possession of sexual organs of such and such kind, but also in a suite of characteristics, ranging from overall physical appearance to pitch of voice, gestures, and characteristic thoughts.[21] The interesting thing they noticed is that the three—sexual organs, capacity, and gender—could conceivably come apart.

Here's just one example. If, as is reported of divine beings in some realms where physical features are absent, and so too, then, no biological sex is present, gendered behaviors are nevertheless expressed, then being female cannot consist in having female sex organs (or the putative female sex capacity).[22] This, furthermore, presents a substantive issue. If not identical, how do these overlapping features relate? How do we determine which features covary in an interesting way with what? And what kind of relation are we using to explore all this?

DOMINANCE AND EXPLANATION

Dominance (*ādhipatya*)—defined by some unhelpfully as "surpassing power" (more about which below)—is the special variety of explanatory relation at issue. For example, the above cosmological example of disembodied yet gendered gods and goddesses was raised as a counterexample to thinking (as some did) that biological sex could express dominance with respect to gender. And dominance is used by Vasubandhu in *The Twenty Verses* to describe, among other things, how things come into view for beings based on past action, as when he says that beings in hell see what they collectively do "on account of the dominant [or, as I shall call it, the "constitutive and determining"] influence of the process of ripening of species-defined shared patterns of activity." In what follows, we'll see why I translate what others speak of in terms of "dominance" as having to do with a "constitutive and determining influence."[23]

What we're after, either way, is a distinctively cosmological way of thinking about life.[24] To understand it, we'll take our bearing from two examples to which Vasubandhu appeals in the second chapter of *The Cutting Edge of Buddhist Thought*. Vasubandhu presents an argument against the explanation offered by the Kashmirian philosophers of the way in which sensory capacities enjoy dominance. I do not think the exegetical situation (and the details of the metaphysical commitments of different Buddhist philosophical traditions) need distract us here from the properly formal point that is at issue in the discussion, which concerns this: how the relation at issue involves an asymmetry between two items, one dominant (or determining) and the other dominated (or determined).

To say that some X is dominant with respect to some Y is not to speak of composition. For example, my hand is not dominant with respect to my grasping something, nor my feet with respect to walking, even though one might think no grasping is possible without my hand, and in that way, depends on it. (Similarly, it is not possible to walk without feet.) That feet are not dominant with respect to walking is because, according to Vasubandhu, walking *just consists in* (or, is not other than) the successive shapes of my feet. Thus, dominance is not the relation of composition.[25]

We might think that this implies that if X is to be dominant with respect to Y, and X cannot be what Y consists in, then X is the cause of Y, X and Y being different. Vasubandhu says that causation is not the right relation. He offers the example of saying that pleasure, as a phenomenon, has the sexual organs as its dominant factor. Again, we might say, there is no bodily pleasure without them, and the kind of pleasure may vary with the kind of organs one possesses. But Vasubandhu stresses that this relation is not it, for X produces Y as a separable event, the separability of which may be understood because pleasure can be and is produced by something else as well.[26]

If we are not dealing with composition or causation, what kind of a relation is intended by dominance? The example of the relationship between the visual faculty and the visual consciousness adduced by Vasubandhu helps.[27] Every instance of visual consciousness is visual. What it is to be a visual consciousness—to be such as to have a type of sensory content peculiar to it—depends on its relationship with the visual capacity.[28] This is a dependence of type, and not a dependence obtaining between tokens of particular types alone. This is the key to distinguishing the relation of dominance from the way in which the dependence of an occurrent episode of visual awareness on its occurrent sensory particular is theorized by Vasubandhu's interlocutors. As they understand it, the latter involves an eminently causal relation between two particulars of independent types.

To clarify this, it is worth turning to the argument introduced in *The Cutting Edge of Buddhist Thought* to distinguish the relation obtaining between the sensory capacity and awareness from the relation between the object and the episode of awareness that is identified in part as "an awareness of that object": "But do the objects of the senses, hue and so on, not exercise dominance in this case with respect to the awareness? This is not dominance. For by dominance we mean surpassing power. The visual capacity exercises influence on all subsequent perceptions."[29] Notice the first formal condition of "surpassing power": it is not limited to a singular causal relation (as in a singular causal claim concerning concrete particulars). Each case of an object's influence on the episode of awareness it conditions involves a singular causal relationship, taken individually. The case of the relationship between the visual capacity and awareness is distinct, however, since it involves a relationship between the visual capacity and every subsequent, possible instance of awareness based on it.

This requires establishing a relationship obtaining at the level of *types* of particulars, and not one entirely grounded on singular causal relationships between concrete tokens of types. On the strength of Vasubandhu's analogy, we may say the following in crude fashion: we have a case of dominance when type Y is shown to depend on type X. But this is not quite right. We want to express not an abstract relationship (where "abstract" is used as the contrary of what is "concrete"). After all, it is always *particulars* of a type X that exhibit the relationship that obtains between types. We need, then, to allow that the relation obtains between types that have an intrinsic affinity, for want of a better word, while not being items of an identical type.

It will help if we associate a type, say X or Y, with sets of properties, and allow that each property includes a range of possible variation—say, to keep with Vasubandhu's example, the phenomenal property of clarity associated with the type "visual awareness." What we want to capture with the help of "dominance" may be cashed out in two steps. First,

(i) Every token instance of a Y-type of thing depends, for being what it is, on there being a Y* type of thing.

In addition, the reason for (i) is this:[30]

(ii) The properties of tokens of Y type things essential to their counting as a Y type thing vary with variations in properties of tokens of Y* type things, which are essential to their counting as Y* type thing.

There is a notion of affinity to be explored here. It is part of the definition of the sensory capacity that it can be affected by a range of conditions. Likewise, it is of the essence of the idea of being conscious that there can be degrees of clarity, for example, and that the possibility of variations in exemplifying this property *is expressive in part of what it is* to experience an instance of consciousness. But Vasubandhu is telling us that the properties in question are not independent. Instead, they vary with variations in the appropriate properties of the visual capacity. The correlation, then, or rather constitutive determination, is one that obtains between these ranges of variation among properties. I should add that by "constitutive" I do not mean to imply anything about the physical makeup of concrete particulars. I mean, instead, to underscore an analytic nexus connecting types identified through analysis. It is through the determining influence of tokens of one type on another that such a nexus is dynamically realized.

A TECHNICAL ASIDE: DOMINANCE, GROUNDING, AND SUPERVENIENCE

This aside may be safely skipped by those incurious about contemporary metaphysical toolkits available to Anglophone philosophers.

I recommend taking it that dominance is a variety of explanation in which "explanans and explanandum are connected, not primarily through some sort of causal mechanism connecting otherwise separable particulars, but through some constitutive form of determination," to adapt a way Kit Fine has spoken of metaphysical grounding.[31] By this I am suggesting that "dominance" is a tool that does some of the work that talk of grounding does in contemporary analytic metaphysics.

What of "supervenience"—the relation that, in slogan form, "there cannot be an A-difference without a B-difference"?[32] One of the uses of this technical word for a generic kind of relationship is to denote a relationship that isolates what is to be explained, without settling the issues that arise from it: for example, whether we are dealing with reduction, composition, identity, or ontologically neutral statements of a relation. I think it would be helpful to say that in isolating a relationship whereby Y and Y* type things, on my way of putting it, express a relation of dominance, one might also say, following Vasubandhu's lead, that Y type things supervene on Y*, which is the converse of saying that Y* type things enjoy *dominance* with respect to Y. We can thus preserve here the two features that talk of supervenience typically involves: *dependence*, such that there can't be Y type things without Y* type things; and *determination*, such that the Y type properties cannot be what they are without the Y* type properties being what they are.[33]

How would speaking of dominance as the inverse of supervenience relate to talk of grounding? Unproblematically, as long as we do not conflate supervenience with reduction.[34] Vasubandhu uses dominance to express a relationship between concrete particulars picked out by theory (and not common sense), the status of which are metaphysically impeccable. Talk of dominance is *not* part of an attempt to resolve commonsense commitments to questionable entities through analysis. As long as one keeps that in mind, one might say either of these two things: "For Y* type things to express dominance with respect to Y type things means that Y* type things serve to explain, or ground Y type things, or that Y type things supervene on Y* type things."

In an astute footnote, Cabezón recommends translating the words expressive of this relation we have just explored with the relevant inflections of the verb "to determine."[35] I agree. To say that "X determines Y" says something far stronger than saying that "X influences Y." Though, as we've seen above, the relation is a bit more involved than this. With an eye on Kit Fine's sense of ground, I translate instances of *adhipati* (and related terms) as "a constitutive and determining influence."

I must confess that while I think this is the right gloss for philosophers, it fails to capture a little of the music of the metaphor that I hear in *adhipati*. I have no way to convey the sense of the sovereign exercise of power in a given domain. For something to be related to something else by *adhipati* is for two spheres to overlap, with what happens in one being subject to the sovereignty and authority of what goes on in another.

Consider the difference it makes to think of one's life as consisting in such overlapping domains. Consider thinking, for example, that the domain of the present falls entirely within the territory and so under the sway of what was done in the past. Or, as Vasubandhu uses the category to say in 18ab of *The Twenty Verses*, think of us as being constitutively open to the influence of one another, as falling, that is, under each other's sway. My translation can't capture the taste of the thought here or why it matters. Translating philosophy is no less wretched than translating poetry.

WORLDS AS CONSTRAINTS

I've tried to present sentience on the Buddhist model as an array of determinable features that, when differently instantiated, constitute life as a multidimensional space of variation.[36] Worlds, as Buddhist philosophers understand these, can be used to flesh out what sentience as such a space of variation involves. Much of the work in the first half of Vasubandhu's third chapter of *The Cutting Edge of Buddhist Thought* is given over to clarifying what this might mean in connection with what the philosopher Michael Thompson has termed "natural historical judgments": judgments of the type "S are/have/do F."

Consider, at random, the following kind of statement from the beginning of the chapter: "For beings of the nonphysical worlds, the psychological continuum develops on the basis of principles such as vitality."[37] That is said in contradistinction to other types of beings whose mental life presupposes the availability of a physical body. Such judgments, which tend to be formulated in a tenseless present tense,[38] map possibilities based on variations in life-forms and their living environments.[39]

The different life-forms (*sattva*) are not only different ways in which a world may be experienced. Life-forms, or different ways of being a living being, with different modes of embodiment and different patterns of being minded, constitute different worlds (*loka*). They are possible modes of subjectivity, regions of being into which one can come to be reborn (*gati*).[40]

To talk of worlds in connection with life-forms is to keep an eye on variations of sentience and thus versions of experience; in contrast, one may also speak of a world in terms of the physical environment that forms what Buddhist philosophers call a shared context, or *bhājana-loka*, a phrase usually translated as "receptacle world." That translation has always seemed to me to suggest that the world as shared context is a mere container. But in Sanskrit, the word *bhājanam* is used, among other things, as a word for utensils, such as pots, plates, cups, or jugs, items with which to serve up foodstuff and drink, items to use in enjoyment and nourishment.[41] But receptacle, after Latin *receptaculum*, indicates a "place to receive and store things," from *receptare*, frequentative of *recipere*, meaning "to hold" or "to contain," and thus may fail to convey the relation that talk of utensils or *bhājana* imply. In what follows, I'll ask you to keep an ear out for the possible resonances of thinking of the world as (a) something made, as is a vessel, *for* use by us, and (b) as something serving as an occasion for experiences to occur, and thus not as something entirely independent of the beings who interact with it.[42]

The nature of the relation will be explored in the next chapter, where we shall take up the conditions for the generation of worlds due to the actions of living beings, thus stressing the relationship between these two senses of world. For now, I recommend thinking of the name *bhājana* as an accented characterization of the physical world, its environing features and locales and objects, one that highlights that the world contributes to, even as it befits, the available range of experiential possibilities with which beings are associated.

HOW LIFE COUNTS: COSMOLOGICAL INDIVIDUALS

Vasubandhu's reader must acquire a sense of how to apply talk of life-forms as worlds to talk of individuals. There is no quicker way to introduce the subject than to see how Vasubandhu redefines death (and thus being alive) in *The Twenty Verses.*

In verse 19, Vasubandhu offers an analysis of what it means to judge that an individual is no longer alive when physical facts may not serve as criteria for our descriptions of living and dying. Death, Vasubandhu says, should be thought of "as the termination of something's continuing to be a particular life-form."[43] To say some X dies is not to say that *everything* to which we might refer when speaking of X ceases to be. In speaking of death with Vasubandhu we must be sensitive to the sortals he has available to him. (By "sortals" I shall mean the features that can serve as the criteria or the continued existence of an item of that kind, and which tell us how to count things of that kind.) The relevant sortal in the case of death, says Vasubandhu, is provided by S's being a particular sort of living being. To say some S dies is to say that that S no longer counts as a being of that particular type or that particular life-form—say a human being, a god, or an animal, as the case may be. But it does not mean that S ceases to be altogether.

That continuity exceeds the unity of a lifetime is one way of incorporating the truth of rebirth, which offers Vasubandhu ways of describing S that go beyond conventions. Vasubandhu can describe S not only as existing from conception to death, but from death to death, and as a continuum involving at least four stages, as per Buddhist cosmological descriptions: there is (1) being in-between our death and a new life; and (2) being conceived and coming into being as a life-form; (3) the state of being a particular life-form, which extends from conception to death; and (4) the state of dying.[44]

To describe us as living beings picks us out insofar as we are creaturely beings, individuated from birth to death as beings of some identifiable life-form. But that is only one of the four morally and psychologically important thresholds available to Vasubandhu to stress when speaking of individuals. Of course, this only makes sense given rebirth, or the fact of one's constituting an extended individual, one whose duration consists of many lifetimes of which a single lifetime would be only a phase. If Vasubandhu's definition of dying takes to heart the lessons of Buddhist commitment to rebirth exerting pressure on his categories and his way of speaking, the upshot is this: there is room for bringing different kinds of things into view when speaking of the being that one is.

Perhaps, stated like this, the point is unsurprising. Even in English, may we not describe ourselves very differently depending on the context and the concepts we use? Describing oneself as an organism and as a person are quite distinct, for example: "When I speak of a person," Shelly Kagan explains, "I have in mind a creature—of whatever biological (or nonbiological!) sort—that has certain characteristic psychological capacities and thoughts, a creature that is rational and self-conscious, aware of itself as existing across time."[45]

For Kagan, and I suspect many contemporary philosophers, being a person might overlap with the sequence we constitute within a lifetime as living creatures, but it does not stretch as far: newborns are not persons; and, as Kagan notes, not all individuals survive until death as persons in this relevant sense.

Buddhist philosophers can agree, while adding a little complexity of their own. They can use "forensic responsibility" as a criterion the way Kagan does to come up with the forensic category of a psychologically continuous subject one may identify over time with the help of a criterion such as *being the same as the agent of* some relevant action.[46] Such a subject is narrower than the individual taken as a living being.

But Buddhists also claim that there can, in principle, be memory across lifetimes. The hypothetical creature, to adapt Kagan, capable of being "aware of itself as existing across *lifetimes*" is neither living being nor person, but what I call a cosmological individual.

To count oneself as a cosmological individual with Vasubandhu, one has to keep in view what the Buddha meant by speaking of such continuities that exceed a lifetime as being "one." Though a matter of considerable debate, as Vasubandhu allows us to see in his *Against Selves*, he defined it to his own satisfaction in terms of *a causal unity of a sequence* obtaining across lifetimes on account of karma, supplemented with the thought that "one" can refer to a collective singular.[47] That's the individual that counts, cosmologically speaking.

Life, I would now recommend, is a partial frame bringing the continuity of such a being into view in certain contexts. To think with life in this way, we must first eschew thinking of it as a metaphysical category. There are, to be sure, altogether too many metaphysical questions that can be posed about life, questions that were entertained by Buddhist philosophers. Take, for example, questions regarding what substantive principle, if any, life might be identified with;[48] or what generic property, if any, our categories for living beings might track.[49] Given that Buddhist metaphysicians eschewed property possessors and substances in general and were predisposed to nominalism in the face of any kind of generic property which our species concepts might be said to track, talk of life could present metaphysical headaches. I recommend setting these aside.

Instead, consider treating "life" with Vasubandhu as a form of description, a way in which to bring something else into view. The faculty of life or vitality (*jīvitendriya*) is defined by Vasubandhu in *On the Five Heaps* in connection with a frame of continuity, a way of selecting a stretch of mental continuity to frame as one through which a particular set of dispositions and factors of action abide. These dispositions, in turn, are individuated as those associated with (or as constituting) a living being as a being of a particular type, in conformity with the constraints set by the consequences of prior action.[50]

To speak of X as alive, then, is to say that there is psychological continuity on the part of a mental continuum of a particular kind. It gets at not only what is present but what is possible and coherent with that individual counting as a being of a particular type. It is also what shows us the nexus that is an individual's present insofar as it is open to the past due to the structuring influence of action.

Which is where we need to now direct our attention.

THINKING WITH COSMOLOGICAL INDIVIDUALS: A BEGINNER'S CASE STUDY

No cosmological individual lives at any stage of its extended life without expressing some life-form. And no individual is wholly bound up with any one life-form. This is the dynamic that informs cosmological descriptions, and which cosmological descriptions use to reveal the world to be far more complex than one's intuitions might have supposed.

Cosmological descriptions, to borrow a phrase from Xuanzang, can "draw forth the past"[51] of a being's actions into one's present. In doing so, they can test intuitions one might unreflectively hold concerning (as I shall call it) the integrity of what is present and salient in a region of space and time.

Let me suggest what I mean with an example. Consider the way an embryo/fetus (call it C) gestating in an organism (call it B) can complicate any simple-minded conviction that there can be only one organism, or living thing, or organizational unity associated with a single region of space and time.[52]

Consider now that such a situation, instead, invites several questions: Are B and C related? If so how? By formal parthood? By material constitution? By simple containment (such that B and C are always separable)?[53] Cosmological descriptions, analogously, introduce complexity. Indeed, they intensify the kind of issues brought into focus by natality.

Cosmological descriptions make us see that just what is going on and how in any given locus is never transparent. The structuring power of action (karma) and the way in which phases of cosmological descriptions intersect with the present can increase the number of actants possibly present in any given locus and widen the scope of causally relevant factors of interaction operative in any locus, entangling the present in a past as well as a future that are not easy to pin down.

For example, imagine if in the above case of gestation, in addition to the mother (B) and embryo/fetus (C), there was a third participant, call it A, who is an earlier phase of a continuum, only one phase of which is formed by C. Imagine now saying that the relationship between B and C—even were we to acknowledge such a relation to involve partial material constitution and C's being a part of B—is not necessarily as important as the relation between B and A; or, perhaps, that because of the influence of A's prior action on C, we have no particular reason to say that C is a part of B any more than we have reason to say that it is a part of the continuum of A.

Things can get a lot more complicated. The pressure that may result was recognized as part of cosmological descriptions and as something that needed to be conceptually explored, as in the following case raised in *The Cutting Edge of Buddhist Metaphysics*: "A being growing in the womb of a dog, a sow, and the like, can die in its embryonic stage and be reborn in any of the five possible contexts of rebirth. Let us suppose then that this embryonic being is replaced by a being in-between death and life that is bound for hell. This intermediate being, if he has the form of a being in hell, will burn the womb of the dog."[54] For my purposes, the ultimate intelligibility of the issues here raised is beside the point. What is very much to the point, however, is to note how in this scenario the cosmological description would allow us to imagine the womb of an animal to be a mere container for a being within it that it has not generated. It does not even stand as a candidate possessor of the being in the way that it stood to be part-possessor with respect to the fetus that has been replaced. The links between potential gestator and the being contained in it—but not gestated by it—are not as strong as the constitutive ties the intermediate being enjoys with beings located in the past and the future. Is much of what we think as being materially related tied by nothing more than relations of proximity and containment? And just how extensively populated by such invisible beings is any region of being? "There is no end to the number of creatures of brief lives who subsist on smells and tastes,"[55] says Vasubandhu in this chapter, intimating that at small scales, life can present itself as an indefinitely dense continuum of beings, of diverse and heterogenous modes of embodiment, possibly co-occupying the same regions, each a part of infinitely dense karmic trajectories of their own.

In addition to forcing us to revisit the connections between beings, places and bodies, and the weight of any constitutive relations between items located in the present, this case also challenges our sense of causal locality. How is the being subject to causal influences from remote locations (past and possibly future) to which its containing context is not subject?[56]

Jointly, these reflections constitute what I called the challenge to the integrity and salience of the present represented by Buddhist cosmological description. In fact, it is a perfect example to try our hand at using Buddhist cosmological concepts.

Dying is no end to continuity, given rebirth, and the next phase must be spatiotemporally continuous, many Buddhist philosophers maintain.[57] Let "a being in-between death and rebirth" (*antarābhava*) be the description of the phase of a cosmological individual. The question is: must the being in-between one form of life and another itself have a form of life associated with it? One answer involves saying that being in-between does not express its own form of life; it is a liminal stage, associated with the form of life that serves as "the destination" (*gati*), the next distinct stage of continuity it serves to constitute. If that is so, as every phase requires a life-form, there will be at least one moment when in some locus there might be incompatible forms of life. And so, the question is posed, Why does the being in-between, bound for hell, not burn up the womb of the animal it occupies?

Vasubandhu presents three responses to this problematic scenario, the first of which misses the point of the thought experiment.[58] The second response maintains that the kind of materiality such a being possesses is "no more tangible than it is visible,"[59] so that a collocation of a being of one type in a being of another needs not be incompatible. To fully appreciate this, we need to take on board

Vasubandhu's comments in the same chapter to the effect that resistance to co-occupation is a rule that applies only to material features of the same type.[60]

While this gives us an example of the revisionary potential of a cosmological description, it is the last response that (in my opinion) is the most revealing. None of the three responses give up on the connection between an individual and a form of life. But the third accepts that taking such concrete scenarios seriously entails real problems. It's just that, as Vasubandhu says, "in any event, the influence of actions prevents this."[61] I read that last phrase as saying that it is simply a brute fact that the world, as structured by action, is such that cases like this will not arise.[62]

I will say more about brute facts in the conclusion of chapter 5, where we will consider features of the world that are basic and resist further explanation. All we need here is to see how the connection between individuals and their forms of life, a connection grounded in action, is one baseline feature of the world. This is like saying that the conceptual connection between being an individual and having a certain form of life is among the most basic ways the world is structured, and the potentially intuition-challenging implications for our sense of what I called the integrity of the present belong to the ground floor of any Buddhist account of what we are like.

VARIETIES OF COSMOLOGICAL DESCRIPTION

Cosmological descriptions are descriptions of an individual as a complex, temporally extended entity spanning lifetimes and as possessing, thereby, many possible contexts of relevance. Such descriptions have revisionary potential. I want to consider the various forms cosmological descriptions might take in connection with psychological or individuating properties of individuals. I will consider more forms than are strictly relevant to the way in which Vasubandhu makes his point in *The Twenty Verses*. But I owe it to the reader to get a feel for how these tools might function and what they can allow one to do.

Wendy Doniger O'Flaherty has noted that while it is fairly typical in South Asian sources for parents to make only a physical contribution to conception, "the Buddhists, however, suggest a primal scene which would have gladdened the heart of Sigmund Freud."[63] Let's set the stage. For our actants, we need a mother and a father. The father contributes semen; the mother contributes blood and the stage for the drama, the womb. Their union, and the subsequent mixing of blood and semen, produces an insensate and not yet living context in the womb favorable to conception. But to stage the drama of life, we require a new actor, a being in-between death and life (*antarābhava*).

Conception involves this being first occupying, and then, through a process that signals this being's end, taking the place of the insensate context favorable for life provided by the parents. Once that happens, a new series forms (*upapatti-bhava-skandha*), and we have what can be described either as a new living individual, or as the next stage in a cosmological individual of which the being in-between life and death formed one liminal stage.

The details of the material constitution of this new series, and the degree to which the material composition of this being makes any contribution to this new series, are as labyrinthine as they are fascinating and intensely debated.[64] What matters for us, however, is the antecedent drama on a wider stage, which I here paraphrase:

> By virtue of the power of actions the being in-between is endowed with divine sight; and though distant, sees the place of his rebirth. There he sees his father and mother. And is troubled. If male, there arises a male passion for the mother; if female, a female passion for the father. And conversely, either hatred for the father or the mother, respectively . . . Thus confounded, and through the desire for sex, it attaches itself in that place, imagining that it is he with whom they unite. When the impurities of semen and blood are released in the womb, the being in between, quickening in joy, enters in entirely and settles there. Then its constituents harden; and then the constituents of the being in between dissipate and disappear—in this way there is formation of life [*upapatti*].[65]

Freud scandalized an era by situating the sexual development necessary to account for human adult psychology far earlier in a human's life than anyone had thought necessary.[66] It was a culturally salient shift of imaginative reach, as was the one that poets (like Thomas Traherne) precipitated in early modern Europe when they shaped the meaning of a (then) new word, "consciousness," by inviting their readers to imaginatively contend with what it is—or rather, may be—like to sense and experience thought's first appearance in the womb (even as generations of philosophers and medical authorities had passed over prenatal life as a context of experience or salience).[67] Vasubandhu's rehearsal of one Buddhist description of conception, as is typical of cosmological descriptions, involves the routinization of a variety of imaginative shift, requiring us to contend with an extended stage of experience and relevance, entailing a redescription of the contexts we think we know.

Part of the rhetorical complexity derives from the way Buddhist texts typically discuss natality, discussions that, as Amy Langenberg notes, "can slip up and down various referential axes—human to nonhuman, sentient to insentient, biological to cosmological—without necessarily calling attention to these various registers."[68] More particularly, Vasubandhu's descriptions feature a rhetorical complexity involving three aspects I'd like to briefly address: wider stages for the explanation or revaluation of a constitutive feature of our lives, the (sometimes tacit) emphasis on what I will call uniformity of reality, and an ability to enact affective styles associated with the different points of view entertained in these descriptions.

Many Buddhist texts provide an account of prenatal sensation and forms of experience, though they do so to different ends, and can stage it in different sites of experience. The description I offered above does not invite us to entertain what it is like to be in the womb. Some descriptions, however, do. Consider the following description, as used in *The Cutting Edge of Buddhist Thought*: "When the embryo is ready . . . there arise in the womb winds from the ripening of action, which causes the embryo to turn . . . toward the portal of its birth. It is difficult to move . . . [When the birth is felicitous] the mother and servants take the newborn baby in their hands, which feel like knives and acid to the body, which now is as exposed as an open wound."[69] Elsewhere, the Buddhist poet Candragomin offers readers an extended lyrical meditation on prenatal sensation in the womb, evoking its visceral textures, conveying that being born is a process so traumatic that it squeezes out all memory: "His memories of time past, as if / slowly, continuously, pressed out of him / in disgust, abandon him there."[70] This gives us a clue. Cosmological descriptions may act as antidotes, being a variety of complex imaginative exercises of recollection, reversing birth, and offering us a chance to shape memory, not only with an aim to "recover" what we have forgotten, but thereby also our forgetting of it.[71]

Reversing the transition from presence of mind to unknowing, cosmological descriptions orient us to the nature of reality (*dharmatā*), which informs my second characteristic. Consider the description of the "hardening" of the constituting features of the being in-between in the womb. We can hear in it an allusion to the process of the "fall" of the first beings at the beginning of a cosmic epoch offered in the same chapter: "Beings initially were luminous, and had joy as their sustenance—then something appears, the savor of the earth, and one eats—the eating made their bodies become coarse and heavy and their luminosity came to an end."[72] Such continuities may be found in other ways. Thus, in the winds that determine the time and manner of birth, we find an echo of the processes that shape the features of the highest peaks in the world;[73] these in turn are continuous with those that structure the transition from one cosmic epoch to another when, as *The Cutting Edge of Buddhist Thought* maintains, not even one atom of the physical world remains,[74] and the world begins again, not from physical atoms, but with winds or forces of motility carrying over special power properties from a different nonphysical region of being, the whole process powered by the past actions of creatures, or karma.

I mention these here because it would seem that the processes that turn on the lights of a cosmic epoch are at work in the smallest dispositions of life in the womb. Generation, whether of individuals, features, or even worlds, recapitulates similar processes and principles.[75] Contemporary cosmologists tell us that there is no special place where things work differently. The universe looks the same in any direction, if we choose a suitable vantage point. On behalf of the Buddhist cosmologist, I would like to point out the replication of structuring principles *at any scale* at which we think of it, from a given point of view—such as the way Buddhas look at things.

Which brings me to my last point and the complex rhetorical stance of this description. Note that the description I quoted above, in a way, assumes the so-called divine (and thus, transempirical) eye of the being in-between. A cosmological description, like the point of view of a being in-between, *sees through* the contexts formed by specific forms of life, having available to it facts otherwise occluded to an embodied observer situated in time and place and restricted in perception by the laws of optics. In adopting a divine eye of such a being, the cosmological description does not, of course, simply recapitulate the confusion of such a being. It does something else. It appears to transmute the confusion and psychologically fraught experiential texture of passage into life into crisper emotional textures: thrill, perhaps, and even a controlled variety of revulsion.

Could we not consider the description as a whole to be something other than a theoretical set piece? Could it not be an enactment on an ascetic's part of experiences conducive to shock and disenchantment? We might be clued in to this transvaluation by considering the way in which the womb is described in the above passage, or the way, a few sentences later, it will be described as a "cemetery."[76] These are not value-neutral descriptions. Even as the being in-between is described as staging a complex variety of enactment of a role, seeking to identify itself with one of its future parents, the ascetic may enact the narrated enactment to produce a complex variety of mimesis with therapeutic effects.[77]

COSMOLOGICAL DESCRIPTION AND STRUCTURAL DESCRIPTIONS

We shall soon see Vasubandhu invite Buddhist philosophers to embed their description of perceptual experience in a cosmological description, involving a wider stage and a more complicated accounting for the possibility of perception than epistemologists typically credit. It will be a story, like all cosmological descriptions, involving past activity. But what kind of cosmological description will Vasubandhu use?

Cosmological descriptions can keep in view actual, categorical features an individual might possess. They may also focus on possibilities, framing a story with either individual features or collective perspectives. And they may seek to have us inhabit, and revalue, the confused perspective of a situated being or take on the point of view of a Buddha. In Vasubandhu's case, I believe we are best served by taking it to be a Buddha's eye view of the collective framing of structural possibilities. To see how we might link features through cosmological description to actions in the past in a more schematic way, it will be necessary to get into the weeds a little, if only momentarily. Getting clearer on this will help set us up to appreciate the shape of Vasubandhu's thesis about mental content. And it will help us understand what we need to do in the next chapters.

When linking beings to the past, some descriptions seek to link features pertaining to an individual, while other descriptions can zoom out, as it were, to take into account features pertaining to a collective and a wider class of particulars. For example, one can use the language of "ripening" or "maturing" (*vipāka*) of action, but such a description would only apply to persons, and then only to the individual result of what an individual has done.[78] In *The Cutting Edge of Buddhist Thought*, the kind of description involved in how a process structures an individual—indeed, how it, in part, constitutes the individual—is distinctive.[79] Particularly when set against descriptions that seek to account for features that are not exclusive to the individual but shared, indeed typically going beyond talk of persons and living beings to include environmental factors—mountains, rivers, and the like.[80] Such features having to do with the collective context of living beings, as I intimated above, are not unlinked to backward-looking descriptions. But these are described as the effect of dominance or determining influence (*adhipatiphala*) and not as maturation (*vipāka*).[81]

I propose thinking of these contextual features, and their being thought of as the aggregate result of collectives, as indicative of an interest on the part of Buddhist cosmologists in "structural descriptions": descriptions that involve many individuals, and which highlight the contextual parameters necessary for the full description of the nature and functionality of those individuals.[82] With this bit of added detail, we can now say the following: with the idea of life (and other intrinsically collective notions such as "being a life-form") as a frame for the description of cosmological individuals, one can think of structural and individual features as coordinating elements central to any Buddhist story of how a form of life relates to its world.

Cosmological individuals are metaphysical collectives of several (psychologically and forensically) distinct persons, linked to one another by actions and the consequences of actions. The things we do constitute ways in which our life can be experienced by ourselves in the future, by virtue of what we do changing us and making us up differently; but what we do also induces changes beyond our mortal frame, making up someone in the future. In the other direction, we are partly constituted by what others have done.

A cosmological description reflects this. It will typically involve, at some level, an appeal to cosmological individuals, relating the processes through which these are structured over time by the consequences of action to the ways in which a cosmological individual can come to express, over time, different forms of life, with different features and dimensions of mindedness. Vasubandhu's description of the case of the hungry ghosts is paradigmatic: "For we know that insofar as these beings are constituted by a process involving the ripening of morally equivalent actions, *all* hungry ghosts, and not just one alone, see a river filled with pus."[83] Notice the collective rather than distributive sense of the class of subjects: the understanding of collectivity here as expressive of a life-form, with a range of mindedness and a range of possible content. One's experiences are constrained by one's having one life-form rather than another. Before thinking of the content that "I" have available to me, such a description would have me attend to the unmarked "we" that may constitute and determine what I can have in view and how.

Notice, also, the backward-looking elements in the description. We are dealing with a community of beings constituted by shared patterns of habituation to have a certain range of content available to them just insofar as they have been constituted to be beings of a certain type. This points the theorist of perception in a certain direction. If one must include "the kind of being one is" into one's account of perception, perhaps one will have to balance static as well as dynamic accounts of the structures of collective possibilities. And this may suggest the general shape of an account applicable to all subjects, not just the damned.

5

MAKING UP WORLDS

In some way all creatures bear traces of their past.

—JENNIFER ACKERMAN, *NOTES FROM THE SHORE*[1]

Recall the words of Inez Serrano in *No Exit*: "Wait! You'll see how simple it is. Childishly simple. Obviously there aren't any physical torments—you agree, don't you? And yet we're in hell . . . We'll stay in this room together, the three of us, for ever and ever . . . [I]n short, there's someone absent here, the official torturer."[2] It looks to be fitting to Sartre's damned persons that to be forced together in a room with French Empire décor is enough to constitute a hell. And, as in a cafeteria, the suffering is all self-service. We're going to have to talk about hell as well. In fact, Vasubandhu even subjects the concept of "official torturers" or "guards in hell" to analytic scrutiny, finding, in Inez's phrase, something missing. But in the following pages we shall be talking rather differently than Sartre or any of his characters were.

Vasubandhu is not just performing a similar service for Buddhist cosmology as Sartre was for premodern descriptions of hell and its descriptions of elaborate tortures, instruments, and suffering. Vasubandhu is not talking about some possible human experiences being *hellish*, nor is he simply offering us an existential redescription of the meaning of suffering. Whether or not it is also true that we could use the arguments allegorically,[3] Vasubandhu is describing how a real life-form in a real world, one very unlike ours—however, alas, intelligible—comes into being.

Hell is a world representing a real possibility and functioning in the capacity of what Robert Sugden calls a credible world.[4] A "credible world" in this case is a theoretical model capable of illuminating what having a world in view involves. No doubt, Buddhist accounts of hell will stretch our imagination, as will the arguments Vasubandhu offers in connection with the possibility of collective experiences of virtual environments that are not explained by objects. But the argument is ingenious, however bizarre to us now in its details and motivations.

Ingenious. And rather involved. In order to do it justice, I have divided my discussion of it into two chapters. In this chapter we'll learn how to speak about the formation of worlds, carrying over our concern with cosmological descriptions from the last chapter. Vasubandhu, recall, will claim the following: instead of our collective ways of being minded being explained due to a commonality of objects, individuated independently of subjects, and causally responsible for inducing in them the experiences characteristic of that environment, we ought to locate what is characteristically had in view in an environment differently. The beings in hell have in view what they do "on account of the constitutive and determining influence of the process of ripening of species-defined shared patterns of activity."[5] This moves us, as we've seen cosmological descriptions do, to recontextualize the present as being under the sway of a still effective past.

At this stage, we are not dealing with argument but redescription. As such, it is crucial to the claims of *The Twenty Verses* and this book. It is easiest to see the shape of redescription and the conceptual distance between Vasubandhu and his Buddhist interlocutors with the application of cosmological description to features of objects and the physical environment. To see which, we must learn to use Vasubandhu's preferred way of underscoring the influence of the past on the present with the help of a *form of description* developed to address the influence of habituation to patterns of activity in the formation of persons. I call this a teleological form of description.

MAKING WORLDS: THE TEXTBOOK ACCOUNT

Introducing the chapter on action in *The Cutting Edge of Buddhist Thought*, Vasubandhu claims that worlds in general, including the world as our shared context, are caused by the actions of beings. The claim offers a glimpse of "textbook" Buddhism. For the claim that collective action structures the possibilities of our shared context would not be news for Buddhist philosophers.[6] Action is a way in which the past enters into texture of our worlds, and the very texture of our lives.

At the beginning of his chapter on action in an early and influential work of Buddhist scholasticism, *The Heart of Buddhist Thought*, Dharmaśreṣṭhin explained the phrase "action decorates and adorns [*citrayati*] the possible forms of life into which one can be born [*gati*] and the various contexts [*sthāna*] in the world [*loka*]" to mean that "each sentient being is endowed with a different kind of body in the five possible forms of life into which one can be reborn, in the three time periods, past, present, and future."[7] Our particular mode of embodiment is a particular style of being minded, the fact of which testifies to the kind of people we have been. Dharmatrāta, who goes on to explain the sense that "decoration and adornment" have in the above phrase, as well as Dharmaśresthin's comments on it, says that action endows "each sentient being with their genealogical kind [*gotra*] in the five possible forms of life into which one can be born. Action is the seed, and the existence of the world sprouts from that, just as a plant sprouts from a particular seed."[8] Our present shared world embodies the interaction of many personal histories.

As we shall see, to speak thus of the relation between a seed and a fruit is possibly to gesture at constitutive relations holding between past and present that may put pressure on some claims and commitments Buddhist philosophers entertain about our shared world in other theoretical contexts. But Vasubandhu does not immediately commit to any controversy when he introduces the topic of action and the first verse of the chapter: "Now, regarding what was discussed earlier—the extensive variety of the worlds consisting in the life-forms of living beings, and the shared context in which they dwell—one might well ask: By whom was this made? It is certainly not the case that it was made by a single agent possessed of prior thought. Rather, it is that 'the constitutive variety of worlds is the result of action' on the part of sentient beings."[9] Elsewhere, Vasubandhu argues that we cannot make sense of what there is as anything but a complex function of dynamically open-ended processes. We cannot treat the world, that is, as a totality or mereological unity, nor may we ground it in anything unitary, such as the mind of God, or some insentient cosmological principle.[10] To cite the actions of many as antecedent is a way of underscoring the constitutive complexity and manifoldness of what there is.

Vasubandhu's appeal to actions involves a backward-looking explanation and picks out a necessary condition for how a certain state of affairs has come to be. It does not on its own tell us what is both necessary and sufficient for action to bring about such a state of affairs; for that, as it turns out, Vasubandhu prefers to use forward-looking concerns with habituation to patterns of action.[11] The former is the domain of cosmological thinking, the latter the domain of praxis and self-cultivation. From here on out, we shall only be concerned with the backward-looking descriptions connected with action, a point whose significance I'll address in the conclusion to chapter 7.

Vasubandhu here links "the variety of worlds" to action. Yaśomitra tells us that by "variety" Vasubandhu refers to the furniture of the world, the various kinds of things that figure in our physical environment—take your mountains, your islands, and so on. At the same time, the word "variety" is also intended to encompass the diversity presented by different classes of beings, defined by the cosmological type (whether individuated as creatures dependent for their experience on material sensory particulars, or not), their regions of beings, their circumstances of generation, and the like.[12]

If such variation, as understood cosmologically, is linked to action, what kind of relation, exactly, do they have in mind as holding between us and our world? In the last chapter we saw Buddhists appeal to a constitutive variety of relation called "dominance." Are even physical features of the world grounded in the constitutive and determining influence of action? If even the physical contexts and environing features given which we live our lives—and not only psychological or personal features—are dependent for their properties on the determining influence of the traces of past actions, then they are not truly independent of us.

OF OBJECTS AGAIN, AND TALKING PAST ONE ANOTHER

But we do not yet know how to speak of this nonindependence or entanglement. In what follows, I'll distinguish between two over-arching ways of assigning a relational status to features, one epistemological and the other cosmological. I will try to show that epistemological ways of handling dependency don't go far enough to capture the way that Vasubandhu, thinking cosmologically, will attempt to entangle beings and their environments in *The Twenty Verses*.

Some Buddhist philosophers argue that the degree to which an item in the world is "beautiful"—we may use here many (potentially) judgment-dependent notions, such as "good," "beneficial," "pleasurable," and so on—is a description-dependent feature of that object and not an independent fact. Such arguments, discussed in chapter 2 as arguments from illusion, usually trade on the fact that different subjects do not enjoy invariant responses in the presence of the same object. That is one way to argue for something's not being independent but entangled with our biased stances as desiring subjects with the capacity to bring sensory inputs under complex descriptions.

Within this variety of epistemological dependency,[13] we may distinguish between two sorts of entangled features. Let us define a metaphysically contrastive concept of an entangled feature as one that results when we describe what we have in view of a thing so as to suggest that we can distinguish our way of having it in view from some way in which the thing is *anyhow*. This would be to imagine treating that thing as an object from some vantage point. Recall my defining object as follows: any putative item in the world (whether physical or mental) that might be recruited to play a causal role in a story tracking the source of content in experiences, and which is thought to possess a nature, linked to the causal powers invoked by us to explain an experience, independently of the experiences with which it is related.

Imagine saying, for example, that certain entangled features (like an object's being beautiful) don't belong to the properties of things, now conceived of as the objects in the ontology of a physical science—or, perhaps, as objects in Buddhist metaphysics. The idea here is that a contrastive sense of an entangled feature is intelligible only in contrast to conceiving of some privileged theoretical lexicon in which we consider all relational features simply to drop out. Which might, in turn, recommend treating an entangled feature as being possibly less real than a nonentangled one.

Alternatively, one can imagine a noncontrastive notion of an entangled feature, as I believe at one time Vasubandhu to have done. In general, Vasubandhu was cautious when handling epistemological arguments from variation precisely because he was wary of the weight assigned to a metaphysically contrastive notion of entangled feature.

Take, once again, the example of pleasure. One argument might run that there are no objective facts about pleasure, just because items thought to be pleasurable do not invariably cause the experience of pleasure in people, nor do they cause pleasure in different people in the same way. The contrast is made between judgment-dependent features, like "being pleasurable," and features having to do with sensible properties amenable to perception, imagined as a description-free instrument.

In response to such an argument, Vasubandhu points out that features can be real and yet dispositional, and that dependence on the state of perceiving subjects is part of their nature, and comes at no cost to their status as real features of the environment.[14] His response allows him to avoid saying things that modern constructivists about dependent (or entangled) features have been known to say: say, that being pleasurable is identical to the property of being disposed to be experienced in a way accounted pleasurable.[15] Vasubandhu has no need to say anything of the sort. For entanglement of a feature with our dispositional bases is no reason for saying *it is unreal*—nor for saying that a feature's manifesting only under certain conditions makes its manifestation any less a matter of the disclosure of real features of the environment.

Would Vasubandhu then be inclined to treat the evidence of Buddhist cosmology as recommending a noncontrastive notion of entanglement? I don't know. There's only so far one can take the argument on the basis of epistemology. Preserving the reality of dependent features, as Vasubandhu does, may recommend not entertaining the kind of privileged point of view from nowhere that metaphysically contrastive ways of handling relational features do. And, just possibly, we won't have any role for objects. But there is nothing to recommend ruling talk of objects out either.

And that is my point. The kind of nonindependence we are gesturing at in the cosmological case of the discussion of living beings and their environmental conditions is not really analogous to the epistemological concerns some Buddhist philosophers use to generate contrastive (or noncontrastive) notions of dependence. For the cosmologist is interested in entangled descriptions of beings and their environments that take into account entanglements that are *logically prior* to concerns grounded in the perceptual contact between already constituted subjects and objects.

Let us define an epistemological structure of dependency (involved in the contrastive entangled object) so as to distinguish it from cosmological dependency. Epistemological dependency says that *certain* properties (being "secondary," as we might put it after Galileo) require perceiving subjects if they are to obtain, while others, possibly, do not. Cosmological dependency says that the features we have available to describe as objects would themselves not obtain were it not for some process that also produces the subjects capable of entertaining them as objects.

The interesting thing is this: it would not be at all obvious to a Buddhist philosopher that these varieties of dependency—epistemological and cosmological—need be in tension. Vasubandhu has to argue that they are. A Buddhist epistemologist may try to maintain that the fact that certain environmental features and beings are produced by some connected process is entirely independent of an epistemological concern with their interaction in the present. For an epistemologist need not be interested in how it is possible that a being can be related to some bit of the environment as a subject is to an object. Granted some such story, an epistemologist need only be interested in the criteria by which we may determine which of some being's determinations of some relevant bit of the environment count as knowledge and which do not. Vasubandhu owes his interlocutors a story of there being a deeper connection and a relevantly deeper connection at that. He must show them that there is no room on a cosmological account of ourselves to structure our relation to our environment in terms of objects and subjects.

TYING BEINGS AND THEIR WORLDS TOGETHER

Vasubandhu must show his interlocutors that the very idea of an object, to borrow a phrase from the philosopher Merleau-Ponty, might be the track left by a certain abstract way of thinking of ourselves, an abstraction undermined by cosmology.[16]

If in *The Twenty Verses* Vasubandhu attempts to show that the cosmological story of the deep history responsible for the twinned generation of beings and their worlds has consequences for any account of how beings and objects relate in perceptual experience, the reason has to do with *the kind of* causal story cosmology requires. And it has to do with the variety of relation that that story suggests obtains between the ways in which things come into view for us and our past.

In the next section, I'll begin to outline the elements necessary to tell the story and to appreciate one of its distinctive features: its reliance on what one might call a teleological form of description. The story will link not only the occurrence of features of a world but *the nature of features* and possible function to facts about us. The tie is not only causal but conceptual.

In the next chapter we shall see why Vasubandhu thinks that such elements recommend simply dropping objects from our description of how beings relate to environments. To prepare for these discussions, I'd like to suggest the shape of my account by adverting to Vasubandhu's way of handling a question he raises immediately after introducing the link between cosmological variety and action: "If it is the case that the variety in which worlds consist is 'the result of action' (as the verse says), then what is the reason for the fact that exceedingly beautiful and pleasing items such as saffron and sandalwood come into being on account of the actions of sentient beings, but not correspondingly beautiful bodies?"[17] Note the conceptual point: how close is the connection between the items in the world and the bodies of sentient beings, and what kind of connection is it? I follow Yaśomitra in taking this to be a question concerned with how items of experience (or enjoyment in general) are related to the enjoyers of experience. How shall we make sense of our bodies being one way, and our available experiences another? The answer is that the relationship is constitutive: "It would not be the case," says Yaśomitra, "that experience of something pleasant as pleasant would be possible without this discrepancy—for the pleasant is that which brings relief."[18]

Putting it like this helps us see how such a discussion is relevant to a concern with modeling how things come into view for us. Are we to individuate what an environment consists in together with its experiencing subjects in a constitutive way, as Vasubandhu and Yaśomitra here suggest doing by speaking of enjoyments?

In a word, yes. The answer stresses the connection between the possible enjoyments (of which worlds consist) and the actions of beings that constitute them: "Given just the actions of a particular type, on the part of beings who (habitually) engage in actions that are not of one moral type alone, it is the case that when their bodies, as conditions of experience that are constitutively unpleasant (consisting in sores, or abscesses) are brought into being, there are items of experience, beautiful and charming, that serve as antidotes (for the unpleasantness of the body). But *both*, the bodies *and* experiential objects of the gods who engage as a rule in unmixed types of actions, are delightful."[19] Vasubandhu, as Yaśomitra suggested, has just tied experienced features in the world to the history of experiencing beings in a rather dramatic way. Some X is experienced as F—some X *is* F, in fact—because being F serves a purpose, or in some way befits the being experiencing X.

This is to draw a normative connection between the range of possible contents and affordances in an environment and the beings who interact with them. A story that shows us how this kind of normative connection comes about might be able to go farther than the merely epistemological point regarding the possibility of noncontrastive entangled features. As I read the thought experiment in the next chapter, Vasubandhu will suggest that to tell the cosmological story aright is to see that we cannot meaningfully apply the language of objecthood onto what comes into view for us. To put the point another way, an epistemologist's way of handling structures of dependency obscures the point the cosmological story is trying to underscore: the ground-floor causal as well as conceptual entanglements of beings and environments involved in the very idea of something that can come into experiential view.

TELEOLOGICAL DESCRIPTION

I said above that part of the cosmological story consists in saying this: "Some X is experienced as F—some X *is* F, in fact—because being F serves a purpose, or in some way befits the being experiencing X." To speak like this involves speaking of features not only in terms of the functions they serve but as adaptations in Charles Darwin's sense. *Functions* and *adaptations* are—or rather, were—not equivalent notions, despite some terminological license taken by evolutionary biologists today. Stephen Jay Gould notes that while it is common to hear the word "adaptation" used to mean "any structure that performs a beneficial task," Darwin himself only used the word "adaptation" for those structures that had evolved over time by natural selection to carry out the particular function in question.[20]

I do not wish to say that we should compare Vasubandhu's concepts directly with Darwin's. Nor will it do to link adaptation with "design," either implicitly or explicitly.[21] The point, rather, is to note that some properties or structures of living beings might come to be as remedies for—which is to say, *for the sake of* alleviating—the suffering of embodied beings. And more generally, some features are understood to occur as they do as adaptations befitting the embodied conditions of beings, or more accurately, as befitting what individuals have done to become these beings and as befitting the environment their actions have made.

That way of putting things places an individual in a life-form and environment within the wider context that is the life of cosmological individuals. We cannot understand the sense of functions as adaptations without taking into account the *longue durée* processes that serve to bring into being the conditions and manage to be characterized by two things: the continued availability of the past in the present—which is a causal problem—and the fact that the present somehow manifests or expresses the past. The latter presents a conceptual question, having to do with a concern regarding the kind of normative connection the process might be thought to secure.

On Vasubandhu's behalf, let's reconstruct a form of description to which he was partial[22] and which was capable of addressing the casual and the normative questions raised by cosmological processes. This will be the type of description I call teleological.

To call it this, perhaps, is tendentious, for several understandable (if ultimately misplaced) reasons. It has been claimed, for example, that Buddhist philosophers are innocent of teleology and/or that they did not invoke teleological explanations. Neither is true. Buddhists can, and indeed have, explained a feature of the world by appealing to a purpose served by that feature. Thus, consider Vasubandhu's response to the implicit question raised early in the first chapter of *The Cutting Edge of Buddhist Thought*, "Why do we have a pair of eyes?" The answer has it that "the production of a pair [of eyes] is for the sake of beauty."[23] In the discussion that follows in Yaśomitra's commentary, we find a complicated exchange involving the concepts of purpose (*prayojana*) and cause (*kāraṇa*), a discussion in which the conclusion that there can be causes (*hetu*) that are not purposes (*prayojana*) has to be argued for: if there is no purpose for X in context C, can X come into being in C?[24]

But purposes and beneficiaries are not what shall concern me here. This brings me to another reason why talk of teleology can be controversial. When speaking of teleology, it is not always clear what we might mean. Here's what I shall take to be criterial: not, as one might expect, explanations that invoke purposes but descriptions that invoke (or are expressive of) finality. That is, I distinguish between a commitment to *final causes* in one's description of phenomena from a commitment to teleological description and explanation.

Let me be clear. I manifestly do not mean to claim (as the critics of Aristotelian philosophy alleged was entailed by a commitment to final causes) that to speak of ends in natural processes is to speak of these natural processes counting as the actions of sentient beings. I do think that an end must be involved for a description of a process to count as teleological, but not that the process thereby counts as an action (or something done *for the sake* of an end).[25]

What remains of the notion of teleological description is nevertheless significant—(expressive) finality, arguably the true target of the criticisms of teleology furnished by proponents of mechanism such as Descartes.[26]

Here's the X-ray of what I mean. Let's say we have a process involving a succession of events (x_1, x_2, . . .). Does it have the kind of structure that will allow us to speak of it as having an initial and a final state (x_1, x_2, . . . x_f)? May we say that it directed at that final state as the end of the process? If the process involves not only a succession of events but a succession of events constituting a sequence of change, terminating itself after reaching a limit, or end, then I think we can speak of this process as teleological.

OF SEEDS AND FRUIT

What will allow us to determine that a sequence of change is aimed at an end? One will have to inspect the kind of relation one finds between initial and final state. Does Vasubandhu know anything like the above process of change? Yes. He presents a mode of description (he particularly favored) in his essay *Against Selves*, where he builds to it as a conclusion. I cite from the translation of Matthew Kapstein: "[The effect arises] from the distinctive feature of the transformation of that continuum; from the completion of the sequence of sprout, stem, leaf, etc., culminating in the flower [which transforms into the fruit] . . . And that has not arisen from exhausted action, and also not immediately. What then? From the distinctive feature of the transformation of that continuum."[27] I find it useful to translate that last sentence thus: "[the fruit arises] from a distinct sequence of intrinsic change" (*saṃtāna-pariṇāma-viśeṣa*).

What we are dealing with is presented as a solution to a problem. "As the fruit arises from a seed" is a particular locution, one to which Vasubandhu has us attend. "So it is said," says Vasubandhu: "It does not arise from an exhausted seed, but neither does it arise immediately."[28] Such a formulation is introduced to isolate a presupposition in speaking of how an action could have an effect on a person over time. If, against Vasubandhu's advice, we modeled causation as a relation obtaining between entirely separable events (the individuation of which does not involve any reference to one another), we run into the problem of the temporal location of the causal power: if the event that serves as a cause is no longer present, how could it cause the effect? And if that event whose causal power is recruited to explain the delayed effect were present, or subsisting in some way, then why should the event picked out as a cause have caused its effect only after a delay? In citing the derivation of a fruit from a seed, what Vasubandhu is offering is a model of "because" that offsets such problems. On this view, the past enters into us by disposing us or constituting us in certain ways over time. It is the wider context of the process as a whole, and its shape, captured by the *directed change* of seed to fruit, that serves as the explanatory context.

The above description is used by Vasubandhu to bring a stretch of events under a unified (albeit analogical) description, picking out phases in a sequence of events to be seeds, thought to initiate processes of change that culminate as if yielding fruit.[29] The constitutive relation between a seed *of* a fruit and the expressive relation a fruit bears to the seed from which it emerges—the ability of a fruit to make manifest what a seed potentially is—lends itself to a description of a sequence in terms of an arrangement of phases, each of which is a phase in a process of coming to completion.[30]

The point of this variety of causal description is to show us how local and concrete stretches of a continuum come to be unified under such processes as the causal description picks out. That's the primary job of a teleological mode of description—to be able to articulate the connections of dependence obtaining between different temporal stretches as aspects or phases of a single process.[31]

VASUBANDHU'S INTERESTING THESIS: A REPRISE

Vasubandhu effectively appeals to such an account in his *Twenty Verses*. Recall how Vasubandhu's explicit statement of his interesting thesis is couched as an ascription of what the Buddha meant by speaking of the two conditions for the occurrence of mental events. This is what he claims the Buddha meant to teach us: "A conscious mental event possessing some specific manifest content, such as some particular hue, for example, comes into being on account of a seed or dispositional power attaining the end of a directed process of change. The Blessed One spoke of these two—the dispositional power and the manifest content—as being, respectively, the two conditions for perceptual experience called the eye and hue, to continue with our example of visual experience." We can now see what Vasubandhu has done. He has subsumed the idea of what a mental event is directed at, what it has in view—its manifest content—under a description. The description has the same form as that of his descriptions of habituation. By invoking a "sequence of directed change," Vasubandhu is likely thinking of such a process of directed change: the process of growth exhibited by a seed, which grows into a plant (through several phases in a sequence of change), and terminates in the production of a fruit, the properties of which vary as a function of variations in the properties of the seed. He has thus contextualized "being directed at content" within the variety of directedness dispositions impart to the sequences we are.

To be able to have some X in view is to be disposed by habituation to be someone for whom X was seeded as a possibility and nurtured over time. This is already to suggest a determining and constitutive variety of inseparable link. But it can become even more explicit. In the cosmological examples, we saw talk of purposes or befitting style characterizations of content. We may find these here as well, as when an interlocutor will say to Vasubandhu that for beings in hell, "these material elements change in such ways that they appear to perform various acts, like shaking their fists *for the sake of inducing fear.*"[32] The emphasis is mine, intended to show how it is that things come into view as befitting the kinds of beings we are, a relationship the constitutive variety of determination of manifest content by habituation makes possible to endorse.

Once we place the mental event within a history of habituation to certain patterns of activity, there may be no further question to ask as to the connection that a mental event enjoys with something like "the" world. Instead, it is the relationship with the past borne along into the present by habit that matters. At least, that's what we shall see Vasubandhu try to show in the next chapter.

Vasubandhu's cosmological commitments, we saw in the last chapter, involve setting "the axis of history at the center of things," to adapt a phrase used by Timothy Ferris to capture the influence Darwin's way of thinking had on natural philosophy.[33] Bert James Loewenberg said of Darwin that "he succeeded in putting the *whole* of past life into *every* aspect of *every* form of present life."[34] In Vasubandhu's case, it is the history of action that shows us how the past gets into the present: into the features of things, into our bodies, and even into the manifest textures of experience.

LOOKING BACK

Vasubandhu's interesting thesis relates what we have in view, like any cosmological feature, to a history of action. According to him, what shows up in perception can be said to express the links that obtain between life-forms and their environment and that are grounded in a shared history.

Vasubandhu directs our attention to recontextualizing the weight of the present and the value of certain features of individuals and their environments in ways consistent with what I called cosmological descriptions in the last chapter. There, I stressed the destabilizing and counterintuitive aspects of Buddhist cosmological descriptions. I said that they put pressure on our commitments to the integrity of salience of the present. Was that a mistake?

Maybe. In a wonderful essay, Matthew MacKenzie has suggested that we can think of the Buddhist cosmological commitments I have canvassed in this chapter rather differently. We do not need to say that they recommend a peculiarly premodern view of the world. Instead, they might be read as advancing a fairly intuitive, phenomenological account of experience with contemporary parallels. In particular, he recommends framing Buddhist claims about action and the connection between mind and world such that a central lesson comes through. The lesson is this: "Through karmic processes we *enact* ourselves—that is, we make and remake ourselves through our actions," and "we also enact our world(s) through karma—that is . . . our patterns of action and reaction bring forth meaningful worlds, which in turn shape these very patterns for better or worse."[35] MacKenzie intends the verb "enact" in a technical sense now associated with a family of views devolving from the work of Francisco Varela, Evan Thompson, and Eleanor Rosch.

Helpfully, MacKenzie quotes Evan Thompson's summary of the program: "The conviction that motivates the enactive approach is that cognition is not the representation of an independent world by an independent mind, but is rather the enactment of a world and a mind on the basis of a history of embodied action."[36] Put this way, it might seem very hard for me to object to anyone's speaking of Vasubandhu's enactivism. It would possibly even be churlish. Nevertheless, there are reasons to be cautious—all of which, I should say, MacKenzie is well aware of, having articulated them already in print in connection with the limitations of what he calls Buddhist reductionism (more about which below). For my purposes, however, I find it useful to go into the matter in a little more detail.

As MacKenzie notes, as a theoretical program, enactivism involves several claims. One of its claims plainly does not apply: perceptual experience *is not itself* considered a form of action (or even activity) by Vasubandhu (nor indeed, by any Buddhist philosopher in his orbit, as far as I know).[37] It is not even clear why action (*karma*) should constrain a Buddhist account of what shows up in perceptual experience: it is, in fact, Vasubandhu who argues that it should, as I'm trying to show in this book.

Nevertheless, it is not in any account of perception or perceptual experience that my worry lies. Vasubandhu, as I read him, could very well agree with the antirepresentationalism enactivists recommend when speaking of cognition.[38] It's just that things are not so simple when it comes to the theoretical focus in enactivism on the distinctive dynamics of autonomous systems, paradigmatically living organisms.

In particular, I am concerned with the possible consequences of the use MacKenzie makes of Vasubandhu's claim that we must look to collective action as the antecedent for the variety in which worlds consist.[39] MacKenzie reads this claim as an enactivist might: "Thus sentient beings enact themselves and their worlds in dynamic interdependence over time."[40] This intertheoretic translation (of "karma talk" by talk of "enacting") might suggest that Vasubandhu intends something like the claim that the dynamic details of a living organism's embodiment matter, paradigmatically so when explaining agency and a suite of functional and behavioral norms.[41] And it might suggest that, in offering his claim, Vasubandhu is guided by the kinds of norms that govern the theoretical activities of enactivists.

It is a matter of determining where a theory would have us attend and why. As I read him, Vasubandhu's way of entangling features of the environment and living beings does not depend on facts in the present, nor is it derived from scrutiny of the dynamic inner workings of an organism with an eye on the way in which an organism structures its environment and itself over time. I believe that Vasubandhu is too much of what MacKenzie calls a Buddhist reductionist—a problematic variety of Buddhist metaphysician, according to MacKenzie, especially when compared with early Buddhists and Madhyamakas—who does not have the resources to make the kinds of claims MacKenzie thinks Buddhists should be making.[42]

My point is not to take sides in this dispute. I just wish for it to be clear why there is no obvious intertheoretic analogue in Vasubandhu's descriptions for enactivism's focus on an organism or emergent structure. For the lesson to be learned does not have to do with Vasubandhu's offering us a rival proposal. It is the fact that an appeal to enactivism can obscure what Vasubandhu may have been trying to do. Intertheoretic comparisons can conceal a very different and no less important norm governing the success of Vasubandhu's descriptions.[43]

I do not know of any description of an organism in Vasubandhu that coordinates an "inside" look into its activities at the scales at which enactivism typically would have us attend. I mean to make a twin claim: firstly, Vasubandhu's redescription does not invite scrutiny of *the inner details* of anything in the present or pertaining to the biological basis of an organism; secondly, it does not involve recruiting into its description anything like the activities of *an organism*. The first point emphasizes explanatory ambition; the second, explanatory resources.

Recall that Vasubandhu's redescription grounds manifest content in processes involving habituation to action on the part of a cosmological individual. Specifically, the content that some individual S has available now (including the sense of being a self) is grounded in the dispositions engendered by some prior being causally related to S. To be sure, the activities S engages in will contribute to the circumstances of some future individual or individuals who will stand as her successors. But the focus of Vasubandhu's description is not on her activities but those of her predecessors.

Vasubandhu offers us no "inside" look into the detailed dynamics of the interactions this individual, being alive, must enjoy with her environment. To be sure, one could lean on Buddhist accounts of momentariness and say that *there must be* a finer level of grain it is possible to achieve in his descriptions. But Vasubandhu does not offer this finer-grained description when making this thesis. Nor does he seem to want to offer any such descriptive purchase on the activities within a single organism to account for the shape of the description he is offering.

For one thing, I believe that he would think our attention to such a sort of thing misplaced. Consider, for example, the case of new life in a womb, which is thought by Buddhist philosophers to be occasioned of two types of matter: semen and blood. What is the relationship between semen and blood, the matter occasioning new life, and the new life that grows once the being in-between joins, and its special variety of matter dissolves and joins in the mix? Vasubandhu offers two proposals: "Some say . . . that the semen and blood, which lack faculties, perish together with the being in the between; that which does possess faculties (the new life) appears in the way that a sprout arises after the destruction of a seed . . . [O]thers say that other elements [are responsible], as in the case of worms on leaves."[44] What must be characterized is the relationship between a complex state of matter with seemingly emergent properties (like capacities for sensation and consciousness) and its constituting conditions that lack them, but from which life appears to have been generated. On both models presented above, I would argue, we are being offered dependence without structure or true emergence.

The first—having us think of "a sprout after the destruction of seed"—begs off from the question of the emergence of structure, complexity, and new properties by simply denying that there actually is continuity of constituting matter. There is only reoccupation.

The second model (that of "worms on leaves") allows for dependence at a time, but without integration, organization, or structure. The emergence of new life (as worms on a leaf) is presented as being the utterly disconnected achievement of some obscure principle.

But the new life, it turns out, is connected. Not to its constituting matter, but to the laws of action, as the explanation says, which is the only time activity is mentioned on either of these biological models. The question was this: Do the material principles [*mahābhūtāni*] of the semen and blood themselves become, by the force of karma, the basis for the faculties of this new being? Or do other material principles, supported by these, arise as a result of action?"[45] The phenomena here are completely passive with respect to the natural forces associated with karma.

How could Vasubandhu say anything else? Apart from the force of karma, there is only one metaphysical creature that he considered to be prima facie intelligible as a possible candidate for underwriting the emergence of new structures and new properties—the Vaiśeṣika idea of a part-possessing whole. Schematically expressed, it looks something like this: "For all *x*, and all (*y*1, *y*2, . . . *yn*), if *x* is a concrete particular composed from actual parts, and (*y*1, *y*2, . . . *yn*) are the proper parts of *x*, then there exists some *z*, such that (1) *x* = *z*; (2) *z* is discrete from (*y*1, *y*2, . . . *yn*); and (3) *z* is physically present in each part (*y*1, *y*2, . . . *yn*) and nowhere else."[46] I think that this is the only metaphysical item Vasubandhu seriously considered that has the organizational unity to count as an organism if alive.[47] It is thought to be an effect, caused by its parts and, residing in these parts, recontextualizing them.

Appropriately enough, Vasubandhu discussed this metaphysical idea at the close of his chapter on cosmology in *The Cutting Edge of Buddhist Thought*,[48] where he discusses how things get started again at the beginning of a new eon after a period of cosmic involution, when not even a single atom (however subtle) remains of the physical universe. One explanation favored by non-Buddhist philosophers involves the emergence of objects out of eternal atoms left over at the end of the epoch. They claim that without atoms, no cause could be found for the emergence of objects. Importantly, they maintain this, in part, because they deny the theory that would have cosmological explanations for the generation of worlds be tied to an account involving power properties, or seeds, being ferried across from another world by wind, ultimately linked to the power of karma.

Vasubandhu thought the sidelining of karma wrongheaded.[49] He thought the concept of a mereologically complex structure problematic. And he thought the account of emergent properties—discussed in connection with the part-possessing whole as a mereological structure—ultimately inexplicable. And he also found, I would argue, the attempt to circumvent the appeal to past action problematic. But not, I'd argue, because karma provides Vasubandhu with a better explanation.

If Vasubandhu does not describe the processes initiated by action as involving the complex self-making activities of individuals, and if he does not analyze the process in terms of mereological structure and emergence, nor ground the process in anything that could serve further *to account* for those features that distinguish his preferred forms of description, this is deliberate. Vasubandhu's account *takes us out of* the organism, as it were, recontextualizing what looks to be a self-sufficient context in a complex trajectory involving sometimes utter dependence on the past lives and activities of other individuals, whose own lives may always be similarly recontextualized.

It is the transindividual trajectory that matters, a trajectory that defies organization and even description.

Like an enactivist, Vasubandhu does emphasize the fragility of boundaries, and the fact that they are made, not given. But, unlike an enactivist, he does not look forward to what is new in what is made. Vasubandhu looks back, with something of the caution of someone like Freud, who once wrote in a letter to his fiancée, "What we once were, [we] in part still remain."[50]

These differences matter. In invoking backward-looking explanations with the help of karma, Vasubandhu might have in mind to reveal a wonder—a limit to reasoning and description that involves neither explanation nor explanandum. If not prediction or explanation, what norms might govern success in description for Vasubandhu? I'll discuss this aspect of the claim in the conclusion to the next chapter, where I'll try to make good on the thought here expressed that Vasubandhu is pointing in a very different direction than is contemporary science. But to what end, we'll see next.

6

TRANSPARENT THINGS, THROUGH WHICH THE PAST SHINES

It is a striking thought that two of the most singular and influential works of philosophy in twentieth-century Europe should have taken up the meaning of "world" for reconsideration.

Wittgenstein began his *Tractatus* by resisting a particular picture, writing that the world is "the totality of facts, not of things." "It is," Max Black wrote, "as if [Wittgenstein] were to say: 'Consider what you mean by all that contingently exists, everything that makes the universe different from what it might have been.'"[1] Which helps us see that the difference between a mere inventory of separable items and a scaffolding of facts is a difference that matters.

The inventory, no matter how inclusive and accurate, leaves something out: the fact that the things in question exist. That is the view Max Black attributes to Wittgenstein,[2] though something more fundamental has gone missing, Martin Heidegger thought. The world should not be understood as an inventory of any manner of occurrent things at all, Heidegger suggested, no matter how structurally rich. List such items in the world as there are, creaturely and insentient, and you will find two things missing: the sort of creature for whom any such list could make any sense as being their world, and the sense it makes for any item in that list to be available in such a creature's world.[3]

Both Wittgenstein and Heidegger are redirecting their reader's attention with such arguments, exposing blind spots in philosophical theories, and the inadequacies of received conceptual tools. I would argue that in the opening of *The Twenty Verses* Vasubandhu is performing the same function for his Buddhist interlocutors. He is reminding them to think about the conceptual lessons that Buddhist cosmology holds for thinking about being in a world. "This object and that object / Never contained the landscape / nor all of its implications," wrote the poet Charles Wright.[4] This is what I hear Vasubandhu saying to his Buddhist interlocutors as well.

In the last few chapters we have set the stage. Given Buddhist cosmological commitments, what beings have available to them to experience as part of belonging to a world is not independent of the processes that made them and their world. But if Buddhist philosophers thus weaken the logical independence of life-form and lived world, they do not necessarily identify them. Yet Vasubandhu does not simply want to say that objects *are in part* constituted by the traces of actions that also serve to define beings. He wants to be done with objects. Let the idea of traces of habituation take their place. How will he argue for this?

One of Nabokov's semi-omniscient narrators once said this: "When *we* concentrate on a material object, whatever its situation, the very act of attention may lead to our involuntarily sinking into the history of that object."[5] Vasubandhu will use the guards in hell to begin a thought experiment that will attempt just such a perspective on the obdurately material objects that appear to us to serve as the ground for episodes in which we are directed at them. That is, we should not skim over the present realities we see. Instead, taking a cosmological point of view, we should learn to voluntarily see through them to the traces of our long history of habituation and see (to adapt the words of Nabokov's recently deceased) objects as "transparent things, through which the past shines."[6]

In this chapter we'll follow this argument through.

COSMOLOGY AND ETHNOGRAPHY

Vasubandhu's interlocutor is committed to the thought that we cannot speak of constraints on experience without objects. Objects provide the interlocutor with his paradigmatic notion of a constraint. A world, then, such as it emerges in the interlocutor's arguments, is expressed as something of a container for an inventory of (paradigmatically physical) objects. By contrast, Vasubandhu's cosmological notion of cosmological constraints invokes a different paradigm of explanation. It is a world—and no mere inventory of objects—that provides for constraints. But to get a feel for Vasubandhu's sense of a world, we may follow his brief yet carefully contoured description of hell:

> All constraints on experience are jointly established as in hell [4bc]. How? Given the fact of beings in hell seeing, among other things, the guards in hell, and being tormented by them [4cd].
>
> As, for instance, it is established that in the hells beings in hell see such things as the guards in hell in accordance with constraints on place and time. The phrase "among other things" above includes such things as dogs, crows, and iron hills moving to and fro.
>
> These visual experiences are enjoyed by all those suffering in hell, not just by one alone; and their collective torment at the hands of these guards in hell is established, even in the absence of there really being any such things as guards in hell, on account of the constitutive and determining influence of the process of ripening of species-defined shared patterns of activity.[7]

The description of hell exemplifies two features: a collective life-form and an environment of possible elements that serve to condition the lives in it. Thus, to speak of a world is to speak of at least two things at the same time:

(i) A class of individuals belonging to a life-form with a particular range of capacities to which are fitted a certain range of available experiences.
(ii) A class of items the presence of which goes into making the sorts of experiences that a class of individuals has available to them definitive of their being in that place (or definitive of their being that sort of life-form, as in the case of denizens of the formless regions of being).

A description of a world needs something more than an inventory of objects picked out from some unspecified point of view. But even more than subjects, it needs an identifiable mode of subjectivity, a certain experiential point of view from which, for example, (ii) might be picked out, and which, furthermore, may be associated with a unifying tenor of description. We need,

(iii) A distinctive experiential register.

What I mean is that there is such a thing as *a style of experience* associated with the description of a recognizable life-form in its characteristic environment. This factor will play a crucial role in Vasubandhu's argument below.

Why have I begun with Vasubandhu's description of hell? Cosmology, as I have presented it in this book, is the study of variation. And Vasubandhu's description of another world, I would argue, practices a kind of sensitivity to variation and difference across life-forms enshrined in Buddhist cosmology as a discipline. If I may be provocative, Vasubandhu's description of hell should be read as being a forebear for the art and skill of recording the difference we owe to anthropology in the middle of the twentieth century. Consider, for example, what Gregory Bateson thought was necessary to be able to think that one could present the whole of a culture other than one's own: "Stressing every aspect exactly as it is stressed in the culture itself, no single detail would appear bizarre or strange or arbitrary to the reader, but rather the details would all appear natural and reasonable as they do to the natives who have lived all their lives within the culture."[8] Bateson thought artists might be able to accomplish the perspectival feat and he believed that an artist would thereby capture an "ethos," or "emotional tone."[9] Ethos is what unifies the many different details into a single whole, without which many features or incidents of that culture would not make sense. For Vasubandhu, the emotional register and the style of experiencing play a similar role. Hell has an associated experiential texture. One could use the word "torment" to get at it, combining the fear and terror that are criterial for experiences to be "of" hell, as we shall hear later. Everything that shows up in the experiences of the beings condemned to hell fits in with this ethos: the eerie mountains, the thorned trees, and the guards in hell.

But here's a potential problem. Are we not allowing our description to draw too much from the vantage point of only one kind of possible experiencer? Surely there is more in hell's environment than can be captured using some such thing as a style of experience? Consider the torturers, or the animals. Does the total emotional palette have to make room for their way of being in this environment, their way of making sense of it? Can one not imagine a description of the environment, for example, that would seek to describe more of the environing features than the experiences of subjects could have in view? The iron mountains moving to and fro, for example? Why are they moving? How? Just why is everything here fitted to terrorize some, if not all, the living beings? Perhaps there are structures that go into making available the experiences and the total style of feeling that informs the way of describing the environment, but that the phenomenological description cannot—without failing to be an ecological description unified by a total palette—make explicit?[10]

We are now gesturing at what Bateson would have called a scientific description. Bateson thought that no study of a culture could be complete "unless it links up the structure and the pragmatic working of the culture with its emotional tone or ethos."[11] I think Vasubandhu would agree that there is work for another mode of description. We saw the form of description he might have to hand in the last chapter: a teleologically shaped story responsible for the generation of beings and their environments.

But Vasubandhu may have been the first to stress the general shape of a problem that may result from worlds possessing scientific descriptions as well as descriptions in terms of ethos: what if they come into tension? For example, what if there are not really any guards in hell—no possible subjects, in fact, whose emotional palette in hell jars with that of the unifying theme of fear and terror given torture? Reporting the experience as suggested by the content, the reports of hell (as with the experiences of some beings in hell) center certain facts about the world and their presence in it as realities. When one finds inconsistencies, this might create room for considering adjustments to our models, including the need to think how certain features get to seem to be the way they do. Anything with a history may be susceptible to subtle perturbations when we change the story or even just the focus of the story. And every manifest aspect in a world, Buddhists tell us—the environment, the subjects, and even the style of experience—has a history.

GUARDS IN HELL

Vasubandhu's account in *The Cutting Edge of Metaphysics* shows us that descriptions of hell feature particular types of beings armed with swords, lances, and javelins. The function of these beings appears to alternate between keeping beings in hell from escaping, and inflicting, with due diligence, a diet of richly imagined torture on their victims.[12] Yet, notwithstanding the availability of vivid depictions highlighting the cruel and practical intelligence of these beings in a variety of contexts, narrative and contemplative, Vasubandhu suggests doubt: "One question suggests another: are the guards in hells living beings or not?"[13]

"As opposed to what?" one might be tempted to ask. It turns out, however, that a proposal was voiced that these beings might not be genuine living beings, but instead some kind of simulacra. By "simulacra" here I intend a generic term for the sense that something seems to be an *x* but is not an *x*. In our case, these beings are not really living beings, but parcels of matter whose nature and whose movements mimic but do not involve life.

Buddhists knew and thought with different categories of simulacra. There are automata, or mechanical devices that can mimic the actions of living beings; there are virtual beings, manifested by the abilities of Buddhas and other adepts to manipulate appearances, capable of appearing to act, converse, even think.[14] The case at hand involves environmental adaptations, parcels of matter that seem to be living beings with agency and purpose to terrorize the beings reborn in hell.[15]

Other philosophers, however, seem to have held that it was necessary and possible for there to be wardens in hell, or sentient beings distinct from the victims in hell, albeit allowing for these guards in hell to be sentient beings with special bodies adapted to hell.[16]

The conceptual parameters for the debate, thus, involved two questions:

(a) Are guards in hell living, sentient beings?

and,

(b) If not living beings, can these be explained through adaptations of the environment?[17]

This debate is not confined to only one Buddhist philosophical tradition.[18] The salience of the debate may not have been confined to one South Asian religious tradition.[19] In fact, the debate is not even confined to South Asia. Augustine, Vasubandhu's contemporary, could write in *The City of God*: "At this point we are confronted with another question: If this fire is not to be immaterial, like the pain of the soul, but material fire, inflicting pain by contact, so that bodies can be tortured by it, then how will there be punishment in it for the evil spirits? It is obviously the same fire which will be used for the punishment of the demons as well as the human beings."[20] As it turned out, there was nothing "obvious" about any of it. Hell and the guards in hell have proved good to think with for a variety of thinkers in antiquity. My goal is limited. I wish to understand why Vasubandhu in particular wanted his interlocutors to think this through.

THOUGHT EXPERIMENTS

I suggest thinking that Vasubandhu uses the case of guards in hell as a thought experiment in a particular sense. The sense of "thought experiment" I have in mind to recommend derives from Thomas Kuhn's belief that a thought experiment is useful when we wish to isolate a problematic presupposition in a paradigm. The thought experiment is a diagnostic stress test.[21]

There is a notion of paradigm on which Buddhist scholastic discourse, particularly cosmological discourse, counts as a paradigm, if by that (after Kuhn) we mean a disciplinary matrix and allow ourselves to extend Kuhn's sense of problem-solutions to include paradigmatic descriptions of the world and exemplary problems concerned with interpretations of those sentences.[22]

Of course, one may think of thought experiments rather differently. Robert Sharf, for example, has written eloquently to the effect that while many have approached Buddhist cosmological "doctrines as the products of intelligent but misguided scholastics struggling to make sense of the universe," hobbled by scripture and "prescientific understanding of the cosmos," it is possible (and perhaps better) to adopt the perspective that these doctrines are frames of reference for pondering conceptual issues like personal identity, responsibility, sentience, and death. And since he says so right after discussing thought experiments, one can suppose that he is recommending a contrast between an approach to Buddhist cosmology that treats it as a series of thought experiments and an approach that would frame it as a conceptual grammar for scripturally informed empirical description.[23]

In my view, there is no contrast to be drawn. A Kuhn-style thought experiment is salient just in case we are dealing with a paradigm of (premodern) description, given which the experiment can explore real possibilities and because of which one may seek to derive readily intelligible and alethically relevant lessons concerning how the world actually is.[24]

Our sense of paradigm need not be an exact analogue to theory in empirical science. Nor do we need an exact analogy to Kuhn's conception of crisis. But we do need to get a feel for the possibility of revising a paradigm. We need to associate cosmology with an area of uncertainty or an "area of trouble" (as Kuhn calls it), one that the thought experiment can explore in order to isolate a root presupposition, the resolution or response to which will have important ramifications more globally.

Guards in hell, I'll attempt to show, provide Vasubandhu with a way to focus an anomaly in Buddhist cosmological descriptions. And the revision of the cosmological paradigm to follow will have knock-on effects in a distinct paradigm, that of Buddhist epistemological theories and their accounts of perceptual content. Vasubandhu's arguments will partially exploit an analogy: an object might be as anomalous an idea in the context of perception as the idea of guards in hell is when describing hell.

WHAT DO YOU MEAN, "DO GUARDS IN HELL EXIST?"

Vasubandhu thinks that hell presents us with a case of collective experience in the absence of objects as causes of content. To be in hell is, indeed, to experience suffering at the hands of the guards in hell. But he also thinks that there are no guards in hell.

Before one may draw any lessons from this possibility, Vasubandhu must answer why anyone should think that guards in hell do not obtain. That flies in the face of received descriptions of hell and also (presumably) contradicts the perceptual reports of those in hell, should they ever be in a position to report on their experience in hell.

Vasubandhu's reason for denying that there are such beings is instructive: "On account of incoherence: Guards in hell do not make sense when taken to be beings in hell." What follows, then, is a conceptual argument, based on a problem with the conditions under which experience in hell is meaningful as an experience in hell. Here is Vasubandhu's conceptual argument:

> [They do not make sense] because they just do not experience suffering there in the same way as do beings in hell. And if you attempt to take it that wardens in hell torment one another, and so count as beings suffering in hell, then it would be impossible to define them apart from those destined to suffer in hell. That is, it would not be possible to say, "These are beings in hell," "these guards in hell." Moreover, there could be no fear if beings of equal strength, size, and shape torment one another. How could beings torment another, given that they cannot endure the burning pain while standing on a ground made up of heated iron? How is it possible for a being not "of" hell to be in hell?[25]

The analysis focuses our attention on a dilemma: guards must be a part of hell if they are to serve their function and yet be sufficiently removed from hell if they are to serve their function.

We are being guided by the ethos of hell that is linked to a particular experiential possibility. In doing so, we are situating our description of that ethos from the vantage point of the beings who suffer in hell, the punishment of whom serves as one of the reasons why the environment is the way that it is. Beings suffering in hell experience pain and terror, and experience these as being caused in them by other sorts of beings *who are unlike them*. That, says Vasubandhu, is constitutive of their experience of fear and terror.

But if it is necessary that the guards in hell be unlike the victims in hell, it is also not possible to make sense of their being entirely different. Recall our discussion of an ecological experience. The phenomenology of a guard in hell ought to reflect the environment it is in. But attempting to square the experiences of the guards in hell with their environment threatens to make them either too much alike or too unlike the victims in hell. That's the dilemma. A guard in hell must and must not suffer in hell if it is to be in hell.

It is worth saying that the idea that there was something anomalous about guards in hell was not confined to the works of systematic thinkers. It appears to have had a rather wide currency, as a popular narrative in South Asia suggests. The story I have in mind is that of King Aśoka's attempt to build a hell on earth under inspiration of Buddhist cosmological depictions of hell. In Xuanzang's telling of the climax of the story, in which the king finally repents for his awful social experiment, the King and his psychotic henchman, the torturer in the king's hell, engage in the following exchange when the King for the first time enters the hell he has made on earth: "The keeper, addressing the king said, 'Mahar̄aja, you too must die.' 'And why so?' said the King. 'Because of your former decree with respect to the infliction of death, that all who came to the walls of the hell should be killed; it was not said that the king might enter and escape death.' The King said, 'The decree was indeed established, and cannot be altered. But when the law was made, were *you* excepted?'"[26] The narrative appears to exploit the anomalous status of the guards in hell explored in Vasubandhu's arguments. But if we can rest assured as to the fact of there having been a cultural salience to such arguments, we do not yet have a sense of what, precisely, that salience consisted in. And we have yet to gauge the general philosophical lesson that stands to be learned from the statement of the anomaly. We do not yet have a sense of what principles the experiment will test, nor what it might be taken to show us.

BEING IN AN ENVIRONMENT

Let's try two distinct (yet coordinate) ways to get a feel for the salience of the anomaly. The first will stay with the ecological dimensions of the problem, which will allow us to explore an example of a general principle that hangs in the balance; the second, which I will develop in the next section, will offer a statement of the principle at a more generalized level, one applicable to perceptual experience more generally.

The ecological version is this: how closely must beings and their environments be related? Vasubandhu seems to think that the answer must be "very closely indeed." For something to be in an environment, it must be capable of exerting a causal influence on the environment. If a being is to have such a causal function in an environment, and if it is to be a living being, then its internal constitution and its experiential life ought to reflect the environment in which it lives. We might be tempted to ask: Why could the inner life of the torturer not have some other affect, some other way of registering the reality of its task and its environment? There might be more subtle forms of pain, or subtle psychological forms of debilitation induced in guards in hell?

This is why we ought not to take the example as an allegory for an environment as ramified as our own human world. The thought experiment has chosen a very carefully defined and rather attenuated environment. Unlike the hellish torture cells of our own world, where torturers will undergo a variety of experiential consequences, in hell all experiences must partake of the global affective palette, stipulated with reference to the experience of victims.

This is what an interlocutor attempts to clear up by asking, "First of all, how are animals born in heaven?"[27] The question motivating the analogy to heaven seeks an example from within Buddhist cosmology to ask: Can there not be more than one type of being in an environment? Is Vasubandhu not guilty of conflating being in the same environment with being the same type of being?

It is possible to think that animals are unfitted for heaven because the life of animals makes no room for anything like the felicities associated with heaven. What Mahāmaudgalyāyana saw of the life of animals in the *Mahāvastu*, for example, and the fact of scarcity of food, society, and security that constitutes their lives,[28] might suggest their being socially and psychologically unfit for life in heaven. Furthermore, some might think that since their appetites are so basic and so geared to survival, the virtues or felicities of food, for example, or any of the finer pleasures constitutive of being in heaven, are things to which they are entirely indifferent. To such portraits of the affective palette of misery one might add the valuation, voiced by some Buddhists, that animals are too impure—being creatures too embodied and too locked in to certain modes of responding to the environment on the basis of sensation—to find a place in true utopias, such as the lands of felicity imagined by some Buddhist texts. For example, we are assured by the word of the Buddha that in the land of felicity that is *Sukhāvatī*, the world of the Buddha of Infinite Light/Life Amitābha/Amitāyus, there are no animals. The birds, exquisite to look at and to hear, are simulacra, produced by that Buddha's power to manipulate appearances.[29]

Vasubandhu's response is instructive. He denies the analogy: "Those animals found in heaven are born there owing to former actions performed in our shared context, actions that conform to the felicities of the world into which they are to be born. And these animals born in heaven experience the felicities that are produced there."[30] This is a strangely touching recognition on the part of Vasubandhu: animals do not only promote pleasure, but they can fully experience it. Their inner life as creatures always fully reflects the environments in which they find themselves. That's the principle that is threatened by the anomalous description of the guards in hell.

Permit me a brief digression. Conceptually, there is a striking thought here, possibly of interest to a sensitive historian of culture. The above arguments (at least conceptually) suggest that the capacities to generate and to experience pleasure are tightly linked, more tightly than are capacities to suffer and to inflict or receive punishment. Unlike the case of experiencing and causing pleasure, the ability to suffer does not appear to entail the ability to punish. And that might be meant to signal that punishment is not in any obvious sense natural to us. What might that tell us? It might suggest that such arguments are part of a larger cultural negotiation of the place and salience of punishment and social forms centered on punishment.[31] I am put in mind of Wendy Doniger's remarks to the effect that "stories about animals are sometimes really about animals . . . but stories about animals also function as parables" of social classifications.[32] I think a historian will find that the same may well be true of cosmological arguments.

But the immediate lesson for Buddhist ecological descriptions of cosmological worlds is this: I said in the introduction that Vasubandhu may be among the first thinkers to recognize that if a description of a world has to keep in view the situated perspective of inhabitants there as well as the causal processes that account for their experience, these might come into tension. One of the things that will have to happen is that we revise some (but not all) of the descriptions to which the inhabitants of the world are likely to acquiesce. Exploring the anomaly and the conceptual form of the revision of the situated perspective of environed beings will give Buddhist philosophers a clue as to the shape their own account of perceptual experience might have to take.

LOGICAL AND PHYSICAL GAPS

Let's generalize the lessons of the ecological anomaly. Vasubandhu's argument is not intended to be exhaustive, merely exemplary. That is, Vasubandhu does not in *The Twenty Verses* revisit every single possible redescription of the guards of hell. In particular, he does not list the following possibility of making sense of guards in hell as living beings recognized in *The Cutting Edge of Buddhist Thought*: "According to one view, [the guards in hell] count as living beings . . . [H]ow are they not burned by fire? Either because of the fire is neutralized (by the force of prior actions), or else because of the special constitution of their bodies."[33] Of the many possible variants on explanations that recommend fine-tuning some aspect of the description of the material condition of the guards in hell and maintaining that there is a transparent insulation between the bodies of the guards in hell and the fires of hell is, I think, a fine metaphor for the logical gap Vasubandhu is keen on exposing.

Here's what I mean by a logical gap. I formulated the problem above as a problem for ecological description. But it is also a problem for experiential reports more basically. It has, for example, the same form as Leszek Kolakowski's question: "What were philosophers after when they inquired whether an object is *outside* or *beyond* an act of perception?"

This is either a topological image or a concern with "belonging to a class." Kolakowski suggests that the spatial image is absurd. It would amount to asking whether the object is spatially situated where the act of perception is. On the other hand, what could it mean to say that "a perceived object is not an element of the act of perception as a whole?"[34] Following Kolakowski's suggestion, I think one thing it could mean, one thing it did mean to Vasubandhu, is that we must provide a description of that object as part of a class without reference to the perceptual act, while coordinating this with its causal power to influence the perceptual act. Describe it as an object, in other words. Vasubandhu may be using the anomaly of the guards in hell—basing his sense of belonging to a world as satisfying the formal condition of "belonging to a class"—to show why this can become a problem. Or, at least, that attempts to repair the anomaly will be revealing.

Vasubandhu's insight here can also be expressed by considering the problem with the help of language his intellectual descendent Dignāga was to provide. Think of what an account of perceptual experience must involve in order to count as an explanation of perceptual experience. Dignāga says that some item can serve as the ground for an experience, its *ālambana*, if it produces a cognition in which there is a manifest aspect of itself. This is because it is defined as the condition (*pratyaya*) for the coming to be of that (appearance).[35] It is thus internal to the very idea of *the explanatory condition of experience* that it serve to coordinate the causal and phenomenological elements of the experience. To put this in the language of sentences about perception rather than perceptual episodes, we can acquire a condition that Vasubandhu and his interlocutor must respect: "If *S* sees *x*, we may say that '*S* sees *x* because of *z*" only if (i) *z* causes the perceptual episode and (ii) *z* can account for why the content takes the form of *x*, its aspect or phenomenological shape." Vasubandhu's thought experiment may be designed to show us that we do not always know what a candidate explanation might even look like.[36]

GOING BEYOND (SIMPLE) OBJECTS

Vasubandhu's question—"How can a being in an environment not be *of* that environment?"—may cut deep. To save the appearances, and eliminate the anomaly, Vasubandhu's interlocutor offers a major revision, practicing a variety of cosmological description of his own: "Take it, however, in the following way: because of the former actions of these beings in hell, particular material elements come to be constituted in hell. These elements are individuated by their color, shapes, size, and power in such a way as to acquire such designations as 'guards in hell.' And these material elements change in such ways that they appear to perform various acts, like shaking their fists for the sake of inducing fear."[37] The redescription keeps guards in hell as contents but not causes. It links the conditions by which subjects and objects are constituted, and softens the independence of the items taken in perception to be autonomous. Why do material elements in hell look like guards in hell? Consider what the perceptual report would look like based on this explanation: "*S*-type beings see 'guards in hell' not because of there being guards in hell, but because of a history of action that makes material elements in hell appear as guards in hell *in order* to induce fear in *S*, as befits the former actions of beings who are now *S*-type beings." That's a rather more complicated perceptual report than the one with which the interlocutor began pushing back against Vasubandhu, all the way back at the beginning of *The Twenty Verses*. Vasubandhu's interlocutor now subscribes to teleological cosmological descriptions and what, in the last chapter, we called befitting style characterizations of content.

But this is not Vasubandhu's proposal. Vasubandhu's interlocutor preserves some room to speak of objects by parceling up a region of space-time into two sorts of features. There are the object-like material elements, defined independently of any entanglement with the deep history of the generation of living beings. And then there are adaptations of these elements, shaped by teleological processes to "look a certain way" to the beings fitted out by action to be in that environment. There is one causal mechanism. The mechanism responsible for adapting the environment to look the way it does is the mechanism responsible for generating subjects for whom the environment is so adapted. But the mechanism, as we shall see, splits into causal tributaries, each requiring further consideration. Let me first consider what is left of the idea of an object on this proposal before turning to Vasubandhu's thoughts regarding the causal mechanism.

Thinking of the scope of possible experience in this bifurcated way might allow some Buddhist philosophers to think that a single region may be associated with several highly ramified property particulars, not all of which are disclosed to every type of being in contact with that region.[38] On this account, determining how to specify the region in terms of objects is complex; for the causal power of regions of space-time (and the properties they contain) must be linked to certain antecedent concerns involving different (possibly intersecting) histories of life-forms. But here is the relevant point. On the scenario just sketched, Vasubandhu's interlocutor must concede that, referring to the inventory of separable causes in the present using objects alone, he has no account of why a given slice of space-time should "look the way it does." He has no way, employing just objects, of satisfying the conditions of a successful explanation of perception. To hook up the causes he has available to use with the way in which things are manifest, he must run his explanation through facts concerning the type of beings whose experiences he is explaining. And he must appeal to their karmic story.

Both the interlocutor and Vasubandhu now seem to share some formal conception of what kind of an explanation is required if we are to link up cause and content when speaking of experiences of a world. But the question now is what role the "materiality" of the intentional content has to play. If any.

At this point in the argument, we need not think that Vasubandhu takes himself to be in a position to prove that we can dispense with objects. Nor is he able to show, as he will be later in the text, that, given some incoherence in the very idea of objects, making sense of experience necessarily involves dispensing with objects. Instead, we have only moved past thinking that an object (or anything object-like) is sufficient or even the most illuminating way to think about what having anything in view involves.

The account we know Vasubandhu to favor involves the persistence of dispositions reinforced through habituation. This process, as Vasubandhu believes, involves no separability of cause and effect. The dispositions serve to constitute the content that manifests them. And the process involves no heteronomy: no generation of material effects from mental events. For Vasubandhu, to cite the process promotes a dual vision. We describe the manifest in terms of what is experienced of the world by a subject from the point of view of being a life-form. But when describing the same process in causal terms, we describe a single sort of thing: the constitutive determination of possible experience by patterns of habituation engendering a certain life-form.

But what is *descriptively* twofold is rendered *ontologically* twofold on his interlocutor's proposal. The interlocutor proposes two further features: (i) including a mechanism by which mental events can generate material effects, in effect yielding teleological ends in nature extrinsic to the process that accounts for them; and (ii) a new relation, that of perceptual contact, which must join together two things: (a) a material locus that serves as the heteronomous effect of a teleological process (adapted to interact with living beings) and (b) the minds of these living beings.

WHERE WE HAVE ARRIVED

Vasubandhu feels that what has been proposed above involves an infelicity of thought, being a variety of speculative imagination: "But the continuing dispositional traces of these actions stick to and remain within the individual mental continua of these beings: they are not found anywhere else. Why not commit to the thought that there is a particular type of causal process involving the mental continuum, such that the result of such a causal process would occur *only* where the traces of actions are? What is the reason for speculating that the result of a process involving the dispositional traces of action occurs where the traces of action do not?"[39] His interesting thesis shares a form with the redescription he has elicited from his interlocutor. But let's be clear. His claim is not that the interesting thesis—on which what comes into view for us must be linked to the kinds of beings we are—enjoys parity with an explanation that credits the causal influence of objects as explanatorily necessary and sufficient. Rather, he claims that there is a kind of parity between his view and a theory that has conceded that the burden of explanatory work is not wholly borne by objects. Vasubandhu's argument has brought us to the point of seeing that we will have to deal with the traces of action, or habituation.

I have used talk of traces, and sometimes habituation, to translate an evocative word, *vāsanā*. One might also point to the metaphorical range of this word and its related meanings—"to linger" or "to dwell"—associated with smell and thus coming to mean "perfume" as well.[40] Yaśomitra once helpfully defines the word in his commentary to *The Cutting Edge of Buddhist Thought* thus: "a function of prior habits, which instantiates as a specific dispositional power of a mental event to be the unaltered cause of [future] activities of body and speech."[41] There can be no account of how we have things in view without our having an account of how, as I phrased it in the introduction, we are poised by the trajectories of past experience we bear within us.

Vasubandhu has extracted that much of an agreement from his interlocutor. And for a moment, just for a moment, Vasubandhu presents the conversation as having arrived at a choice between two variants of a similar form of description, one of which has more elements. Vasubandhu presents his own conceptual reoccupation of objects and restriction to talk of habituation, and nothing else, as being more natural in some sense. Lighter, I would say.

Of course, the proposals are not equivalently weighted. As his interlocutor quickly reminds Vasubandhu, there are scriptural utterances that might tell against Vasubandhu's views. Notwithstanding, that is, Vasubandhu's cosmological redescription of perceptual experience, the reason a Buddhist philosopher might nevertheless insist on a conceptual place for objects is that the Buddha has explicitly taught that there are two types of conditions for episodes of intentional awareness: "If what is manifest as sensory particulars, hues, and the like, were just an instance of experiential awareness, and not an object characterized as a sensory particular, then the Buddha would not have said that there exist sensory conditions qua objects, including such particulars as hues."[42] The Buddha did not speak without reason, and one reason why he spoke like this might just be that there are such things as objects.

This appeal to scripture requires of Vasubandhu a two-pronged response that I cannot explore in this book. First, it requires of Vasubandhu a claim that the Buddha could not have meant his assertion of there being two kinds of conditions for intentional awareness in any literal sense, just because the very concept of objects is incoherent. This argument will show that having something in view necessarily cannot be explained as a function of the causal influence on us of objects.

But secondly, Vasubandhu must account for the Buddha's having spoken as he has of the conditions of awareness. Vasubandhu requires a model of exegesis very different from the naïve (or perhaps resolute) semantics of his interlocutor. Both arguments are required if Vasubandhu's conceptual connection between perception and habituation to action can be recommended to his fellow Buddhists. More importantly, both arguments are required if Vasubandhu's account is to count as a reconstruction of the Buddha's own considered view.

A reader interested in seeing what recommends the revision of both our common sense and the prima facie sense of what the Buddha meant is advised to explore the arguments of *The Twenty Verses* in greater detail. They will give reasons for not taking the Buddha at his word.

But they will not offer an explanation of the shape the correct account of experiential content must take. Only a cosmological argument can show that, it would seem. And perhaps only a cosmological account can help us orient to what the correct description will reveal of reality.[43]

VENERATING REALITY

Without the appeal to scripture, Vasubandhu and his interlocutor might manage a delicate balance between them. They have agreed on the need for a form of description that entangles subjects and their worlds through befitting teleological-style descriptions featuring habituation. They disagree as to how to best characterize such entanglement. For Vasubandhu, habituation manifests as what comes into view. For the interlocutor, habituation results in changes to the material occasions with which we come into relation in perceptual experience.

As I indicated, *The Twenty Verses* does not stop with Vasubandhu's interesting thesis; nor does it end with his rhetorical appeal to parity between types of redescription. Why, then, freeze-frame, as it were, and dwell on this moment of the text? Briefly, because I believe that the appeal to apparent commensurability of forms of description and the implicit appeal to comparative lightness suggest a moment of metatextual gravity: we are possibly being alerted here to the kind of intellectual practice in which Vasubandhu has been engaged. Furthermore, it just might allow us to get a feel for the world to which he took himself to be responsible in theory.

As we have it here, the debate appears to show Vasubandhu declare for (as Indian philosophers would call it) lightness in theorizing—what I would call explanatory transparency. But lightness (or, in a European context, simplicity) is frequently taken to be a (vexed) virtue to which one might appeal when assessing the explanatory success of theories. It is often vexed because there are a variety of ways of articulating what simplicity consists in, and it is not always clear, in every domain, whether simplicity gives us a more accurate picture than does complexity.[44] So too, with the impression of explanatory transparency. Vasubandhu appears to be saying that we should not invoke any phenomenon in our theory for which we do not have a transparent mechanism. I quoted him above as saying that "the continuing dispositional traces of these actions stick to and remain within the individual mental continua of these beings: they are not found anywhere else." This might give the impression that Vasubandhu believes in one or both of the following: that there are no cases of interaction without a specifiable causal mechanism or pathway; that indicating a causal pathway or mechanism comes to the same thing as explaining a phenomenon. But we should not assume either.

We should not assume that Vasubandhu's redescription is intended to give us better *explanatory* purchase on what there is. But what else might a redescription seek to do? This is where some historical work is necessary. And it is useful to step back and take in Vasubandhu's intellectual world from a wider vantage point. An appeal to lightness might be part of securing an appropriate responsiveness to reality. To see what this might mean, I shall try to reconstruct what I call the norm of reality in theory on the basis of Buddhist appeals to a principle of reality (*dharmatāyukti*). The latter principle is one to which Buddhist philosophers claimed they could appeal when reasoning. I will use it to elicit the norms that can help us tell descriptions that succeed from descriptions that don't.

By reconstructing a connection between lightness and norms of description, I wish to explore the intuitive sense many have that we are in fact speaking about a world when we invoke something like brute facts, facts that resist further explanation or description.[45] It is historically variable when, in point of fact, and with what sort of feature of the world, one is confronted with a sense of reality. Variable too will be which attitudes are appropriately directed at one's having reached such limits. Thus, exploring how and when brute facts are evoked might be a way to spot these historically variable senses of what the world is like.

You'll see what I mean as we go on. My point of departure emphasizes lightness in the context of an acknowledged failure of causal explanation. I'll begin by noting that Vasubandhu has arrived somewhere like this intellectual balance between competing descriptions involving karma before. In the context of this other case, he and his interlocutors were concerned with a description of the same kind of process, a directed sequence of change, in connection with the contested status of a curious item in the theoretical toolkit of some Buddhist scholastics. We will need a little background to appreciate it. I'll first provide the background for the second concept—that of covert action—and then reconstruct a situation where contested claims made about situations described with the help of that concept occur, and to which Vasubandhu responds by appealing again to the apparent lightness of his own use of sequences of directed change. Finally, I'll use that situation to reconstruct a norm of reality and a norm of description.

To begin, let's consider the notion of overt actions: actions of speech or gestures of one's body, for example. Overt actions, say Buddhist philosophers, may intimate to another that I am doing something, or that these events have been brought about with an antecedent intent. Such overt actions, therefore, are *vijñaptis*, here meaning "communicative events."

But in performing some overt actions, some Buddhists maintain, I may do something else. This something else is a variety of (concatenation of) change one induces in oneself by acting overtly with a sufficiently good or bad intent; unlike overt actions, this is *covert*, intimating nothing. While not a mental phenomenon, it is not material in the sense of occupying space and resisting co-occupation. Lastly, it is not episodic, but something that occurs seriatim, like a flow, enacting a concatenation of ethically evaluable change in one's embodied being over time. For what we do to ourselves in performing overt actions structures our embodied experience over time and may be assessed as being either skillful or unskillful. Thus, such phenomena are treated as being a variety of action, albeit noncommunicating, covert actions (*avijñapti-karman*).[46]

It is with reference to this contested category that Vasubandhu was once moved to appeal to simplicity. He did so because of cases where there is a genuine mystery that his fellow Buddhist theorists of covert actions were grappling with, problems we would call problems of action (or more properly inter-action) at a distance.[47] As discussed by them, the problem generally involves the delayed (sometimes posthumous) predication of an action to an agent, as in the following types of cases.

> *Scenario 1.* Agent A determines to kill C. Agent A has the intent to kill C but hires B to do it. Agent A commits overt actions in hiring someone to kill C. But this is not the same thing as having brought about the killing of C. As long as C is not killed, Agent A has not brought about the killing of C. Agent A does not know when C is killed, or even if C is killed. Many long years pass. B kills C. At that time, the theory states that "what Agent A has done" changes from having intended to kill C to having brought about the killing of C.[48]

The change is not a mere change in description, for the change brings about real consequences by virtue of the merit or demerit thought to accrue to certain actions.

Another case appealed to in this context has to do with the belief in the ritual efficacy of donations used by specific beneficiaries.

> *Scenario 2.* A person A gives a gift to a person S in a monastery with the intent that S uses it. Every time S uses the gift, or is otherwise changed by it, the

merit that accrues to person A for having given the gift changes by increasing, no matter where person A is, or what person A is doing."[49]

The general form of the worry is that "what was done" at a particular time, by a particular person at any given time in one given spatial location, may change certain events indefinitely after the time of the original act in some indefinitely far removed locus. Buddhist philosophers wanted to explain this.

Vasubandhu agreed that such situations need to be accommodated. And he agrees with parts of the proposal. To take the example from case 1, "If Agent A has ordered B to kill C, and after some time T, when Agent A is now a different person, A*, B kills C unbeknownst to A*, and A* is really changed,"[50] then Vasubandhu agrees that:

(a) There is something connecting Agent A at time T and person A*.

and,

(b) This something must be such as to be sensitive to changes in loci indefinitely far removed in space and time from C as well as B.

Vasubandhu's proposal will connect Agent A and A* by a mental process. The theorist of covert action says that there must be something like covert action to account for (a) if (b) is to be possible. Vasubandhu disagrees. His own proposal of mental change, and that of covert action, he says, are "just as incomprehensible" (*asaṃjñāyamānah*),[51] or "difficult to understand" (*durbodha*), in the words of the commentator. What does this mean?

Let me offer this reconstruction of what it might have meant for Vasubandhu to think this: one must resist appealing to further structure in pursuit of explanations where, firstly, an explanation is not provided by the further structure and, secondly, especially so in a case where explanation cannot, in any event, be provided.

The theorist who wishes to use covert actions seeks to explain (b) with some new way of characterizing (a). But his physical characterization of (a) burdens the explanatory power of both Vasubandhu's theory and his own with a second problem, the problem of the interaction of mind and body, which does not resolve the first. Worse, it potentially conceals the fact that both explanations are actually incomprehensible. Why should that be worse? In *The Twenty Verses* it can sound as if he believes that descriptions like (a) are explanatorily transparent. For insofar as descriptions of Vasubandhu's position invoke the mechanism of habituation, they eschew the kind of untethered distal effects or the burden of inexplicable mechanisms that talk of interaction seems to promote. In other words, there is nothing to keep us from understanding. I'll come back to this impression in a moment. What's important for now is that in *The Cutting Edge of Buddhist Thought*, Vasubandhu may well have believed that concealing the theoretical situation in this way—either as the interlocutor does in *The Cutting Edge of Buddhist Thought*, or as I have just done on behalf of *The Twenty Verses*—may potentially violate a norm: a norm concerned with expressing (and thus venerating) reality.

Let's take a brief step back. Much of the engagement with Buddhist philosophy has focused on sentences of type (a) and problems of personal continuity (of which there are appreciably many) connecting Agent A and person A*. But it is with case (b) that Vasubandhu orients himself in *The Cutting Edge of Buddhist Thought*, for it is cases of this sort that appear to show him and his interlocutors something important about what the world most fundamentally is like. Scenario 2, for example, is credited by Vasubandhu to past masters, and the example of the gift is introduced by him on their behalf with the following: "This is *dharmatā*," meaning "reality," which Yaśomitra glosses as "the beginningless power of karma."[52]

The case of the gift in scenario 2 exemplifies reality, but not, therefore, I hasten to add, some modern notion of lawlike regularity. Many modern reconstructions of Buddhist philosophy have been guided by the intuition that to think of the world as possessing a theoretically articulable order is for it to exhibit lawlike regularity. But as the philosopher Alison Peterman reminds us, there are (and have been) other models of order. There were "two distinguishable . . . and distinguished" notions of order in the early modern period, Peterman claims, only one of which is law-likeness—or regularity in our sense. The other she calls coordination. According to regularity, "individuals behave similarly across time and space, and as a result we can predict and control them."[53] Philosophical explanation takes the form of general rules. This is the norm that philosophers reconstructing Buddhist philosophy are likely to use. Peterman, however, continues: "But a different kind of order is nature's *coordination*. Individuals in nature seem to respond to each other as if they could perceive and communicate with one another. They make small adjustments in their motions based on differences in the states of a wide variety of other bodies, accommodating and harmonizing with one another, often at a distance. It was not obvious to natural philosophers of the period that what explains the one explains the other."[54] The cases above express reality through the interaction and coordination of individuals, loci, and times, not so much by generalizable regularities. This is the sort of thing that is expressed by our cases above. Reality is shown by patterns of interaction that are a function of karma, the ways the past (and our entangled present) may enter into and constrain our lives, some of which defy belief.

It may appear as if Vasubandhu's appeal to habituation in *The Twenty Verses* is an appeal to a mechanism that he and his interlocutors can fully specify and completely understand. I do not believe that this is so. And far from eschewing interaction in *The Twenty Verses*, he will go on to use his characterization of the way in which the past enters into and constitutes what we have in view to underscore rather than to dismiss the impression that interaction defies explanation. For Vasubandhu repeatedly goes on to advert to the various ways in which, for better or worse, our lives are entangled with one another's by virtue of what we may do and have done to one another. At the same time, it becomes increasingly unclear to what, if any, mechanisms Vasubandhu may appeal to account for this once he has so thoroughly eschewed reference to physical pathways for influence. The impression one increasingly gets as *The Twenty Verses* draws to its close is that reality outstrips our explanatory grip. And that impression seems deliberate.

My initial inclination was to say that what we are witnessing in the last verses of *The Twenty Verses* is a tacit appeal to something like brute facts, features of the world that resist easy characterization or explanation. I thought then that I would have to reconstruct or invent a language of attitudes to such facts and the different ways in which they might be made explicit in analysis. I had forgotten the thematization of this in Indian Buddhist scholastic principles of reasoning. What I needed, as Richard Nance reminded me, was the Yogācāra scholastic conception of the four principles of reasoning; in particular, we shall need the principle of reality.

The four principles of reasoning (*yukti*), invoked in works such as the *Śrāvakabhūmi* and the *Saṁdhinirmocanasūtra*, among others, present four "tools for the investigation of Buddhist teaching":[55] they are the principle of dependence, the principle of efficacy, the principle of valid proof, and the principle of reality (*dharmatā-yukti*). It is only the last that will concern me here.

Each tool involves a practice, and the fourth is no exception. Using this practice (*yoga*) of reasoning, as the *Śrāvakabhūmi* has it, "one longs for, [but] does not ponder or discursively reflect on, the established reality, the inconceivable reality, the abiding reality of dharmas as they actually exist."[56] Of this Nance notes that the practice does not consist in thinking or discursive reflection: "Rather, we are directed to apply ourselves with devotion, adherence, or veneration (*adhi* + √*muc* Tib. *mos par byed*) to reality as such (*dharmatā*), which is said to be inconceivable (*acintya*). We are thus presented with a concept of reasoning that incorporates veneration for that which we do not, and perhaps cannot (short of Buddhahood), comprehend."[57] This principle of reasoning concerns our orientation to reality in terms of our awareness of the reach of reasons. This is what I mean by speaking of a norm of reality: the norm tells us that we must seek to be true to what the world is really like, but that we should not necessarily seek to capture it in our descriptions and procedures of reason.[58] The norm specifies not explanation, but perspicuous characterization in aid of veneration as a goal, keeping reality as reality—and thus as a wonder—in view.

I think this is a norm tacitly introduced (however briefly) as the interlocutor's views and Vasubandhu's hover in precarious balance for just a moment. And I believe that it is a norm tacitly in play in the rest of *The Twenty Verses*. At least, I believe readers should contemplate the analogy to be drawn with the cases of interaction without physical mechanisms subsequently invoked in *The Cutting Edge of Buddhist Thought* and consider that, by Vasubandhu's lights, a limit may have been reached once one has characterized the conceptual link between what comes into view and habituation. It is a limit that the interlocutor transgresses by speculating or imagining explanations involving the material elements—the word is Vasubandhu's (using the verbal root *kḷp-*)— in search of further explanation or grounding for what Vasubandhu's description characterizes but does not explain.[59] What's at stake, again, is a richly felt attentiveness on the part of these philosophers as to what they think reality most basically is like.

I offer these reflections tentatively. I am unsure of Vasubandhu's explicit commitment to the principle and norm of reality, though as I say, I do believe that he is guided by something like it here and in many other places in his work. (I'll bring it up again in the conclusion to this book.) We are, however, only at the beginning of our study of such modal notions as possibility and impossibility and conceivability and inconceivability in connection with Buddhist scholasticism[60]. So, for now, let me put it this way: there are moments when authors in historical works effectively turn to one another, and so turn to us as well, saying, *But this is what the world is like.* We need to learn how to listen for such moments.

7

WAKING UP AND LIVING ASLEEP

Our words and actions should not be like those of sleepers.

—HERACLITUS[1]

The unwise sleep, the sage is always awake.

—*ĀCĀRĀṄGA SŪTRA*[2]

"What do we have to do with dreams and illusions?" asked King Candraprabhā in a story named after him in the *Divine Stories*.[3] Candraprabhā distrusts the claims of dreams, even so-called true dreams, as dreams that foretell the future would come to be known in Sanskrit.[4] It is not unreasonable to think that my arguments in the last three chapters have asked you to cultivate an analogous distrust. Have I not asked you to leave dreaming and illusions behind for more involved "alternating contexts" of possible experience? As it turns out, however, Vasubandhu has some further use for dreams.

In this chapter we shall consider Vasubandhu's appeal to literal episodes of dreaming at the close of *The Twenty Verses* to discuss the epistemological consequences of his thesis; and we shall consider his use of an analogy to dreams (and waking up from dreams) to model what knowing something consists in. At the beginning of *The Twenty Verses*, as in this book, dreams feature as one among many contexts for possible experience. Now we shall consider dreaming and waking as a structure to make sense of the forms of experience available to us.[5]

I want to understand not only what Vasubandhu is saying about our situation as sentient beings in the world. I also want to know what the analogy to dreaming and waking might imply for the status of his own theoretical enterprise, and for our relationship to it as readers potentially transformed by it.

THE EPISTEMOLOGICAL CONSEQUENCES OF VASUBANDHU'S INTERESTING THESIS

What Vasubandhu has accomplished by appealing to cosmology is this: he has suggested that if Buddhists take their own accounts of life-forms and their worlds seriously, there might then not be a further mystery regarding the connection between mind and world. As I put it in the introduction, to be able to exhibit mindedness is just to be the kind of being that it befits one's history of action to be, the kind of being that is fitted to the environment one's actions have contributed to making.

But the view has consequences for Buddhist epistemology. Consider the assignment of epistemic status to the distinction between literal episodes of waking and dreaming. For example, imagine someone asking a reader why they thought I had disagreed with Paul Griffiths's interpretation of Vasubandhu, and hearing them reply: "Because I *saw* the relevant endnote." Surely that's different from hearing them say: "I dreamt it." The former appeals to an epistemic status that the latter does not enjoy. Can Vasubandhu credit this way of speaking?

Not simply. Vasubandhu recognized that one consequence of his thesis is that waking experience cannot be described as enjoying distinctive epistemic weight. In verse 16ab of *The Twenty Verses* he comes right out and says so. Where the epistemic status of waking experience is concerned—should the epistemic status of waking experiences be defined solely with respect to the issue of whether or not perception puts us directly in touch with a world that is independent of us—one is not in any better situation than when dreaming: "Perceptual judgment—or cognitive awareness regarding perceptual evidence—is analogous to what happens in dreams and similar experiences [16ab], occurring even in the absence of objects."[6]

The train of argument beginning here does not seek to remove grounds for talk of perceptual experience entirely. It does, however, attempt to resituate its weight. To see how exactly, we need to appreciate the overarching view against which Vasubandhu sets himself.

His interlocutor appears to be working with the assumption that to describe an experience as perceptual is to say that the experience puts us in touch with its content in an especially direct way. Consider a claim that would have the authority of perception reside in this: to say of an experience of X that it is a perception of X is to claim that one is in touch with an existing X. That is one way to understand Vasubandhu's interlocutor's belief that "the existence or nonexistence of something is determined on the strength of epistemic criteria, and of all such epistemic criteria, perceptual evidence is the weightiest."[7]

Some Buddhists enshrined the authority of perception with respect to existence by resorting to a casual theory of perception: "Perceptual acquaintance is the awareness that derives from that object" (*tato 'rthād pratyakṣam*)—the object at which the awareness event is directed.[8]

Thus, causation may here be taken to secure the weighty link between perception and existence:

P is perceived if and only if the experience of P is caused by P.
Only existent concrete particulars can be causes.
If P is perceived, then P exists.[9]

Some premodern philosophers thought that Vasubandhu once subscribed to this way of cashing out the authority of perception. Others demurred.[10] Whatever the truth might be, Vasubandhu's views in *The Twenty Verses* cut against thinking that the above picture offers anyone an especially direct link between perception and existence.

Vasubandhu even thinks that his interlocutor cannot believe that it is the ostensibly perceptual experience itself that secures the kind of link between object and experience on which the authority of perception depends. At least, such a link is not secured experientially. I'd like here to explain Vasubandhu's reasoning in a fairly schematic way as it points to a structural feature of our epistemic situation. I will call it his commitment to knowledge as involving dynamic contexts. I shall first reconstruct what I mean by this in the neighborhood of moments at a very small scale, but this will offer us a glimpse of the large-scale structures of knowing to which Vasubandhu will appeal with the help of an analogy to dreaming and waking.

Confining our attention to the small scale for now, there are three overall features of which to keep track. To take our bearings with Vasubandhu, consider that what counts as perception in the following debate will not be some cognitively silent input that can interact with our cognitive machinery entirely in the dark, so to speak. Instead, consider the epistemically relevant thought, *This was seen by me*, or, *I saw this*.[11] If we consider that our account of perceptual acquaintance will have to make room for an event of that sort, then perception as an alethically relevant phenomenon, firstly, may not be an event but a process, the causal story of which might begin in cognitively "silent" sensory contact but which will have to be appraised in terms of a conceptually articulate cognitive achievement.[12]

Secondly, the relation between perceptual knowledge and perceptual input is not, then, best modelled along the lines of a real relation. For, a Buddhist might not be able to maintain that there is any actual item that survives as the same object from start to finish.[13]

And thirdly, the possible sources for available experiences issuing in perceptual judgment of the form "I saw X," and what goes into structuring and texturing the feel of such experiences, is much wider than a simpleminded model of perception as grounded sensory contact might allow us to see.

When Vasubandhu reminds his interlocutor that Buddhist scholastics have reason not to treat sensation as knowledge in the absence of perceptual judgment, he is inviting his interlocutors to consider the implications of the dynamics of cognition in terms of two sorts of transitions, ontological and epistemic. The first source of dynamism has to do with the Buddhist theory of momentariness, a thesis affirming intrinsic change and which says this: what looks to us like a temporally extended happening should be resolved into a sequence of causally connected, qualitatively similar, instantaneous occurrences, none lasting longer than the time it takes for them to begin.[14] The second source of dynamism has to do with Vasubandhu's here exploiting a distinction that his interlocutor is likely to find intuitive, one between sensory and broadly cognitive content.

There are, thus, *two sets* of variations of which to keep track: there is the causal sequence of intrinsic change that any X consists in; and then there is the variation due to the sequence of distinct cognitive and epistemic capacities brought to bear on X, interacting in complex ways.

Keeping in mind both sets of dynamism, to know anything sensory involves complex operations with respect to the continued availability and the classification of content. To be in sensory contact with some X is different from having it be grasped in some preliminary way; and this is distinct, in turn, from its being made available downstream of sensory contact. Because of momentariness, to have X available downstream of input may require having it be represented in some way (by way of subsequent episodes having the phenomenological form of the former).[15] And this is distinct in turn from what goes into having the input explicitly being labelled in the form, *this is* X.[16]

Thus, knowledge of X is always achieved at a temporal and epistemic remove from X. And because the recollection (and cognitive retrieval) on which the above processes depend begin with experiences and not with objects, and take place in a diverse set of possible contexts not all of which are strictly speaking sensory (as Vasubandhu considers in verse 17b), we are not always in a position to infer from memory of some experience that we must have been in contact with the item we remember experiencing.[17] From all this, we may take away that knowledge exhibits the following structure: X in some epistemic context C cannot be known until reconstructed in a later context C', and which forms a culminating part of C. This, I take it, is evident in small-scaled processes, as in the domain of events that last a vanishingly small time and are continuously changing. Is any such structure of knowledge apparent at larger scales?

ZOOMING OUT

Yes, but to see it we must first explore a metaphorical way of redescribing ourselves. The metaphor is this: if we are as good as dreaming insofar as we take ourselves to be in touch with a world of independent objects, we are as good as asleep when it comes to being in any kind of epistemic standing with respect to ourselves. We do not know our own minds, as we come to learn at the end of *The Twenty Verses*:

> —*In what sense does even knowing one's own mind not conform to its object?*
> On account of unknowing . . . On account of our unknowing with respect to what Buddhas know, both knowledge of our own mind and knowledge of the minds of others fail to conform to their objects: they fail to conform to their objects insofar as these kinds of knowing involve content that appears falsely. They involve content that appears falsely on account of the fact that these modes of knowing have not yet abandoned the conceptual construction of that which grasps and that which is grasped.[18]

I'll have more to say about the cognitive and practical scope of Buddhas, or what Buddhas know, below. But it is important to know that whatever else may fall under the cognitive scope of Buddhas, Buddhas know us and our minds. They can see, and not only speak of, the causal mechanisms responsible for making us up.

Vasubandhu says of our experiences that they are available to us on account of our habituations to patterns of activity. That is not how it seems to us. They seem, instead, to derive from the objects they appear to be about. And that's not the only way in which our experience appears to steer us wrong. Vasubandhu also notes that our experiences are available to us *as structured* by a particular kind of disposition, given which we interpret our experience in terms of a discrete item that is grasped in experience and in terms of a discrete and separable item that serves as the agent of grasping content.[19] Typical types of things that fulfill this schema of insistence on our part might be the idea of freestanding objects that are grasped, and the idea of an agent (either a self, or perhaps the senses, or even the awareness itself) as an agent that grasps. Importantly, even the idea of "internal" objects, if used to explain our experiences, could count as an instance of the concept of that which is grasped. In fact, any model that consists in *a kind of relation* between distinct items is an instance of thinking of experience in terms of the twofold conception of grasper and grasped.

This twofold structure, the concepts of grasper and grasped, which informs the phenomenological experience of beings relevantly like us, also tags ways in which we are inclined to interpret experience. They are an insistent way of taking up experience, dispositions we allow to persist through certain patterns of habituating to our experience. It is also the case, however, that such dispositions infuse the phenomenological evidence of our available intentional states. They appear "as" items in our experience. What if there were no such things?

This is *not* the empirical thesis that many of our beliefs about our own psychological states, events, and so on might be fallible, perhaps even more often that one might be tempted to suppose. Rather, the problem here is global, pertaining to the structural conditions for the possibility of our empirical beliefs about ourselves. In other words, our habituation to such dispositions makes available a certain style of experience, a certain way of being open to the world whose very conditions of possibility render that content occlusive with respect to how things really are.

That we are primed by unknowing—a motivated cognitive mode that actively serves to conceal from us what we are truly like[20]—may be described in a static or dynamic mode. Let's begin with the static picture. Of our experiences, Vasubandhu says that "they involve content that appears falsely on account of the fact that these modes of knowing have not yet abandoned the conceptual construction of that which grasps and that which is grasped."[21] There is a stance from which our minds may be known a certain way. We do not occupy that stance. And our way of structuring experience occludes the truth of that stance.

But we may use the metaphor of sleep and waking to set this more dynamically, redescribing our current situation to suggest a connection between what we are like now and the stance we may come to occupy: "Even so, those asleep with a sleep of the lingering traces of habituation to unreal conceptual constructions—seeing, as one does in a dream, objects that do not exist—are not yet awake."[22] Of course, such metaphorical appeal may be appraised as being more or less apposite. An interlocutor notes that, "if, analogous to the case of dreaming, the mental events of even those who are awake were to have unreal objects as their content, then it follows that people would come to understand their unreality by themselves. But this is not the case."[23]

To appeal to dreaming and waking is to appeal to a structure. Vasubandhu has some such account for small-scaled processes. Does he have one for our life as a whole? For dreams and awakening to serve as master metaphor for moving from one epistemological situation to another, we shall need, for one thing, what Vladimir Nabokov once called "the mysterious mental maneuver needed to pass from one state of being to another."[24]

But we shall need more than this, as we shall see below when we explore two puzzles that stand in the way of understanding Vasubandhu's metaphor. I call them the puzzle of periodicity and the puzzle of alethic relevance. It is only after we reread Vasubandhu in light of the puzzles that we shall see how Vasubandhu's small-scaled structure of knowledge is recapitulated on a larger scale.

THE PUZZLE OF PERIODICITY

We know that dreams can serve to model the idea of recontextualizing frames of description. Cosmological contexts and dreaming have precisely such transitions in common. Which is why Vasubandhu can cite a scripture that says of those emerging from the cosmological form of life associated with the unconscious gods—and so coming into possession of conscious states—that "they die, like a person awakening from sleep."[25]

But these are periodic and repeatable transitions. It is a striking thought that a repeatable occurrence should serve to orient us to an *irreversible* achievement. As long as we are alive, we wake up, eventually to fall asleep again, and so until we are no more. Why should coming into knowledge be treated like waking up from sleep?

The periodic metaphor, we have seen, was available and used by Buddhist authors. So too, however, is the nonperiodic sense of final achievement, enshrined in a verb, *buddh-*, from which we get the participle "buddha." As my epigraphs suggest, there is also a long history of associating wisdom with wakefulness and knowledge. Although, curiously, this is not often invoked as the chief meaning of the achievement in question. A convenient place to see this is in Yaśomitra's reflections on the word *buddha* early in his commentary to the first chapter of *The Cutting Edge of Buddhist Thought*: "In the word *buddha* the participial affix is employed in the sense of an agent. He is the *buddha* because of the blossoming [*vikāsana*] of his cognitive faculty [*buddhi*].

Thus, the sense is expanding out [or, being opened (*vi-buddha*)] like an opened lotus flower."[26]

It is only as the second meaning that we find "awakened" (*pra-buddha*): "like one awakened from sleep, for one is awakened [*buddha*] when either sleep or ignorance [*avidyā*] departs. Others say that the affix has the sense of both the agent and the direct object, since a Buddha is one who awakens himself."[27] (We may note here that the Tibetan translation of "Buddha" [*sang rgyas*] is said to reflect both semantic explanations, *prabuddha* [*sang*] and *vibuddha* [*rgyas*].)[28]

But neither explanation shows us why we should not press the metaphor. Why should the meaning of "waking up" ever have come to be associated with something like a nonreversible epistemic achievement? For that matter, why should blossoming out not also connote eventual clasping shut? Are these metaphors not seriously misleading?

THE PUZZLE OF ALETHIC RELEVANCE

My second puzzle is derived from Margaret Macdonald's observation that "just as waking up is not a method of discovery, so falling asleep is not falling into error."[29] Of course, it has often been thought that waking up can be a context of discovery—when one discovers, for example, that one has been asleep. Surely *that* is not an uncommon experience? But this might only tell us that one was in a certain kind of context distinct from one in which one now finds oneself. It does not on its own suffice to assign epistemic weight or even direction to the change.

So, even if the Buddha is one who woke himself up, as Macdonald shows, there is something else one needs in order to find the ubiquitous analogy made between awakening and discovery appropriate. We need not just causal continuity but epistemic continuity. And that requires thinking of experiences offered in dreaming and waking contexts as alethically tied together in some way. (We do not, however, need to take on board here the stringent—and perhaps peculiarly hypermodern—skepticism concerning whether or not there even are relevant experiences in dreams.)

What would that look like? A heroine in a famous work of Sanskrit romance, Subandhu's *Vāsavadattā*, knew one way of connecting dreaming and waking experiences and tried to communicate this in a letter to her beloved. Dreaming and waking, she noted, can sometimes be related as conjecture and either confirmation or falsification in a subsequent context of discovery: "A girl in love can't still her heart, even when she has witnessed her lover's feelings with her own eyes—a girl who has come to experience his feelings in a dream just can't be sure."[30] To experience something as if in a dream is to enter into a stance of possible conviction with respect to what is experienced: one can only "fasten, or secure conviction" by tying it down (*draḍhayati*, to use her word) on waking, in which context one might either confirm or deny what one has seen. But may we think of all episodes of waking upon dreaming like this?

Not generally, someone like Sextus Empiricus could argue. Waking and dreaming are evidential contexts in which one can experience different and often incompatible appearances, true. In waking, X can appear to be F; in dreaming, X can appear to be F*. But what does that tell us except, as Sextus says, that "different appearances come about depending on sleeping or waking. When we are awake we view things differently from when we are asleep, and when asleep differently from the way we do when we are awake; so the existence or non-existence of the objects becomes not absolute but relative—relative to being asleep or awake."[31] Once one has drawn the distinction between waking and dreaming as evidential contexts, it is hard to find a truly independent reason to judge one context as any truer or any more authentic than another.[32] More pertinently, once one sees this, as Michael Veber wisely notes, one might have to suspend judgment as to whether waking and sleep are entirely disconnected or connected contexts of possible experience. Which is a point that the Chinese philosopher Zhuangzi made long before, and in connection with the possibility of using dreams to model life as movement through a succession of different contexts of experience.

To follow the third-personal narrative from the *Book of Zhuangzi*, take the locution "X becoming Y" to also mean "X dreams, and in the context of the dream, experiences themselves to be Y/or a Y-sort of thing." Here is Zhuangzi's anecdote compressed:[33] "Zhuang Zhou once dreamt—and then was a butterfly. The butterfly did not know about Zhou. Suddenly it awoke—and then it was fully and completely Zhou." The text says that *there is* a distinction to be drawn between being Zhou and being a butterfly. These are distinct evidentiary situation affording their own complex experiences and perspectives. In fact, there is being Zhou and becoming a butterfly in a dream; there is being Zhou again; and there is the epistemic perspective exemplified by the point of view of the narrator.

As Lu Zhi argued, it is not obvious how we are to say which of these evidentiary situations are true or false, right or wrong, authentic or inauthentic, without begging the question.[34] Sextus may well have approved of the way the anecdote ends: "One does not know whether there is a Zhou becoming a butterfly in a dream or . . . a butterfly becoming a Zhou in a dream." We may conclude that experience involves change, but there is seemingly no fixed direction to the changes nor can changes be assigned definitive (and contrasting) epistemic or metaphysical weight.

VASUBANDHU'S REFINED ANALOGY

Sensitized by our puzzles, we may now return to Vasubandhu's analogy with the suspicion that it might be more demanding than I had let on: "This is not indicative, since when dreaming, one who has not yet awakened does not understand the unreality of the content experienced [17cd]. Even so, those asleep with a sleep of the lingering traces of habituation to unreal conceptual constructions—seeing, as one does in a dream, objects that do not exist—are not yet awake: they do not truly understand the nonexistence of these objects."[35] This will not solve both puzzles. But it will help.

When Vasubandhu says that we are as good as asleep, it is because there is something about what is happening now that we do not and cannot know in our current evidentiary situation. But we can move into a stance from which we can learn something about the evidentiary situation that is ours. That is, we will not only come into a context wherein we can have new or different experiences. The new context takes the prior context as its content. It takes, in fact, what it is to have experience as its content, revising thereby what we thought we knew in connection with having experience as such.

Vasubandhu finds such a model in the epistemic structure developed by Yogācāra Buddhists to make sense of the transformative experience of what is radically different from our own case. To which he adds some further refinements: "There is a variety of awareness transcending ordinary modes of awareness that is nonconceptual and which serves as an antidote to conceptual construction. When someone is awakened through acquiring this variety of awareness, and because of making real and coming face-to-face with the purified mode of ordinary awareness which follows it, they truly understand what is the case: the unreality of ostensibly physical occasions of content. This situation is our own."[36] This adds a further element. Yogācāra Buddhists stress that awakening involves a process. And they would have us draw a distinction between, as Paul Griffiths puts it, "the awareness which occurs at the moment of awakening to Buddhahood" and "the [subsequent] awareness which makes it possible for Buddha to function in the world after awakening has occurred."[37] On this model, we should construe awakening as involving three epistemic contexts: there is the context one is in (C); there is the context of experience that relates to the former in some epistemically relevant way, typically by challenging or revising the interpretations of C available in C (call this second context ~C); and then there is a subsequent context of experience that integrates the second and the first, recontextualizing what experiences are available and their salience (C*).

In the above paragraph, Vasubandhu says that the transformative experience is an antidote. By this he does not only mean that it is causally effective. He does mean that, but also that it is an epistemically relevant state, the experience of which calls into question one's prior understanding of experiences. In his commentary to *The Thirty Verses*, Sthiramati understands Vasubandhu to say that this is because the transformative context shows us the reality of what we think we know but our understanding of which is vitiated by the structure of subject and object we impose on it.[38] The new context then allows us to complete our understanding of experience by recontextualizing it. And the reason it represents an irreversible or final achievement has to do with the fact of reality being the object of knowledge. It is not simply that one comes to understand this or that context of experience. One comes to understand something constitutive about what experience as such involves. This experiential process ensures that the alethic relevance of awakening does not only lie in the challenge it poses to our prior understanding of experience. So thoroughly does the new recontextualize the old, it changes the structure and meaning of experience; after awakening, we shall not be able to experience the same way again.

This all might be made far more problematic, given just how radically distinct in kind the awakening experience is thought to be. From the perspective of experiences such as ours, structured the way they are, the idea of nonduality seems unintelligible. I'll have (only a very little) more to say about this when discussing what "reality" means below. For now, I wish merely to say this much: what we are dealing with here used to be called a dialectical model (and often erroneously ascribed to Hegel), consisting in thesis, antithesis, and synthesis.[39] Think of the content involved in this dialectical process in terms of the hermeneutic significance of experience.

What I mean is that on a hermeneutic model, invoking the structure of awakening is not limited to raising skeptical challenges. The claim, instead, is that just as one does not know one is dreaming unless one wakes up, one may not know what one's current evidentiary situation really is until one moves into another context. Consider, then, the claim to be a potential generalization of a model for what knowledge (and falsity) in experience involves. Experiencing X might be like dreaming X in the following sense: ordinarily, we experience X without knowing what X is; in fact, our ability to bring to our discriminative capacities to bear on what we experience is muted. Ostensibly, this is analogous to experience when asleep. Thus, to know X we must, *as it were*, wake up to X, or go from *merely* experiencing X to a state where one understands what experiencing X involves, thus recontextualizing the nature and meaning of X.[40] The dialectical version adds two refinements. The hermeneutic process involves a variety of inconsistency, on which the nature of contents and our orientation to these must be challenged by a new context; this challenge, in turn, once integrated into experience, changes it utterly. Experience, transformed, continues without end.

SĀRAṆA WAKES UP

Before raising the minor puzzles for myself, I used to think Vasubandhu's analogy treating the entirety of our lives as a variety of sleep simple. I am now no longer sure about its implications for Vasubandhu's theoretical project. Nor am I clear about its implications for ways in which readers might relate to Vasubandhu's work. I will try to be honest about my puzzlement and about the limitations of this book.

We have asked, "What are the conditions we have to meet in order to entitle describing oneself as Vasubandhu recommends with the help of the structure of awakening?" Now we shall ask a different sort of question. How does Vasubandhu think about this structure in connection with an ideal epistemic subject? Or, for that matter, in connection with his reader?

I will begin by considering a story of awakening and transformation to which Vasubandhu appeals in his comments to verse 19. There, he is tasked with illustrating the intelligibility of descriptions of action when our vocabulary drops all reference to extra-mental factors. In reply, he appeals to narratives of forced transformation, only one of which will concern me here, the story of Sāraṇa, the son of King Udayana of Vatsa who became a disciple of Mahākātyāyana. Vasubandhu does not narrate the story, but it is found in his fellow northwesterner Kumāralāta's once well-known collection of philosophical stories from the third century CE, *Kalpanāmaṇḍaṭikā*, sometimes also known as the *Collection of Exempla* (*Dṛṣṭāntapaṅkti*).

The story begins when Sāraṇa journeyed to Ujjain in the Kingdom of Avanti with his teacher. I offer a summary of the story, one I have prepared after consulting the excellent rendition of Édouard Huber.[41]

> Sāraṇa was beautiful, and the women of King Pradyota who had come into the woods on a picnic became enamored of him. King Pradyota, aroused by spring and his environs, went looking for them. Only to find them enthralled with the young monk.
>
> He interrogated Sāraṇa. On learning that he had not yet attained any stage of excellence in the Buddhist path, he began to suspect Sāraṇa of having made love to his wives.
>
> In his anger, Pradyota was unjust: he had Sāraṇa stripped of his clothes and mercilessly beaten until he was comatose. When Sāraṇa regained consciousness, he was ashamed. Then fearful. And angered. Gathering the shreds of his clothes, he returned to his master, who saw that he looked bloodied and bruised all over, like a black plum.
>
> Then Mahākātyāyana tried to talk Sāraṇa out of his desire for vengeance, born as it was out of humiliation, fear, and anger. He tried to get him to see past the body as the locus of value and practical concern. But

Sāraṇa was obdurate. He wanted to renounce his monastic vows, to reclaim the throne of his father, and to wage bloody war against King Pradyota.

After the appeals of his fellow monks and that of his preceptor Mahākātyāyana failed, Mahākātyāyana at last appeared to relent. He asked Sāraṇa to wait one more night. Then Mahākātyāyana placed a hand on Sāraṇa's head, and through his mental power, caused Sāraṇa to fall into a deep sleep, and induced in him a dream in which Sāraṇa believed himself to journey far away from his teacher.

Sāraṇa reclaimed his throne, and in time, gathered a huge army, and began a bloody battle against the king who had humiliated him. But he saw the fortunes of war turn against him. Pradyota was victorious and Sāraṇa was captured. Sāraṇa saw himself sentenced to death.

He was tortured through the night. And the night seemed to him in his anxiety and horror interminable. As he waited for dawn, he heard the demonic executioners sharpening their swords right by his head. All through the night these sounds and the laughter of the executioners terrorized him. But in the morning, as he was led to the execution ground, he saw Mahākātyāyana enter the city, dressed as a monk, holding the begging bowl, on his way for alms.

Sāraṇa cried out, declaring the error of his ways, his recognition of his folly, and his commitment to the Buddhist way of life. At that moment, the swords in the hands of his demonic executioners transformed before him into blue lotuses. Weeping, Sāraṇa cried out to his master, as the demons urged him to, and Sāraṇa committed himself in speech to take refuge in him.

Sāraṇa was inconsolable, however. He believed himself to have renounced his vows, and thus having rendered void his chance at freedom from suffering. Mahākātyāyana attempted to persuade him that this was a dream created by his own power, that all this had not actually happened. Sāraṇa would not believe it. In order to convince him, Mahākātyāyana created rays of light that shone out from his upraised right hand.

There is much in this story that resonates with Vasubandhu's concerns at the close of *The Twenty Verses*—most pointedly, the story's commitment to virtual realism. Witness the juxtaposition of two kinds of loci for events and action: there is the domain of the physical, the body of the suffering Sāraṇa, and the frame for the intelligibility of his own plans for revenge. Then there is the domain of the virtual, created by the power of Mahākātyāyana's mind that could so affect Sāraṇa. As part of the virtual environment of the story, we would have to include the dream life of Sāraṇa, a frame of the story from which we do not, notably, unambiguously emerge in the narrative: it is the scene of Sāraṇa's denouement and the stage for Mahākātyāyana's powers. The latter can enter into the dream he has created for Sāraṇa, walking and altering the dream. His presence in that virtual environment *does not* seem to involve a fiction.

We shall want to say that Sāraṇa's second life, a seeming fiction made virtually real in a dream, is the reason and the stage for the actual Sāraṇa's transformation and concrete felicity, one which, notwithstanding its being grounded in a dream, has lasting effects for actual Sāraṇa. This needs to be unpacked, since it exploits a narrative technique of embedded narrative frames that are popular in South Asia, particularly when exploring the possibilities of dreaming and waking through narrative.[42]

In the outer frame, in which much of the story had taken place, Mahākātyāyana induces Sārana to sleep. Sāraṇa falls asleep, and this brings into view the crucial embedded frame, the dream of Sāraṇa, in which the rest of the narrative takes place. The dream is a virtual reality made by Mahākātyāyana and the stage of action for the rest of the narrative. It is where Mahākātyāyana is shown to act, and where Sāraṇa experiences real change because of what his virtual self, present in this virtual realm, experiences.

We can articulate this with the language of alternating contexts of experience used above in connection with skepticism as well as with the hermeneutic model of dreaming and waking:

a. In context of possibility C, a range of experiences occur to Sāraṇa suggesting that P about himself (such as that he is a monk, has certain modes of conduct that befit him, and so on).
b. In context of possibility C*, the virtual reality that follows upon C, a range of experiences occur to Sāraṇa, suggesting that ~P (such as his not being a monk, giving up on his ethical commitments, and so on.)
c. When Sāraṇa wakes up, he is in context C**, in which some things suggest to him that P, and some things (those that happened in C*, and which have affected him and which he can remember), suggest ~P.

Sāraṇa is depicted as not being able to determine what has happened or intelligibly frame the situation to himself. Sāraṇa finds it intelligible within the frame of his dream that everything that is happening is really happening. In fact, crucially, we are told that *he initially finds it unintelligible that what had happened—all that has happened to him—was really just a dream.*

No doubt, we can say that this has a rhetorical function. Speaking of early modern France, Jean Starobinski says that the play becomes (or *appears* to become) believable just in case it includes a character who ostensibly refuses to believe in the appearances he encounters. In the baroque era this ultimate illusion was expressed symbolically by the play within a play.[43] Whether or not the background social conditions for such a cognitive device are the same in South Asian antiquity as they were in Montaigne's early modern Europe, it is the frame story that allows one to turn a story of dreams and waking into a metapoetic and metacognitive tool to explore the conditions of representation and believability.

But the situation the story presents us with is not the kind of evidentiary conflict described by Zhuangzi and Sextus Empiricus. Our story tells us something else. Sāraṇa cannot choose because he lacks a crucial variety of evidentiary factor, one that is available in none of the above frames of reference. What Sāraṇa lacks (and what the story's dramatization of his indecision attempts to make more credible to us) is the causal description of what has happened to him as well as an appreciation for the salience of it. What he lacks is what the story (and other stories like this) put before us: a new conceptual grammar and the correct frame for adjudicating what is possible and what is not, given which one can come to follow and entertain how such a phenomenon is so much as possible. Mahākātyāyana in the narrative knows how, as does the narrator of the story. And it is made available to a reader of the story sooner than it is to Sāraṇa.

The relevant causal description involves the processes and powers by which the virtual realm (C*) was generated. Thus, Sāraṇa will only come to believe that what has happened to him was a dream, however salient, when he comes to learn something even more cognitively challenging. He must come to believe, as must the reader, that Mahākātyāyana is really capable of creating a virtual realm in which real, lasting changes are possible. He must come to believe in reality as it is disclosed in Buddhist tales, a reality consisting in wonder, power, and possibility.[44] A world in which what causes can bring about often exceeds the intelligibility of our descriptions.

Nietzsche thought that the hallmark of a dream was that "anything is possible at each moment."[45] Not, surely, anything.[46] Sāraṇa learns from his virtual life in the extended dream that Mahākātyāyana made for him that he only thought he knew what was and what was not possible. Reality is larger and otherwise than he was inclined to think, and becoming acquainted with it turned out to be transformative.

But there are two potential models at work here, based on two things one might mean by reality and involving (at least) two corresponding senses of "becoming acquainted with" in the above sentence. In one scenario, one may think of becoming acquainted with reality as acquiring new sentences to use to refer to phenomena whose occurrence one had no reason to suspect. In another scenario, one may become acquainted with reality by learning new possibilities for experience with a transformative intent. I'll explore both below, using the second to suggest an important possible disanalogy between Sāraṇa's situation and that of a reader of Vasubandhu's *Twenty Verses.*

THINKING ABOUT AND EXPERIENCING REALITY

In his comments on verse 10d of *The Twenty Verses,* Vasubandhu contrasts two kinds of cognitive domains and two kinds of cognitive subjects. On the one hand, there are naïve beings relevantly like us, whose experience is structured like ours with reference to that which grasps and that which is grasped. However, the cognitive scope of Buddhas, we are told, is not like ours.

What else can we say about it?

If we use stories such as Sāraṇa's as models, Vasubandhu's *Twenty Verses* may effectively function the way Buddhist narratives of karma do. As Amber Carpenter has it, "Over hundreds of tales of previous lives of the Buddha, and of his accomplished followers . . . we are enabled to see our familiar world in an unfamiliar way—namely, as the Buddha sees it."[47] With that in mind, perhaps the first thing to say is that the idea of the scope of the Buddhas recommends thinking of the incompleteness of our forms of experience. Experience, as we know it, is an incomplete context because there are truths about what we experience and truths about our experience of these that we do not know merely by enjoying experiences. We do not see ourselves as Buddhas do.

Keeping in mind Vasubandhu's having thought of the scope of Buddhas in connection with the Buddha's omniscience elsewhere, and connecting these, in turn, with the fine details of karmic processes linking the past and present, here's another thing we might say.[48] A Buddha's eye view of things may be taken to function so as to serve as a guarantor for truths of generic types of sentences concerning karmic processes to which Vasubandhu appeals but which lie beyond our ken to specify in any fine detail or to evaluate. We do not know our own minds, and do not see ourselves as Buddhas do, partly because we do not think of our forms of experience and available content being constrained and determined by the past or karma. Perhaps Vasubandhu appeals to a Buddha's eye view to guarantee not only that there is another way of envisioning ourselves but also the truth of his proposed revision, and the ultimate validity of sentences of the sort he would have us use in *The Twenty Verses* to describe ourselves and our sphere of possibilities.

Granted, that might be a distinctively reductive way to cash out the idea of a narrative vision of reality insofar as we are reducing karmic narratives, their invitation to take up a Buddha's eye view of ourselves, and their associated presentations and possible experiences of reality, to a list of propositions about the world and a list of acceptable attitudes to such propositions. I don't mean to imply such a reduction. The ability to tell (and to follow) new stories with the help of which to redescribe oneself is surely more complicated. All I wish to do is to put forward the following idea: karmic stories involve what I called a new conceptual grammar. Were we to justify that grammar, asking for the criteria favoring one sort of narrative and its associated grammar of possibilities over another, one may have to appeal to something like the Buddha's omniscience, taking up his point of view as an epistemically significant and not merely ameliorative stance.

But this brings us to a third thing to say about the scope of Buddhas in *The Twenty Verses*. Perhaps the language of a Buddha's eye view, and the related notion of omniscience, is meant to promote a variety of humility, possibly even skepticism about metaphysics rather than assurances. Look at the conclusion of *The Twenty Verses*: "Which is to say that this, in all its aspects, cannot be thought through by the likes of me, since it goes beyond the scope of reasoning. For whom, then, can it in its entirety be said to be the scope of knowledge and action? To answer that, this text concludes with this: it is the scope of Buddhas."[49] Perhaps we are to read that as cautioning against identifying the orientation this work recommends with respect to available content with a set of sentences about what is true and what is not. One might read this in connection with the norm of reality expressed in the last chapter: at some point, we must seek an end to justification and allow our sentences to evoke, but not explain reality as something beyond our ken, something we can recognize as being worth calling reality precisely because it goes beyond what we, but not what Buddhas, may know.

But perhaps Vasubandhu is also thereby saying something else. Imagine thinking that "going beyond the scope of reasoning" has the following rhetorical function: no matter what we say, there may be another way to recontextualize the claims we make on behalf of what the Buddha meant. For the sentences we may have to attribute to the Buddha regarding what is the case are infinite, and various, given his changing what he says when speaking to different people in different contexts, and the possibly infinite pedagogical contexts in which the Buddha has been (and possibly continues to be) involved. The mere possibility of this puts pressure on what we identify as the truth conditions for his utterances. There is always the possibility of having to revise, even contradict, the meanings we may reconstruct for him and thus the provision of any statements purporting to offer *the* meaning (and *the* truth conditions) for what the Buddha taught as reality can never be final.[50] To say that the infinity associated with the scope of Buddhas calls into question the metaphysical and epistemological status of any statements of a Buddhist philosopher finds an echo in the way Maria Heim has recently presented the reliance on the immeasurability of the teaching and the omniscience of the Buddha in the work of Vasubandhu's contemporary, Buddhaghosa.[51] Perhaps it is not so much a norm of reality as it is the unending labor of interpretation and recontextualization that Vasubandhu evokes at the end. And if so, perhaps "reality," far from being brought into view in some reverential way, or being underwritten by appeal to the perspective of Buddhas, is meant to lose its intuitive metaphysical sense.

No doubt, there is much interpretive work to be done. And much philosophical fine-tuning must be achieved before one can try to assess what these models really entail, which of them are consistent with one another, and which of these we shall need to present a complete picture of Vasubandhu's work.[52] We also need an abundance of caution. Though Vasubandhu does not say anything to explicitly warrant caution in *The Twenty Verses*, I urge it nonetheless with respect to the interpretative models above, at least if they are to be used to get a feel for the sense of reality at stake in Vasubandhu's notion of the scope of Buddhas.

What we have presented has involved thinking primarily with the help of sentences, their meanings, and the idea of their ostensible connection with (parts of) reality (or their lack thereof). But elsewhere, in *The Thirty Verses*, Vasubandhu urges us to abandon something adjacent to such ways of talking of sentence-shaped bits of our thought and world when he advises us on how best to take on the view he recommends. This is relevant here because what Vasubandhu says in the *Thirty Verses* has to do with what forms his analytical target in *The Twenty Verses*, the very structure of experience as it is manifest to us.

This structure may be taken to be a precondition for certain ways of understanding what matching utterances with reality entails. On Vasubandhu's view, experience offers itself as something that (a) does not merely seem to us to be a certain way, but also as something separable from us: be it items in the world or stretches of our own mental life at a different time; (b) what experience represents to us as being the case are the causes of what our experiences seemingly are about; and (c) such a structure seems to inform the very concept of our experience. But if Vasubandhu's claim is that anything that is made possible by *this* structure, or anything that reinforces it, is problematic, this calls into question one family of views for finding intelligible a naïve concept of truth and so something like the above models for relating to reality. I have in mind theories of correspondence that would have truth consist in relations obtaining between representations and nonmental items.[53] If the very idea of sentences as candidates for truth in this sense might be parasitic on the structures that manifest our experience, Vasubandhu ought to recommend caution—just because the structure of what is manifest to us counts as one of the preconditions for the structure of our knowledge of the world presupposed by some ways of concerning oneself with the truth of utterances.

While I believe that Vasubandhu does raise the issue of the structure of the manifest in *The Twenty Verses* in his comments on verse 10 (when advancing the contrast between the way in which our experiential scope is constructed and the way a Buddha's is), he does not develop the point. Vasubandhu's conclusion to *The Thirty Verses* is another matter: "Placing anything before oneself," he says there, "even thinking 'This is nothing but the presentation of content,' insofar as it is a perceptual apprehension, one fails to situate oneself in that."[54] The "that" is the condition of there being nothing but presentation of content, here presented not as a proposition, or a fact, but rather as a way of experiencing. And, consequently, Vasubandhu would have us concern ourselves with its reality very differently than the way we do when regarding sentences, their meanings, and truth.

It is helpful to distinguish between two senses of reality. Consider, first, the use of the word "reality" in the following sentence written by the philosopher G. E. Anscombe in connection with Wittgenstein's *Tractatus*: "The principal theme of the book is the connection between language, or thought, and reality."[55] "Reality" here has the sense of an independent substantive. This sense of "reality," characteristically at issue when we speak of the truth or falsity of our utterances, is very different from the (grammatically) dependent sense of reality at issue when speaking of, say, "the reality of X" or the "quiddity of X," and so on. But it is this latter sense of reality (as expressed by a family of words—such as *paramārtha*, *dharmatā*, *dharmadhātu*, *tathatā*, among others[56]) that Vasubandhu takes to be at issue in *The Thirty Verses*.

Let us consider some conceptual preliminaries, however, before exploring what it means to speak of the reality of experience (as we shall have to). The grammatically dependent sense of reality involves a relation. But what kind? We should think of it as analogous with the relation between a type and its tokens, suggests Vasubandhu, leaning on the way in which being impermanent, or being an instance of pain, or being without self (*anityatā*, *duḥkhatā*, *anātmatā*) are thought to characterize concrete particulars.[57] To be a concrete particular is to be impermanent; and all impermanent things are impermanent in the same way, notwithstanding their other differences. That shows us that "reality of X" functions a little like "nature of X." That in turn helps us understand a further criterion for anything to count as worthy of being called the reality of something: "On account of existing thus at all times" (*sarvakāla*).[58]

This can be taken in two ways, temporally and modally. Consider Vasubandhu's recognition in *The Cutting Edge of Buddhist Thought* that one can use "always" (*sarvadā*) in connection with talk of the nature of something without entailing that the nature of X eternally exists or that X exists separably from its nature.[59] Relatedly, I recommend taking it that Vasubandhu is suggesting that "the reality of X"—or, something's "being thus" (*tathatā*) in Sanskrit—is properly so-called on account of X's being thus *invariably*, always so, in the sense of constitutively so: to be an X, any kind of X, is to exhibit the reality criterial for being an X.

Sthiramati explains Vasubandhu's point with reference to different ways of classifying persons based on their achievements along the path of self-cultivation: "That is to say, it is present at all times thus [*tathā*] [whether one is] in the state of an ordinary person, a disciple, or one beyond training."[60] The changes to which one is subject on the path of self-cultivation do not touch the constitutive reality of being an experiential subject that is here at issue. I say "experiential subject," for as Sthiramati immediately goes on to quote Vasubandhu as saying, the reality we are speaking of is the fact or condition of there being nothing but presentation of content (*vijñaptimātratā*),[61] or "the reality of thought" (*cittadharmatā*), to use Sthiramati's subsequent gloss.[62]

There are further subtleties of which to be mindful once we fully take on board the fact that we are speaking of the reality of mind. For it will turn out to be an experiential reality, a phrase by which I mean two things: it is a reality concerning our experience of things, which, though necessarily the case for our experience to count as an experience, is not for that actualized or brought into view in every experience. Furthermore, to entertain the reality of experience is not like entertaining a proposition about reality, where reality is understood in a substantive sense. To entertain the reality of an experience—to actualize it by bringing into view—alters experience.

To understand this, we shall need to return talk of "reality" to its context in what Vasubandhu calls the three natures or three modes of being (*trisvabhāva*). These are the metaconceptual tools Vasubandhu (and Yogācāra philosophers more generally) use to interpret the nature of experiences, once experiences are described as episodes involving presentation of content and just the presentation of content, without reference to objects as causes.[63]

The mental is multidimensional, to describe which one has to take into account the various stances we may occupy with respect to it: we may describe mental events with an eye to their contents; their being events involving causal process; or in terms of what Vasubandhu calls their reality, which is defined in terms of the first two modes.

Describing experience, one encounters an ambiguity: we may speak of it as process and as product. To describe experience in terms of what is experienced—the product—gives one the first mode. Speaking of experience in terms of a causal process, on the other hand, gets one the second of the three modes of being. Vasubandhu speaks of the mental as involving a process of construction and he speaks of content as what is constructed. To understand this, we may follow Vasubandhu's criteria for the use of *vikalpa*. A mental episode or sequence of episodes involving some X as content counts as involving a case of *vikalpa*, or construction,

(i) when the episode is not a function of the causal influence of some independently specifiable X (or something X-like) upon an individual, but rather,
(ii) the availability of X is not independently given, but dependent on a mental process of which the episode is a part, and, for the most part, *due to* such a process,
(iii) the intelligibility of X—the full description of what X *is*—requires reference to such a process, and
(iv) one may bring the process, but not X—the content made available by it—directly under a causal description.[64]

Construction provides for content as well as structure. In fact, Sthiramati, elsewhere, points out that the principal sense of "construction of what is unreal" (*abhūta-parikalpa*) is the constitution of content in terms of subjects and objects:[65] all mental processes—including sensory experiences—may be described as being *processes* of *vikalpa*, or construction; *therefore*, all content counts as unreal when taken as a candidate for reality independently of the process. But it counts as real (or literally, fully realized [*parinispanna*]), when we learn to look past the contents to the process, seeing it as always having been free of the constructed structure.[66]

The process always being utterly free of subject and object, as Sthiramati puts it, is the mode of being fully realized or perfected or actualized. But what does "always being utterly free" mean? I do not wish to get here into the metaphysics of modality. Let me avoid the considerable interpretive work that must be done here and say only what we need to take away for now. To attribute the reality of being free from structure just means that such experience as we know is not necessary in the following sense: we can be otherwise. The fact that present structures of experience can be unmade is presently a fact about experience. But what freedom is thereby intimated has to be realized. We have to make it real through an experientializing process. Which means, as it turns out, that we have to inhabit reality and not think about it.

MAKING IT REAL

As long as we orient ourselves to what is being taught by Vasubandhu as a proposition and not as a horizon, the constructed structure of experience will not loosen its grip: "To the extent that awareness is not situated in the fact of there being nothing but presentation of content, the proclivity predisposing us to the twofold structure of grasping does not cease."[67] Sthiramati glosses this to say, "To the extent that awareness is not situated in the *nature of thought*, here signaled by the phrase 'nothing but presentation of content'—that is, when awareness, instead, continues to find traction in apprehending that which is grasped and that which grasps."[68]

Situating ourselves this way has ameliorative and epistemic consequences. It changes us. And this change can show us the inadequacy of our concepts. This is surely what Vasubandhu means by stating with the Yogācāra tradition at the close of *The Thirty Verses* that awakening involves an utter transformation of (our dispositional) basis and characterizing this transformation in terms of the subsequent nonapplicability of the concepts of mind and intentional apprehension. Speaking of the resultant experiential state, he says "it is without mind, without apprehension, and it is a cognitive state that is transcendent."[69] This is a verse Sthiramati introduces as a response to the following question: "If thought dwells thus in the fact of there being nothing but mental events, how is it then defined?"[70] He understands Vasubandhu to mean that after awakening and our transformation, the kind of experience that typifies our lives thus far—involving that which grasps (here indicated by the term "mind") and that which is grasped (here indicated in an abbreviated and elliptical way, Sthiramati thinks, with the term "apprehension")—fails to describe the distinctive kind of cognitive state achieved.[71]

I am inclined to take Vasubandhu's point slightly differently, perhaps more emphatically: what characterizes us after realization cannot be described in terms of "mind," which as a concept is restricted to our experiential conditions and history of action. On this view, to speak of a mind (*citta*) is to speak of what is exemplified by a life-form defined as Vasubandhu thinks by the continual availability of certain forms of habituation. We come to a limit to Vasubandhu's interesting thesis regarding habituation: it does not exhaust what is real of mind, in the sense that it does not show us all that is possible. The concept of experience as presentations of content constrained by habituation does not apply to the kind of distinctive modality of being that results upon awakening. The way we talk is adequate to the ways in which our history thus far has allowed us to experience.

Being in touch with reality, in some sense, must involve a kind of *overlooking* of what we are habituated to see. It must involve an overlooking of object-centered presentation of content, and a disciplined avoidance of attempting to make of the reality of our minds an intentional object within the structure of experience to which we are habituated. The destabilization begins with losing sight of all objects to which we are related. Here is Vasubandhu's claim in *The Thirty Verses*, as introduced by Sthiramati and paraphrased by him:

> One might ask: "But then how does one let go of grasping on the part of awareness? How is one situated in the nature of thought?" In order to address these questions, it is said [by Vasubandhu]: "But when an instance of cognition in no way involves the apprehension of an intentional object, then it is situated in the fact of there being nothing but presentation of content—on account of there no longer being grasping, given the absence of that which is grasped (28)." At such time as when an instance of cognition does not apprehend, does not see, does not take note of, does not grasp, does not adhere to or dwell on intentional objects that are external to thought—be these intentional objects acquired from exposure to the doctrine, contexts of oral instruction, or intentional objects that are natural to and constitutive of sensory experience—intentional objects of the sensory capacities, such as hue, or sounds, and so on. Which is to say, when an instance of cognition instead sees things as they are (and not as one born congenitally blind), at that time there is the relinquishing of grasping on the part of an active awareness and one is situated in the nature of thought.[72]

As many have noted of Yogācāra, to let go of objects is not a thesis, nor yet a proposition. It appears here in the guise of a preliminary step in a practice. Where it ends, I cannot quite say.[73] Nor, to the best of my knowledge, does Vasubandhu ever really volunteer more.

Sāraṇa wakes up by coming out of an experience in which he led a virtual existence. He thought he was in contact with others. With the exception of Mahākātyāyana, he was not. To make sense of his experience, I suggested above, he must learn how to tell an extraordinary story replete with new possibilities of power and wonder. Vasubandhu's description asks of us something even more extreme. It too can be read as giving us a Buddha's eye view and as enlarging our sense of what we believe to be possible. But the way in which the past is understood to constitute us, and the number of revisions this imposes on our self-understanding and our sense of the world seems more acute. Does this make any difference to what it means to know?

Not so much in *The Twenty Verses* perhaps. But in *The Thirty Verses*, he asks us to inhabit experience as guided by his philosophical commitments; to situate ourselves within it, in fact, which just might prove more demanding than was Sāraṇa's transformative experience. Sāraṇa's experience does not result in his lastingly losing either his narrative or conceptual grip on reality. He can learn new terms, new types of events, and new stories. He retains a kind of narrative grasp on reality. But Vasubandhu's proposal works differently. Making reality present, he thinks, transforms us utterly, in ways our concepts and narratives might not be able to keep up with. At least not from the inside, so to speak.

In the course of the book, I have focused on the kind of backward-looking gestures at causal descriptions invoking the past in the present. This is the kind of view the Buddha has of our lives. But in *The Thirty Verses*, this is not the most important perspective. To make what is true of us real involves a practice that looks to what is possible, turning our face toward what is required of us to become like a Buddha. This book, however, except for this chapter, has looked the other way with *The Twenty Verses*.

In doing so, I have asked you to dwell with one kind of reality and not another. I mean this in a Buddhist sense, for texts are realities in which one can dwell. *The Sūtra of the Utmost Radiance*, a popular Mahāyāna work, begins by saying that the Buddha taught it while living in the *dharmadhātu*, a realm of reality that is soon glossed with the phrase "the profound scope of Buddhas" (*gaṃbhīra buddhagocara*). This is a term we now know rather well. But with this phrase, Natalie Gummer tells us, the text explicitly goes on to name itself. The Buddha, apparently, dwells in the text he is teaching.[74]

This makes sense. Aren't texts a context in which awakening can take place? Or, conversely, can't texts be contexts that reinforce our long sleep?

What of Vasubandhu's texts? At the time of writing, I cannot say that I know which of Vasubandhu's texts better embodies the sense of reality that mattered to him. It is as if one text looks at the world and asks us to imagine a new vantage point, though entertaining this only at the level of argument and redescription. The other foregoes all argument, seeking instead a path from here to there in a categorical map of experience. The vast cosmological vistas that give *The Twenty Verses* its texture are replaced in *The Thirty Verses* by an interplay of intrapsychic processes and functions. The stage is different, as are the players and possibly the play. It is as if *The Twenty Verses* were written to convince us that we are asleep, and *The Thirty Verses* to show us how, within the dream, we might begin to wake up.

As Vasubandhu's own words disavow our conventions and yet fail to be adequate to the place to which they would have us get to, it can seem as if there is a transitional quality to *The Twenty Verses* as well, as if such a work were in its own way a realm of hypnagogic transition. But in which direction shall we describe such a transition as taking place for contemporary readers?

"I felt," Bertrand Russell said of another inventive work, "as many others have felt—that *The Monadology* was a kind of fantastic fairy tale, coherent perhaps, but wholly arbitrary."[75] I hope you will not any longer find Vasubandhu's *Twenty Verses* arbitrary, but I don't think anyone would object to my saying that Vasubandhu's work can also elicit from people a sense that it is possessed of what one might term (after Nicholas Rescher) "an aura of strangeness."[76] A reality-testing strangeness, such as can happen on the borders of sleep and waking or waking and sleep. No doubt, given different senses of what the world is really like, different readers will be led to evaluate the direction of the transition through which Vasubandhu's text leads us very differently.

CONCLUSION

The Future of Past Systems of Possibility

"As was his practice, from time to time the venerable Mahāmaudgalyāyana would journey through the realms of hell, journey through the animal realm, and journey through the realms of hungry ghosts, gods, and humans"[1]—thus begins *The Story of Sahasodgata* in *The Divine Stories*. It is one of the most effective openings for any short story that I know, perhaps only rivalled by the terse beginning of its close cousin, the story that introduces the *Mahāvastu*: "Now, the venerable Mahāmaudgalyāyana often went on a visit to hell."[2]

The effect of saying that he went "often" and "as was his practice" in juxtaposition with such destinations is uncanny. Why should anyone wish to travel to such places? How does one even get there? And why go there more than once?

Vasubandhu, like Mahāmaudgalyāyana, is a traveler. Or so I would argue given the intellectual journey that is *The Twenty Verses*. But why did Vasubandhu have us visit the realms of the hungry ghosts and hell? Mahāmaudgalyāyana sometimes seems to me an anthropologist among the damned. Going beyond a confirmation of received Buddhist truths of action and consequence, he even collects the poems of hungry ghosts,[3] thereby allowing readers the opportunity to direct their attention to the unsuspected forms suffering can take and to the various ways in which it can be experienced by those we typically overlook.

What would Vasubandhu have us take away from his intellectual journey?

Taking that question as a guide, my conclusion will provide a brief summary of what we have learned in this book. But there is more than one conceptual journey of which to keep track. Along with Vasubandhu's journey to the realms of Buddhist cosmology, there is the distance between Vasubandhu's sense of reality and our own. I will consider what traversing both these distances might involve below.

WHAT IT MEANS

This book has argued the following: Vasubandhu has used Buddhist accounts of hungry ghosts and the experiences of those suffering in hell to contextualize Buddhist accounts of perception within Buddhist cosmology. Doing this has allowed him to bring together Buddhist accounts of perception and action and thus mind and world in a very particular way. Just how particular may be seen by considering a very different view.

Aristotle believed that action and perception are two distinct, even contrary processes. As C. D. C. Reeve summarizes the view, "each of these"—he is speaking of action and contemplation—"involves the transmission of form, either from the world to the soul, as in the case of perception and understanding, or from the soul to the world, as in desire and action."[4] Vasubandhu's thesis suggests something quite distinct. Instead of two separable kinds of processes—one running from mind to world (through action), and another from world to mind (through perception)—there is only one kind of process, with distinct phases, or moments. Perceptual uptake of the world is the culmination of a process of habituation to action, one that accounts for our having available anything to take up as content.

There are more or less revisionary ways to entangle perception and action. One might maintain, for example, that we ascribe the power to act only to those with the power to perceive, and vice versa.[5] But this is still short of affirming Vasubandhu's interesting thesis. Vasubandhu is effectively claiming that, in some quite literal sense, in perception we see the traces of what has been made by living beings to whom we are connected by a history of cause and effect. Perception discloses a constructed context of which we are a part.

To describe this, Vasubandhu thinks, we must forego looking for proximate causes of perceptual experience. We must forego thinking that perception relates us to anything ultimately separable from us. For perception to be grounded in and constrained by action is to have it that subjects and their environments are best accounted for by a single variety of process, beginning in action and culminating in perceptual disclosures of an only ostensibly independent world.

This way of putting it makes no concession to what one might term methodological individualism. To think otherwise is a temptation that results from ignoring Vasubandhu's commitment to the resources of Buddhist cosmology. We must remember the cosmological individual, the succession of lives linked over time through cause and effect, and recall that each life is lived at a particular place as a particular life-form. Vasubandhu and his interlocutors believe that our experiences are constrained by our cosmological history and by our relationship to our ecological niche.[6] The disagreement between Vasubandhu and his co-religionists has to do with whether we can capture this dependency by speaking of our being constrained by an array of objects, specified (as if) independently of the experiential profile of any one particular life-form. Vasubandhu believes not.

Certainly, Vasubandhu's point is not to say that the individual subject has complete freedom with respect to what they can experience. Experiences are not unconstrained by deep and proximate contexts. This is the lesson of the curious case of the guards in hell. Like beings in hell, we are in the grip of what is manifest to us on the basis of constraints we mislocate and mischaracterize when we think that our experiences are constrained by an array of objects in the present, specified (as if) independently of the experiential profile of any one particular lifeform.

Focusing on life-forms and cosmological individuals with the resources of Buddhist cosmology provides Vasubandhu with two kinds of constraints.[7] He suggests that we are, first of all, constrained as individuals by the life-form our individual life now exhibits. For our current life-form, like all life-forms, has associated with it a particular experiential profile that makes possible a certain range of experiences, attitudes, and affordances, and excludes others.

Secondly, there is a constraint provided by the past to which, in Leszek Kolakowski's memorable characterization, we belong and which we are unable to change even "while it fills the whole of our existence."[8] We are sometimes encouraged to believe that the only way in which we can make sense of being constrained by what is the case—and thereby by something beyond us—is by having recourse to a spatial metaphor that objects exemplify with ease: we are constrained *just in case* we are responsive to what is "out there." Following Vasubandhu's cosmological example suggests otherwise. An individual is constrained to experience what is available as a being of a particular type. And we are to make sense of our exemplifying one or another life-form, say Buddhist theorists, through a history of action. But the actions are not those performed by the subject whose experiences are in question; they are performed by beings in the past with whom the subject is causally continuous but not self-identical. The gap between mind and world to which some theorists look in order to preserve intuitions about how the world comes into view can't be realized through a spatial metaphor alone. We are not responsive only to what is located in things "outside" of us. Rather, in experience we are responding to a variety of collective history we have forgotten.

TALKING TO THE DEAD, INTERPRETING THEM FOR THE LIVING

If only the value of history in philosophy was as evident to us as the role of the past was for Vasubandhu. This book was written as an exercise in the history of philosophy, understood as an exercise in the difficult art of conducting dialogues with the dead, to borrow Edwin Curley's memorable phrase.[9] What are the criteria for success for such an enterprise?

The polymath al-Jāḥiẓ once claimed that we must not only speak to the dead—we must do so while also serving as interpreters for the living.[10] Have I made it possible for Vasubandhu to find conversation partners, those with whom his views and the resonances of his interesting thesis might reverberate? I'll offer two suggestions, the first of which looks in the direction of Vasubandhu's past, while the second looks to Vasubandhu's possible futures. The point in both cases will be to show possibilities for what his thesis might be taken to mean.

I have claimed that there is something innovative in Vasubandhu's account. This is a characterization that concerns the state of Buddhist philosophy in his immediate milieu, the world of Buddhist scholasticism in the north and the northwest of the subcontinent and as conducted in Sanskrit.

We might also claim of Vasubandhu's account, however, whether he knew this or not—whether or not he even could have been in a position to know this—that it effectively recapitulates one of the conceptual innovations associated with the philosophers of the traditions coalescing around the city state of Kosala in antiquity (around 500 BCE).

I have in mind to connect Vasubandhu here with Lauren Bausch's reconstruction of the concept of embodied apperception (*saṃjñā*, in the Sanskrit of the Kāṇva recension of the *Bṛhadāraṇyaka*, *saññā* in the Pāli of the *Suttanipāta*). On Bausch's account, this is a mode of knowing that perceives reality in conjunction with karmic retribution: "The *saṃjñā/saññā* mode of knowing is conditioned by past karma, which is stored first before flowing into the sensory faculties, where it constructs apperception."[11] I can't see that Vasubandhu would disagree with this. In a way, Vasubandhu has made explicit the consequences for any account of perception that takes the history of karma and the history of Buddhist accounts of karma seriously. And his making the consequences of Buddhist commitments to such a cosmological context explicit can seem a little like a return of the philosophically repressed.

I offer the above as a point of possible departure for future historians of South Asian philosophy. But the past is not the only place to seek a relevance for Vasubandhu's thesis. Consider one lexically similar proposal from a possibly surprising source. Doesn't Karl Marx sound a little like Vasubandhu when he says that "[man's] whole human attitude to the world—sight, hearing, smell, taste, touch, thought, contemplation, and sensation" is grounded in the priority of action? Marx says such things to counter thinking that mind can be treated as being anything but a part of nature.[12] He stresses that we are active beings in order to make the following point, as summarized by Leszek Kolakowski on the basis of Marx's *Paris Manuscripts*: "Man's relationship to the world is not originally contemplation or passive perception, in which things transmit their likeness to the subject or transform their inherent being into fragments of the subject's perceptual field."[13] Or consider the more striking claim that "perception is, from the beginning, the result of the combined operation of nature and the practical orientation of human beings."[14] Can Kolakowski's Marx be the way for Vasubandhu to speak to us today? Of course, that depends. Is the making of social environments over time an analogue to the making of cosmological niches on the Buddhist account?

Much will depend on what one means by action and what one means by a life-form.[15] For example, Marx does not think of human activity as the natural activity of what he calls species being.[16] Even if he thinks of man as a human natural being, he does not think of man as a *merely* natural being. The concept of action here limits us to speak of humans as more than natural beings, beings who express normativity and purpose in their action—uniquely so, according to Marx. Merely natural beings do not act in this sense; they do not, that is, make history.

Would Vasubandhu restrict the world-making notion of action to humans? Should we? Marx may have gone wrong in withholding the normative notion of action when speaking of animals and their environments. But perhaps Vasubandhu is wrong to act as if his normative conception of action, karma, self-evidently extends to encompass all manner of forms of life and their living ways of environing themselves? Think of the different varieties of actions and the different ways of coupling perception and action of which we shall have to take account in order to describe the ways that organisms at even the smallest scales can impress themselves on their environment, and so alter their own place and trajectory within it. Will just one notion of action do the trick?[17] Just one notion of "world"? It's all very well for Vasubandhu to have said that "there is no end to the number of creatures of brief lives who subsist on smells and tastes,"[18] by which he meant to indicate that life involves an infinitely dense continuum at every scale. But does his own theory of the link between perception and karma do justice to the lives of such creatures? Was it ever intended to?

Philosophers working with Vasubandhu in the future may emphasize his use of life-forms as a category of natural history in order to be able to have Vasubandhu's thinking align with the direction of biologically informed contemporary philosophy of mind. This will require, at the very least, no longer using human action as an implicit norm. On the other hand, one might wish to take Vasubandhu's account in an altogether different direction, thinking, along with Marx (his predecessors, or any number of other philosophers since then) of worlds in a different way: as social worlds, conventions, ways of life, or lifeworlds. Such notions center on the kind of normativity and richness of meaning that human worlds appear to exhibit. It's not a zero-sum game, of course. One might try out first one approach, then another. Or, like the Japanese Zen philosopher Eihei Dōgen, blend them, as when he spoke of there being "worlds in all four directions . . . not only over there, but also right here beneath your feet, even in a single drop of water."[19] Confoundingly, Dōgen appears to want to hold together aspects of the natural-historical idea of environments as well as the lifeworlds (grounded in an idea of the virtues of each world's own "household customs").

Is some caution warranted? Vasubandhu's intellectual descendent, Dharmakīrti, can help us see why. Dharmakīrti's insight was that the concept of a collective way of life (as in our belonging to a social world) is not the same kind of concept as that of belonging to a life-form. Both involve the idea of "being an X." But he had in mind the epistemological point that the conditions for the use of these concepts is different. To recognize someone as belonging to the social lifeworld of being a Brahman, say, or a healer, or a merchant, to use Dharmakīrti's examples, requires of us two things: first, that we be sensitive to something about another's way of being in the world that is intrinsically description dependent; and second, it requires of us socialization in order to be able to be sensitive to those description-dependent and meaning-rich features in the first place.[20] To see someone as a social type of X, say, is not as evident as seeing that something belongs to a species. Coming into an awareness of the difference between, let us say, humans and dogs, does not require socialization.

To be described as being human, then, unlike being described as being a Brahman or a Kashmiri, might not center the normative or meaning-rich features of one's life. Though that's not the whole story. (How could it ever be, for philosophers?) Dharmakīrti does think that there is an analogy to be made between being a distinct type of person through habituation and being a distinct species, as in his appeal to the famous verse that has a mendicant, a libidinous man, and a dog exhibit three distinct responses in judgment regarding the body of a beautiful woman; seeing it spontaneously, and respectively, as a corpse, as a lovely woman, and as food.[21] This is to make a (social) ontological point concerning the way in which we make ourselves and our environments over time, emphasizing as well the epistemological consequences of being an X, and so belonging to a social world. The three—the monk, the lecher and the dog—live in or express what one might call different karmic worlds. On this conception, whether or not they do actually exhibit different life-forms does not appear to matter, given how the response of every one of them is incompatible with the responses of either of the others.[22]

We can speak of karmic worlds to capture the machinery responsible for the generation of worlds as well as the epistemological consequences of there being such worlds. As long as we see that karmic worlds are sense involving and sense excluding. To belong to a karmic world is minimally to belong to a recognizable way of *seeing* under an interpretation: seeing (or better, taking) X to be Y. Two things are criterial: firstly, that one's habits and purposes shape one's life in such a way that these manifest even in what appears to be the most basic patterns of sensory receptivity to one's environment; and secondly, that being habituated differently would have resulted in different patterns of available content and action.[23]

I spoke earlier as if the interpreter of Vasubandhu will face a choice and have to either distinguish natural and social worlds entirely or elide any distinction between them. But Dharmakīrti's use of karmic worlds shows us that this might be the wrong lesson to take from the history of Buddhist thought. Dharmakīrti's is a more relaxed, possibly even pragmatic criterion, on which having a praxis, a way of life, can either be or fail to be equivalent to a natural-historical world in terms of its epistemological effects depending on our theoretical purposes. This renders the distinction between social and natural world less absolute, as does the confounding use to which Dōgen can put talk of worlds. The confounding aspects of it, it is important to see, are possibly of ameliorative and therapeutic value. Let's see an example.

Writing in 1240 CE, Dōgen said,

> When dragons and fish see water as a palace, just as when humans see palaces, they do not view it as flowing. And if some onlooker were to explain to them that their palace was flowing water, they would surely be just as amazed as we are now to hear it said that mountains flow. Still, there would undoubtedly be some dragons and fish who would accept such an explanation of the railings, stairs, and columns of palaces and pavilions . . . Although human beings have understood what is in seas and rivers as water, just what kind of thing dragons, fish and other beings understand and use as water, we do not yet know.[24]

Living beings don't just happen to live where they do. A collective way of being a living being and the elemental habitat associated with such a way can constitute a region of being: a distinctive way of living, embodying a distinctive mode of understanding of the conditions of life, one that individual beings can come to acknowledge over time.[25] Dōgen intimates that this can happen when we allow ourselves to try to imagine inhabiting our environment differently, as part of a region of being for another form of life; more particularly, it can happen by imagining how alienating it can be for an individual living, associated with a distinct region of being, to adopt our sense of its habitat.

Why does that matter? Let me limit my answer to considering just the lesson Dōgen has to teach those who may wish to take Vasubandhu's insights further. The idea of a region of being in Dōgen's hands is intended to cut through the distinction between social and natural worlds. We can use it to bring ourselves to see that other lives may well be as socio-normatively complex as our own. Or, to put the point equivalently, it may well be that our life, our norms of making sense included, is just as natural as any other.

Dōgen's point concerns our metaconceptual distinctions, such as the distinction between social and natural environments—a distinction one might be tempted to draw, for example, between our built environments, rich in sense and significance, and the so-called attenuated, seemingly featureless world of the natural elements merely lived in by other life-forms; or the distinction between socio-normative forms of (human) praxis and mere causally describable animal behavior. What if these may wind up being of a piece with the sense-making apparatus appropriate only to one region of being? Furthermore, when Dōgen says that "one should not be limited to human views"[26] and that "we do not yet know" what we may need to know, this might apply at a meta level as a criticism of any project, such as Vasubandhu's, that seeks a sideways-on account of the generation of worlds.

It's a point worth making. Dōgen's example of water as a habitat that sustains overlapping but exclusive regions of being linked to life-forms ultimately derives from a text that was important to Vasubandhu as well, the *Mahāyānasaṃgraha*: "The sea itself has no disparities, yet owing to the karmic differences of gods, humans, hungry ghosts and fish, gods see it as a treasure trove of jewels, humans see it as water, hungry ghosts see it as an ocean of pus, and fish see it as a palatial dwelling."[27] Yet, unlike Vasubandhu, Dōgen does not seek to embed these karmic worlds in an encompassing causal context or structure of variation: "The waters which vary in accordance with the different types of beings do not depend on body or mind; they do not arise from karma," he says.[28] A karmic story, very possibly, is a story couched in a theoretical vocabulary appropriate to the normative (indeed, moralizing) standards of just one region of being, one we may well need to go beyond.

I find that to be a potentially liberating line of thought, though I limit myself to deriving with its help only a modest methodological allegory. Even though couched in similar language and derived from a shared tradition, Buddhist philosophers like Vasubandhu, and Dharmakīrti, and Dōgen (among others) could use ostensibly the same concepts in similar-sounding claims to very different ends in different contexts. Depending on how one defines these concepts, how one motivates the illustrating examples, and why, Vasubandhu's thesis can acquire different meanings, even if one uses seemingly identical sentences to express that thesis—just as it has over time in the premodern world, and as it will, hopefully, continue to do. However, future interpreters should recall what Dōgen says of the different ways in which worlds come into view according to the type of being that sees them: "These different ways of seeing are the condition under which water"—or any region of being—"is killed or given life."[29]

CONCEIVABILITY AND "THE" WORLD

Vasubandhu chooses to motivate his thesis with the help of examples that will seem exotic to most contemporary (Anglophone) philosophers. I have argued that we should not try to update these examples without first attempting to understand them as Vasubandhu and his interlocutors would have, as credible models of real worlds. Here, I wish to consider the implication of the following thought: the examples are epistemically distant from us, but Vasubandhu's use of them need not be. To see this, we must set aside two possible mischaracterizations of what Vasubandhu is doing. Once we do this, we can thereby see an interesting way in which a historian of philosophy might look to Vasubandhu and his thought experiments as nonignorable antecedents for our own form of intellectual activity, notwithstanding other varieties of distance that might separate us. By implication, this might also suggest a way to understand the kind of activity we have been engaged in during the course of this book.

I'll begin with an example used by Saul Kripke in *Wittgenstein on Rules and Private Language*, that of an integer function *quus*, which has the same value as our *plus* for all argument pairs both members of which are less than 57, but the value 5 for all other pairs. To this supposition, Kripke added the following comment: "The set of responses in which we agree, and the way they interweave with our activities, is our *form of life*. Beings who agreed in consistently giving bizarre quus-like responses would share in another form of life. By definition, such another form of life would be bizarre and incomprehensible to us."[30] We can imagine such a form of life if no a priori argument excludes it. The questions I wish to entertain now are these: Should we think of Vasubandhu's (to many) "bizarre" cosmological examples and his life-forms as such abstractly imagined possible forms of life? Is Vasubandhu's having entertained such examples indicative of his having belonged to a form of life different from our own? What would that mean?

John Haugeland says of Kripke's form of life that he cannot be sure that he can imagine it. And he is not sure that he ought to have to try to imagine a merely abstract possibility, given the historical examples of other, concretely exampled cultures in which systems of arithmetic are found. A philosopher, Haugeland suggests, must first work with the set of actual variations in our concepts that history and anthropology furnish us with. For it is only when one does so that one will begin to find evidence of a factor that constrains the variation of which our concepts are capable as well as the limits of what we can imagine, a factor that goes missing when we indulge merely abstract possibility. The factor that goes missing is what Haugeland calls "the world itself—the real world that we all live in."[31]

I think that the distinction between merely abstract possibilities and actual variability in concepts is a useful one. Though I must say that I do not believe that we have anything like a secure grasp on the set of actual variations in the concepts used by different human communities, evidence of which continues to be furnished by philology, history, and anthropology, among other disciplines. Nor do I believe that we are entitled to consider talk of "the world itself" to be secure merely given *our* determination of patterns of invariance in such a hypothetical (because still incomplete) set. But I do think it is helpful to say that Vasubandhu is not merely offering his interlocutors an abstractly imagined case—a merely possible case—one defined as possible given that no a priori argument excludes it. Nor is he offering them an ethnographic report of what other people believe. Rather, as I hope you will agree after this book, Vasubandhu is exploring his world, "the world itself" as he and his co-religionists imagine it to be.

He does this in *The Twenty Verses* in two ways: firstly, by calling attention to alternate contexts of possible experience and exploring these with the help of Buddhist cosmological accounts of different lifeforms; and he does so by reflecting on Buddhist cosmology, with its central commitment to alternate contexts of possible experience, as a distinctive system of possibility and style of reasoning with implications for concepts in other Buddhist technical discussions (such as "perception" in epistemology) and common-sense assumptions (as in the case of Sāraṇa's possession and dream). By the compound phrase "system of possibility and style of reasoning" I mean to speak of a connected set of concepts and discursive tools in a given discourse (at a given time) that constrains the descriptions of phenomena that are available to be entertained as being possibly true or false, scrutable or inscrutable, explicable or inexplicable, and so on.[32] What I mean to say is this: Vasubandhu is not only advancing one or another set of propositions about the world. He is calling his interlocutors' attention to the fact that they work within a system of possibility. And he is using such an acknowledgment to make explicit a sense of reality that he and his co-religionists share.

As is discussed over the course of this book, this is achieved through explorations of rival intuitions concerning what is possible—articulating it with an awareness of its revisionary potential with respect to common-sense (or untutored) intuitions, on the one hand, and rival philosophical approaches on the other, and by appealing to paradigmatic cases of possibility that evade explanation. To put things this way immediately suggests the attraction of Vasubandhu's thought experiments for any philosopher or student of the history of ideas impressed by the difference between mere abstract possibility and concrete human variation. There is a difference between our having, on the one hand, evidence of (perhaps only) tacitly held conceptions of the world that we have to make explicit, and our possessing, on the other hand, examples of (alternative) systems of possibility and associated styles of reasoning that have been made explicit by philosophers working at a different time and in a different tradition. The attractiveness of Vasubandhu's case lies in his having given us an example of the latter. He does not only exemplify conceptual variation—he actively explores it.

That there have been other, concretely exampled systems of possibility—and thus other conceptual repertoires given which talk of "the world" acquires quasi-historical and variable sense—is a thesis that is not particularly entertained in contemporary philosophy.[33] It is even less common to credit that there have been philosophical attempts on the part of others in distinct cultures and times to explore actual variations in our concepts that different systems of possibility present. Our unearned confidence in the universality that attaches to our intuitions in our parochial use of conceptual tools in a couple of languages is only exceeded by the institutionalized form of sanctioned ignorance of the greatest part of serious thought in other cultures, in other languages, at different times.

With regard to treating Sanskrit Buddhist scholastic thought of the north and northwest of the subcontinent of the fifth century CE as an example of thought conducted within a different system of possibility, there are two forms of incuriosity against which I have set myself in this book. (I make no distinction here between forms of incuriosity sustained by indifference or by overfamiliarity.)

The first form of incuriosity is simply the incuriosity about what it is like for laymen and intellectuals alike to inhabit a world whose contours are different from our own. "The late antique [Mediterranean] body," Peter Brown once reminded his readers, "was embedded in a cosmic matrix in ways that made its perception of itself profoundly unlike our own."[34] And "we need," he went on to argue, "to look back, once again, to those high, imagined peaks of the cosmos against which all ancient [Mediterranean] people, Christians and non-Christians alike, viewed their society and their own persons."[35] What is true of antique Christianity is true of Buddhism of that time as well.

True, many contemporary Anglophone readers can treat the ancient Mediterranean world with the kind of familiarity and intimacy that necessitates correction because of the generations that devoted considerable intellectual effort to the recovery and reconstruction of that ancient world. Creating the conditions for contemporary readers to acquire intimate familiarity with the intellectual worlds of ancient South Asia is surely a worthy goal for scholars. Might that not recommend attending only to what is most continuous with contemporary philosophy, setting the demons and guards in hell and assorted exotica to one side? I would welcome such work, at least if undertaken "in the hope," as Steven Collins liked to say, "that [it] will be read in conjunction with other forms of historiography."[36] One should hope that one's reader will be provided with many books, of different sorts and written in a plurality of voices. By all means, let us then engage with what is familiar. But let us also allow, as Sheldon Pollock once put it, that there is no shame in premodernity.[37]

In stressing what is likely to be unfamiliar to contemporary philosophers, I have also wished to address a second variety of incuriosity. The ancients did not simply inhabit other worlds. They thought in them and thought about them. Does thinking in other intellectual worlds mean something different from thinking in our own? Can "to think" be a verb like "to love," one that may acquire subtly different saliences and meanings in different cultural and historical contexts?[38]

I do not think that we should be in any hurry to answer this. Not until we possess many more attempts at describing the experience of thought on the part of individual philosophers in the ancient world than we now possess.[39] It might be that the inner life of philosophers from the past can look to be the same as ours when intellection is reduced to the familiar manipulation of the well-worn tools of our trade, analysis and argument. But we need not forever restrict our attention thus to claims or definitions and arguments for and against them.

To be sure, this book too has featured an interest in intellectual toolkits. I have discussed not only the dreams, demons, and guards in hell that occupied Vasubandhu's attention, but also the epistemic machinery—the concepts, arguments, and thought experiments of Buddhist cosmology—that he brought to bear when thinking about them. This is at it should be. But at the same time, I hope that I have also succeeded in suggesting a distinct target for the historian's attention: the historically variable ways in which one can be oriented in thought.

I have written this book with the following question in mind: How would Vasubandhu characterize and assess the nature and salience of thought in his own practice?[40] What did he take himself to be doing in composing a work like *The Twenty Verses* or developing and defending the views that he did therein? I do not have anything like a complete answer at present, though I hope to have indicated something of the various norms that might be brought to bear when thinking of the conditions of success or failure of Vasubandhu's form of intellectual activity. Thus, we have spoken not only of what it might mean to think in connection with the Buddhist scholastic norm called the principle of reality, but also of the various senses of the concept of "reality" one may encounter in Vasubandhu's work.

I have, furthermore, attempted to steer clear of the temptation to think that systems of possibility are paradigmatically sets of propositions documenting what is held to be actual. I have tried, instead, to follow the wisdom of Robert Musil: "To pass freely through open doors, it is necessary to respect the fact that they have solid frames. This principle . . . is simply a requisite sense of reality. But if there is a sense of reality . . . then there must also be something we can call a sense of possibility."[41] I have tried to cultivate a feel for Vasubandhu's sense of reality by cultivating a feel for what, in his system of thought, was possible and what was not. I remain, however, conscious of just how much more remains to be done.

To take but one example, such a sense of reality, or feel for modality, cannot be separated out from a possible aesthetics. I mean to say that there is a link between a sense of reality, the issue of possibility, and aesthetics as a disciplined way of attuning and shaping one's attention. I can explain with the help of an example.

After an inconclusive attempt to understand the ontological status of mirror images, Vasubandhu exclaims: "Indeed, the powers of phenomena are beyond reckoning!" (*acintyo hi dharmāṇaṃ śaktibhedaḥ*).[42] That mirrors "respond" to the presence of objects by mirroring them, that magnets attract iron, or that "moonstones" liquefy in moonlight (to use further examples that Yaśomitra adduces to generalize Vasubandhu's point) are examples that induce in the analyst a way of comporting to possibilities.

At the close of chapter 6, I spoke of how moments like this are thought by Buddhist scholastics to express a norm of description, one invoking the principle of reality by showing us a limit to what can be comprehended by our concepts and in our descriptions. What does this have to do with aesthetics? Just this. There is something it is like to invoke, and to acknowledge, such norms. The literary critic Daṇḍin in his *Mirror of Literature* uses a verse with a functionally identical exclamation as Vasubandhu's to illustrate the emotion and trope of wonder as known to aesthetics in Sanskrit: "Bodyless Eros, with five flowers for arrows, has conquered the world: that's impossible—or else, marvelous are the powers of things."[43] We arrive at wonder, Daṇḍin suggests through this verse, after traversing the disjunction that obtains between, on the one hand, being entitled to disbelieve in something because it fails to conform to the requirements reason sets on intelligibility, and allowing the world, on the other hand, to serve as the ultimate arbiter for what is and what is not possible.

But Daṇḍin illustrates the point I wish to make here, not only by using a verse to specify the modal issue but by enacting a lesson. To see that possibility can outstrip conceivability is to do more than to exercise one's intellect or to come to inhabit a propositional attitude. Wonder is just one example of a norm that can straddle intellectual and aesthetic concerns, suggesting perhaps that works of intellect and analysis might have been produced in accordance with such norms—norms that may have served as a variety of affective scaffolding in the intellectual environment of a text, shaping an intellectual's responsiveness to the content of sentences and the formal procedures designed to manipulate such sentences in analysis and argument. Intellectual praxis may have involved attunement to moods with identifiable savors as much as it did analysis and argument, moods associated with, though not reducible to, sentential contents, and serving as orienting states for comporting oneself to one's intellectual community and to the world brought into view (in certain normatively regulated ways) in analysis and argument.

I have tried to write this book mindful of the lesson to be drawn from this. To enter into another intellectual world, to know one's way around a work produced in another system of possibility, might require what being able to enter into works of drama or poetry requires, what convincingly entering and losing oneself in any world made with words requires—a connoisseur's hard-won feel for and acquaintance with taste and value.

THE NARROW ROAD

This brings to me the close of this book and a more honest way of stating my interest in Vasubandhu's works. While some of the questions with which I began have, from time to time, kept me up at night, none of them compelled me to write once I was up the next day. Perhaps it will seem antiquated. But my orientation to the materials of my study has not been unlike that of another traveler. This man was once faced with a humanizing connection with a past to which he was, at the time of recording his thoughts, only tenuously connected. Here he records his experience of what he came upon after long travel, and what he could then only dimly perceive: "Many are the names that have been preserved for us in poetry from ancient times; but mountains crumble and rivers disappear, new roads replace the old, stones are buried and vanish in the earth . . . time passes and the world changes. The remains of the past are shrouded in uncertainty. And yet here before my eyes was a monument which none would deny had lasted a thousand years. I felt as if I were looking into the minds of the men of old."[44] This is from the Japanese poet Bashō's *Narrow Road to/of the Interior*; and this is how he ends this remarkable passage, reporting what he thought then: "This was one of the pleasures of travel and of growing old."

Some works of philosophy in antiquity are monuments; some are environments. And there can be pleasure in intellectual travel to them, even as there are virtues to spending time in them. Such virtues have been variously described: in terms of the pleasure of making friends with persons of antiquity, in the Chinese philosopher Mencius's phrase with regard to the classics; in terms of the pleasure of coming to see the faces of the ancients through their writings, to use the Song-era literary critic Ye Xie's way of putting it.[45] Such descriptions more typically accompany works of literary merit, but there is no reason not to speak thus of works of philosophy. In his monumental works and in the byways of his essays, Vasubandhu of Peshawar waits for us still. I will be content if I have suggested only a little of the joy and the wonder that's to be found in trying to meet him there.

APPENDIX

THE TWENTY VERSES OF VASUBANDHU IN TRANSLATION

PART ONE: ABOUT THIS TRANSLATION

This appendix offers readers of this book a translation of *The Twenty Verses*, by which, as in the body of the book, I mean the verses of Vasubandhu as well as his prose autocommentary.

In the translation to follow, the verses are represented by text marked **in bold** and identified with a number and letter. The verse form used by Vasubandhu has four feet in Sanskrit, here represented as is custom by the roman letters a through d. Thus **18d**, for example, names the fourth foot of the eighteenth verse.

To make things easier, I have tried to accentuate the dialogical framing of thought in the commentary by indenting an ostensible interlocutor's voice, and *putting the statements made within this stance in italics*, marking it off with an em dash. There are places where the voice of an interlocutor is presented in verse. In such instances, ***the thought is marked off in italics and bold type.*** In the main body of the text, I cite my translation without these typographic markers out of aesthetic concerns. Here, I hope they will help facilitate rather than hijack a reader's attention.

On the dialogical style, Matthew Kapstein's comments on another essay by Vasubandhu are apposite: "To orient the reader to Vasubandhu's argument, earlier translators have attempted to assign each passage to a specific interlocutor, and so construing the text as a dialogue throughout. Though Vasubandhu's work clearly does betray its origins in earlier dialogic works, it seems to me that dialogue here is by and large left implicit, and that many passages can best be interpreted as the internal dialogue of a single thinker."[1]

Though the dialogue can feel quite explicit in *The Twenty Verses*, this need not be in tension with the suggestion that Vasubandhu, in addition to being in dialogue with other people, may also be thinking with himself, insofar as he is exploring views from intellectual vantage points he has traversed before through his own intellectual career.

To assist readers, I have offered my own subdivisions of the text in parenthetical subheadings to highlight, as gently as possible, the way in which different arguments in the text may be organized. My subdivisions are these:

1. The Initial Intelligibility of the Claim
2. The Case of the Guards in Hell
3. What the Buddha Said, and Meant
4. The Internal Architecture of Objects
5. The Weight of Perception
6. The Consequences of Revisionary Philosophy

I have derived them from a particular picture of what a work such as *The Twenty Verses* might be attempting to do. It is possible to approach *The Twenty Verses* as an example of what Vasubandhu has elsewhere treated as one of the tasks of interpretation, namely warding off objections to one's interpretation of something the Buddha meant.[2] In effect, Vasubandhu outlines for us what is involved in the *rational reconstruction* of the meaning of the Buddha's utterances. I have tried to lay out and to defend this approach to *The Twenty Verses* elsewhere. Here, I will only state what I think this entails.

To defend an utterance under a particular interpretation, or P, as what the Buddha, all things considered, meant to teach as his considered view of things, one must do the following:

a) Show that P is not prima facie implausible.
b) Show that anything else said by the Buddha that is inconsistent with P can be accounted for so as to come out as being consistent with P.
c) Show how P fulfills accepted criteria determining whether or not some teaching ought to count as a part of the Buddha's overall therapeutic aims and commitments.

d) Show not only (a), but also that *one cannot but* consider P to be what the Buddha meant, on pain of saddling him with a contradiction or other variety of incoherence entailed by ~P.

My book has explored the implications of the meaning Vasubandhu reconstructs for the Buddha in verse 9; I have not pursued all that a rational reconstruction must do if it is to be successful. But I have offered my own subdivisions of the text to highlight the way in which I believe different arguments in the text do try to serve this goal. I take it, then, that (a) is fulfilled in my sections 1 and 2; (b) in section 6, not limiting oneself to the Buddha's utterances, but including basic commitments involved in what one might call a Buddhist worldview; (c) in section 3; (d) in section 4, with section 5 serving to complete the argument by examining just what one is entitled to conclude on the basis of the kind of arguments found in section 4. I have found it useful to consider section 5 as the place where Vasubandhu is exploring the relationship between rational reconstruction and epistemology as methods available to Buddhist philosophers.

I should say, no programmatic concern with reconstruction informs the translation itself. Whether or not one is convinced that this is the most productive way to read *The Twenty Verses*, I hope that the division of the text into sections will facilitate one's sense of how arguments in the text might hang together. Additionally, I hope that readers will take up different ways of emphasizing the coherence of the work that is still consistent with the subdivisions I have used in my translation.[3]

The Twenty Verses is a short text, and it is a vast one. The range of concerns in it, both quantitatively and qualitatively, is almost forbidding, and, in my opinion, unprecedented by anything else of similar scope composed by Vasubandhu. No doubt, this will be the primary source of disorientation for a reader, one only strengthened by one's possible cultural unfamiliarity with the cosmology and narratives that frame the work in the beginning and last verses of the work respectively. I think this range is deliberate in two senses. Not only is it the case that we are encouraged to take variability of possible experiences as basic, but I now read *The Twenty Verses* as mapping a path for us through Vasubandhu's vast and rather varied oeuvre, signposting through enthymematic arguments his considered thoughts on problems motivated elsewhere in more detail. Were we to follow such a path, I believe that we would emerge with a richer sense of what constellation of issues, precisely, entails his considered view, and with a more fully fleshed out sense of their salience for him. No translation can offer one *all that*, though this book has attempted to do so with one issue, namely cosmology, and I hope to return to this endless work another time with a running commentary. All in all, then, I offer this translation as a companion for this book, and as a possible spur to future work that will follow Vasubandhu through the many doors *The Twenty Verses* contains.

A word about the sources for my translation, and the criteria that have guided my decisions. I have used as my basis for translation the superb new critical edition of the Sanskrit provided by Jonathan A. Silk.[4] I have also retained Silk's numbering, beginning with verse 2, which follows the numbering of earlier editions of the text that do feature an introductory verse. That the appearance is quixotic cannot be denied. I have allowed it to stand to facilitate cross-references with the work of others.

My translation is by no means the first translation of this important work.[5] Not only is it not the first translation, I have no ambition for this translation to serve as the final word. In making it I have had a specific purpose in mind. I wished to produce a readable and accurate (if not entirely transparent) translation for the use of readers of this book and for philosophically inclined readers new to Buddhist scholastic prose.

By a "transparent translation" I have in mind to emphasize the virtues exemplified by translations produced by philologists for the use of other philologists. Such translations, typically produced when attempting to justify one's interpretation of points at issue, seek to preserve the lexical, syntactic, and rhetorical features of the original. Particularly when supplemented by the use of calques, neologisms, or unusual and unidiomatic English terms, such efforts, ironically enough, largely serve to produce opacity through creating ponies to the original that are unreadable to all but initiates or those for whom the Sanskrit (or other original language) is in any event available.[6] I have taken as my inspiration, instead, the attempt to provide what Lawrence J. McCrea and Parimal G. Patil call "translation without brackets," the guiding principle for which goes something like this: "When . . . material is both implied by context and necessary for understanding the passage, we include it without brackets."[7]

I have found this principle (and the example they have set us) liberating. In dispensing with brackets, I have allowed my judgment as to the shape and flow of the argument to enter into the translated text, without defending my choices in every instance on the page. To ease readability, I have also, on occasion, translated *the function* and not only *the dictionary meaning* of certain particles and phrases used by authors of Sanskrit scholastic prose. The result of not, as it were, pausing in the middle of conveying what a sentence means to justify myself is hopefully easier for a reader. If not *readable*, I do hope that it is at least easier on the eyes.

I have tried to generate idiomatic, and yet precise translations of the technical function of certain terms. These might not be at first apparent without consideration of the function of certain technical terms in contemporary Anglophone philosophy. It should not distract the reader of this book. In only two places, namely the commentary to **10ab** and **12ab**, have I allowed myself the liberty of enumerating the members of a category (the "two sets of six conditions for experiential awareness," and "the six possible dimensions of orientation in space") only mentioned by Vasubandhu, exhibiting these in the form of a table and a list, respectively, in order to allow a reader to follow some of the details of the argument. In the discussion of verse **16**, I have allowed the translation to incorporate two distinct varieties of emphasis possible with the use of the word *pratyakṣa*—which can, in some contexts, mean what is perceptually evident, as well as the episode of perception—and this gives the discussion a slightly more paraphrastic tenor than might be thought desirable. I find it useful, however, for a reader new to this material to "hear" the different directions in which the argument might pull, depending on which variety of emphasis one allows oneself to follow. The argument, I think one will find, goes through with either emphasis.

Glossary

I have not provided a full glossary for this translation. Nevertheless, there are a few words, phrases, and names that it will be helpful to have glossed to facilitate reading.

Mahāyāna. Literally, "the great vehicle," and the first word of this text. It is a self-appellation for what *The Princeton Dictionary of Buddhism* describes as "a movement that began some four centuries after the Buddha's death, marked by the composition of texts that purported to be his words."[8] The content of these texts varies, but there is often a shared didactic emphasis on a Buddha's awakening and the ethical and cognitive prerequisites for such awakening. And as far as Vasubandhu is concerned, Mahāyāna works cannot be discounted as being taught by the Buddha.[9] He also takes them to be criterially committed to the teaching that things do not possess independent identities. He begins this text with a canonical utterance found in a variety of Mahāyāna works, most likely ultimately to be traced to the *Daśabhūmika-sūtra*.[10]

Threefold world. This is standard way of speaking of the entire range of possible existence and experience as understood by Buddhist cosmology. The three divisions are made as follows: (1) there is the *kāmadhātu*, or *kāmaloka*, wherein existence and experience as a being are conditioned by sensory contact and desire; (2) there is the *rūpadhātu*, in which one is still embodied, but differently than are sensing, desiring beings (one might think here of certain classes of divine beings); (3) and lastly there is the *ārūpyadhātu*, wherein utterly nonembodied forms of experience are thought to play out.

City of Celestial Musicians. This does not name a fictional place. That is, it is not a place described as possible or actual in some discourse, but one that turns out not to pick out anything concrete. Acknowledging that this figure does not occur in the earliest Buddhist literature, the author of the *Large Treatise on the Excellence of Wisdom* (*Mahāprajñāpāramitā-śāstra*) explains it in terms suggestive of what we would describe as a fata morgana, a superior mirage; in particular, it may mean a mirage of a city seen at the horizon and produced at certain times in the day.[11]

Sāraṇa and **Mahākātyāyana.** Vasubandhu is referring to two characters: Sāraṇa, the son of King Udayana of Vatsa, and Mahākātyāyana, a famous disciple of the Buddha. His reference to them is to a story from the collection of philosophical stories, *The Kalpanāmaṇḍaṭikā*, authored by Vasubandhu's intellectual forebear, Kumāralāta. For more on the story, see chapter 7 of this book.

Vemacitra was a king of Titans (or anti-gods—Asuras) in Buddhist stories. The story of his defeat and transformation to which Vasubandhu alludes is discussed in detail by Sylvain Lévi in an article that also discusses the reference to **Upāli**, a famous layperson who lived at the time of the Buddha and who became a disciple of the Buddha. Vasubandhu is citing an important dialogue featuring Upāli that contrasts Jaina and Buddhist philosophical approaches to the moral assessment of actions, the *Upāli Sūtra*.[12]

PART TWO: *THE TWENTY VERSES*

The Mahāyāna Buddhist tradition teaches that all that is connected with the threefold world is just presentation of content, since there is a canonical utterance: "O Sons of the Conqueror, the threefold world is nothing but thought."

"Thought," "mind," "awareness," and "presentation of content" are coextensional synonyms. In the above quotation, "thought" is used so as to include all mental functions.

The adverbial qualification "just" is used for the sake of ruling out objects: just this episode of awareness arises, having an object as its manifest content. Just in the way there is the visual experience of nonactual hair or double moons on the part of those suffering from ocular disease, but there is no actual object whatsoever.

(1. The Initial Intelligibility of the Claim)

One might object to the above as follows:

***—If a mental event presenting content can occur without being caused by an object, the following do not make sense: spatiotemporal constraints; the fact that there is no restriction to a single individual; and the exercise of causal functions.* (2)**

This objection states the following: "If a mental event presenting something like hue as its content can occur in the absence of objects such as a particular spread of hue, it does not occur *because* of an object such as a specific spread of hue. Why then does the presentation of content occur in a particular place, and not everywhere? Why does it occur only in that place at a particular time, and not always? Why does it occur to all those present in that particular place at that time, and not to just one alone?

Fine hairs, for example, appear only to those who suffer from an ocular disease, but not to others. Why is it that the function of hair, or bees, for example, is not discharged by the hair and the bees and other things seen by those who have such an ocular disease, whereas it is not the case that such functions are not discharged by their real counterparts in other contexts? Why is it that the food, drink, clothes, poison, weapons, among other things seen in a dream, do not have the causal efficacy to satisfy, respectively, hunger, thirst, and so on, that their counterparts outside of a dream do?

Not being actual, the city of Celestial Musicians does not possess the causal powers of a city, whereas real cities do. If the above contents resemble what is not actual insofar as they lack any correlated objects, you can't make any sense of the following: constraints on the place and time of experiences; the fact that there is no restriction of content to an individual; and the exercise of causal functions."

That's what the objection argues. But it is not the case that we can't make any sense of the above on our proposal. Since **constraints like spatial location are established, as in the case of dreaming. (3ab)** First of all, how is it that in a dream, even in the absence of a correlated object, particular things—whether bees, gardens, women, men, or what have you—are seen only in particular places, and not everywhere, and seen in these particular places only at particular times, not at all times? From this it follows that one can have spatiotemporal constraints on experience even in the absence of objects.

Furthermore, as with the hungry ghost world, there is no restriction of content to individuals. (3bc)

The phrase "hungry ghost" in "as with the hungry ghost world" above should be treated as a collective singular, meaning: "As with the many individuals making up the community of hungry ghosts."

How does the example work? **Given that they all**, collectively and in the same way, **see such things as a river filled with pus. (3cd)** For we know that insofar as these beings are constituted by a process involving the ripening of morally equivalent actions, *all* hungry ghosts, and not just one alone, see a river filled with pus. We say "such things as a river filled with pus" because along with a river filled with pus they also see the river filled with urine, feces, and so on, and see the river guarded by beings holding staffs and swords.

Thus, the fact that there is no restriction of content to individuals is established even when there is no object.

The performance of a characteristic causal function is established as in the case of a wet dream. (4ab) Take the example of a wet dream, defined by the emission of semen in the absence of sexual intercourse. In this way, to begin with, one can use these and other examples to establish the fourfold constraint on experiences, beginning with the spatiotemporal constraints, one at a time. **On the other hand, all constraints on experience are jointly established as in hell. (4bc)** How?

Given the fact of beings in hell seeing, among other things, the guards in hell, and being tormented by them. (4cd)

As, for instance, it is established that in the hells beings in hell see such things as the guards in hell in accordance with constraints on place and time. The phrase "among other things" above includes such things as dogs, crows, and iron hills moving to and fro.

These visual experiences are enjoyed by all those suffering in hell, not just by one alone; and their collective torment at the hands of these guards in hell is established, even in the absence of there really being any such things as guards in hell, on account of the constitutive and determining influence of the process of ripening of species-defined shared patterns of activity.

Similarly, it should be understood that the fourfold constraint on experiences in its entirety is established in other worlds as well.

(2. The Case of the Guards in Hell)

—But why do we not wish to take it that the guards in hell, or the dogs and crows there, are real living beings?

On account of incoherence: guards in hell do not make sense when taken to be beings in hell.

This is because they just do not experience suffering there in the same way as do beings in hell. And if you attempt to take it that wardens in hell torment one another and so count as beings suffering in hell, then it would be impossible to define them apart from those destined to suffer in hell. That is, it would not be possible to say, "These are beings in hell," "these guards in hell."

Moreover, there could be no fear if beings of equal strength, size, and shape torment one another. How could beings torment another, given that they cannot endure the burning pain while standing on a ground made up of heated iron? How is it possible for a being not "of" hell to be in hell?

—First of all, how are animals born in heaven? If they are, then analogously there could be guards in hell, taking it that these guards would be specific varieties of animals or hungry ghosts.

Since they do not experience the suffering produced in hell, the case of the guards in hell is not analogous to either the case of animals born in heaven or that of hungry ghosts. (5) For those animals found in heaven are born there owing to former actions performed in our shared context, actions that conform to the felicities of the world into which they are to be born. And these animals born in heaven experience the felicities that are produced there; but beings such as the guards in hell do not, however, experience hellish suffering. Therefore, the possibility that real animals or hungry ghosts in hell are present in hell does not make sense.

—Take it, however, in the following way: because of the former actions of these beings in hell, particular material elements come to be constituted in hell. These elements are individuated by their color, shapes, size, and power in such a way as to acquire such designations as "guards in hell." And these material elements change in such ways that they appear to perform various acts, like shaking their fists for the sake of inducing fear, in the way that mountains aspected like rams appear to come and go in that environment, or thorns in a forest or iron-thorned trees appear to turn themselves down and then upwards, so inducing fear. It is not the case, therefore, that the guards in hell are wholly and entirely impossible.

If you admit that it is because of the former actions of beings in hell that material elements in hell come to be in the ways you have described above, and you accept the fact of a process of change, why not admit such a process on the part of mind? (6) Which is to say, what reason do you have not to admit that the relevant causal process is an entirely mental process of a change, one initiated by the former actions of those beings? In particular, why speculate about the material elements?

Furthermore, you imagine the dispositional traces of actions to occur in one place and their result in another. What reason do you have not to concede that the results of action occur just where the dispositional traces are? (7)

This is the argument: the coming into being of material elements, and the causal processes that transform them, are on your account imagined to be of a particular type, one conforming to the former actions of those beings in hell which serve as the causal antecedent of both the elements and the process that transforms them. But the continuing dispositional traces of these actions stick to and remain within the individual mental continua of these beings: they are not found anywhere else. Why not commit to the thought that there is a particular type of causal process involving the mental continuum, such that the result of such a causal process would occur *only* where the traces of actions are? What is the reason for speculating that the result of a process involving the dispositional traces of action occurs where the traces of action do not?

—The reason is scripture.

(3. What the Buddha Said, and Meant)

—If what is manifest as sensory particulars, hues, and the like, were just an instance of experiential awareness, and not an object characterized as a sensory particular, then the Buddha would not have said that there exist sensory conditions qua objects, including such particulars as hues.

This is not a reason, since **the existence of ostensibly physical conditions of experience such as hues was stated as a function of an implicative communicative intent. It was also directed at those beginners in need of training, just as in the case of the phrase "The being that is reborn." (8)**

Take the statement, "There exists a being that is reborn." This was asserted by the Blessed One constrained by an implicative intent, with a view to affirming the noninterruption of mental continuity in the future. This statement of the Buddha's is one that we know cannot have been literally meant, on the evidence of the following scriptural utterance: "There does not exist here either a being or a self, but only impersonal phenomena possessed of causes." Thus, although the Blessed One did speak of the existence of the conditions of sensory experience such as hues, as it is directed at individuals who need to be guided by such instruction, statements of this kind are implicative.

—What is the implicative intent in the present case?

A mental event, having something as its manifest content, eventuates based on a corresponding dispositional power, or seed, proper to it: the

sage characterized these two aspects of the mental event as being the twofold conditions of sensory experience. (9)

What does this state? A conscious mental event possessing some specific manifest content, such as some particular hue, for example, comes into being on account of a seed or dispositional power attaining the end of a directed process of change. The Blessed One spoke of these two—the dispositional power and the manifest content—as being, respectively, the two conditions for perceptual experience called the eye and hue, to continue with our example of visual experience.

—*What are the virtues of teaching like this, constrained by such an implicative intent?*

For the following reason: in this way there can be an introduction to the selflessness of persons. (10ab) This is what serves as the reason. When one teaches in this way, one can gain access to the selflessness of persons. Here's how.

The six types of experiential awareness—sensory and cognitive—function based on two sets of six conditions.

Capacities	*Occasions and Types of Content*
Eye	Hues
Ear	Sounds
Nose	Smells
Tongue	Tastes
Body	Textures
Mind	Cognitive content

Having discerned that there does not exist any *unitary* agent of seeing in the case of visual awareness, nor any respective agent for any of the types of episodes of experiential awareness up to and including cognitive awareness, those in need of instruction in the teaching of the selflessness of persons are introduced to the fact of persons not being selves.

Moreover, teaching in another way introduces the selflessness of phenomena. (10bcd) "Teaching in another way" means "teaching that there is nothing but presentation of content."

—*How does this lead to understanding the selflessness of phenomena?*

One can get there by coming to understand the following thought: this is just an instance of the presentation of content, having as its manifest content phenomena such as hues, and the like; but no corresponding phenomenon *defined* independently as being a hue, and so on, exists.

—But if no individual, whatsoever, exists, then there is no such thing as just an instance of the presentation of content. So how is this fact of there being nothing but presentation of content established?

It is emphatically not the case that the fact of phenomena not possessing independent identities can be got at by claiming that "No phenomenon, whatsoever, exists."

Rather, the fact of phenomena not possessing independent identities can be introduced in terms of phenomena being without **a constructed identity. (10d)** Consider such phenomena for which an essential nature, such as grasper and grasped is constructed by the naïve: the selflessness of such phenomena, or, the fact of these phenomena not possessing independent identities, concerns the identity that has been constructed for them by the naïve. But this does not touch on that identity which is inexpressible and which serves as the theoretical and practical scope of Buddhas.

So, there is a way to introduce the fact of phenomena not having independent identities even on the part of the doctrine that there is nothing but presentation of content—namely, in terms of the absence of that identity which is constructed for one event by another mental event, characterized, as are all mental events, by the presentation of content. Contrast this with an unrestricted denial of the existence of phenomena in each and every respect.

Contrariwise, were it the case that one mental event were to have another mental event *as its object*, this would mean that the fact that there is just presentation of content could not be established, on account of mental events involving the presentation of content being possessed of objects.

(4. The Internal Architecture of Objects)

—How should one understand that the Blessed One spoke of the existence of the sensory conditions of experiential awareness such as visible hue with the kind of implied intent you have reconstructed for him? How should one understand, moreover, that there just do not exist any objects that individually come to serve as the physical and causal conditions for our awareness of such things as visible hue?

Since **the ostensibly physical object is not a unity, nor is it a manifold consisting in minima; or an aggregation: since the minimal part cannot be proven. (11)**

What does this assert? Any sensory condition, such as hue and the like, that could become the physical occasion and object of an episode presenting content such as hue is possibly either something unitary, as the philosophers of the Vaiśeṣika tradition imagine a part-possessing form to be; or, a manifold consisting in minima; or an aggregation of minima.

First of all, the ostensibly physical sensible object is not a unity: because there is no apprehension anywhere at all of a part-possessing form that is separate from its parts. Neither is it a manifold, because minimal parts are not individually apprehended. Nor is it the case that those minimal parts, once aggregated, come to be the ostensibly physical sensory object: since a minimal part is not established as a variety of unitary concrete particular.

—*Why is it not so established?*

Through the simultaneous conjunction with six, the minimal part has six parts. (12ab) Given simultaneous conjunction with six other minimal parts through the six dimensions of possible orientation in space—namely, up and down, front and back, left and right—the consequence is that the minimal part must have six parts: on account of the impossibility of one thing occupying a place occupied by another.

On account of the six co-occupying the same place, the cluster would have the measure of a single minimal part. (12cd)

Consider the following alternative possibility: let the place of one minimal part serve as the place where six minimal parts occur. In such a case, because all occupy the same place, the entire cluster would have the measure and extent of a single minimal part—since these minimal parts cannot exclude one another. In this scenario, no *cluster* of any sort would show up in experience.

The philosophers of Kashmir associated with the tradition of *The Vibhāṣa* here interject:

—"*There is absolutely no conjunction of minima—since they do not have any parts. Let's be done with the absurdity that would entail! But aggregations, on the other hand, do conjoin with one another.*"

Let us ask of them whether or not the aggregations of minima are separable from those minima: **Given that there is no conjoining of minima, what is it that is being conjoined when those minima are aggregated? (13ab)**

And it is not merely owing to their partlessness that the conjunction of minima cannot be established. (13cd)

Should you now claim that even aggregations do not conjoin with one another, then you should not say that the partlessness of minima is the reason that the conjunction of minima cannot be established: for the conjunction of aggregations that have parts cannot be affirmed either.

Therefore, minima cannot be established as a variety of singular concrete particular, whether or not you accept the conjunction of minima.

It does not make sense to take something that has actual spatial parts to be simple. (14ab) For if a minimal part has spatial parts—given its having a forward part just insofar as it has a back part—how can it make sense that this kind of minimal part, whose identity consists in having such parts, is simple?

Contrariwise, how could there be shade or obstruction? (14c) If no individual minima possessed actual spatial parts, then, when the sun is shining, how is it that in one place there is shade while there is sunlight in another? For that minimal part, treated as a simple, would not have any further spatial part where light would not be present.

And how could a minimal part obstruct another were there no distinction of spatial parts? For, on such an account, when some B enters into the space of some A, there is no remaining spatial part of A in which there could be resistance to B. In the absence of any resistance exhibited by minimal parts, the entire aggregate of minima would reduce to the dimension of just one minimal part on account of having the same location, as argued above.

—Do you not, then, accept that these two, shade and obstruction, are predicated of a cluster, and not a minimal part?

Do you, for your part, accept that the cluster of which one would predicate shade and obstruction is something other than the minimal parts?

—No, we would not say that.

If the cluster is not something distinct, the two cannot be predicated of it. (14d) If you do not wish to have the cluster be something other than the minimal parts, then it surely follows that the two, shade and obstruction, cannot be its properties.

—This is speculation regarding arrangement. Why such anxiety over whether or not the ostensibly physical object is a minimal part or an aggregation? The defining characteristic of such sensible things like hue, for example, has not been negated.

What, then, do you take to be their defining characteristic?

—Being the physical occasion for the sensory systems, such as vision and the like, and being blue, and so on.

This is precisely what is being determined: consider the physical occasion for vision, for example, which you exemplify with the colors blue, yellow, and so on—is it a single concrete particular, or many?

—What follows from this?

We've already discussed the flaws that result when it is treated as something multiple. **If the physical occasion for vision were unitary, there could not be gradual motion; neither would simultaneous apprehension and nonapprehension be possible; neither could there be the simultaneous occurrence of various distinct things; nor could there be unseen minuteness. (15)**

That is, if one conceives the occasion of visual sensation, such as a hue like blue, for example, to be impartite and not manifold, and if one conceives it to be a unitary concrete particular, then the following would be true:

(i) Gradual traversal of—or, continuous motion across—the earth becomes impossible: for a single step would have to traverse the whole.

(ii) Nor would it be the case that one would apprehend the facing part of something at the same time as one fails to apprehend its nonfacing part: for it does not make any sense to speak of both apprehending and not apprehending, at the same time, the exact same unitary and impartite thing.

(iii) You could not find in a single place such discrete and various things as elephants, horses, and so on: because it follows from the above proposal that one thing would be precisely where another is. For another thing, we apprehend the palpable absence of two discrete things in the gap between them. So, we're now forced to ask: how then does it make sense to take it that a single place is both occupied and not occupied by two discrete things?

(iv) Lastly, take the case of minute aquatic creatures that exhibit the same features as large ones, just on a smaller scale. If you imagine these small-scaled creatures to be distinct concrete particulars solely on the basis of differences in characteristics, and not otherwise (say, on the basis of magnitude), these creatures will prove not to be imperceptible.

Given the above arguments, it is necessary to conceive of distinctions in terms of minimal parts. But the minimal part is not established as something unitary. Given that it is not so established, it follows that such things as hue are not established as being the physical occasions for their corresponding sensory capacities, such as vision. Thus, the fact that there is nothing but presentation of content is proved.

(5. The Weight of Perception)

—The existence or nonexistence of something is determined on the strength of epistemic criteria, and of all such epistemic criteria, perceptual evidence is the weightiest. Given the nonexistence of objects, how could there be a cognitive episode of awareness with the following content: "This experience of mine is an instance of perceptual evidence," or, "This is right before my eyes"?

Perceptual judgment—or **cognitive awareness regarding perceptual evidence—is analogous to what happens in dreams and similar experiences (16ab)**, occurring even in the absence of objects, as was previously intimated.

And to add to the above, **the object is not *actually seen* at such time when there is cognitive awareness regarding perceptual evidence. How then can one affirm an object's being perceptually evident, or, that the episode counts an instance of perceptual evidence? (16bcd)**

This is the additional argument: when a cognitive episode regarding perceptual evidence—a cognitive episode, that is, with the content "I am enjoying an instance of perceptual evidence"—comes about, at such time the object is not actually *seen*. This is for two reasons: firstly, there is the fact that the analytic work of discerning or judging involved in such a cognitive episode can only derive from *cognitive* awareness; and, secondly, there is the fact of strictly visual awareness having ceased to be operative by the time cognitive awareness comes into play.

Granted all of this, how then can one want to affirm the object's being perceptually evident, or, that the episode counts as an instance of perceptual evidence? In particular, this is especially pressing for one who advances the momentariness of all things; it must be especially pressing, that is, for any philosopher who believes that instances of hue, flavor, and the like, have entirely ceased to be operative at the time cognitive awareness comes into play.

—What was not experienced previously cannot be experientially remembered by a subsequent episode of cognitive awareness—thus, necessarily, it must come about because of an experience of an object, and that kind of experience is called "seeing." *It's in this way that one can commit to the perceptually evident status of physical occasions for experience, beginning with such things as hue.*

This idea that there is experiential memory *of an object* that has been previously experienced has not been established, since, **as was previously stated, a mental event occurs having as its manifest content such things as objects. (17ab)** I have already discussed how even in the absence of an object, a mental event such as visual awareness comes about having as its manifest content such things as objects. **Experiential memory comes about on the basis of such an event. (17b)**

On account of some such mental event presenting content, there occurs a nonsensory and cognitive mental episode. This episode, linked to the mental function of experiential memory, enjoys the former mental event as its content; it also involves the conceptual categorization of that former mental event's content, such as hue and the like. Thus, from the occurrence of experiential memory one cannot conclude that there is such a thing as *the* immediate *experience of an object.*

—If, analogous to the case of dreaming, the mental events of even those who are awake were to have unreal objects as their content, then it follows that people would come to understand their unreality by themselves. But this is not the case. Therefore, it is not the case that all cases of our experiential uptake of objects is as in a dream—without, that is, objects.

This is not indicative, since **when dreaming, one who has not yet awakened does not understand the unreality of the content experienced. (17cd)** Even so, those asleep with a sleep of the lingering traces of habituation to unreal conceptual constructions—seeing, as one does in a dream, objects that do not exist—are not yet awake: they do not truly understand the nonexistence of these objects.

There is a variety of awareness transcending ordinary modes of awareness that is nonconceptual and which serves as an antidote to conceptual construction. When someone is awakened through acquiring this variety of awareness, and because of making real and coming face-to-face with the purified mode of ordinary awareness that follows it, they truly understand what is the case: the unreality of ostensibly physical occasions of content. This situation is our own.

(6. The Consequences of Revisionary Philosophy)

—Let us grant that mental events presenting objects as their manifest content occur on the part of individuals solely as a consequence of specific processes of change that are proper to those individuals, and not on account of a particular object. Consider now the fact that the presentation of content that individuals may enjoy is constrained and shaped by whether one associates with true or false friends, whether one hears true or false doctrines: how do you establish these constraints, given that there is no real association with friends, be they true or untrue, nor, on your account, could one learn anything through instruction?

Mental events presenting content are constrained with respect to one another by virtue of the fact of mutual influence. (18ab) Because all beings exert a constitutive and determining influence on the mental events of each other, it comes about that there is a mutually effected constraint on the presentation of content in accordance with circumstances. "Mutually" here means "reciprocally."

Thus, a distinct mental event occurs in one individual on account of a specific mental event occurring on the part of another individual, and not because of a distinct object.

—Were mental events presenting content not to be possessed of objects even in the case of those who are awake and just in the way that they are not for those asleep, why are the consequences of what is done—consequences that can be either desired or undesired, based on whether the conduct is wholesome or unwholesome—not equivalent for those who are asleep and those who are not?

Since **thought in sleep and dreams is afflicted and overcome by torpor—that's why the consequences of what is done by those asleep and those awake are not equivalent. (18cd)** This is the cause for the situation presented above, not the real existence of objects.

—If all this is just presentation of content, then no one has a body or voice. How, then, does the death of sheep and other creatures violently handled by butchers come about? Or, if their death is not a function of anything these butchers have done, why are butchers connected to the morally censorable act of taking a life?

Killing is an unnatural deformation brought about by particular mental events on the part of others—just as, for example, the elision of memory undergone by some is brought about by the mental powers of demons and the like. (19)

The analogy is this: for some people, deformations of natural psychological processes come about due to possession by spirits, visions, dreams, or elision of memory. And these are caused by the mental power of either demonic beings or human beings with extraordinary powers. For example, Sāraṇa was induced to experience a dream through the empowering control of the noble Mahākātyāyana; or consider how the Titan Vemacitra was overcome by the disordered hostility of the forest sages.

On analogy with such cases, killing should be understood to involve the following: influenced by specific mental events on the part of certain beings, there comes to be a certain unnatural deformation in some other being that interrupts or blocks its life, and owing to which there is death—defined as the termination of something's continuing to be a particular life-form.

Else, how did the Daṇḍaka forest's being depopulated and empty come about on account of the anger of the sages? (20ab)

If one does not concede that the death of beings is influenced by specific mental events of others, then why did the Blessed One, demonstrating the fact that mental violence is among the most censorable forms of violence, ask the householder Upāli: "O Householder, have you heard how these forests, the Daṇḍaka, Mataṅga, and Kaliṅga were emptied and rendered ritually pure?"

He replied, "I have heard, O Gautama, that it was through the sages' malice of mind."

Contrariwise, how could the greatly censorious nature of mental violence be demonstrated by this narrative? (20cd)

Take the following way of construing it: "The beings dwelling there were destroyed by demons who were pleased by these sages, but they were not killed directly on account of a censorable instance of malice of mind on the part of the sages." On that interpretation, how is it demonstrated by this action that mental violence is a greater moral violation than physical or verbal violence? That is only established based on the killing of so many by a censorious act of malice of mind alone.

—If all this is just presentation of content, then do those who know other minds know the mind of another, or not?

What turns on this question?

—If they do not know, how can they count as those who know other minds?

Let them therefore count as knowing other minds: **the epistemic state of those who know other minds does not conform with its object.**

—How so?

It is analogous to knowing one's own mind. (21abc)

—In what sense does even knowing one's own mind not conform to its object?

On account of unknowing—it is analogous to the cognitive scope of Buddhas. (21cd) The scope of Buddhas, or what Buddhas know, is constitutively inexpressible. On account of our unknowing with respect to what Buddhas know, both knowledge of our own mind and knowledge of the minds of others fail to conform to their objects: they fail to conform to their objects insofar as these kinds of knowing involve content that appears falsely. They involve content that appears falsely on account of the fact that these modes of knowing have not yet abandoned the conceptual construction of that which grasps and that which is grasped.

The fact of there being just presentation of content is of profound depths, its divisions and details without end. Given this, **I have furnished this demonstration of the fact of there being nothing but presentation of content insofar as my own capacities permit; in its entirety it is beyond thought. (22abcd)** Which is to say that this, in all its aspects, cannot be thought through by the likes of me, since it goes beyond the scope of reasoning.

—For whom, then, can it in its entirety be said to be the scope of knowledge and action?

To answer that, this text concludes with this: **it is the scope of Buddhas. (22d)**

For this, in all its aspects, is the scope of Buddhas: on account of their not being obstructed with respect to knowing all things to be known, in all ways.

NOTES

INTRODUCTION

1. The phrase derives from Jonathan Lear, "Leaving the World Alone," *Journal of Philosophy* 79 (1982): 382–403; 385–386. Such use is typically restricted to human cases and involves meaning-rich content. I shall use it in a more general sense. I have been well served by the history of consciousness in Timothy M. Harrison, *Coming To: Consciousness and Natality in Early Modern England* (Chicago: University of Chicago Press, 2020).
2. Peter Godfrey-Smith, *Other Minds: The Octopus, the Sea, and the Deep Origins of Consciousness* (New York: Farrar, Straus and Giroux, 2017).
3. One could describe such a view as "ecological," after J. J. Gibson's use of this word to gesture at the complementarity of animal and environment. See J. J. Gibson, *The Ecological Approach to Visual Perception* (Boston: Houghton Mifflin, 1986). I will try to refrain from using such connections in this book, attempting over time to derive my characterizations of Vasubandhu (to the extent possible) with concepts that he either used or had available to him.
4. Maria Heim, *Voice of the Buddha: Buddhaghosa on the Immeasurable Words* (Oxford: Oxford University Press, 2018), 42.
5. For book-length philosophical attempts to generate such a picture, one might consider beginning with Jonathan C. Gold, *Paving the Great Way: Vasubandhu's Unifying Buddhist Philosophy* (New York: Columbia University Press, 2015). See also the earlier (and unjustly neglected) efforts in Thích Mãn Giác, *The Philosophy of Vasubandhu* (Los Angeles: College of Buddhist Studies, 1989); Le Manh That, "The Philosophy of Vasubandhu" (PhD diss., University of Wisconsin, 1974). Scholars can now agree that there is a narrow circle of works that were authored by the same person, a circle within which I have circumscribed my interpretive claims on behalf of Vasubandhu. But there is an outer circle of works ascribed to Vasubandhu, on which there is little or no consensus. I have nothing to add to the difficult issues this wider corpus entails. For the complicated textual situation, see Matthew T. Kapstein, "Who Wrote the Trisvabhāvanirdeśa? Reflections on an Enigmatic Text and Its Place in the History of Buddhist Philosophy," *Journal of Indian Philosophy* 46, no. 1 (2018): 1–30; H. Buescher,

"Distinguishing the Two Vasubandhus, the Bhāṣyakāra and the Kośakāra, as Vijñānavāda-Yogācāra Authors," in *The Foundation for Yoga Practitioners*, ed. U. T. Kragh (Cambridge, MA: Harvard University Department of South Asian Studies, 2013), 368–396.

6. More generally, all translations from Sanskrit, unless otherwise indicated, are my own. To keep this work accessible and given the constraints of space, I have not included the Sanskrit, but I have pointed to existing translations (typically the most easily accessible translation) where available for comparison with my own. Thus, for example, when citing from my own translation of *The Twenty Verses* (included in the appendix), I cite the corresponding passages in the edition and translation in J. A. Silk, *Materials Toward the Study of Vasubandhu's Viṁśikā (I): Sanskrit and Tibetan Critical Editions of the Verses and Autocommentary; An English Translation and Annotations* (Cambridge, MA: Harvard University Department of South Asian Studies, 2016).
7. Amber D. Carpenter, "Transformative Vision: Coming to See the Buddha's Reality," in *Buddhist Literature as Philosophy, Buddhist Philosophy as Literature*, ed. Rafal K. Stepien (Albany: State University of New York Press, 2020), 35–61; 46. Her next example, that of a gymnasium of the soul, is even more evocative and connects with themes of practices of self, which I take up at the end of chapter 7.
8. I am here adapting a phrase from Elizabeth Barnes, *The Minority Body: A Theory of Disability* (Oxford: Oxford University Press, 2016), ix.
9. I have not wished to over-specify a mechanism of error when speaking of these examples. For important clarifications, see Paul J. Griffiths, *On Being Mindless: Buddhist Meditation and the Mind-Body Problem* (LaSalle, IL: Open Court Press 1991), 81–82. See also Junjie Chu, "A Study of Satimira in Dignāga's Definition of Pseudo-Perception (PS 1.7cd–8ab)," *Wiener Zeitschrift für die Kunde Südasiens* 48 (2004): 113–149; 114.
10. Vasubandhu associates hungry ghosts with a primary dwelling (*mūlasthāna*) five hundred leagues underground where Yama (in Brahmanical lore, the ruler of the dead) dwells as their king. Hungry ghosts who are found elsewhere have been dispatched (*visṛtā*) from there. See Leo M. Pruden, trans., *Abhidharmakosabhasyam of Vasubandhu* (Berkeley, CA: Asian Humanities Press, 1988–1990), 2:460. I owe to Andy Rotman (in personal conversation and based on his forthcoming work on hungry ghosts) the following references: *Eric Huntington, Creating the Universe: Depictions of the Cosmos in Himalayan Buddhism* (Seattle: University of Washington Press, 2019), 40. On typologies of different types of hungry ghosts (including those that distinguish between hungry ghosts that do and do not coexist with humans), see Daniel M. Stuart, "A Less Traveled Path: Meditation and Textual Practice in the *Saddharmasm rtyupasthana(sutra)*" (PhD diss., University of California, Berkeley, 2012), 50–51. For my purposes, the crucial point is that there can be environmental overlap and overlap in the attitudes of human and hungry ghost to the experiential contents typically available to the latter.
11. On the history of these beings in Buddhist cosmology, with notes on their wider South Asian counterparts among the dead (in connection with rites that are designed to turn the departed into ancestors), see David Gordon White, "'Dakkhiṇa' and 'Agnicayana': An Extended Application of Paul Mus's Typology," *History of Religions* 26, no. 2 (November 1986):

188–213. See also Adeana S. McNicholl, "Celestial Seductresses and Hungry Ghosts: Preta Narratives in Early Indian Buddhism" (PhD diss., Stanford University, 2019).

12. Cf. Silk, *Materials*, 41.
13. As I will often have reason to quote from another of Vasubandhu's works, the magisterial *Abhidharmakośa* (in some six-hundred verses) and commentary thereon (here, at times, treated as a single work), let me briefly explain why I will refer to it with (the sadly) unusual rendering, *The Cutting Edge of Buddhist Thought*. Though the title is frequently translated by scholars with *kośa* meaning "treasury"—which it often enough can mean in Sanskrit—this is not what Vasubandhu himself says. He has in mind *kośa* in the sense of a sheath of a sword, as he makes clear in his commentary to verse 1.2cd, where he offers two ways of resolving the compound title: "'The Sheath of the [Sword That Is the] Abhidharma'" and "'[The Sword] Whose Sheath Is the Abhidharma.'" I wish to highlight this metaphorical weaponization of knowledge and its function with a comparable intellectual metaphor used in our own time, though technically I suppose it should be noted that the reference is to the Sarvāstivāda Abhidharma canon as the cutting edge of Buddhist systematic thought. On the title, see Bruce Cameron Hall, "Vasubandhu on Aggregates, Spheres, and Components: Being Chapter One of the Abhidharmakośa" (PhD diss., Harvard University, 1983), 47; Alexis Sanderson, "The Sarvāstivāda and Its Critics: Anātmavāda and the Theory of Karma," in *Buddhism into the Year 2000*, ed. Dhammakaya Foundation (Bangkok: Dhammakaya Foundation, 1994), 33–48; 43.
14. *Kośa*, commentary on 4.58d; cf. Pruden, *Abhidharmakosabhasyam of Vasubandhu*, 2:634. For "mercy of/struck by" I am taking into account the variant readings, *abhinunnā* and *abhitunnā*.
15. See Roy Tzohar, "Imagine Being a Preta: Early Indian Yogācāra Approaches to Intersubjectivity," *Sophia* 56, no. 2 (2017): 337–354.
16. Can one not imagine, for example, a phenomenologist among the hungry ghosts realizing that the experience of frustration intrinsic to their situation might suggest that their experiences are *erroneous representations* of the kind of causes which underwrite human experience? On differing explanations of whether this is meant to show that the hungry ghosts enjoy erroneous representations, or rather to call in question the very idea of representations, see José Cabezón, *Dose of Emptiness: An Annotated Translation of the "Stong Thun Chen Mo" of Mkhas Grub Dge Legs Dpal Bzang* (New York: State University of New York Press, 1998), 341, 334–345. See also Daniel Cozort, *Unique Tenets of the Middle Way Consequence School* (Ithaca, NY: Snow Lion, 1998), 116.
17. See the discussion in John Locke, *An Essay Concerning Human Understanding*, ed. Peter H. Nidditch (Oxford: Clarendon Press, 1979), 389. Unlike Locke's case of inverted color content, we are here dealing with different communities of people; furthermore, we are not stipulating that the inversion of content be indiscernible (nor requiring that the behavior of those with inverted content be indistinguishable). Lastly, the content thought of as inverted in the Buddhist case would not count as simple in Locke's sense of that term. It is not obviously immune from assessment in terms of its being true or false.
18. This will not generalize, but I have been inspired here by a fairly common account of the way in which hungry ghosts experience content—as in verse 95 of the *Suhṛllekha*; Padma Tendzin, *Suhridlekha* (Varanasi: Central Institute of High Tibetan Studies, 2002).

19. I will go into this in much greater detail in chapters 4 through 7. I would, however, like to note that Xuanzang at least agrees with this being the central lesson when he says, "In reality, if a consciousness manifests itself as a region or land, it is because that region can serve as a support or be of some use to its material bodies. Hence the consciousness will manifest itself as a region as long as that region can support those bodies or be of some use to them." He later adds that this account should be extended to descriptions of the way in which different lifeforms (hungry ghosts, human beings, gods) do not have available to them the same experiences. See Wei Tat, *Ch'eng Wei-Shih Lun: Doctrine of Mere Consciousness* (Hong Kong: Ch'eng Wei-Shih Lun Publication Committee, 1973), 147.
20. Quoted in Branka Arsić, *On Leaving: A Reading in Emerson* (Cambridge, MA: Harvard University Press, 2010), 101.
21. Ben-Ami Scharfstein, *A Comparative History of World Philosophy from the Upanisads to Kant* (Albany: State University of New York Press, 1998), 414.
22. Leaning on Hilary Putnam's now infamous thought experiment, B. K. Matilal thought of Vasubandhu's life-forms as "brains in a vat," tricked out by the know-how of a mad scientist of the future to enjoy the full range of human experiences of the world. B. K. Matilal, *Perception: An Essay on Classical Indian Theories of Knowledge* (Oxford: Clarendon Press, 1986), 231.
23. See chapter 5 of Shlomo Biderman, *Crossing Horizons: World, Self, and Language in Indian and Western Thought* (New York, Columbia University Press, 2008). John Dunne, however, has suggested that these karmic worlds (as he calls them) may have been used by Buddhist philosophers in ways analogous to the philosophical use of possible worlds in contemporary philosophy. The entire issue deserves closer study, given the complexity attendant on contemporary understandings of what is at issue in possible world descriptions. See John D. Dunne, *Foundations of Dharmakīrti's Philosophy* (Somerville, MA: Wisdom Publications, 2004), 186n61. In chapter 5, I'll mention a few cases where Buddhists have been explicit about thinking modally with something called Buddha fields, and in the conclusion to the book briefly take up different ways a few different Buddhists have construed the kind of examples adduced by Vasubandhu.
24. Nelson Goodman, *The Structure of Appearance* (Cambridge, MA: Harvard University Press, 1951), 4–5. I am also thinking of David Wiggins saying that "it is perfectly notorious that not every story corresponds to a possible world." David Wiggins, *Sameness and Substance Renewed* (Oxford: Oxford University Press, 2001), 66.
25. I draw on Vincent Eltschinger, "Turning Hermeneutics Into Apologetics—Reasoning and Rationality Under Changing Historical Circumstances," in *Scriptural Authority, Reason and Action*, ed. Vincent Eltschinger and Helmut Krasser (Vienna: Österreichischen Akademie der Wissenschaften, 2013), 71–147; especially 73–76. See also the work on which the above essay draws, Sara L. McClintock, *Omniscience and the Rhetoric of Reason, Śāntarakṣita and Kamalaśīla on Rationality, Argumentation, and Religious Authority* (Somerville, MA: Wisdom Publications, 2010).
26. Kumārila Bhaṭṭa, for example, explicitly turned away from any argument in Vasubandhu's tradition that takes its bearing from the nature of objects, preferring instead to discuss only such arguments as could be warranted on the basis of the deliverances of perceptual

experience. As Sucaritamiśra reads it, this is a refusal to accept that the argument from atomism can have a weight independent of arguments from perception. See verses 17–18 of chapter 3 (*Nirālambana-vāda*) of the *Ślokavārttika* in Ganganath Jha, *Slokavartika: Translated from the Sanskrit with Extracts from the Commentaries Kasika of Sucarita Misra and Nyayaratnakara of Partha Sarthi Misra* (Delhi: Sri Satguru Publications, 1983), 121. I think this can be extended to include arguments involving revisionary metaphysical commitments.

27. Quoted in Alice Ambrose, "Wittgenstein on Mathematical Proof," *Mind* 91 (1982): 264–272; 264.
28. Li Zhi, *A Book to Burn and a Book to Keep (Hidden): Selected Writings*, ed. Rivi Handler-Spitz, Pauline C. Lee, and Haun Saussy (New York: Columbia University Press, 2016), 264.
29. Quoted in Zhi, *A Book to Burn*, 264n4.
30. Martin Heidegger, *Being and Time*, trans. John Macquarrie and Edward Robinson (New York: Harper Perennial, 2008), 251.
31. A superb resource—judicious, meticulous, and well-nigh exhaustive—for those wishing an introduction to Vasubandhu's *Twenty Verses* as a form of idealism may be found in Birgit Kellner and John Taber, "Studies in Yogācāra-Vijñānavāda Idealism I: The Interpretation of Vasubandhu's *Viṃśikā*," *Asiatische Studien* 68, no. 3 (2014): 709–756.
32. Such care is warranted, for the mind, as a cognitive instrument, is also considered a capacity analogous to sensory capacities. In my remarks above I have been guided by an argument that, in his commentary to Vasubandhu's *Thirty Verses*, Sthiramati believes can be pressed against Vasubandhu's view. The argument runs as follows: "An external object is admitted to be a causal condition—the kind of condition that an intentional object of a mental event is—by virtue of producing an event having itself as content, and not by virtue of being *simply a cause*: since in that case there would be no entailment of a distinction from other causal conditions (such as the immediately preceding mental event, among other conditions enumerated by Buddhist philosophers)" (my translation). Hartmut Buescher, *Sthiramati's Triṃśikāvijñaptibhāṣya: Critical Editions of the Sanskrit Text and Its Tibetan Translation* (Vienna: Verlag der Österreichischen Akademie der Wissenschaften, 2007), 42.
33. I will explain my choices for this translation as we go on in the book, particularly in chapter 6. But for now, one might take the relevant clause to say this: "Due to a seed which has attained a particular transformation" (*svabījāt pariṇāmaviśeṣaprāptāt*). In Kellner and Taber, "Studies in Yogācāra-Vijñānavāda Idealism," 741. The points will go through here regardless.
34. Cf. Silk, *Materials*, 85.
35. Importantly, Vasubandhu's appeal to dispositional powers is analogized with the case of experiential memory: "What is being a seed? With respect to an individual [*ātmabhāva*], it is the power [*śakti*] for an afflictive experience to arise born from a prior afflictive experience, as is the capacity for experiential memory to arise born from prior experiential awareness [*anubhava-jñāna*], and the capacity for sprouts, and the like, to produce a grain of rice bred from a prior grain of rice." From the commentary to *Kośa* 2.36d; translation after William S. Waldron, *The Buddhist Unconscious: The* Ālaya-vijñāna *in the Context of Indian Buddhist Thought* (New York: RutledgeCurzon, 2003), 74. See also Sean M. Smith, "A Buddhist Analysis of Affective Bias," *Journal of Indian Philosophy* 1 (2019): 1–31.

36. Cited in Stephen Jay Gould, *Ever Since Darwin: Reflections in Natural History* (New York: W. W. Norton, 1979), 25.
37. This *more-and-less than human* form of mind, then, involves a kind of generality, which can result in a thinning out of the specific natural-historical force of the life-form we now express. But it is entirely different from the generality that attaches to Kant's notion of "rational being." Any being, either alien (a form of life in radically different conditions, perhaps so causally remote from our own that it is best treated as independent of our own case) or imaginary, can be thought to satisfy the requirements for counting as a rational being on Kant's view. One could then theorize what it means to count as such without taking into account any of the constitutive differences between different forms of life that, on Vasubandhu's view, ought to constrain our thinking. My remarks here, down to the vocabulary I have used, have been stimulated by Michael Thompson, "Forms of Nature: 'First,' 'Second,' 'Living,' 'Rational' and 'Phronetic,'" in *Freiheit: Stuttgarter Hegel-Kongress 2011*, ed. Gunnar Hindrichs and Axel Honneth (Frankfurt: Vittorio Klostermann, 2013), 701–735.

1. PRESENTATION, OBJECTS, REPRESENTATIONS

1. If one wishes to use "intentionality" to describe the fact of being directed at content, I ask the reader to keep in mind that we shall have to mean what some philosophers might term "concrete intentionality," to use Galen Strawson's phrase. Concrete intentionality has to do with "intentionality considered as a real, concrete phenomenon, something that can be correctly attributed to concrete entities like ourselves and dogs—to concrete states we are in or concrete occurrences in us." Galen Strawson, *Real Materialism and Other Essays* (Oxford: Clarendon Press, 2008), 281.
2. In his introduction to *The Twenty Verses*, Vasubandhu says this: the basic claim is that "the adverbial qualification 'just' is used for the sake of ruling out objects: just this episode of awareness arises, having an object as its manifest content . . . but there is no actual object whatsoever." Cf. J. A. Silk, *Materials Toward the Study of Vasubandhu's Viṁśikā (I): Sanskrit and Tibetan Critical Editions of the Verses and Autocommentary; An English Translation and Annotations* (Cambridge, MA: Harvard University Department of South Asian Studies, 2016), 31. More basically, at the end of 10d it is implied that any notion of objects as sources of content is incompatible with Vasubandhu's view. Silk, *Materials*, 79.
3. As discussed by Hayden White, the view is comparative: philosophy and lyric poetry resist translation in a way that narrative does not. See Haydn White, "The Value of Narrativity in the Representation of Reality," *Critical Inquiry* 7, no. 1 (Autumn 1980): 5–27; 6.
4. Cf. Silk, *Materials*, 31.
5. My comments are based on the first set of Vasubandhu's explanations of the three terms for mind presented in *Kośa* 2.34a–b; Leo M. Pruden, trans. *Abhidharmakosabhasyam of Vasubandhu* (Berkeley, CA: Asian Humanities Press, 1988–1990), 1:205. Thus, Vasubandhu refers to the verb *manute*, from the root *man*, indicating thinking while he glosses *vijñāna* with the verbal

form *vijānāti*, which Yaśomitra explains as the discernment, in particular, of the intentional object that serves as the content of an episode of awareness (*vijānāty ālambanamiti vijñānam*). A discussion of this may be found in William S. Waldron, *The Buddhist Unconscious: The* ālaya-vijñāna *in the Context of Indian Buddhist Thought* (New York: RoutledgeCurzon, 2003), 219n17. See also William Montgomery McGovern, *A Manual of Buddhist Philosophy*, vol. 1, *Cosmology* (London: Kegan Paul, Trench and Trubner, 1923), 132–134. Vasubandhu goes on to offer another semantic explanation for the different words *manas*, *vijñāna*, and *citta* immediately in the same text, and offers yet another account in *On the Five Heaps*; see Artemus B. Engle, *The Inner Science of Buddhist Practice: Vasubandhu's Summary of the Five Heaps with Commentary by Sthiramati* (Ithaca, NY: Snow Lion, 2009), 239.

6. Vasubandhu distinguishes between explanations here. Some would have the factor be called *citta* because it serves as the means by which actions and states evaluated according to moral criteria "accumulate" (as Yaśomitra makes clear: *kuśalam akuśalaṃ vā cinotīty arthaḥ*); others explain the word by pointing to the fact that the factor is constituted by the traces of intentional action of different moral kinds. See comments on *Kośa* 2.34ab in Pruden, *Abhidharmakosabhasyam of Vasubandhu*, 1:205.
7. Vasubandhu is one such philosopher, as he makes clearer elsewhere. In *On the Five Heaps*, he declares a distinction between episodic mental events and a continuous mental process. See Engle, *The Inner Science of Buddhist Practice*, 329. In *The Thirty Verses*, Vasubandhu distinguishes between three types of mental processes. For background to these different models, which are *not* presupposed in *The Twenty Verses*, see William S. Waldron, "How Innovative Is the Ālayavijñāna? The Ālayavijñāna in the Context of Canonical and Abhidharma Vijñaana Theory Part II," *Journal of Indian Philosophy* 23, no. 1 (March 1995): 9–51; Jowita Kramer, "Some Remarks on the Proofs of the Store Mind (*Ālayavijñāna*) and the Development of the Concept of *Manas*," in *Text, History, and Philosophy*, ed. Bart Dessein and Weijen Teng (Leiden: Brill, 2016), 146–169; for an account of how Vasubandhu uses the expanded model of mental process to offer a revised model of self-consciousness, see Jonardon Ganeri, "Subjectivity, Selfhood and the Use of the Word 'I,' in *Self, No Self? Perspectives from Analytical, Phenomenological, and Indian Traditions*, ed. Mark Siderits, Evan Thompson, and Dan Zahavi (Oxford: Oxford University Press, 2010), 176–192.
8. All mental—and only mental—events exhibit intentionality, that is, contentfulness (in Sanskrit, *sālambanatā*), and all and only mental events further involve a mode by which intentional content is apprehended and engaged (*ākāra*). See *Kośa* 2.34b–d in Pruden, *Abhidharmakosabhasyam of Vasubandhu*, 1:205; for a crisp statement, see Harivarman's comment: "If a dharma can take objects (**ālambana*), it is named *citta*." In Qian Lin, "Mind in Dispute: The Section on Mind in Harivarman's *Tattvasiddhi" (PhD diss., University of Washington, 2015), 237. See also Jonardon Ganeri, *Attention, Not Self* (Oxford: Oxford University Press, 2017), 9; see Evan Thompson, *Waking, Dreaming, Being: Self and Consciousness in Neuroscience, Meditation, and Philosophy* (New York: Columbia University Press, 2017), 35–37.
9. I shall stay silent on the ontological status of these mental functions, and the very real difficulty that modelling the distinction between mind and mental functions presented to Buddhists. Except to say this: Dhammajoti notes Saṁghabhadra's contention that in his

time, the fifth century CE, the issue was vexed. See K. L. Dhammajoti, *Entrance into the Supreme Doctrine: Skandhila's Abhidharmāvatāra* (Hong Kong: University of Hong Kong, 2008), 129n10. Harivarman devoted an entire section of his **Tattvasiddhi* to the controversy (see Lin, "Mind in Dispute"). For thinking of the mind as a determinable frame I have been inspired by the discussion of *citta-viśeṣa* in Harivarman's argument (developing on Śrīlāta)—without necessarily taking on board the associated ontological commitments. See Lin, "Mind in Dispute, 252, 256.

10. In *On the Five Heaps*, Vasubandhu asks: "What is an instance of awareness? The presentation of intentional content" (*vijñānaṃ katamat? ālambanam vijñaptiḥ*). See Engle, *The Inner Science of Buddhist Practice*, 239. In *The Cutting Edge of Buddhist Thought* (1.16a), Vasubandhu defines awareness as directed presentations, or presentations directed at particular sensory occasions (*viṣayaṃ viṣayaṃ prati vijñaptiḥ*). See Bruce Cameron Hall, "Vasubandhu on Aggregates, Spheres, and Components: Being Chapter One of the Abhidharmakośa" (PhD diss., Harvard University, 1983), 84. See also Hugh B. Urban and Paul J. Griffiths, "What Else Remains in Śūnyatā? An Investigation of Terms for Mental Imagery in the Madhyāntavibhāga-Corpus," *Journal of the International Association of Buddhist Studies* 17, no. 1 (1994): 1–26; Ah-Yueh Yeh, "The Characteristics of 'Vijñāna' and 'Vijñapti' on the basis of Vasubandhu's *Pañcaskandhaprakaraṇa*," *Annals of the Bhandarkar Oriental Research Institute* 60 (1979): 175–198; Bruce Cameron Hall, "The Meaning of Vijñapti in Vasubandhu's Concept of Mind," *Journal of the International Association of Buddhist Studies* 9, no. 1 (1986): 7–23.
11. Engle, *The Inner Science of Buddhist Practice*, 267–268. The outsourcing of the function (*kriyā*) of experiential (or, qualitative) awareness to feeling (*vedanā*), rather than to mentality simpliciter, is older. See the arguments in Lin, "Mind in Dispute," 86. For a fuller defense of the claim made here, see Sonam Kachru, "The Mind in Pain: The View from Buddhist Systematic and Narrative Thought," in *The Bloomsbury Research Handbook of Emotions in Classical Indian Philosophy*, ed. Maria Heim, Chakravarthi Ram-Prasad, and Roy Tzohar (London: Bloomsbury Academic, forthcoming).
12. Ned Block, "On a Confusion About a Function of Consciousness," *Behavioral and Brain Sciences* 18 (1995): 227–247; 227; 230; see. Ganeri, *Attention, Not Self*, 51.
13. As Galen Strawson might put it. See Galen Strawson, *Selves: An Essay in Revisionary Metaphysics* (Oxford: Oxford University Press, 2011), 268–270.
14. Quoted in Timothy Sprigge, *James and Bradley: American Truth and British Reality* (Chicago: Open Court, 1993), 442n2 (emphasis mine). Timothy Sprigge interprets this to mean "that there is *nothing but* experience." Bradley's locution, which inspired Timothy Sprigge's reformulation of Schiller's words, was this: "We may say, in other words, that there is no being or fact outside of that which is commonly called psychical existence" (441).
15. Quoted in Sprigge, *James and Bradley*, 441–442.
16. Such a thesis does, however, acquire prominence with Prajñākaragupta (active eighth century CE), given his repeated invocation of claims to the effect that "existence" means "(perceptual) apprehension" (as expressed in phrases such as *upalambhaḥ satteti vyavasthā, upalambhaḥ satteti vyavasthā, tata upalambhaḥ sattocyate*, and more, discussed in M. Inami, "Nondual Cognition," in *Religion and Logic in Buddhist Philosophical Analysis*, ed. H. Lasic,

E. Franco, and B. Kellner [Vienna: Verlag der Österreichischen Akademie der Wissenschaften, 2011], 177–196; 191n49). Prajñākaragupta is underscoring here Dharmakīrti's claim that "existence is just perception" (*sattvam upalabdhir eva*) made in the course of the latter's discussion of nonapprehension (*anupalabdhi*) in his commentary to *Pramāṇavārttikam* 1.3ab. See Catherine Prueitt, "Shifting Concepts: The Realignment of Dharmakīrti on Concepts and the Error of Subject/Object Duality in Pratyabhijñā Śaiva Thought," *Journal of Indian Philosophy* 45 (2017): 21–47; 27n8; John D. Dunne, *Foundations of Dharmakīrti's Philosophy* (Somerville, MA: Wisdom Publications, 2004), 85n2.

17. Terms loaded with epistemological significance are ubiquitous: "idea," "percept," "sense-datum," "image," "appearance," and so on. A useful summary is provided in Ben-Ami Scharfstein, *A Comparative History of World Philosophy from the Upanisads to Kant* (Albany: State University of New York Press, 1998), 413. Scharfstein settles on the term "representation" as the right comparative phrase to gloss Vasubandhu's definitions of *vijñapti*.
18. See N. Simonsson, "Reflections on the Grammatical Tradition in Tibet," in *Indological and Buddhist Studies, Volume in Honour of Professor J. W. de Jong on His Sixtieth Birthday*, ed. L. A. Hercus et al. (Canberra: Australian National University, Faculty of Asian Studies, 1982), 531–544. For an explicit reflection on the connection between the sense of "thing" and "purpose" in the Mīmāṃsā tradition, see Francis X. D'Sa, *Śabdapramāṇyam in Śabara and Kumārila: Towards a Study of the Mīmāṃsā Experience of Language* (Vienna: Indologisches Institut der Universität Wien, 1980), 21–22. For Vātsyāyana's clarification of *artha* as purpose and object on *Nyāyasūtra* 1.1.24, see Dunne, *Foundations of Dharmakīrti's Philosophy*, 46.
19. A. S. Barwich has discussed an ostensibly generic idea of objecthood but one that is really tied to vision as involving three criteria: stimulus representation, perceptual constancy, and figure-ground segregation. Ann-Sophie Barwich, "A Critique of Olfactory Objects," *Frontiers in Psychology* 10, no. 1337 (2019): https://doi.org/10.3389/fpsyg.2019.01337.
20. I am following *The Cutting Edge of Buddhist Thought* on *Kośa* 9ab, where the category *rūpa* is enumerated and where *artha* is the general word for the sensory particulars serving as the causal conditions and objects for events of sensory awareness. See Hall, "Vasubandhu on Aggregates, Spheres, and Components," 61–62.
21. See *Kośa* 1.20ab in Hall, "Vasubandhu on Aggregates, Spheres, and Components," 77.
22. Hall, "Vasubandhu on Aggregates, Spheres, and Components," 69–70.
23. Rhys Davids, *The Questions of King Milinda, Part I* (Oxford: Clarendon Press, 1890), 86–87.
24. I am here inspired by the discussion of the semantic inflation of "object" in Hilary Putnam, *The Threefold Cord: Mind, Body, and World* (New York: Columbia University Press, 1999), 7–8.
25. See the discussion on *Kośa* 1.29 in Hall, "Vasubandhu on Aggregates, Spheres, and Components," 116. Strictly speaking, *ālambana* ought to be translated only as "intentional content" when one has in place Vasubandhu's arguments that one can experience nonexistent *ālambana*. For Vasubandhu's arguments, see Collett Cox, "On the Possibility of a Non-Existent Object of Consciousness: Sārvāstivādin and Dārṣṭāntika Theories," *Journal of the International Association of Buddhist Studies* 11, no. 1 (1988): 31–89.
26. For theories according to which *viṣayas* play such a substantive role in the generation of awareness, see Cox, "On the Possibility of a Non-Existent Object of Consciousness," 34–35.

27. Prahlad Pradhan, *Abhidharmakośabhāṣya of Vasubandhu* (Patna: K. P. Jayaswal Research Institute, 1967), 299.
28. Silk, *Materials*, 117.
29. Strictly speaking, the difference in descriptions of content is made on the basis of distinguishing between causal and noncausal relations: the distinction Vasubandhu draws in Sanskrit involves a distinction between just speaking of X as content (or "just a basis," *ālambana-mātra*), as distinct from X's being an efficient cause (*janaka*), whose individuation would require an identity separate from that of the mental event whose content it provides. For this understanding of an item serving as a generative cause (*janaka-kāraṇa*), see also Vasubandhu on the category of *sahabhū-hetu* in Kenneth K. Tanaka, "Simultaneous Relation (Sahbhū-hetu): A Study in Buddhist Theory of Causation," *Journal of the International Association of Buddhist Studies* 8, no 1 (1985): 91–111.
30. The ontological issue of independence should not be conflated with the epistemic concern with "externality," a concern that would come to dominate the reception of Yogācāra after Vasubandhu. On the difference this can make, see Jonathan C. Gold, "No Outside, No Inside: Duality, Reality and Vasubandhu's Illusory Elephant," *Asian Philosophy* 16 (2006): 1–38.
31. For reliance on relations, see Kathleen Akins, "Of Sensory Systems and the 'Aboutness' of Mental States," *Journal of Philosophy* 93, no. 7 (July 1996): 337–372; 339, 344. "The problematic assumption in the philosophical treatment of intentionality," Mark Johnston writes, "has the structure of a mental (or brain) representation being contingently related, be it by causation or by individuating description or whatever, to an item represented." Mark Johnston, *Saving God: Religion After Idolatry* (Princeton, NJ: Princeton University Press, 2009), 144. Bruce Cameron Hall and Richard Hayes have argued against saddling Vasubandhu with representationalism. See Brigit Kellner and John Taber, "Studies in Yogācāra-Vijñānavāda Idealism I: The Interpretation of Vasubandhu's *Viṃśikā*," *Asiatische Studien* 68, no. 3 (2014): 712, 735n90.
32. Whether the explanation is premodern (as we shall immediately see) or modern, as when one speaks of encoding information in states inside an organism to stand in for items outside the organism. This is also why I am not comfortable with the confidence, expressed in some quarters of Anglophone philosophy, that representation and intentionality are synonymous.
33. In what follows, I am deeply indebted to Thomas M. Lennon, "Locke on Ideas and Representation," in *The Cambridge Companion to Locke's "Essay Concerning Human Understanding,"* ed. L. Newman (Cambridge: Cambridge University Press, 2007), 231–257. While Locke's use of "representation" (and the debates it spawned) are not exhaustive, they are instructive.
34. Comment to 3cd; cf. Silk, *Materials*, 41.
35. Cf. Silk, *Materials*, 41.
36. When, for example, Vasubandhu's interlocutor suggests that material elements in hell are adapted due to karma to appear as the purposive movements of living beings. Silk, *Materials*, 55.
37. Comment to 3cd; cf. Silk, *Materials*, 41.
38. Though speaking counterfactually, I do not think that Vasubandhu himself would recommend saying so. At the very least, we would have to refine the link between thinking that "X represents Y" and that "X resembles Y." The karmic process of maturation through which certain factors can lead to distal effects, or *vipāka*, is said by Vasubandhu to get its name

from emphasizing dissimilarity (*visadṛśaḥ*): "*vipāka* is a *pāka*, or result dissimilar from its cause." The dissimilarity that matters has, often enough, to do with differences in the moral appraisability and status of the result when compared with the cause. See Pruden, *Abhidharmakosabhasyam of Vasubandhu*, 1:275; see also 1:356–357n370. On resemblance and representation, see below.

39. See verse 9ab and comments thereon; Silk, *Materials*, 67–69.
40. Nicholas Shea, *Representation in Cognitive Science* (Oxford: Oxford University Press, 2018), 4–6.
41. Johnston, *Saving God*, 141n7; Andy Clark, *Being There: Putting Brain, Body, and World Together Again* (Cambridge, MA: MIT Press, 1997), 144–147. A version of this argument is made by Lambert Schmithausen, who points out that it also has the advantage of not precluding subconscious mental processes and their contents. Lambert Schmithausen, "Aspects of Spiritual Practice in Early Yogācāra," *Journal of the International College for Postgraduate Buddhist Studies* 11 (2007): 213–244; 213n2. This is discussed in Kellner and Taber, "Studies in Yogācāra-Vijñānavāda," 735n90.
42. I have been informed by thoughts about inter-theoretic identification in Evan Thompson, "Jonardon Ganeri's Transcultural Philosophy of Attention," *Philosophy and Phenomenological Research* 101, no. 2 (September 2020): 489–494.
43. Robert B. Brandom, *A Spirit of Trust: A Reading of Hegel's Phenomenology* (Cambridge, MA: Harvard University Press, 2019), 38.
44. Pradhan, *Abhidharmakośabhāṣya of Vasubandhu*, 473. Following Yaśomitra's gloss, *tadākārateti nīlādiviṣayākāratety arthaḥ*. See U. Wogihara, ed., *Sphuṭārthā Abhidharmakośavyākhyā* (Tokyo: Sankibo Buddhist Book Store, 1989), 712.
45. Birgit Kellner, "Changing Frames in Buddhist Thought: The Concept of Ākāra in Abhidharma and in Buddhist Epistemological Analysis," *Journal of Indian Philosophy* 42 (2014): 275–295; 279–280.
46. Brandom, *A Spirit of Trust*, 39 (emphasis in original).

2. HOW NOT TO USE DREAMS

1. Heraclitus, "Fragment no. 89," quoted in Plutarch, "Superstition," in *Moralia*, vol. 2, trans. Frank Cole Babbit, Loeb Classical Library 222 (Cambridge, MA: Harvard University Press, 1928), 463.
2. See "the dreaming argument" in René Descartes, *Meditations on First Philosophy: With Selections from the Objections and Replies*, ed. John Cottingham (Cambridge: Cambridge University Press, 1996), 65.
3. Hobbes sometimes took this to involve a truism but appears to have changed his mind. See Thomas Hobbes, *Leviathan*, ed. J. C. A. Gaskin (New York: Oxford University Press, 1998), 12–13; W. Von Leyden, "Descartes and Hobbes on Waking and Dreaming," *Revue Internationale de Philosophie* 10, no. 1 (1956): 95–101; 98–99.
4. Victor H. Mair, *Wandering on the Way: Early Taoist Tales and Parables of Chuang Tzu* (Honolulu: University of Hawai'i Press, 1998), 62.

5. See Myles Burnyeat, *The Theaetetus of Plato* (Indianapolis, IN: Hackett, 1990), 280.
6. Cicero, *Academica* II, XV, 48; quoted in Stephen Menn, *Descartes and Augustine* (Cambridge: Cambridge University Press, 1998), 233–234.
7. Menn, *Descartes and Augustine*, 225–229.
8. For more on this, see Sonam Kachru, "Dream Argument," in *The Encyclopedia of Philosophy of Religion*, ed. Stewart Goetz and Charles Taliaferro (New York: John Wiley, forthcoming).
9. I am dealing here only with reconstructions that attempt to find a complete argument within the opening of the text and believe that dreams (or an equivalent example centered on the experience of an individual) can make Vasubandhu's case for him. For other approaches, see Brigit Kellner and John Taber, "Studies in Yogācāra-Vijñānavāda Idealism I: The Interpretation of Vasubandhu's *Viṃśikā*," *Asiatische Studien* 68, no. 3 (2014): 709–756.
10. Ethan Mills, "External-World Skepticism in Classical India: The Case of Vasubandhu," *International Journal for the Study of Skepticism* 7, no. 3 (2017): 147–172.
11. B. K. Matilal, *Perception: An Essay on Classical Indian Theories of Knowledge* (Oxford: Clarendon Press, 1986), 229. See the reconstruction in Hisayasu Kobayashi, "On the Development of the Argument to Prove Vijñaptimātratā," in *Religion and Logic in Buddhist Philosophical Analysis: Proceedings of the Fourth International Dharmakīrti Conference*, ed. Helmut Krasser et al. (Vienna: Verlag der Österreichischen Akademie der Wissenschaften, 2011), 299–308. On this reconstruction, see Kellner and Taber, "Studies in Yogācāra-Vijñānavāda Idealism," 735–736n94.
12. See Jürgen Hanneder, "Vasubandhus Viṃśaikā 1–2 anhand der Sanskrit-und tibetischen Fassungen," in *Indica et Tibetica: Festschrift für Michael Hahn*, ed. Konrad Klaus and Jens-Uwe Hartmann (Vienna: Wiener Studien Zur Tibetologie und Buddhismuskunde, 2007), 207–215; 211. See also Kellner and Taber, "Studies in Yogācāra-Vijñānavāda Idealism," 735–736.
13. Cf. J. A. Silk, *Materials Toward the Study of Vasubandhu's Viṁśikā (I): Sanskrit and Tibetan Critical Editions of the Verses and Autocommentary; An English Translation and Annotations* (Cambridge, MA: Department of South Asian Studies, Harvard University, 2016), 31.
14. Cf. Silk, *Materials*, 31.
15. Cf. Silk, *Materials*, 73.
16. I am leaning on a distinction that was to be drawn later in the tradition by describing experience in terms of "what is manifest" (*yat-khyāti*) as distinct from "how something is manifest" (*yathā-khyāti*), as the *Trisvabhāvanirdeśa* (attributed to Vasubandhu) does in its second verse. On the date of this work and its attribution, see Matthew T. Kapstein, "Who Wrote the Trisvabhāvanirdeśa? Reflections on an Enigmatic Text and Its Place in the History of Buddhist Philosophy," *Journal of Indian Philosophy* 46, no. 1 (2018): 1–30.
17. H. W. Bodewitz, *Jaiminīya Brāhmaṇa 1.1–65: Translation and Commentary, with a Study of Agnihotra and Prāṇāgnihotra* (Leiden: E. J. Brill, 1973), 167; Eviatar Shulman, *Rethinking the Buddha: Early Buddhist Philosophy as Meditative Perception* (Cambridge: Cambridge University Press, 2017), 146.
18. Vasubandhu, indicating the reasons the scholars of the Vibhāṣā may have to privilege in some way the category of *rūpa*, or visible form, offers this as one explanation: "Even in the world, what is observed as 'this,' 'here,' 'there,' that, not the others, is considered 'form.'" Thus, conventionally, the pronouns of proximity like *idaṃ* ("this here"), or *iha* ("here") are

used with reference to what the Buddhists classify as physical phenomena. See comment to *Kośa* 1.24 in Bruce Cameron Hall, "Vasubandhu on Aggregates, Spheres, and Components: Being Chapter One of the Abhidharmakośa" (PhD diss., Harvard University, 1983), 105.

19. Wittgenstein once considered what would be involved in restricting "this" to mean the visual field "as such" and not any single object seen and he declared it "senseless" when compared to the traditional usage of the demonstrative. Here, in contrast, the claim is not whether we could gesture at the visual field taken on its own without also picking out something seen. Instead, it is whether or not we could restrict "this" to the event of seeing something, allowing ourselves reference to what is seen, but restricting the interpretation of what is seen to be something at the very least of a piece with the event of seeing, something wholly phenomenal. See Ludwig Wittgenstein, *The Blue and the Brown Books* (Oxford: Blackwell, 1958), 64.
20. A superb discussion of the later Buddhist philosopher Prajñākaragupta's awareness of the indeterminacy of evidence governing the use of a demonstrative can be found in Matthew T. Kapstein, "Buddhist Idealists and Their Jain Critics on Our Knowledge of External Objects," *Royal Institute of Philosophy Supplement* 74 (2014): 123–147; especially 135–136. Kapstein translates Prajñākaragupta's point thus: "If one attempts to demonstrate an object ostensibly, it is not seen, for there is no 'seeing of an object.'" (Prajñākaragupta's comments on verse 321 of Dharmakīrti's *Pramāṇavārttika* may be found in Rāhula Sāṅkṛtyāyana, *Pramāṇavārttikabhāṣyam* [Patna: Tibetan Works Series, 1953], 349–352.) This is not the argument Vasubandhu uses here, though it is perhaps not inconsistent with the argument I am reconstructing for him.
21. In some cases, in fact, and contrary to the thrust of the epistemological argument reconstructed on behalf of the Yogācāras by Brahmanical epistemologists, the dream argument has been found useful precisely because it can call into question the presumptive authority of phenomenal experience. For example, according to the influential (and Yogācāra-influenced) Gauḍapāda, that in virtue of which waking experience is analogous to dreams—the manifest structure of experience in terms of subject and object—is indicative of waking and dreaming experience sharing a common root in illusion and not reality. That points to an ontological difference between what is real and what is manifest in our experience. See III.29–31 in Vidushekhara Bhattacharya, *The Āgamaśāstra of Gauḍapāda* (Delhi: Motilal Banarsidass, 1989 [1943]), 66–67. (A conversation with Michael Allen led me to this reference.) More generally, things can get very complicated very quickly when one attempts to spell out just what we are being asked to entertain by the variety of dreaming argument I am (diagnostically) reconstructing for Vasubandhu. See J. J. Valberg, *Dream, Death and the Self* (Princeton, NJ: Princeton University Press, 2007).
22. Irad Kimhi, "Causation and Non-Reductionism" (PhD diss., University of Pittsburgh, 1993), 35–36.
23. For a historical sense of the conditions under which this is possible (though one restricted to European thought narrowly construed), see Myles Burnyeat, "Idealism and Greek Philosophy: What Descartes Saw and Berkeley Missed," *Philosophical Review* 91, no. 1 (January 1982): 3–40; Hubert Dreyfus and Charles Taylor, *Retrieving Realism* (Cambridge, MA: Harvard University Press, 2015), 7–8. For a preliminary attempt at telling a story about South Asian

historical possibilities (with reference to Yogācāra), see Sonam Kachru, "Ratnakīrti and the Extent of Inner Space: An Essay on Yogācāra and the Threat of Genuine Solipsism," *Sophia* 58, no. 1 (2019): 61–83.

24. Silk, *Materials*, 129.
25. Artemus B. Engle, *The Inner Science of Buddhist Practice: Vasubandhu's Summary of the Five Heaps with Commentary by Sthiramati* (Ithaca, NY: Snow Lion, 2009), 236.
26. Sthiramati glosses the term in his commentary to *On the Five Heaps* as well in his commentary to *The Thirty Verses*. Engle, *The Inner Science of Buddhist Practice*, 308; Sylvain Lévi, *Un système de philosophie bouddhique: Matériaux pour l'étude du système Vijñāptimātra* (Paris: Honoré Champion, 1932), 100.
27. *Mahāyānasaṃgraha* II.6. This translation is adapted from an unpublished draft of Paul Griffiths's translation from the Tibetan. See also Étienne Lamotte, *Mahāyānasaṃgraha, La Somme du Grand Véhicule d'Asaṅga, Volume II: Translation and Commentary* (Louvain: Bureaux du Muséon, 1938–1939), 92–93; John P. Keenan, *The Summary of the Great Vehicle* (Berkeley, CA: Numata Center for Buddhist Translation and Research, 2003), 38.
28. See *Mahāyānasaṃgraha* II.7: "Can this be understood by those who have not awakened to the true nature of things? It can be understood by scripture and argument."
29. For an account of how the analogy to dreams in Yogācāra works could come to be treated as a "model through which any conscious state can be explained," at least from the perspective of Brahmanical authors and with particular reference to Śaiva philosophers in Kashmir, see Isabelle Ratié, "The Dreamer and the Yogin: On the Relationship Between Buddhist and Śaiva Idealisms," *Bulletin of the School of Oriental and African Studies* 73, no. 3 (2010): 437–478; 453–454. This reconstructed argument is typically not used by the Buddhist authors for whom it is reconstructed, neither before nor after Digṅāga's reformulation of Buddhist philosophy as epistemology. See John Taber, "Kumārila's Refutation of the Dreaming Argument: The *Nirālambanavāda-adhikaraṇa*," in *Studies in Mīmāṃsā*, ed. R. C. Dwivedi (Delhi: Motilal Banarsidass, 1994), 27–52; 28–31. An exception may be found in Prajñākaragupta, who seems to offer the argument as a Buddhist argument and to defend its intelligibility against criticism. See Hisayasu Kobayashi, "Prajñākaragupta on the Two Truths and Argumentation," *Journal of Indian Philosophy* 39 (2011): 427–439; 428. It may prove relevant to Ratié's remarks that Prajñākaragupta is writing in Kashmir.
30. As discussed in Kellner and Taber, "Studies in Yogācāra-Vijñānavāda," 736–737.
31. Comments on *Madhyāmakahṛdayakārikāḥ* 5.13, in Malcolm David Eckel, *Bhāviveka and His Buddhist Opponents*, Harvard Oriental Series 70 (Cambridge, MA: Harvard University Department of South Asian Studies, 2009), 232–233n36.
32. *Nyāyasūtrabhāṣya* on 4.2.33; see Ganganath Jha, *Gautama's Nyāyasūtras (With Vātsyāyana-Bhāṣya)* (Poona: Oriental Book Agency, 1939), 489. This is an argument that likely uses Vasubandhu's own acknowledgment of this point. See Silk, *Materials*, 121.
33. I owe this reconstruction to Joel Feldman, "Vasubandhu's Illusion Argument and Parasitism of Illusion upon Veridical Experience," *Philosophy East and West* 55, no. 4 (October 2005): 529–541. See p. 535, where Feldman discusses Uddyotakara's basically assimilating this particular argument to the class of arguments based on *upalabdhi*, a type of argument Dharmakīrti

would have classified as an argument proceeding on the basis of conceptual relations grounded in the definitions of phenomena (with the nature of something serving as its reason). This argument, then, like the Mīmāṃsā reconstruction discussed below, tries to fix the nature of the mental on the basis of the experience in dreaming.

34. We owe a late (and very clear) presentation of this argumentative strategy to the thirteenth-century philosopher and scholar Vedānta Deśika in his *Sarvārthasiddhi* on his *Tattvamuktākalāpa* 4.13: "The Yogācāras and others establish that all instances of cognition, just insofar as these count as instance of cognition, fail to correspond to their object—this is argued for by appealing to the case of dreaming and similar examples. And they teach that the state of corresponding to objects is un-established in all cases, and in need of rejection." See Elisa Freschi, "Veṅkaṭanātha's Engagement with Buddhist Opponents in the Buddhist Texts He Reused," *Buddhist Studies Review* 33, no. 1–2 (2016): 65–99; 73.
35. See Arindam Chakrabarti, "Dream and Love at the Edge of Wisdom: A Contemporary Cross-Cultural Remapping of Vedānta," in *The Bloomsbury Research Handbook of Vedānta*, ed. Ayon Maharaj (London: Bloomsbury Academic, 2020), 445–472. Compare the presentation of the argument for the view ascribed to philosophers (like Vasubandhu) of the Yogācāra tradition in the *Śābara-bhāṣya* 1.1.5, which I have translated here while keeping in mind the incommensurability between the Mīmāṃsā use of certain technical terms from the point of view of Buddhist philosophers: "All instances of cognition are without an object [*nirālambana*], like dreams; for in dreams it is the essential nature of thought that is indicated, that is, that thought is intrinsically without objects; waking cognition, like the cognition of a pillar, is a cognition—hence waking cognition is also without an object."
36. See Matilal, *Perception*, 229. He uses the Mīmāṃsā argument to underwrite the skeptical edge based on modal considerations: "If it is possible for awareness to create its own object, and then to grasp it (as in a dream), then everything that we seem to be aware of *could be* on the same footing, 'a making of awareness' [a *vijnapti*] only."
37. In his *Prajñapradīpa*, Bhāviveka offers to his reconstructed philosopher of the Yogācāra tradition a peculiar variant: "Consciousness is empty of objects, such as 'Caitra' . . . because it functions at a particular time, like dream consciousness." This would have dreaming fix what is criterial for mentality by suggesting that anything that is episodic (as experience is in a dream) must therefore also (like dreaming) not enjoy real content. This argument is not, however, taken seriously, whether by Bhāviveka or his reconstructed interlocutors. See Malcolm David Eckel, "Bhavaviveka's Critique of Yogācāra Philosophy in Chapter XXV of the *Prajñāpradīpa*," in *Miscellanea Buddhica*, ed. C. Lindtner (Copenhagen: Akademisk Forlag, 1985): 25–75; 61.
38. Chakravarthi Ram-Prasad, "Dreams and Reality: The Śaṅkarite Critique of Vijñānavāda," *Philosophy East and West* 43, no. 3 (July 1993): 405–455; see also Chakravarthi Ram-Prasad, "Dreams and the Coherence of Experience: An Anti-idealist Critique from Classical Indian Philosophy," *American Philosophical Quarterly* 32, no. 3 (1995): 225–239.
39. See Leszek Kolakowski, *Metaphysical Horror* (Chicago: University of Chicago Press, 2001), 105. Kolakowski, not unlike many, associates this kind of insulation with Cartesianism. This might be. But we should not associate it with Descartes himself. See Lilli Alanen,

"Descartes's Dualism and the Philosophy of Mind," *Revue de Métaphysique et de Morale* 94, no. 3 (1989): 391–413; Gary Hartfield, "Transparency of Mind: The Contributions of Descartes, Leibniz, and Berkeley to the Genesis of the Modern Subject," in *Departure for Modern Europe: A Handbook of Early Modern Philosophy (1400–1700)*, ed. Hubertus Busche (Leipzig: Felix Meiner Verlag, 2011): 361–375.

40. As old as the oldest *Upaniṣad*; see the *Bṛhadāraṇyaka Upaniṣad* 2.1.18 in Patrick Olivelle, *The Early Upanisads: Annotated Text and Translation* (New York: Oxford University Press, 1998), 63.
41. On Prabhācandra's thought experiments with "I thoughts," see Jonardon Ganeri, *The Self: Naturalism, Consciousness, and the First-Person Stance* (Oxford: Oxford University Press, 2012), 57–60. For mind as inner space in late Yogācāra, see Kachru, "Ratnakīrti and the Extent of Inner Space." Interestingly, virtual subjects in medieval Sanskrit narratives do not necessarily enjoy (epistemically) transparent experiences, often finding themselves having to reinterpret what they think they know: having, as it were, to wake up even in dreams. For narrative experiments with virtual spaces, dreaming, and subjectivity, see Wendy Doniger O'Flaherty, *Dreams, Illusions and Other Realities* (Chicago: University of Chicago Press, 1984); David Shulman, *More Than Real: A History of the Imagination in South Asia* (Cambridge, MA: Harvard University Press, 2012); and many of the essays in Christopher Key Chapple and Arindam Chakrabarti, eds., *Mind, Morals, and Make-Believe in the Mokṣopāya (Yogavāsiṣṭha)* (Albany: State University of New York Press, 2015).
42. See Feldman, "Vasubandhu's Illusion Argument"; Mills, "External-World Skepticism."
43. J. L. Austin, *Sense and Sensibilia* (Oxford: Oxford University Press, 1962), 45; 20.
44. The conflict of appearance may be generated from reports from a single subject at different times, or different subjects at one time and concerning a single object, crediting an object with incompatible properties. In deference to contemporary usage, I shall discuss "arguments from illusion," with the caveat that such a general moniker forces the idiomatic sense of "illusion" to overlap with "hallucination." I have sometimes distinguished sensory error, or hallucinations, from conflicting appearances, but these are grouped together often enough in both Buddhist and contemporary arguments from illusion. Austin is critical of such conflation. For a more charitable view of it, see David Hilbert, "Hallucination, Sense Data and Direct Realism," *Philosophical Studies* 120 (2004): 185–191. I recognize that there is something artificial in my lumping together the full range of arguments available to Vasubandhu and arguments used by others to reconstruct arguments for Vasubandhu as arguments from illusion.
45. *Mahāyānasaṃgraha* II.14a in Karl Brunnhölzl, *A Compendium of the Mahāyāna: Asaṅga's Mahāyānasaṃgraha and Its Indian Commentaries* (Boulder, CO: Snow Lion, 2018), 1:185.
46. H. Buescher, *Sthiramati's Triṃśikāvijñaptibhāṣya: Critical Editions of the Sanskrit Text and Its Tibetan Translation* (Vienna: Verlag der Österreichischen Akademie der Wissenschaften, 2007), 108.
47. This is consistent with an argument reported by Saṃghabhadra; see Noboyoshi Yamabe, "On the School Affiliation of Aśvaghoṣa: 'Sautrāntika' or 'Yogācāra'?" *Journal of the International Association of Buddhist Studies* 26, no. 2 (2003): 225–255; 239. I do not think that Vasubandhu would have argued for the premise that mental events count as instances of

conceptual construction in this way; in fact, I think it is his arguments in the *Viṃśikā* on which he was relying when he made this claim. On the different responses to this verse (apparently owing to Dharmapāla) that have generated what Yoshifumi Ueda called "two streams of Yogācāra," see Yoshifumi Ueda, "Two Main Streams of Thought in Yogācāra Philosophy," *Philosophy East and West* 17 (1967): 155–165. I rather suspect that Sthiramati's argument presented here (as an argument from illusion) might be an attempt to join Vasubandhu's thoughts on awareness counting as *vikalpa* with a longer history of arguments for the place of construction (or judgment) in experience on the basis of arguments from illusions in the *Mahāyānasaṃgraha* and those discussed in K. L. Dhammajoti, *Abhidharma Doctrines and Controversies on Perception* (Hong Kong: Centre of Buddhist Studies, University of Hong Kong, 2007), 44–46.

48. Buescher, *Sthiramati's Triṃśikāvijñaptibhāṣya*, 110.
49. Buescher, *Sthiramati's Triṃśikāvijñaptibhāṣya*, 110.
50. This is a paraphrase of an example offered by the *Mahāvibhāṣā* in his reconstruction of an argument to the effect that our thoughts (unlike, say, our sensations) do not *track* external objects. For a translation and discussion of this argument, see Dhammajoti, *Abhidharma Doctrines and Controversies*, 44. Compare this with another case: a mendicant, a libidinous man, and a dog have three experiential commitments regarding the body of a beautiful woman; seeing it, respectively, as a corpse, as a lovely woman, and as food. Though the kind of example remains fairly coherent across different instances of its use—a case of conflicting appearances of a single object among different observers—there is an astonishing variety of work to which this example is put even before it is run together with the kind of work to which more explicitly cosmological examples are put in the *Mahāyānasaṃgraha*. This topic deserves a careful history of its own. See Yamabe, "On the School Affiliation of Aśvaghoṣa"; and John D. Dunne, *Foundations of Dharmakīrti's Philosophy* (Somerville, MA: Wisdom Publications, 2004), 184–186.
51. I have benefitted from the discussion of highest common factors in Hilary Putnam, *The Threefold Cord: Mind, Body, and World* (New York, Columbia University Press, 1999), 154.
52. The first case has to do with evaluating the ontological status of mirror images in *The Cutting Edge of Buddhist Thought* (verse 3.11), and it involves considering whether or not mirror images can count as concrete particulars. See Robert Kritzer, "Rūpa and the Antarābhava," *Journal of Indian Philosophy* 28 (2000): 235–272; 243–245. Vasubandhu considers a schema for the argument (associated with the *Mahāvibhāṣā*) that involves stating that mirror images cannot count as real on account of their exemplifying two (contrary) appearances in the same locus. But concrete and sensible physical phenomena cannot co-occupy the same locus by definition. The problem is this: Which pairs of appearance conflict in the way the argument requires and just how is "conflict" to be adjudicated in the case of visible matter? It turns out to be nontrivial. Vasubandhu tries running the argument through with the following pairs: the visible matter of the surface of the mirror and the reflected image; different reflected images on the surface apparent to observers situated in different vantage points, such as people on either bank of a river; light and shade, given a mirror in the shade reflecting sunlight. The arguments are inconclusive, and I read the inconclusive attempt to generate an argument that will stick and allow us to conclude that mirror images are not

real indicative. Perhaps Vasubandhu is demonstrating the *failure* of such an argument strategy and calling attention to the resistance of what is manifest to this kind of treatment.

53. In his comments on *Kośa* 6.3, cf. Gelong Lodrö Sangpo, *Annotated Translation of Louis de La Vallee Poussin, Abhidharmakośabhāṣya: The Treasury of the Abhidharma and Its (Auto)commentary* (Delhi: Motilal Banarsidass Publishers, 2012), 3:1888.
54. Étienne Lamotte, *Le Traité de la Grande Vertu de Sagesse de Nāgārjuna (Mahāprajñāpāramitāśāstra)*, vol. 2, *Chapitres 16–30* (Louvain: Publications de l'Institut Orientaliste de Louvain, 1981), chap. 20, n139.
55. Kimhi, "Causation and Non-Reductionism," 35–36.
56. Austin, *Sense and Sensibilia*, 47.
57. As does A. K. Chatterji, *The Yogācāra Idealism* (Varanasi: Banaras Hindu University, 1962), 78–79.

3. THE PLACE OF DREAMS

1. Epicurus, *Epicurus: The Art of Happiness*, trans. George K. Strodach, foreword by Daniel Klein (New York: Penguin, 2012), 89.
2. Epicurus, *Epicurus*, 86.
3. Epicurus, *Epicurus*, 26.
4. Jennifer M. Windt, *Dreaming: A Conceptual Framework for Philosophy of Mind and Empirical Research* (Cambridge, MA: MIT Press, 2015); Evan Thompson, *Waking, Dreaming, Being: Self and Consciousness in Neuroscience, Meditation, and Philosophy* (New York: Columbia University Press, 2017).
5. This might well rehearse (and reframe) the notion of a spatiotemporal constraint in Vasubandhu's metaphysics that has an effect, an event like the growth of a shoot or the event of food being cooked, constrained to arise in a particular place and a particular time by its cause. See comments on *Kośa* 3.19d in Leo M. Pruden, trans., *Abhidharmakosabhasyam of Vasubandhu* (Berkeley, CA: Asian Humanities Press, 1988–1990), 2:401. As explained there, it is part of the cornerstone of Buddhist commitments to the causal intelligibility of the world.
6. J. A. Silk, *Materials Toward the Study of Vasubandhu's Viṁśikā (I): Sanskrit and Tibetan Critical Editions of the Verses and Autocommentary; An English Translation and Annotations* (Cambridge, MA: Department of South Asian Studies, Harvard University, 2016), 35.
7. As will become clearer, my language is indebted to Michael Heim, *Virtual Realism* (New York: Oxford University Press, 1998), particularly so with respect to the use made thereof by David Chalmers, "The Virtual and the Real," *Disputatio* 9, no. 46 (2017): 309–352; 312. Like Chalmers, I favor talk of environments over systems, but wish the reader to note the modifications required to make use of this in connection with a philosopher who had no knowledge or anticipation of digital technology.
8. Comment to 3ab; Silk, *Materials*, 37.
9. See the bibliography collected in note 1 of Cecily M. K. Whitely, "Aphantasia, Imagination and Dreaming," *Philosophical Studies* (September 2020): https://10.1007/s11098-020-01526-8.

10. Jennifer M. Windt, "The Immersive Spatiotemporal Hallucination Model of Dreaming," *Phenomenology and the Cognitive Sciences* 9 (2010): 295–316.
11. Silk, *Materials*, 117.
12. See discussion (attributed to Dharmaguptakas) on *Kośa* 1.42: "*tathā hi tasminn utpanne rūpaṃ dṛṣṭam ity ucyate, na vijñātam.*" See Prahlad Pradhan, *Abhidharmakośabhāṣya of Vasubandhu* (Patna: K. P. Jayaswal Research Institute, 1967), 31; Bruce Cameron Hall, "Vasubandhu on Aggregates, Spheres, and Components: Being Chapter One of the Abhidharmakośa" (PhD diss., Harvard University, 1983), 160; Gelong Lodrö Sangpo, *Annotated Translation of Louis de La Vallee Poussin, Abhidharmakośabhāṣya: The Treasury of the Abhidharma and Its (Auto)commentary* (Delhi: Motilal Banarsidass Publishers, 2012), 1:291.
13. "*Yat tāvat jñānam darśanam api tat,*" in Dvarikadas Shastri, *Abhidharmakośa and Bhāṣya of Ācārya Vasubandhu with Sphūtārthā Commentary of Ācārya Yaśomitra* (Varanasi: Bauddha Bharati Press, 1987), 1040; see Pruden, *Abhidharmakosabhasyam of Vasubandhu*, 4:1095.
14. Masaaki Hattori, "The Dream Simile in Vijñānavāda Treatises," in *Indological and Buddhist Studies: Volume in Honor of Professor J. W. de Jong on His Sixtieth Birthday*, ed. A. L. Hercus et al. (Canberra: Australian National University Faculty of Asian Studies, 1982), 235–241. I am indebted to Dan Arnold for bringing this work to my attention.
15. See Hattori, "The Dream Simile," especially 237. Hattori cites the *Mahāyānasaṃgrahabhāṣya*, commentary on verse IX.30, where the enjoyment (*upabhoga*) of the content of the external senses is likened to a dream. Hattori also cites a commentary ascribed to Vasubandhu on the *Mahāyānasaṃgraha* and the simile of a dream, wherein Vasubandhu is cited as saying "that just as we have disagreeable or agreeable experience in a dream despite the fact that there is no real object, even so we have diversified experience although there is no real object to be experienced."
16. Jowita Kramer, "Descriptions of 'Feeling' (*vedanā*), 'Ideation' (*saṃjñā*), and 'the Unconditioned' (*asaṃskṛta*) in Vasubandhu's *Pañcaskandhaka* and Sthiramati's *Pañcaskandhakavibhāṣā*," *Rocznik Orientalistyczny* 65, no. 1 (2012): 120–139; 121.
17. Kramer, "Descriptions of 'Feeling,'" 121.
18. As Sthiramati puts it in his commentary to Vasubandhu's *Triṃśikā*, "Affect is threefold, because of the different ways of making evident the [qualitative] nature [*svarūpa*] of an object—as something pleasurable, painful, or as something distinct from these" ("sā punar viṣayasyāhlādaka-paritāpaka-tadubhayākāra-viviktasvarūpa-sākṣātkaraṇabhedāt tridhā bhavati"); H. Buescher, *Sthiramati's Triṃśikāvijñaptibhāṣya: Critical Editions of the Sanskrit Text and Its Tibetan Translation* (Vienna: Verlag der Österreichischen Akademie der Wissenschaften, 2007), 54. Sthiramati offers more extended comments elsewhere; see Artemus B. Engle, *The Inner Science of Buddhist Practice Vasubandhu's Summary of the Five Heaps with Commentary by Sthiramati* (Ithaca, NY: Snow Lion, 2009), 267.
19. Treat it as a methodological hypothesis, given Sthiramati's contention that "in both everyday discourse and theoretical contexts, the term 'experience' [*anubhava*] is recognized as meaning 'that which makes something directly evident' [**viviktasvarūpa-sākṣāt-karaṇa*]. It is not understood in terms of being either a result or a cause"; Engle, *The Inner Science of*

Buddhist Practice, 268. That *vedanā* is *constitutively* experiential renders it unlike other mental features, unlike even the presentation of content that defines the mental frame.

20. On the plausibility of thinking that one might soon be able to televise dreams, see Jennifer M. Windt, "Reporting Dream Experience: Why (Not) to Be Skeptical About Dream Reports," *Frontiers in Human Neuroscience* 7, no. 708 (November 2013): https://doi.org/10.3389/fnhum.2013.00708.
21. Sthiramati is offering an explanation for the order in which the heaps (*skandhāḥ*) that form the basis of our sense of self are listed—from features having to do with our embodied reality (*rūpa*), which Sthiramati interprets in terms of items that exhibit resistance to co-occupation, to awareness (*vijñāna*), which Sthiramati sees as an intrinsically nonspatial type of thing, something that is the most "subtle" because of its not invoking the properties of material objects. Engle, *The Inner Science of Buddhist Practice,* 147. Sthiramati is here following the first of the explanations for the ordering of the heaps in Vasubandhu's *Cutting Edge of Buddhist Thought*, in his comments to *Kośa* 1.22bd.
22. In Engle's translation: "Feelings are more course in their mode of occurrence [*pracāraḥ*] than the other three remaining heaps. Like conception and the rest [of the heaps that are essentially mental in nature], feelings do not have any physical location. However, because of the coarseness of their appearance, it can still be said that a location is discerned in relation to them—as when one says, '[I experience] a feeling in my hand,' or '[I experience] a feeling in my head.'" Engle, *The Inner Science of Buddhist Practice,* 147.
23. Cf. Silk, *Materials*, 43.
24. The trouble will have to do with the way we understand (1). Chalmers has an account on which they reduce to digital objects. But if they are separably individuated from experiencers, this would not work with Vasubandhu's brand of virtual realism. I'll discuss (4) below. See David Chalmers, "The Virtual and the Real," 310.
25. See verses 124–133 of the *Bahyārthasiddhi*, quoted in Masaaki Hattori, "*Bāhyārthasiddhi* of Śubhagupta," *Journal of Indian and Buddhist Studies* 8, no. 1 (1960): 395–400; 398.
26. See Hattori, "*Bāhyārthasiddhi* of Śubhagupta," 398. In what follows, I will take up an epistemic point raised against Vasubandhu. This would have it that in the dream, the dreamer could not be credited with knowledge of the object (*arthaniścaya*) that prompted his course of action, but it is only knowledge that counts as a criterion to establish the presence or absence of objects. This is, of course, a point about the criteria for the *validity* of our experience in dreams, and not solely about the individuation of mental events in the absence of objects.
27. Though not the same, compare this with the argument for virtual objects being digital objects in Chalmers, "The Virtual and the Real," 311.
28. For an account in the *Mahāvibhāṣā* of the different reasons one can enjoy content in dreams, an account to which Vasubandhu would have had access, see Robert Ford Campany, *The Chinese Dreamscape: 300 BCE–800 CE*, Harvard-Yenching Institute Monograph Series 122 (Cambridge, MA: Harvard University Asia Center, 2020), 61. The reasons include (a) other beings (gods, spirits, sages, and so on); (b) past events, insofar as one sees what one has previously

thought about or habitually done; (c) signs of what will come to pass; (d) what one is longing for or worrying about; (e) illness.

29. Quoted in Ian Hacking, *Historical Ontology* (Cambridge, MA: Harvard University Press, 2002), 242.
30. From the *'Ārā' al-hind* in Bruce B. Lawrence, *Shahrastānī on the Indian Religions* (The Hague: De Gruyter Mouton, 2012), 44.
31. Matthew T. Kapstein, *Reason's Traces: Identity and Interpretation in Indian and Tibetan Buddhist Thought* (Somerville, MA: Wisdom Publications, 2001), 127.
32. Consider the spatiotemporal intuition of continuity that Vasubandhu relies on when explaining what continuity of a life between death and birth might consist in: "Existence in the phase of dying and existence in the phase of being born count as a continuous sequence, the second being posterior to the first, and produced in a place other than the first without any discontinuity." On *Kośa* 3.12b, see Pradhan, *Abhidharmakośabhāṣya of Vasubandhu*, 121; Sangpo, *Annotated Translation of Louis de La Vallee Poussin*, 2:960. Or, as Vasubandhu says elsewhere, "phenomena which occur as a sequence are seen to be present in distinct places without discontinuity, just as is true of a sequence of rice [formed when one transports rice to a distant village by passing through all the intervening villages]." *Kośa* 3.11ab; Pradhan, *Abhidharmakośabhāṣya of Vasubandhu*, 120; Sangpo, *Annotated Translation of Louis de La Vallee Poussin*, 2:958.
33. Catherine Wilson, "Vicariousness and Authenticity," in *The Robot in the Garden: Telerobotics and Telepistemology in the Age of the Internet*, ed. Ken Goldberg (Cambridge, MA: MIT Press, 2001), 64–90; 75.
34. E. R. Dodds, *The Greeks and the Irrational* (Berkeley: University of California Press, 1951), 121.
35. Dodds, *The Greeks and the Irrational*, 102. For a better sense of the more involved (and analytically robust and ethnographically sensitive) taxonomy we shall need of the ways in which dreams can come to matter and the ways in which talk and thought of dreams may come to be organized in a culture, see Campany, *The Chinese Dreamscape*, 6.
36. Patrick Olivelle, *The Early Upanisads: Annotated Text and Translation* (New York: Oxford University Press, 1998), 63.
37. *Bṛhadāraṇyaka* 4.3.9, in Olivelle, *The Early Upanisads*, 113.
38. As in the *Pratyutpannasamādhisūtra*, see Paul L. Swanson, *T'ien-T'ai Chih-I's Mo-Ho Chih-Kuan: Clear Serenity, Quiet Insight* (Honolulu: University of Hawai'i Press, 2018), 3:1619–1621.
39. Both Buddhist and non-Buddhist sources from the first century of the Common Era reveal that at this time there is something of an uptick in a related concern: the decipherment and interpretation of dreams significant for the future. See Paul Harrison, "Mediums and Messages: Reflections on the Production of Mahāyāna Sūtras," *Eastern Buddhist* 35, no. 1/2 (2003): 115–161; 135–136. The dimension of portents, messages, or communications in dreams came to be dubbed "true dreams" (*satyasvapna*) in later epistemological traditions. See Keijin Hayashi, "The Term 'True Dream (Satyasvapna)' in the Buddhist Epistemological Tradition," *Journal of Indian Philosophy* 29 (2001): 559–574. The narrative exemplification of this idea can be found in stories of life-altering experiences in dreams (one of which we will examine in

chapter 7), or even in some scriptures, when it is revealed, for example, that Buddhas could be encountered, and learned from, in dreams, or when it is intimated that one's practice of contemplative exercises or the internalization of a text may continue in dreams. See Harrison, "Mediums and Messages," 120, 140.

40. For the views in the Pāli *Vinaya* that sexual experience in dreams (unlike masturbation) does not breach monastic rules of discipline (though indicating a state with karmic results), see Steven Collins, "The Body in Theravāda Monasticism," in *Religion and the Body*, ed. Sara Coakley (Cambridge: Cambridge University Press, 1997), 185–204; 190, and citations therein. For comparative purposes, one might look to concerns with nocturnal emissions in Christian monasticism and testimony of inner states; see Kyle Harper, *From Shame to Sin: The Christian Transformation of Sexual Morality in Late Antiquity* (Cambridge, MA: Harvard University Press, 2013), 240; David Brakke, "The Problematization of Nocturnal Emissions in Early Christian Syria, Egypt, and Gaul," *Journal of Early Christian Studies* 3, no. 4 (1995): 419–460.
41. Bhikkhu Bodhi, "The First Sanghādisesa Rule for Bhikkhus: The Vinaya Piṭaka and Its Commentarial Exegesis," https://www.suttas.net/english/vinaya/bhikkhu-bodhi/the-first-sanghadisesa-rule-for-bhikkhus--by-ven.bodhi.pdf, quoted in José Ignacio Cabezón, *Sexuality in Classical South Asian Buddhism* (Somerville, MA: Wisdom Publications, 2017), 184n486.
42. Following the summary in Cabezón, *Sexuality in Classical South Asian Buddhism*. He cites P. V. Bapat and A. Hirakawa, *Shan-chien-P'i-P'o-Sha: A Chinese Version by Saṁghabhadra of Samantapāsādikā* (Poona: Bhandarkar Oriental Institute, 1970), 360.
43. See the discussion of *Shan-chien-P'i-P'o-Sha* in Campany, *The Chinese Dreamscape*, 59. He cites Bapat and Hirakawa, *Shan-chien-P'i-P'o-Sha*, 356–358.
44. On the debate, see Louis de La Vallée Poussin, "The Five Points of Mahādeva and the Kathāvatthu," *Journal of the Royal Asiatic Society* 1, no. 42 (1910): 413–423.
45. The morally relevant yet publicly nonevident changes induced in us by our acts of omission and commission are said to hold even when we are not awake (and in this sense fully conscious). Whether or not *such* continuity obtains is not a function of our being "conscious" in the sense of being awake. See the discussion of this on *Kośa* 4.4b, translated in Sangpo, *Annotated Translation of Louis de La Vallee Poussin*, 2:1301.
46. Quoted in Bart Dessein, "Of Tempted Arhats and Supermundane Buddhas: Abhidharma in the Krishna Region," in *Buddhism in the Krishna River Valley of Andhra*, ed. Sree Padma Holt and A. W. Barber (Albany: State University of New York Press, 2008), 41–80; 58, 76n137.
47. After Dessein, "Of Tempted Arhats," 58.
48. After Edward Conze, *The Large Sutra on Perfect Wisdom with the Divisions of the Abhisamayālaṅkāra* (Delhi: Motilal Banarsidass, 1979), 432–433; quoted in Harrison, "Mediums and Messages," 137–138.
49. Harrison, "Mediums and Messages," 138.
50. Steven Collins cites Dabba Mallaputta, who replied to his accusations of impropriety by saying that he was not aware of having intercourse in a dream, leave alone while awake (*Vinaya* II.78); and he cites the Buddha characterizing the "highest brahmin" of old as having nothing to do with sex "even in dreams" (*Suttanipāta* 293). Quoted in Collins, "The Body in Theravāda Buddhist Monasticism," 200.

51. Peter Brown, *The Body and Society: Men, Women and Sexual Renunciation in Early Christianity* (New York: Columbia University Press, 2008), 231–232; quoted in Collins, "The Body in Theravāda Buddhist Monasticism," 201.
52. Pruden, *Abhidharmakosabhasyam of Vasubandhu*, 1:222.
53. Victor H. Mair, *Wandering on the Way: Early Taoist Tales and Parables of Chuang Tzu* (Honolulu: University of Hawai'i Press, 1998), 62.
54. Hayashi, "The Term 'True Dream,'" 567.
55. Hayashi, "The Term 'True Dream,'" 567–568.

4. COSMOLOGY FOR PHILOSOPHERS

1. Andy Rotman, *Divine Stories: Divyāvadāna, Part 2* (Somerville, MA: Wisdom Publications, 2018), 18.
2. Samuel Beckett, *Proust and Three Dialogues with Georges Duthuit* (London: J. Calder, 1965), 18–19.
3. The point was made in Bas C. van Fraassen, "'World' Is Not a Count Noun," *Noûs* 29 (1995): 139–157; I am indebted to Alexandre Declos, "Goodman's Many Worlds," *Journal for the History of Analytical Philosophy* 7, no. 6 (2019): https://doi.org/10.15173/jhap.v7i6.3827; see p. 5. See also Roy Tzohar, *A Yogācāra Buddhist Theory of Metaphor* (New York: Oxford University Press, 2018), 195–197.
4. For a superb introduction to Buddhist cosmology, see Eric Huntington, *Creating the Universe: Depictions of the Cosmos in Himalayan Buddhism* (Seattle: University of Washington Press, 2019). Philosophers will also want to consult the comprehensive and analytically trenchant introduction in William McGovern, *A Manual of Buddhist Philosophy*, vol. 1, *Cosmology* (London: Kegan Paul, Trench and Trubner, 1923), 39–183. Of course, it is not necessary to compare the Buddhist use of "world" (*loka*) only with contemporary Anglophone idioms and intuitions constraining the use of "world." For medieval Arabic intellectuals, such as Ibn Qutayba, worlds—*ālam*, or "world" in Arabic, typically being used in the plural in such contexts—are thought of as diverse modes of knowing afforded by diverse (cosmological) life-forms, humans, jinn, and angels. See Nora S. Eggen, "A Multiverse of Knowledge: The Epistemology and Hermeneutics of the *'ālam* in Medieval Islamic Thought," in *Conceptualizing the World: An Exploration Across Disciplines*, ed. Helge Jordheim and Erling Sandmo (New York: Berghahn Books, 2019), 40–53; esp. 42. My thanks to Jane Mikkelson for this reference.
5. As evident in the beginning of chapter 3 of *The Cutting Edge of Buddhist Thought*, where Vasubandhu states that earlier (in chapter 2) the fact of mindedness—meaning, the mental frame and higher mental functions—being constrained by the three kinds of realms of experience was already taught: "kāma-rūpa-ārūpya-dhātu-naiyamyena cittādīnāṁ kṛto nirdeśaḥ," in Shastri, *Abhidharmakośa and Bhāṣya of Ācārya Vasubandhu with Sphūtārthā Commentary of Ācārya Yaśomitra* (Varanasi: Bauddha Bharati Press, 1987), 379. The word for relations I have in mind is *sambandha*, which Yaśomitra supplies in his commentary. Shastri, *Abhidharmakośa and Bhāṣya of Vasubandhu*, 379.

6. Paul J. Griffiths, *On Being Buddha: The Classical Doctrine of Buddhahood* (Albany: State University of New York Press, 1994), 96–97; 129–130.
7. As Xuanzang notes in the *Ch'eng Wei-Shih Lun*: "Furthermore, it is only in this Buddha-world that we conventionally establish names, phrases, and syllables as dependent on sound. It is not the case in other Buddha-worlds, because in those worlds, these three are established in dependence on light, odor, taste, etc." Wei Tat, *Ch'eng Wei-Shih Lun: Doctrine of Mere Consciousness* (Hong Kong: Ch'eng Wei-Shih Lun Publication Committee, 1973), 36. (My thanks to James MacNee for this reference.) For the use of Buddha fields in thought experiments in the *Laṅkāvatārasūtra*, see Sonam Kachru, "As If a Stage: Towards an Ecological Concept of Thought in Indian Buddhist Philosophy," *Journal of World Philosophies* 5, no. 1 (2020): 1–29; 15–18. I leave for another time comparison with the complex (narrative, analytic, and contemplative) uses of other worlds (as versions of the world one is in and believes to be actual) as enacted in the *Yogavāsiṣṭha*. See Swami Venkatesananda, *Vasiṣṭha's Yoga* (Albany: State University of New York Press, 1993), 67; 576.
8. See Daniel M. Stuart, "Becoming Animal: Karma and the Animal Realm Envisioned Through an Early Yogācāra Lens," *Religions* 10, no. 6 (2019): 363, https://doi.org/10.3390/rel10060363; Paul Harrison, "Mediums and Messages: Reflections on the Production of Mahāyāna Sūtras," *Eastern Buddhist* 35, no. 1/2 (2003): 115–161; 120–122.
9. Rupert Gethin, "Cosmology and Meditation: From the Āgañña-sutta to the Mahāyāna," *History of Religions* 36, no. 3 (1997): 183–217; Robert Sharf, "Is Nirvāṇa the Same as Insentience? Chinese Struggles with an Indian Buddhist Ideal," in *India in the Chinese Imagination: Myth, Religion, and Thought*, ed. John Kieschnick and Meir Shahar (Philadelphia: University of Pennsylvania Press, 2014), 141–171; José Ignacio Cabezón, *Sexuality in Classical South Asian Buddhism* (Somerville, MA: Wisdom Publications, 2017), 17–79; 350–369.
10. See Sara L. McClintock, "Ethical Reading and the Ethics of Forgetting and Remembering," in *A Mirror Is for Reflection: Understanding Buddhist Ethics*, ed. Jake H. Davis (New York: Oxford University Press, 2017), 185–202. See also Andy Rotman, *Hungry Ghosts* (New York: Simon and Schuster, forthcoming), dedicated in part to the use made of hungry ghosts in the cycle of hungry ghost stories in the *Avadānaśataka* to explore moral psychological concepts (such as meanness and greed [*mātsarya*]) and as exercises in ethical self-fashioning.
11. Mark Ridley, *How to Read Darwin* (New York: W. W. Norton, 2005), 6.
12. As Vasubandhu does when distinguishing beings into male and female, for example, in his comments on *Kośa* 2.1b. See Shastri, *Abhidharmakośa and Bhāṣya of Vasubandhu*, 136.
13. As Vasubandhu does when characterizing the range of environmental features and factors, for example, in his comments on *Kośa* 4.1a. See Shastri, *Abhidharmakośa and Bhāṣya of Vasubandhu*, 567. Yaśomitra immediately qualifies Vasubandhu's use (of X—*vaicitrya*) by explaining it with an enumeration of distinctions (of A, B, C, . . .) with the help of *bheda*. This resolves the two words as continuous, being merely different, perhaps, in that *vaicitrya* implies but does not spell out an enumeration and connotes a different affective range.
14. Ridley, *How to Read Darwin*, 10.

15. Cabezón, *Sexuality in Classical South Asian Buddhism*, 26–27.
16. As in the longer *Sukhāvatīvyūhasūtra*, in Luis O. Gōmez, *The Land of Bliss: The Paradise of the Buddha of Measureless Light: Sanskrit and Chinese Versions of the Sukhāvatīvyūha Sutras* (Delhi: Motilal Banarsidas, 2002), 85–86. In one commentary attributed to Vasubandhu, topographic relief is thought to make room for evaluative attitudes, "affirmation," and "negation." See Roger Corless, Takahiko Kameyama, and Richard K. Payne, "A Commentary on *The Upadeśa on the Sutras of Limitless Life with Gāthās on the Resolution to be Born* Composed by the Bodhisattva Vasubandhu," *Pacific World* 17 (2015): 69–235; 98. This topographic penchant may possibly reflect a central Asian apocalyptic motif expressing the belief that justice makes no distinctions. See Bruce Lincoln, "'The Earth Becomes Flat': A Study of Apocalyptic Imagery," *Comparative Studies in Society and History* 25, no. 1 (January 1983): 136–153.
17. Recently, the relation has come in for some scrutiny. See Cabezón, *Sexuality in Classical South Asian Buddhism*, 356n896.
18. The twenty-two capacities can be mapped onto six basic sentience-constituting categories, as follows: "The basis of thought (i.e., the six sensory modalities that condition awareness); that which is responsible for sorting beings into contraries (i.e., the sexual systems); that by which the basis endures (i.e., the faculty of life); that by which the basis is defiled (the five types of sensation); the prerequisites for the purification of the basis (i.e., the faculties orienting one to ethical praxis, such as faith, and so on); and that by which the basis is purified." See *Kośa* 2.5 in Leo M. Pruden, trans., *Abhidharmakosabhasyam of Vasubandhu* (Berkeley, CA: Asian Humanities Press, 1988–1990), 1:158.
19. Leonard Zwilling and Michael J. Sweet, "Like a City Ablaze: The Third Sex and the Creation of Sexuality in Jain Religious Literature," *Journal for the History of Sexuality* 6, no. 3 (January 1996): 359–384; 374.
20. Zwilling and Sweet, "Like a City Ablaze," 374–375.
21. For a superb introduction to the promise and power of Buddhist scholastic tools to think about these issues, see Cabezón, *Sexuality in Classical South Asian Buddhism*, 350–367, esp. 357. For gender, see the commentary to 2.2cd on being female: "tatra strībhāvaḥ stry-ākṛtiḥ svaraceṣṭāḥ abhiprāyāḥ"; Prahlad Pradhan, *Abhidharmakośabhāṣya of Vasubandhu* (Patna: K. P. Jayaswal Research Institute, 1967), 36. See also Gelong Lodrö Sangpo, *Annotated Translation of Louis de La Vallee Poussin, Abhidharmakośabhāṣya: The Treasury of the Abhidharma and Its (Auto) commentary* (Delhi: Motilal Banarsidass Publishers, 2012), 1:469.
22. See Sangpo, *Annotated Translation of Louis de La Vallee Poussin*, 1:466. See Cabezón, 360n906.
23. Cf. J. A. Silk, *Materials Toward the Study of Vasubandhu's Viṁśikā (I): Sanskrit and Tibetan Critical Editions of the Verses and Autocommentary; An English Translation and Annotations* (Cambridge, MA: Harvard University Department of South Asian Studies, 2016), 47. Silk chooses "domination" to capture the explanation at issue.
24. It should certainly not be confused with a way of thinking of antecedence unhappily called *adhipati-pratyāya* (which in turn is part of a descriptive and explanatory rubric called the six causes [*hetu*] and four conditions [*pratyaya*]). The way this idea is explained, any X antecedent to any other Y may be described in terms of X being the condition that is called an

adhipati of Y. This is because it is explained as being a particular type of cause, a *kāraṇa*, in 2.62d, and this leads us to the following definition in 2.50a: "All factors are *kāraṇa-hetu* with regard to all [others], with the exception of themselves." The only rule is that it cannot serve as a condition for itself. As stated, it seems less like a definition of a useful variety of condition or relation and more like an illustration of the post hoc fallacy. If one thinks that if B follows A therefore A is cause, condition, or antecedent relation for B, then why not say that everything before B serves as such a condition? In fact, Buddhist philosophers of the Sarvāstivāda tradition, though not the Theravāda, do embrace saying this. See Pruden, *Abhidharmakosabhasyam of Vasubandhu*, 1:255, 1:303. For the virtues of speaking like this, and for distinguishing this way of speaking from the sense of dominance being explored here, see McGovern, *A Manual of Buddhist Philosophy*, 191.

25. This argument, and the argument in the next paragraph, are paraphrastic restatements of Vasubandhu's arguments developed on *Kośa* 2.6; Pradhan, *Abhidharmakośabhāṣya of Vasubandhu*, 40. See Sangpo, *Annotated Translation of Louis de La Vallee Poussin*, 1:473.
26. "The reproductive organs are not faculties with respect to sexual pleasure, since sexual bliss is effected by the regions on the body taken to be the male and female sexual capacities." Pradhan, *Abhidharmakośabhāṣya of Vasubandhu*, 41. On these faculties, see Sangpo, *Annotated Translation of Louis de La Vallee Poussin*, 1:473, 1:709n58.
27. Where the Kashmirians go wrong, Vasubandhu believes, is in identifying the relation of dominance with a specific causal relation obtaining between concrete particulars (*asādhārana-kāraṇatva*). See the introduction to *Kośa* 2.2ab, Pradhan, *Abhidharmakośabhāṣya of Vasubandhu*, 36.
28. *Kośa* 2.2ab states that "rather, the six modalities of awareness enjoy dominance on account of exercising dominance with respect to the apprehension of content proper to each modality." Cf. Pruden, *Abhidharmakosabhasyam of Vasubandhu*, 1:155.
29. From the comment to *Kośa* 2.2ab. Cf. Pruden, *Abhidharmakosabhasyam of Vasubandhu*, 1:156.
30. Comment to *Kośa* 2.2ab: "Conscious apprehension can be specified as being sharp or obscure, strong or weak, and the like, on the basis of the sensory modality, but not on the basis of its proper sensible." See Pruden, *Abhidharmakosabhasyam of Vasubandhu*, 1:156. See also *Kośa* 1.45ab; Pruden, *Abhidharmakosabhasyam of Vasubandhu*, 1:125.
31. Kit Fine, "Guide to Ground," in *Metaphysical Grounding*, ed. Fabrice Correia and Benjamin Schneider (Cambridge: Cambridge University Press, 2012), 37–80.
32. Brian McLaughlin and Karen Bennett, "Supervenience," in *Stanford Encyclopedia of Philosophy*, ed. Edward N. Zalta (Stanford University, Winter 2018 edition), https://plato.stanford.edu/archives/win2018/entries/supervenience/.
33. See Jonardon Ganeri, "Emergentisms, Ancient and Modern," *Mind* 120, no. 479 (July 2011): 671–703; 679.
34. See Kit Fine, "The Question of Realism," *Philosophers' Imprint* 1 (2001): 1–30; 15n21.
35. Cabezón, *Sexuality in Classical South Asian Buddhism*, 356–357n896.
36. In contemporary animal science, a case has been made for a similar way of thinking of consciousness in animals using a multidimensional framework. See Jonathan Birch,

Alexandra K. Schnell, and Nicola S. Clayton, "Dimensions of Animal Consciousness," *Trends in Cognitive Sciences* 24, no. 10 (October 2020): https://doi.org/10.1016/j.tics.2020.07.007.

37. Comment on *Kośa* 3.3c–d. See Pruden, *Abhidharmakosabhasyam of Vasubandhu*, 2:368.
38. Michael Thompson, *Life and Action: Elementary Structures of Practice and Practical Thought* (Cambridge, MA: Harvard University Press, 2012), 65.
39. The distinctions that obtain between kinds of beings function in some ways analogously to distinctions of natural kinds, but they are more general than our current (or even conventional Sanskrit) biological distinctions of individual species. Thus, gods and humans express different life-forms, but the difference between bees and bears does not count as a difference in life-forms, for they belong to a single one—that of animals. Also, if one believes that a biological kind is picked out with reference to the transmission of form through sexual reproduction, then these kinds are not strictly biological. The concept of birth involved here is far more general; see *Kośa* 3.8cd–3.9, and commentary thereon. Pruden, *Abhidharmakosabhasyam of Vasubandhu*, 2:380–381; see also 2:396.
40. I have refrained from using variants of "life-world." The idea of life-form here is not primarily intended to limn the context of meaningfulness or sense as evoked and found in the active life of beings, as is "life-world." See Hans Blumenberg, *Lebenszeit und Weltzeit* (Frankfurt: Suhrkamp, 1986), 48. The tissue of sense associated with the phenomenological idea of a life-world is referred back to the norm-involving activity of subjects, and is understood to involve a complex variety of semantic or attitude dependency. To offer a comparative gloss on such a notion, we would do better to track the Buddhist use of *vyavahāra*, or the world of social transaction. (Though classically [a?] *vyavahāra* does not appear to be motivated so as to model variation over time.) The term "life-forms" attempts instead to describe conditions for experience that are far more basic, not primarily understood as a function of meaning-making and meaning-finding activities. But see the conclusion, where someone like Dōgen could disagree.
41. As for example, in the *Amarakośa* (2.9.34), where along with *āvapanam* (vessel, or jar), and *pātram* (drinking vessel, bowl or cup, or utensil more generally), *bhājanam* is used as a synonym for such objects.
42. The closest we get to an illustration of the analogical work this word as an image might be thought to promote for Vasubandhu is in a sustained analogy for the enumeration of the order of the heaps that serve as the conditions for *I* thoughts: (*Kośa* 1.22): "Or [the enumerated order can be explained] via [analogical] meaning, that is, the list beginning with 'the utensil': for the heaps, beginning with form [and including feeling, judgments, dispositions and awareness] are like the utensil, the food, the flavoring ingredient (spices or sauce, perhaps), the cook and the eater, respectively." See Pruden, *Abhidharmakosabhasyam of Vasubandhu*, 1:83: if the body may thus be analogized with a utensil as context of experience, perhaps, then, the world understood as a utensil is a way of gesturing at its being (ultimately) part of our mode of embodiment.
43. Cf. Silk, *Materials*, 133.
44. *Kośa* 3.37d (see also 3.10); Pradhan, *Abhidharmakośabhāṣya of Vasubandhu*, 151. On the difference between being conceived as a life-form (*upapatti*) and manifesting (as the state of a

being in-between death and conception is said to do), see discussion of *Kośa* 3.10 in Pruden, *Abhidharmakosabhasyam of Vasubandhu*, 2:383.

45. Shelly Kagan, *How to Count Animals, More or Less* (Oxford: Oxford University Press, 2019), 6.
46. See, for example, the extensive discussion on *Kośa* 4.72ab; Pradhan, *Abhidharmakośabhāṣya of Vasubandhu*, 242–243. For a translation, see Sangpo, *Annotated Translation of Louis de La Vallee Poussin*, 2:1409. The idea would be expressed in terms of having the same psychological basis (*āśraya*), which is a more restrictive notion than continuity.
47. On the argument of what the Buddha had in view in speaking of trans-life continuity and identity, see the discussion on how to interpret the Buddha saying "I, indeed, at that time, on that occasion, became the teacher named Sunetra," and the answer that we should construe such identity statements as "I [in this lifetime] am the same X as that [living individual in a former life]"—in terms of the unity of a single continuum, and not the unity of persisting principle. Pradhan, *Abhidharmakośabhāṣya of Vasubandhu*, 472. See Matthew T. Kapstein, *Reason's Traces: Identity and Interpretation in Indian and Tibetan Buddhist Thought* (Somerville, MA: Wisdom Publications, 2001), para 6.6, 366. For the justification of the use of singular terms as collective singulars (according to which a word like "one" can be used for *collectiva*), see Pradhan, *Abhidharmakośabhāṣya of Vasubandhu*, 468. Kapstein, *Reason's Traces*, 361.
48. See *Kośa* 4.73ab, Pruden, *Abhidharmakosabhasyam of Vasubandhu*, 2:650. For subtle debates about the univocity of terms for life (a "breathing thing" versus a "living thing"), see Giulio Agostini, "Buddhist Sources on Feticide as Distinct from Homicide," *Journal of the International Association of Buddhist Studies* 27, no. 1 (2004): 63–97; 69n16.
49. For arguments concerning the type and status of the concept of *nikāya-sabhāga*, the ostensible resemblance of living beings described in terms of their being of the same species, or form of life, see the discussions on *Kośa* 2.41a, examined at length in Collett Cox, *Disputed Dharmas: Early Buddhist Theories of Existence: An Annotated Translation of the Section on Factors Dissociated from Thought from Saṅghabhadra's* Nyāyānusāra (Tokyo: International Institute for Buddhist Studies, 1995), 108–109, 112n6, 128, 131.
50. On the basis of *On the Five Heaps*: "What is the faculty of life? It is a fixed duration on the part of the dispositional factors, which in turn is a function of prior actions given a particular form of being"; "What is *nikāyasabhāgatā*? The fact of living beings being alike in terms of their conditions of individuation." See Artemus B. Engle, *The Inner Science of Buddhist Practice: Vasubandhu's Summary of the Five Heaps with Commentary by Sthiramati* (Ithaca, NY: Snow Lion, 2009), 238. For views expressed in the *Abhidharmakośabhāṣya*, see Cox, *Disputed Dharmas*, 128, 131n21.
51. In Xuanzang's description of dying (in his translation of *Kośa* 3.13), as Ernest Brewster shows, one finds the use of *yin* (引) to describe how dying "draws forth spiritual fruit," or the "totality of the karma that is borne by a sentient being and transforms it into either a spiritual reward or a karmic retribution." See Ernest Billings Brewster, "The Yoga of Dying: Xuanzang on the Nature of Death" (PhD diss., Harvard University, 2018), 400.
52. For comparison, see J. H. Smith's discussion of the revisions Leibniz's metaphysics imposes on the "one body one substance" principle of commonsense and Aristotelian intuitions.

Justin E. H. Smith, *Divine Machines: Leibniz and the Sciences of Life* (Princeton, NJ: Princeton University Press, 2011), 139.

53. For a treatment of this testing the intuitions of philosophers working in Anglophone contexts in English, see Elselijn Kinga, "Were You a Part of Your Mother?" *Mind* 128, no. 511 (July 2019): 609–646.
54. *Kośa* on 3.13a–b; Pruden, *Abhidharmakosabhasyam of Vasubandhu*, 2:390; Shastri, *Abhidharmakośa and Bhāṣya of Vasubandhu*, 420. The case is derived from the *Mahāvibhāṣā*, as quoted in Brewster, "The Yoga of Dying," 401n16.
55. For more on this, see Sonam Kachru, "Things You Wouldn't Think to Look for in One Place: A Note on an All-Too-Brief Example on Life and Matter in Abhidharmakośabhāṣyam ad 3.14c," *Journal of the American Oriental Society* 137, no. 4 (2017): 669–678; 677.
56. I have been influenced by the intuition Einstein once invoked by speaking of "independent existence," defined in an article that he sent to Max Born (in 1948): "It is . . . characteristic of . . . physical objects that they are thought of as arranged in a space-time continuum. An essential aspect of this arrangement . . . is that they lay claim, at a certain time, to an existence independent of one another, provided these objects 'are situated in different parts of space' . . . [t]he following idea characterizes the relative independence of objects (A and B) far apart in space: external influence on A has no direct influence on B." Quoted in Max Born, *The Born-Einstein Letters* (New York: Walker, 1971), 168–173.
57. For more detail on this, see Robert Kritzer, "Rūpa and the Antarābhava," *Journal of Indian Philosophy* 28 (2000): 235–272.
58. The first response involves saying that it is not necessary that beings in hell possess a form that is incompatible with the environment provided by the womb of an animal. It is not necessary, that is, that every being in hell be on fire, and so the dilemma need not arise. This, I venture to say, is not helpfully said, for the fact that it need not arise does not preclude that it can arise. Pruden, *Abhidharmakosabhasyam of Vasubandhu*, 2:390.
59. Pruden, *Abhidharmakosabhasyam of Vasubandhu*, 2:390.
60. Some support for such cases is found by Vasubandhu in natural philosophical reports of creatures that dwell in molten metal. See Kachru, "Things You Wouldn't Think to Look for in One Place."
61. Pruden, *Abhidharmakosabhasyam of Vasubandhu*, 2:390.
62. For a similar concern, see also Rhys Davids, *The Questions of King Milinda, Part I* (Oxford: Clarendon Press, 1890), 104.
63. Wendy Doniger O'Flaherty, ed., *Karma and Rebirth in Classical Indian Traditions* (Berkeley: University of California Press, 1980), 34. She cites James P. McDermott, "Karma and Rebirth in Early Buddhism," in the same volume, 171–172. See also Cabezón, *Sexuality in Classical South Asian Buddhism*, 368.
64. Kritzer, "Rūpa and the Antarābhava," 249–250.
65. Pradhan, *Abhidharmakośabhāṣya of Vasubandhu*, 126. See also Pruden, *Abhidharmakosabhasyam of Vasubandhu*, 2:395. For a longer version in the *Mahāvibāṣā*, see Kritzer, "Rūpa and the Antarābhava," 249–250.
66. Philip Rieff, *Freud: The Mind of the Moralist* (New York: Viking Press, 1959), 149.

67. Timothy Harrison, *Coming To: Consciousness and Natality in Early Modern England* (Chicago: University of Chicago Press, 2020), 162–207. My thanks to Jane Mikkelson for referring me to this book and for many discussions.
68. Amy Paris Langenberg, *Birth in Buddhism: The Suffering Fetus and Female Freedom* (London: Routledge, 2017), 32–33.
69. *Kośa* 3.19ac; cf. Pruden, *Abhidharmakosabhasyam of Vasubandhu*, 2:400.
70. "Pūrvasmṛti-vraṇam-ivolbaṇadoṣapākaṃ bhinnaṃ jahāti ghṛṇayeva nipīḍyamānaḥ," *Śiṣyalekha*, verse 21cd. See also Michael Hahn, *Invitation to Enlightenment* (Berkeley, CA: Dharma Publishing, 1998), 66–67.
71. For Vasubandhu's thoughts on memory and forgetting in connection with birth and cosmology, see Pruden, *Abhidharmakosabhasyam of Vasubandhu*, 2:398. On the ethical dimensions of this, see McClintock, "Ethical Reading."
72. *Kośa* 3.98; Pruden, *Abhidharmakosabhasyam of Vasubandhu*, 2:488. Cabezón, *Sexuality in Classical South Asian Buddhism*, 27–29.
73. Take the explanation for the four different precious substances that make up Mount Meru (*Kośa* 3.49d–50a; Pruden, *Abhidharmakosabhasyam of Vasubandhu*, 2:453): "The waters which have fallen on the sphere of gold are rich in different potentialities: under the action of the winds that possess different efficacies, they disappear and make room for different jewels. It is thus that water is transformed into jewels . . . the gold, silver, jewels, and the land thus formed are brought together and piled in heaps by the winds that are produced by the force of actions. They make up the mountains and the continents." I have elided here Vasubandhu's long and interesting discussion of the Sāṃkhya conception of transformation (*pariṇāma*) as a change in properties on the part of a property possessor. On Meru, see I. W. Mabbett, "The Symbolism of Mount Meru," *History of Religions* 23, no. 1 (August 1983): 64–83.
74. *Kośa* 3.100ab; see Pruden, *Abhihdharmakosabhasyam of Vasubandhu*, 2:491. I am leaning on the Mahīśāsaka description.
75. See the remarks in Cabezón, *Sexuality in Classical South Asian Buddhism*, 355. On the uniformity of nature in Buddhist theory, see McGovern, *A Manual of Buddhist Philosophy*, 166–167.
76. *Kośa* 3.19a–c; see Pruden, *Abhidharmakosabhasyam of Vasubandhu*, 2:400.
77. In offering a description of birth above, I omitted from the description one of the possibilities, which is that of infelicity: "Sometimes, whether due to the unfavorable conditions of the mother's diet, or due to karma, the embryo perishes. Then a midwife, having applied medicinal ointment to her hands, places her hands—in which she holds a sharpened blade—into this hideous wound, this foul-smelling, wet and impurity-choked womb. She pulls out the embryo after cutting it limb by limb. And the individual life associated with the embryo by virtue of a [special kind of] karma goes somewhere else." Compare with Pruden, *Abhidharmakosabhasyam of Vasubandhu*, 2:400. Note the rhetorical complexity here: whose point of view (and values) is this meant to enact, given that there is no occupant of the womb for us to identify with? On the sources on which Vasubandhu is here drawing (such as the *Garbhāvakrāntisūtra*), and the possible uses of the distinctive Buddhist imaginaire of birth and imagined points of view enacted therein, see Amy Paris Langenberg, "Love, Unknowing, and Female Filth: The Buddhist Discourse of Birth as a Vector of Social Change for Monastic

Women in Premodern South Asia," in *Primary Sources and Asian Pasts*, ed. Peter C. Bishop and Elizabeth A. Cecil (Berlin: Walter de Gruyter, 2020), 308–340; 314–315.

78. This formulation is adapted from McGovern, *A Manual of Buddhist Philosophy*, 202. See also Changhwan Park, "The Sautrantika Theory of Seeds (bija) Revisited: With Special Reference to the Ideological Continuity Between Vasubandhu's Theory of Seeds and Its Srilata/Darstantika Precedent" (PhD diss., University of California, Berkeley, 2007), 37–38; on *Kośa* 2.57c, see also Steven Collins, *Self and Society: Essays on Pali Literature and Social Theory: 1988-2010* (Chiang Mai: Silkworm Books, 2013), 158.
79. "But it does not make sense that ripening or coming to completion [*pāka*] be applied to the other types of causes. For by 'ripening' [*pāka*] is meant something born of a sequence of directed change [*santatipariṇāmaviśeṣajaḥ*], extending as far as [but not beyond] the result [*phala*] [of that sequence of directed change]." Pradhan, *Abhidharmakośabhāṣya of Vasubandhu*, 90.
80. "Why are nonsentient phenomena [*asattvākhya*]—mountains, rivers, and the like—not considered to be an effect of *vipāka*? Do they not arise from wholesome or unwholesome actions?" See Pruden, *Abhidharmakosabhasyam of Vasubandhu*, 1:289. The answer to this question states that nonsentient phenomena are by nature shared (*sādhāraṇatva*), as others are also able to enjoy them. But the effect of *vipāka*, by definition, is not shared (*asādhāraṇa*), for it is not the case that another person ever experiences the effect of the ripening of an action undertaken by another. See also McGovern, *A Manual of Buddhist Philosophy*, 200.
81. "But why does another person experience the effect of dominance? This is because sentient beings partake of this effect in common on account of its being brought into being by actions that are shared [*sādharaṇakarmasaṃbhūtva*]." Commentary to *Kośa* 2.57. See Pruden, *Abhidharmakosabhasyam of Vasubandhu*, 1:289.
82. I have been considerably influenced by Sally Haslanger, "What Is a (Social) Structural Explanation?" *Philosophical Studies* 173 (2016): 113–130.
83. Cf. Silk, *Materials*, 41.

5. MAKING UP WORLDS

1. Jennifer Ackerman, *Notes from the Shore* (New York: Penguin, 1996), 106.
2. Jean-Paul Sartre, *No Exit and Three Other Plays* (New York: Vintage International, 1989), 17.
3. Jan Westerhoff, *Twelve Examples of Illusion* (Oxford: Oxford University Press, 2010), 103–104.
4. Robert Sugden, "Credible Worlds: The Status of Theoretical Models in Economics," *Journal of Economic Methodology* 7, no. 1 (2000): https://doi.org/10.1080/135017800362220.
5. J. A. Silk, *Materials Toward the Study of Vasubandhu's Viṁśikā (I): Sanskrit and Tibetan Critical Editions of the Verses and Autocommentary; An English Translation and Annotations* (Cambridge, MA: Harvard University Department of South Asian Studies, 2016), 47.
6. For a valuable summary and background, see Lambert Schmithausen, *Plants in Early Buddhism and the Far Eastern Idea of the Buddha-Nature of Grasses and Trees* (Lumbini: Lumbini International Research Institute, 2009), 276.

7. From *The Heart of Buddhist Metaphysics* (*Abhidharmahṛdayaśāstra*), ad 3.1a–b, after Wataru S. Ryose, "A Study of the *Abhidharmahṛdaya*: The Historical Development of the Concept of Karma in the Sarvāstivāda Thought" (PhD diss., University of Wisconsin, 1987), 114. It used to be common for Western scholars to use the reconstructed Sanskrit name Dharmaśrī, but for several Japanese scholars to use Dharmaśreṣṭhin, the latter being preferable (as argued by Bart Dessein). See Johannes Bronkhorst, *Buddhist Teaching in India* (Somerville, MA: Wisdom Publications, 2009), 100n209; and Charles Willemen, Bart Dessein, and Collett Cox, *Sarvāstivāda Buddhist Scholasticism* (Leiden: Brill, 1998), 174.
8. Dharmatrāta, **Miśrakābhidharmaśāstra* (on *Abhidharmahṛdayaśāstra* 3.1a–b), after Ryose, "A Study of the *Abhidharmahṛdaya*," 115.
9. Prahlad Pradhan, *Abhidharmakośabhāṣya of Vasubandhu* (Patna: K. P. Jayaswal Research Institute, 1967), 161. This verse—"the constitutive variety of worlds is the result of action [4.1a–b]"—has been discussed by several philosophers. See Johannes Bronkhorst, *Karma and Teleology: A Problem and Its Solutions in Indian Philosophy* (Tokyo: International Institute for Buddhist Studies, 2000), 67–77; Paul J. Griffiths, "Notes Towards a Critique of Buddhist Karmic Theory," *Religious Studies* 18, no. 3 (1982): 277–291.
10. *Kośa* 2.64cd. See Richard P. Hayes, "Principled Atheism in the Buddhist Scholastic Tradition," *Journal of Indian Philosophy* 16 (1988): 5–28. For the sense it makes for Vasubandhu to have also directed the argument against the principle *pradhāna*, and for understanding an older definition of this Sāṃkhya principle as a variety of totality of all that exists—a mereologically complex unity—see Johannes Bronkhorst, "On the Nature of pradhāna," in *Expanding and Merging Horizons: Contributions to South Asian and Cross-Cultural Studies in Commemoration of Wilhelm Halbfass*, ed. Karin Preisendanz (Vienna: Austrian Academy of Sciences Press, 2007), 373–381.
11. Vasubandhu begins the next chapter, chapter 5, as follows: "We have said above [in verse 4.1a of the *Cutting Edge of Buddhist Thought*] that 'the constitutive variety of worlds is the result of action.' But it is because of the dispositional proclivities [*anuśaya*] that actions accumulate. In the absence of dispositional proclivities, actions are not capable of turning out a new life." Pradhan, *Abhidharmakośabhāṣya of Vasubandhu*, 274. That is, actions are *not* a sufficient condition. Pace Griffiths, "Notes Towards a Critique," 281. It's a small point, but vital. For forward-looking concerns with action, one must look to patterns of behavior to which beings become habituated. In his *The Thirty Verses*, Vasubandhu adds one further condition, namely, the persistence of dispositions to credit our phenomenological experience to a present relation between that which grasps and that which is grasped (*dvayagrāhavāsanā*). I'll discuss this in chapter 7. Even setting aside forward-looking accounts, Vasubandhu is clear that no single action, nor any explanation relying on actions alone, can explain all the circumstances that go into making one's present life. See the discussion on *Kośa* 4.95b; Leo M. Pruden, trans., *Abhidharmakosabhasyam of Vasubandhu* (Berkeley, CA: Asian Humanities Press, 1988–1990), 2:678.
12. Yaśomitra writes, "Tatra sattva-vaicitryaṃ dhātu-gati-yony-ādi-bhedena. Bhājana-vaicitryaṃ merudvīpādibhedena." U. Wogihara, ed., *Sphuṭārthā Abhidharmakośavyākhyā* (Tokyo: Sankibo Buddhist Book Store, 1989), 345.

13. My comments here have been informed by suggestive remarks in a memo by J. J. Gibson, "A Preliminary Description and Classification of Affordances," in *Reasons for Realism*, ed. E. S. Reed and R. Jones (Hillsdale, NJ: Lawrence Erlbaum Associates, 1982), 403–406.
14. Vasubandhu's specific rejection of an argument attempting to claim that there could not be any such intrinsically pleasurable item in the world based on a dispositional account of the causes of pleasure is a response to the following argument: "[There is nothing intrinsically pleasurable] on account of the fact that there are not invariant causes of pleasure. Things that are causes of pleasure, such as food and drink, coolness or warmth, become causes for pain when increased, or if enjoyed at a different time. They should therefore be taken to be causes of pain, and not pleasure." See the long commentary to *Kośa* 6.3; Gelong Lodrö Sangpo, *Annotated Translation of Louis de La Vallee Poussin, Abhidharmakośabhāṣya: The Treasury of the Abhidharma and Its (Auto)commentary* (Delhi: Motilal Banarsidass Publishers, 2012), 3:1888. Against this, as we saw in chapter 3, Vasubandhu says that there is no rule stating that causes may not have finely grained contextual conditions—for something to serve as a cause does not require that it function at all times and in all places. The context is formed by Vasubandhu's arguments to the effect that the Buddha did not mean to deny that there was such a thing as pleasure, but instead to claim that pleasure qua pleasure is dissatisfying.
15. See Mark Johnston, "The Authority of Affect," *Philosophy and Phenomenological Research* 63, no.1 (July 2001): 181–214; 195.
16. "The natural object is the track left by this generalized existence," as Merleau-Ponty says. M. Merleau-Ponty, *Phenomenology of Perception*, trans. Colin Smith (London: Routledge and Kegan Paul, 1962), 311.
17. Pradhan, *Abhidharmakośabhāṣya of Vasubandhu*, 161.
18. "Sati caivaṃ viṣayopabhogaḥ sambhavati, āśrayaramyatve hi kasya pratīkārāya ramyaviṣayopabhogaḥ syāt"; Dvarikadas Shastri, *Abhidharmakośa and Bhāṣya of Ācārya Vasubandhu with Sphūtārthā Commentary of Ācārya Yaśomitra* (Varanasi: Bauddha Bharati Press, 1987), 567.
19. Pradhan, *Abhidharmakośabhāṣya of Vasubandhu*, 161 (my emphasis).
20. Stephen Jay Gould, "Challenges to Neo-Darwinism and Their Meaning for a Revised View of Human Consciousness," Tanner Lectures on Human Values, Clare Hall, Cambridge, April 30 and May 1, 1984, www.tannerlectures.utah.edu, p. 66.
21. I have benefitted from the distinction between "adaptedness" and "adaptation" drawn by John O. Reiss, *Not by Design: Retiring Darwin's Watchmaker* (Berkeley: University of California Press, 2009), 258. Adaptedness gets at "the relation between organisms that have a particular lifestyle and morphological or physiological features that appear to be correlated with that lifestyle." But unlike the theologians Reiss is considering, adaptedness in the Buddhist case would not be measured—if subject to measure at all—with respect to intended ecological roles in such a way that the adaptedness for the role could be explained by any intention that so adapted it. Reiss, *Not by Design*, 128.
22. See Jonathan C. Gold, *Paving the Great Way: Vasubandhu's Unifying Buddhist Philosophy* (New York: Columbia University Press, 2015), 51–56.
23. *Kośa* 1.19d; Pradhan, *Abhidharmakośabhāṣya of Vasubandhu*, 12–13. I discuss the case in more detail in Sonam Kachru, "The Traces of the World in the Tracks of the Philosophers," in *Reasons*

and Lives in Buddhist Traditions: Studies in Honor of Matthew Kapstein, ed. Dan Arnold, Cécile Ducher, and Pierre-Julien Harter (Somerville, MA: Wisdom Publications, 2019), 323–338; 324–326.

24. See *Kośa* 1.30b–d. See Bruce Cameron Hall, "Vasubandhu on Aggregates, Spheres, and Components: Being Chapter One of the Abhidharmakośa" (PhD diss., Harvard University, 1983), 124. If there are no odors and tastes in some region of being, and no desire on the part of the inhabitants there for odors or tastes, could there be corresponding faculties for odor and taste? For a discussion of the arguments and the background concerns, see José Ignacio Cabezón, *Sexuality in Classical South Asian Buddhism* (Somerville, MA: Wisdom Publications, 2017), 353n886.
25. I understand that this distinction holds even where the process (it being such as to have an end) is understood to involve, at some appreciable degree of remove, facts about sentient beings who do indeed act for ends. Note that as a consequence, my notion of a "teleological description" is considerably weaker than Jonathan Bennett would have us recognize as necessary for a genuine type of distinctive explanation. See Jonathan Bennett, "Leibniz's Two Realms," in *Leibniz: Nature and Freedom*, ed. Donald Rutherford and J. A. Cover (Oxford: Oxford University Press, 2005), 135–156.
26. I have been considerably helped and influenced by the discussion of final ends and directed change in Dennis Des Chene, *Physiologia: Natural Philosophy in Late Aristotelian and Cartesian Thought* (Ithaca, NY: Cornell University Press, 1996), 168–200.
27. Matthew T. Kapstein, *Reason's Traces: Identity and Interpretation in Indian and Tibetan Buddhist Thought* (Somerville, MA: Wisdom Publications, 2001), 374 (bracketed changes for emphasis).
28. Kapstein, *Reason's Traces*, 374.
29. After Kapstein, *Reason's Traces*, 374.
30. Of course, however instructive and suggestive, the organic analogy used to bring a sequence under a description is not apt in every single respect. The organic example might suggest that there ought to be no terminus, but rather, an unrelenting and cyclic process of generation, as fruit in turn gives rise to seeds, and these in turn yield further fruit, and so on. Vasubandhu tells us that the analogy is indeed imperfect, and he does not have quite such a cyclical analogy in mind. See Kapstein, *Reason's Traces*, 374.
31. I am indebted for this way of framing the work of teleological descriptions to Michael Thompson, *Life and Action: Elementary Structures of Practice and Practical Thought* (Cambridge, MA: Harvard University Press, 2012), 78.
32. Cf. Silk, *Materials*, 55.
33. Timothy Ferris, *The Whole Shebang: A State-of-the-Universe(s) Report* (New York: Simon and Schuster, 1997), 174. To center one's account around the axis of the cosmological past, as Vasubandhu has done, may also be as conceptually impactful. We are not best served, I think, by attempting to reidentify (in an intratheoretic fashion) Vasubandhu's redescription of content and habituation in terms of received Buddhist models of the relational conditions for perceptual experience then available to him. For a sense of the complexity that can result from such attempts, and for Xuanzang's caution against infelicitous literalism when thinking of Vasubandhu's redescription, see Wei Tat, *Ch'eng Wei-Shih Lun: Doctrine of Mere Consciousness* (Hong Kong: Ch'eng Wei-Shih Lun Publication Committee, 1973), 261.

34. Quoted by Ferris, *The Whole Shebang*, 174; Loewenberg is quoting from Charles Darwin, *Darwin*, ed. Philip Appleman (New York: W. W. Norton, 1970), 1 (emphasis in original).
35. Matthew MacKenzie, "Enacting Selves, Enacting Worlds: On the Buddhist Theory of Karma," *Philosophy East and West* 63, no. 2 (April 2013): 194–212; 194.
36. Quoted in MacKenzie, "Enacting Selves, Enacting Worlds," 197.
37. Though a typically sophisticated discussion of the matter is found in *The Cutting Edge of Buddhist Thought* regarding the structure of awareness events. The worry is this: should any sort of happening (much less full-blown actions)—expressible by a verbal form in Sanskrit—be attributed to awareness? Is the structure of an event at all captured in the grammatical form this would suggest? See Hall, "Vasubandhu on Aggregates, Spheres, and Components," 160.
38. As he could agree, I suspect, with the phenomenological claims MacKenize makes for a karmic arc, an extension of Merleau-Ponty's "intentional arc." If MacKenzie also means to say, as Hubert Dreyfus does, that the connection of mind and world involves not representations but the manifestation of skills and habits stored as dispositions, then there is striking continuity with Vasubandhu's way of making the point. See Hubert L. Dreyfus, "Intelligence Without Representation—Merleau-Ponty's Critique of Mental Representation: The Relevance of Phenomenology to Scientific Explanation," *Phenomenology and the Cognitive Sciences* 1 (2002): 367–383. On the intentional arc in connection with Buddhism, see also Dan Lusthaus, *Buddhist Phenomenology: A Philosophical Investigation of Yogācāra Buddhism and the Ch'eng Wei-Shih Lun* (London: Routledge, 2002), 29–31. I do not agree with MacKenzie, however, that the claims made for karma by Vasubandhu in the chapter on cosmology are *phenomenological* claims. Buddhist cosmology goes far beyond any variety of phenomenological program of which I am aware.
39. MacKenzie, "Enacting Selves, Enacting Worlds," 203.
40. MacKenzie, "Enacting Selves, Enacting Worlds," 204.
41. Dave Ward, David Silverman, and Mario Villalobos, "Introduction: The Varieties of Enactivism," *Topoi* 36 (2017): 365–375; 368.
42. MacKenize is fully seized of this. "Enacting Selves, Enacting Worlds," 199. See also Matthew MacKenzie, "Enacting the Self: Buddhist and Enactivist Approaches to the Emergence of the Self," *Phenomenology and the Cognitive Sciences* 9, no. 1 (2010): 75–99; especially 84–85.
43. The negative part of this claim, the view that descriptions involving karma are neither observation statements nor (analogues to contemporary scientific) theories framed with respect to empirically observable phenomena—a wonder, perhaps, that this has to be said at all—has recently been forcefully articulated by Evan Thompson, *Why I Am Not a Buddhist* (New Haven, CT: Yale University Press, 2020). See especially p. 54. I am only concerned here with the details of Vasubandhu's world. Whether or not one can (or should event attempt to) contrive versions of premodern descriptions to accord with contemporary and empirically informed theorizing, I leave for others to debate.
44. See Robert Kritzer, "Rūpa in the Antarābhava," *Journal of Indian Philosophy* 28 (2000): 235–272; 250, which cites Pradhan, *Abhidharmakośabhāṣya of Vasubandhu*, 127.3–9. See also Robert Kritzer, "Semen, Blood and the Intermediate Existence," *Journal of Indian and Buddhist Studies* 46, no. 2 (March 1988): 30–36.

45. See Kritzer, "Rūpa in the Antarābhava," 250, which cites Pradhan, *Abhidharmakośabhāṣya of Vasubandhu* 127.3–9.
46. I have modified Matthew Kapstein's definition of "strong conjunction" in his analysis of Buddhist mereological principles to more closely track the Vaiśeṣika (and Nyāya) view, which is less intuitive than it is made out in secondary literature. See Kapstein, *Reason's Traces*, 184. See the superb treatment in D. N. Shastri, *Critique of Indian Realism: The Philosophy of Nyāya-Vaiśeṣika and Its Conflict with the Buddhist Dignāga School* (Delhi: Motilal Banarsidass, 1997), 306.
47. Infamously, Vasubandhu considered unintelligible the Sammatīya proposal to think of persons as "depending upon the heaps" (on which our sense of self is based) but being neither identical nor different from these. Vasubandhu couldn't understand whether what was meant was that one has as one's intentional content the heaps when one thinks of a person, or that the heaps are causally responsible for the person—either way, he believed, this would mean that persons were not a variety of identifiable concrete particular. See Kapstein, *Reason's Traces*, 351. To explain this relationship, the Sammatīya appeal to the analogy of fire and fuel (Kapstein, *Reason's Traces*, 351–352). Interestingly, on Amber Carpenter's reading, the Sammatīya proposal makes sense precisely if we think of a complex variety of emergent and recontextualizaing fact, one holding together otherwise disparate parts (at a time and over time). See Amber Carpenter, "Persons Keeping Their Karma Together: The Reasons for the Pudgalavāda in Early Buddhism," in *The Moon Points Back*, ed. Koji Tanaka, Yasuo Deguchi, Jay L. Garfield, and Graham Priest (New York: Oxford University Press, 2015), 1–45. And this relationship is also what MacKenzie, basing himself on Candrakīrti's understanding of it, uses to make sense of "an enacted self." See MacKenzie, "Enacting Selves, Enacting Worlds," 201–202. It is just not a relationship that Vasubandhu believed was available to him.
48. In his commentary on *Kośa* 3.100ab, for which see Pruden, *Abhidharmakosabhasyam of Vasubandhu*, 2:490–494.
49. Mark Siderits, *Buddhism as Philosophy: An Introduction* (London: Ashgate, 2007), 109–111; see also Sonam Kachru, "Minds and Worlds: A Philosophical Commentary on Vasubandhu's Twenty Verses" (PhD diss., University of Chicago, 2015), 380–382.
50. Ernest Jones, *Sigmund Freud: Life and Work* (London: Hogarth, 1953–1957), 1:191. I have it from A. D. Nuttall, *Dead from the Waist Down: Scholars and Scholarship in Literature and the Popular Imagination* (New Haven, CT: Yale University Press, 2003), 57.

6. TRANSPARENT THINGS, THROUGH WHICH THE PAST SHINES

1. Max Black, *A Companion to Wittgenstein's Tractatus* (Cambridge: Cambridge University Press, 1971), 37. Notoriously, there are problems of interpretation and scope. See Peter M. Sullivan, "The Totality of Facts," *Proceedings of the Aristotelian Society* 100 (2000): 175–192.
2. Black, *A Companion to Wittgenstein's Tractatus*, 30.

3. Michael Inwood, *Heidegger: A Very Short Introduction* (Oxford: Oxford University Press, 2000), 31–32.
4. Charles Wright, "Sitting Outside at the End of Autumn," in *Negative Blue: Selected Later Poems* (New York: Farrar, Strauss and Giroux, 2000), 3.
5. Vladimir Nabokov, *Transparent Things* (New York: Vintage International, 1989), 1 (emphasis in original).
6. Nabokov, *Transparent Things*, 1.
7. Cf. J. A. Silk, *Materials Toward the Study of Vasubandhu's Viṁśikā (I): Sanskrit and Tibetan Critical Editions of the Verses and Autocommentary; An English Translation and Annotations* (Cambridge, MA: Harvard University Department of South Asian Studies, 2016), 47.
8. Gregory Bateson, *Naven: A Survey of the Problems Suggested by a Composite Picture of the Culture of a New Guinea Tribe Drawn from Three Points of View* (Stanford, CA: Stanford University Press, 1958), 1.
9. Bateson, *Naven*, 2.
10. One must also keep in mind the limitations inherent in stressing the desirability of (the fiction) of a description in terms of an ethos. The French philosopher Jacques Rancière, inadvertently echoing the Buddhist point that shared worlds "result from the sedimentation of a certain number of inter-twined acts," also points out a limitation with cosmological descriptions—just insofar as a hasty description can miss the fact that a "common world is never simply an ethos." If there is unity, rather, as one can see when one adopts a description in terms of the political accomplishments of actors, it is an achievement, one always involving "a polemical distribution of modes of being and occupations." Jacques Rancière, *The Politics of Aesthetics*, trans. Gabriel Rockhill (New York: Continuum, 2004), 42. As with the anthropologist's other worlds, it is perhaps simpler for Vasubandhu to find such consistent styles of feeling or unifying tones in worlds other than one's own. Ours, for Vasubandhu, is by definition "mixed." But even here, it is only fair to say that a cosmological description does not keep in view the dimension of sociopolitical interaction, make of that what one will. My thanks to Adrienne Ghaly for bringing this work to my attention.
11. Bateson, *Naven*, 2
12. J. J. Jones, *The Mahāvastu* (London: Luzac, 1949), 1:8–9.
13. *Kośa* 3.59a–c; see Prahlad Pradhan, *Abhidharmakośabhāṣya of Vasubandhu* (Patna: K. P. Jayaswal Research Institute, 1967), 164. This question introduces the debate.
14. Genuine automata in Buddhist literature are often intriguingly enough described in Buddhist literature as deriving from Rome (*roma-viṣaya*)—as in the account in the *Lokapaññati* of automata commissioned by Ajātaśatru to guard the Buddha's relics, a story that even claims for Rome the privilege of being where Indian engineers hoped to be reborn; or Greece (*Yavana-deśa*), as in the Bhaiṣajyavastu of the *Mūlasarvāstivādin Vinaya*. See John S. Strong, *The Legend and Cult of Upagupta: Sanskrit Buddhism in North India and South East Asia* (Princeton, NJ: Princeton University Press, 1992), 187; John S. Strong, *Relics of the Buddha* (Delhi: Motilal Banarsidass Press, 2007), 134–135. On virtual beings, see the discussion in *Bodhisattvabhūmi* in A. B. Engle, *The Bodhisattva Path to Unsurpassed Enlightenment: A Complete Translation of the*

Bodhisattvabhūmi (Boulder, CO: Snow Lion, 2016), 116; and in *The Cutting Edge of Buddhist Thought* (*Kośa* 7.49–51c), Leo M. Pruden, trans., *Abhidharmakosabhasyam of Vasubandhu* (Berkeley, CA: Asian Humanities Press, 1988–1990), 4:1169–1171.

15. Pradhan, *Abhidharmakośabhāṣya of Vasubandhu*, 164.
16. Pradhan, *Abhidharmakośabhāṣya of Vasubandhu*, 164.
17. See Pruden, *Abhidharmakosabhasyam of Vasubandhu*, 2:534n409; the debate derives from the *Abhidharma-vibhāṣā-śāstra*, fascicle 7, Taishō vol. 28, text no. 1546, p. 48, a5–25.
18. See the discussion in the *Kathāvatthu*; Shwe Zan Aung and Rhys Davids, trans., *Points of Controversy, or Subjects of Discourse* (London: Pali Text Society, 1979), 345–346.
19. Hermann Jacobi, *Jaina Sūtras* (Delhi: Motilal Banarsidass, 1964), 2:280–282; Albrecht Wezler and Shujun Motegi, *Yuktidīpikā: The Most Significant Commentary on the Sāṃkhyakārikā* (Stuttgart: Franz Steiner Verlag, 1998), 218–219.
20. Augustine, *Concerning the City of God Against the Pagans*, trans. Henry Bettenson (London: Penguin Books, 2003), 985. Hell appears to have been useful to think with in a number of contexts. Gershom Scholem reports Moses de Leon asking: "How is it possible for the soul to suffer in Hell, since Neshamah [the soul proper] is substantially the same as God, and God therefore appears to inflict punishment upon Himself?" Gershom Scholem, *Major Trends in Jewish Mysticism* (New York: Schocken Books, 1974), 241; see 406n125.
21. Thomas S. Kuhn, "A Function for Thought Experiments," in *The Essential Tension: Selected Studies in Scientific Tradition and Change* (Chicago: University of Chicago Press, 1964), 240–265.
22. Thomas S. Kuhn, *The Structure of Scientific Revolutions*, 2nd ed. (Chicago: University of Chicago Press, 1970), 181–191.
23. Robert Sharf, "Is Nirvana the Same as Insentience? Chinese Struggles with an Indian Buddhist Ideal," in *India in the Chinese Imagination: Myth, Religion, and Thought*, ed. John Kieschnick and Meir Shahar (Philadelphia: University of Pennsylvania Press, 2014), 144–145.
24. Again, this is because of cosmology incorporating varieties of causal description. The case of thought experiments conducted with Buddha fields, as I intimated in chapter 5, is different and more closely connected with the sense of thought experiments using possible worlds in contemporary philosophy. Narratives and contemplative exercises present still other varieties of thought experiments, if we allow such experiments to go beyond "argument" narrowly construed and allow for varieties of imaginative practices. For an example of a narrative thought experiment in Buddhism, see Jonardon Ganeri, *The Concealed Art of the Soul: Theories of Self and Practices of Truth in Indian Ethics and Epistemology* (Oxford: Oxford University Press, 2012), 214–215; for an example of a contemplative visionary experiment, see Daniel M. Stuart, "Becoming Animal: Karma and the Animal Realm Envisioned Through an Early Yogācāra Lens," *Religions* 10, no. 6 (2019): 363.
25. Cf. Silk, *Materials*, 49.
26. Samuel Beal, *Si-Yu-Ki, Buddhist Records of the Western World: Translated from the Chinese of Hiuen Tsiang (A.D. 629)* (London: Kegan and Paul, 1906), 2:87 (emphasis in original).
27. Cf. Silk, *Materials*, 51.
28. After Jones, *The Mahāvastu*, 22.

29. Luis O. Gōmez, *The Land of Bliss: The Paradise of the Buddha of Measureless Light: Sanskrit and Chinese Versions of the Sukhāvatīvyūha Sutras* (Delhi: Motilal Banarsidas, 2002), 83; 17; 147.
30. Cf. Silk, *Materials*, 53.
31. Buddhist thought in South Asia (as elsewhere, no doubt) has involved sophisticated and complex thought concerned with power and punishment, such as in the *Aśokāvadāna*, from which I have already cited, but also in a number of other texts and modes. I list here material from which one may take up this suggestion further. Michael Zimmerman, "A Mahāyānist Criticism of *Arthaśāstra*: The Chapter on Royal Ethics in the *Bodhisattva-gocaropāya-visaya-vikurvana-nirdeśa-sūtra*," *Annual Report of the International Research Institute for Advanced Buddhology at Soka University for the Academic Year 1999* 3 (2000): 177–211; Michael Zimmerman, "Only a Fool Becomes a King: Buddhist Stances on Punishment," in *Buddhism and Violence*, ed. Michael Zimmerman (Lumbini: International Research Institute, 2006), 213–242; especially 218. Michael Zimmerman, *The Immorality of Punishment* (New York: Broadview Press, 2011).
32. Wendy Doniger O'Flaherty, *The Hindus: An Alternative History* (New York: Penguin, 2009), 267–269.
33. Pradhan, *Abhidharmakośabhāṣya of Vasubandhu*, 164.
34. Leszek Kolakowski, *The Presence of Myth*, trans. Adam Czerniawski (Chicago: University of Chicago Press, 1989), 9.
35. From the commentary to *Examining Intentional Content* (*Ālambanaparīkṣā*) 2a, after Erich Frauwallner, "Dignāga's Ālambanaparīkṣā," in *Kleine Schriften* (Wiesbaden: Franz Steiner Verlag, 1982), 340–358; 342.
36. Vasubandhu will raise the issue more explicitly later in his arguments, in verses 11–15 of *The Twenty Verses*, when he asks his interlocutor to coordinate the details of any putative physical description of the sensory field of view with the phenomenological evidence of the field *in* view in our experience (for a detailed account, see Sonam Kachru, "Minds and Worlds: A Philosophical Commentary on Vasubandhu's Twenty Verses" [PhD diss., University of Chicago, 2015], 364–376). Vasubandhu exploits the following problem: coordinating the phenomenological description of objects with a metaphysical explanation grounded in a physical characterization *that can explain* our phenomenological characterizations requires meeting the two criteria necessary for any factor to count as a concrete particular in a Buddhist ontology—mereological simplicity and a distinctive causal power. The details are absorbing, but here we are only dealing with an anticipation that the problem of inconsistent descriptions is potentially in play when specifying the nature of a constituent element in an experiential context. But it is instructive that this is anticipated. While it is only the later argument that gives us the necessity for revision, it is the argument from guards in hell that suggests *the shape the revision of our naïve account must take.*
37. Cf. Silk, *Materials*, 55.
38. For Buddhist accounts of ramified content that were developed in Tibet, see José Ignacio Cabézon, *Dose of Emptiness: An Annotated Translation of the "Stong Thun Chen Mo" of Mkhas Grub Dge Legs Dpal Bzang* (New York: State University of New York Press, 1998), 341, 334–345.
39. Cf. Silk, *Materials*, 59.

40. On the metaphorical range of *vāsanā* in a wider South Asian context, see David Shulman, "The Scent of Memory in Hindu South India," in *The Smell Culture Reader*, ed. Jim Drobnick (Oxford: Berg, 2006), 411–427. For an excellent account of Vasubandhu's views on action and habituation, see Karin Meyers, "The Dynamics of Intention, Freedom, and Habituation According to Vasubandhu's *Abhidharmakośabhāṣya*," in *A Mirror Is for Reflection: Understanding Buddhist Ethics*, ed. Jake H. Davis (New York: Oxford University Press, 2017), 239–257.
41. "Kā punariyaṃ vāsanā nāma śravakāṇām? yo hi yat kleśacaritaḥ pūrvam tasya tatkṛtaḥ kāyavākceṣṭāvikāra-hetu-sāmarthya-viśeṣaś citte vāsaneti ucyate." *Kośa* 7.32d; Dvarikadas Shastri, *Abhidharmakośa and Bhāṣya of Ācārya Vasubandhu with Sphūtārthā Commentary of Ācārya Yaśomitra* (Varanasi: Bauddha Bharati Press, 1987), 1093.
42. Cf. Silk, *Materials*, 61.
43. For what follows, I am deeply grateful to Richard Nance. He engaged with a very rough draft of this section in (an initially anonymous) reader report, correctly divining the intention behind these remarks, helpfully pushing back against some of what I was tempted to say, and pointing me to the right sources that could help me refine what was worth saying.
44. Elliott Sober, "What Is the Problem of Simplicity?" in *Simplicity, Inference, and Modelling*, ed. Arnold Zellner, Hugo A. Keuzenkamp, and Michael McAleer (Cambridge: Cambridge University Press, 2002), 13–32; John Dupré, "The Lure of the Simplistic," *Philosophy of Science* 69, no. S3 (September 2002): https://doi.org/10.1086/341852.
45. Elly Vintiadis and Constantinos Mekios, *Brute Facts* (Oxford: Oxford University Press, 2018), 1.
46. See Alexis Sanderson, "The Sarvāstivāda and Its Critics: Anātmavāda and the Theory of Karma," in *Buddhism into the Year 2000*, ed. Dhammakaya Foundation (Bangkok: Dhammakaya Foundation, 1994), 38; Thomas Lee Dowling, "Vasubandhu on the Avijñapti-Rūpa: A Study in Fifth-Century Abhidharma Buddhism" (PhD diss., Columbia University, 1976).
47. Sanderson, "The Sarvāstivāda and Its Critics," 44. European philosophers have long been preoccupied with action at a distance, formulated sometimes as a concern with whether a body can act where it is not. Here, along with this concern, we will have to add another dimension, which is this: can something register being acted on without a body?
48. A reconstruction that I have developed based on the sketch of the argument on distinguishing a complete action from the beginning of the action found in Pruden, *Abhidharmakosabhasyam of Vasubandhu*, 2:561; 2:564–565.
49. Based on Pruden, *Abhidharmakosabhasyam of Vasubandhu*, 2:563–564. See Sanderson, "The Sarvāstivāda and Its Critics," 39, for the category of *paribhogānvayam puṇyam*. Vasubandhu quotes it as being the opinion of the ancient masters. See Dowling, "Vasubandhu on the Avijñapti-Rūpa," 96.
50. Here I am guided by remarks Vasubandhu makes to his interlocutor at the conclusion of the debate. Pruden, *Abhidharmakosabhasyam of Vasubandhu*, 2:566.
51. Dowling, "Vasubandhu on the Avijñapti-Rūpa," 171.
52. Dowling, "Vasubandhu on the Avijñapti-Rūpa," 96–97.
53. Alison Peterman, review of *The Well-Ordered Universe: The Philosophy of Margaret Cavendish*, by Deborah Boyle, *Notre Dame Philosophical Reviews*, March 4, 2019, https://ndpr.nd.edu/news/the-well-ordered-universe-the-philosophy-of-margaret-cavendish/.

54. Peterman, review of *The Well-Ordered Universe* (emphasis in original).
55. Richard Nance, "On What Do We Rely When We Rely on Reasoning?" *Journal of Indian Philosophy* 35, no. 2 (April 2007), 149–167; 154.
56. Nance, "On What Do We Rely," 155–156.
57. The phrase is *na cintayati na vikalpayati*. See Nance, "On What Do We Rely," 156.
58. The *Bodhisattvabhūmi* advocates that the practitioner introduce a partition between those phenomena that are accessible to being captured by reasons and those that are not, allowing that the latter should be venerated as being accessible to Buddhas; see Nance, "On What Do We Rely," 156n29.
59. Cf. Silk, *Materials*, 57. The phrase I have in mind is *bhūtāni kalpyante*.
60. For example, I am here papering over the following problem: when does Vasubandhu think that something inexplicable offers a genuine case of venerating reality rather than a conceptual confusion? For the need for more study of modal analysis, see my remarks on Vasubandhu's way of removing mystery in connection with a curious fact reported about turtles in Roman and Indian Buddhist natural historical reports; Sonam Kachru, "The Traces of the World in the Tracks of the Philosophers," in *Reasons and Lives in Buddhist Traditions: Studies in Honor of Matthew Kapstein*, ed. Dan Arnold, Cécile Ducher, and Pierre-Julien Harter (Somerville, MA: Wisdom Publications, 2019), 323–338; 328-332.

7. WAKING UP AND LIVING ASLEEP

1. Quoted in Marcus Aurelius, *Marcus Aurelius: Meditations*, trans. Gregory Hays (New York: Modern Library, 2003), 47.
2. Hermann Jacobi, *Jaina Sūtras* (Delhi: Motilal Banarsidass, 1964), 1:28.
3. Andy Rotman, *Divine Stories: Divyāvadāna, Part 2* (Somerville, MA: Wisdom Publications, 2018), 123.
4. Keijin Hayashi, "The Term 'True Dream (Satyasvapna)' in the Buddhist Epistemological Tradition," *Journal of Indian Philosophy* 29 (2001): 559–574.
5. For reasons explored in prior chapters, I cannot follow Paul Griffiths in seeing that "[Vasubandhu's] major attempt at explaining the intersubjective and collective nature of our experience centers upon the image of the dream *or* the collective hallucination." Paul Griffiths, *On Being Mindless: Buddhist Meditation and the Mind-Body Problem* (LaSalle, IL: Open Court Press, 1991), 83 (my emphasis). At the same time, Griffiths's discussion of the metaphor of awakening in verse 17 of the *Viṃśikā* makes some of the points made here.
6. J. A. Silk, *Materials Toward the Study of Vasubandhu's Viṁśikā (I): Sanskrit and Tibetan Critical Editions of the Verses and Autocommentary; An English Translation and Annotations* (Cambridge, MA: Harvard University Department of South Asian Studies, 2016), 113.
7. Introducing verse 16; cf. Silk, *Materials*, 111.
8. Following Frauwallner: "Die Wahrnehmung ist eine Erkenntnis durch ebenden Gegenstand." Erich Frauwallner, "Vasubandhu's Vādavidhiḥ," *Wiener Zeitschrift für die Kunde Süd-Und Ostasiens und Archiv Für Indische Philosophie* 1 (1957): 104–147; 120. My paraphrase is

intended to capture the following gloss provided on the definition, for which the Sanskrit is preserved by different philosophers, such as Jinendrabuddhi: "yasyārthasya yad vijñānaṁ vyapadiśyate, yadi tatā eva tad bhavati, nārthāntarād bhavati, tat pratyakṣaṃ." See Masaaki Hattori, *Dignāga, On Perception: Being the Pratyakṣapariccheda of Dignāga's Pramāṇasamuccaya* (Cambridge, MA: Harvard University Press, 1968), 116n2.10.

9. I reconstruct this from the comments on the causal theory of perception in the *Vādaviddhi*, as it goes on to explain how the emphasis on causation as a criterion for perceptual contact serves to exclude erroneous perceptions as well as experience of conventions (content that cannot be described as being or as directly presenting concrete particulars). Frauwallner, "Vasubandhu's Vādaviddhiḥ," 120.
10. As did the Buddhist philosopher Diṅnāga when arguing against this definition of perceptual acquaintance in his *Pramāṇasamuccaya*: "There is no doubt that the *Vādavidhi* is either not Vasubandhu's own work, or that it does not present the pith of his thought. The reason has to do with his statements elsewhere being at variance." See Hattori, *Diṅnāga, On Perception*, 32–35. Vācaspatimiśra took the definition to be Vasubandhu's own. Whereas in the *Nyāyavārttika* of Uddyotakara the author goes unspecified, Vācaspati makes the identification explicit in his *Nyāyavārttika-tātparyaṭīkā*, crediting the definition as deriving from Vasubandhu (*vāsubandhavaṁ*). For the former, see *Nyāyavārttika*, ed. Vindhyesvariprasad (Benares: Kashi Sanskrit Series, 1916), 40.16; for the latter, see *Tātparya-ṭīkā*, ed. R. S. Dravid (Varanasi: Chowkhamba, 1925), 96.4.
11. See Brigit Kellner and John Taber, "Studies in Yogācāra-Vijñānavāda Idealism I: The Interpretation of Vasubandhu's *Viṃśikā*," *Asiatische Studien* 68, no. 3 (2014), 744n111.
12. This is to look at the point made above from the other direction, as it were. The idea of a *pratyakṣa-buddhi*, a perceptual thought that completes a process of perceptual experience beginning with sensory perception narrowly defined (*indriyāśrita-pratyakṣa*) is part of the Mahāvaibhāṣika conception of perceptual knowledge. As Dhammajoti writes: "From the *Nyāyanusāra* we learn . . . that the Sarvāstivāda school holds that a sensory perception as a *pratyakṣa* experience is fully accomplished only in the second moment, on recollection." K. L. Dhammajoti, *Abhidharma Doctrines and Controversies on Perception* (Hong Kong: Centre of Buddhist Studies, University of Hong Kong, 2007), 139; for the arguments of Śrīlāta, see 156.
13. The consequences of perceptual experience being a process taking up many moments (and the ensuing argument from a time lag) might be differently evaluated depending on one's metaphysics of tensed properties: for the Sārvāstivāda, who eschew the connection between existence and the present (and thus are not presentists), the argument is far more involved. See Dhammajoti, *Abhidharma Doctrines and Controversies*, 153. See also Mark Siderits, *Buddhism as Philosophy: An Introduction* (London: Ashgate, 2007), 133–135. For a contemporary version of this argument, attempting to show a role for non-existent objects in any account of intentional content on the basis of temporal and counterfactual cases, see Colin McGinn, "The Objects of Intentionality," in *Consciousness and Its Objects* (Oxford: Clarendon Press, 2004), 220–249; especially 233.
14. For Vasubandhu's arguments for momentariness, see Alexander von Rospatt, *The Buddhist Doctrine of Momentariness: A Survey of the Origins and Early Phase of This Doctrine Up to Vasubandhu* (Stuttgart: Franz Steiner Verlag, 1995), 178–195; especially 183–192.

15. K. L. Dhammajoti, "Ākāra and Direct Perception (pratyakṣa)," *Pacific World Journal* 3 (2007): 245–272; Birgit Kellner, "Changing Frames in Buddhist Thought: The Concept of Ākāra in Abhidharma and in Buddhist Epistemological Analysis," *Journal of Indian Philosophy* 42 (2014): 275–295. On the accounts that Ābhidharmikas can offer with respect to the application of sorting and classification, see Evan Thompson, "What's in a Concept: Conceptualizing the Non-Conceptual in Buddhist Philosophy," in *Reasons and Empty Persons: Mind, Metaphysics, and Morality: Essays in Honor of Mark Siderits*, ed. Christian Coseru (London: Springer, forthcoming).
16. For more detail, see Robert Sharf, "Knowing Blue: Early Buddhist Accounts of Non-Conceptual Sense Perception," *Philosophy East and West* 68, no. 3 (July 2018): 826–870.
17. Cf. Silk, *Materials*, 117.
18. Cf. Silk, *Materials*, 141.
19. This is in verse 19 of Vasubandhu's *Triṃśikā*: "The lingering traces of action, along with the lingering traces of the twofold grasping, bring into being another life, as a result of a process of maturation when the prior maturation ceases." On the idea of the twofold grasping as a distinct kind of disposition that, in addition to the dispositional traces of action, is necessary for rebirth, Sthiramati is helpful: "Karma is mental action that can bear the predicates meritorious, non-meritorious or immovable. The 'lingering dispositional traces of action' are capacities placed in the mental process that is the storehouse [*ālaya*] by actions, serving to bring about a future individual. The twofold grasping is the grasping of that which is grasped, and the grasping of that which grasps. With respect to these, the conception of 'that which is grasped' is a judgment to the effect that 'there is something to be grasped that inhabits one's own mental continuum and is entirely distinct from awareness.' And the conception of 'that which grasps' is the conviction that the aforementioned thing that is grasped is cognized by awareness, or known, or grasped." H. Buescher, *Sthiramati's Triṃśikāvijñaptibhāṣya: Critical Editions of the Sanskrit Text and Its Tibetan Translation* (Vienna: Verlag der Österreichischen Akademie der Wissenschaften, 2007), 112. Sthiramati might be over-specifying what Vasubandhu meant to include under the possible models for the schema of the twofold conceptions. See the excellent discussion of the rich range of models for these terms in Jonathan C. Gold, "No Outside, No Inside: Duality, Reality and Vasubandhu's Illusory Elephant," *Asian Philosophy* 16 (2006): 1–38.
20. I recommend treating *ajñāna* in *The Twenty Verses* (verse 21) as Vasubandhu does *avidyā* in *The Cutting Edge of Buddhist Thought*. (Elsewhere, Vasubandhu argues for these being synonymous. For references, see Kachru, "Minds and Worlds: A Philosophical Commentary on Vasubandhu's Twenty Verses" [PhD diss., University of Chicago, 2015], 554–555n151.) With respect to the latter, because of its being causally effective, it is argued that such unknowing cannot be treated as the mere absence of knowledge; absences can't, for Vasubandhu, be causes. The argument is presented in comments introducing and discussing *Kośa* 3.28c–d. Crucially, not only must unknowing not be treated as a variety of absence, but we have to treat it as that which has knowledge as its contrary. It is what is opposed to knowledge, just as an enemy is not only someone who is not a friend, but someone who works against one. For the twin conditions that unknowing has to meet, see Leo M. Pruden, trans.,

Abhidharmakosabhasyam of Vasubandhu (Berkeley, CA: Asian Humanities Press, 1988–1990), 2:419–420. See also 422 for Vasubandhu's thoughts on this being a functional characterization of unknowing, rather than one that specifies which determinate content and mode of engagement it should, in fact, be associated with.

21. Silk, *Materials*, 123.
22. Silk, *Materials*, 123.
23. Silk, *Materials*, 121.
24. Vladimir Nabokov, *Transparent Things* (New York: Vintage International, 1989), 104.
25. Pruden, *Abhidharmakosabhasyam of Vasubandhu*, 1:222.
26. Dvarikadas Shastri, *Abhidharmakośa and Bhāṣya of Ācārya Vasubandhu, with Sphūtārthā Commentary of Ācārya Yaśomitra* (Varanasi: Bauddha Bharati Press, 1987), 5.
27. Shastri, *Abhidharmakośa and Bhāṣya of Ācārya Vasubandhu*, 5.
28. On *rgyas*, see Kalu Rinpoché, *Jamgön Kongtrul: The Treasury of Knowledge: Book Six, Part Three: Frameworks of Buddhist Philosophy* (Boulder, CO: Snow Lion, 2007), 314n186.
29. Margaret Macdonald, "Sleeping and Waking," in *Journey into Philosophy: An Introduction with Classic and Contemporary Readings*, ed. Stan Baronett (New York: Routledge, 2017), 80–90; 84. It was originally published in *Mind* 62, no. 246 (1953): 202–215.
30. A. V. Williams Jackson, *Vāsavadattā: A Sanskrit Romance* (New York: Columbia University, 1913), 26.
31. Quoted in Michael Veber, "A Different Kind of Dream-Based Skepticism," *Synthese* (2018): https://doi.org/10.1007/s11229-018-01910-2.
32. See Veber, "A Different Kind of Dream-Based Skepticism."
33. Evan Thompson, *Waking, Dreaming, Being: Self and Consciousness in Neuroscience, Meditation, and Philosophy* (New York: Columbia University Press, 2017), 389.
34. Thompson, *Waking, Dreaming, Being*, 391–393.
35. Cf. Silk, *Materials*, 123.
36. Cf. Silk, *Materials*, 123.
37. Paul J. Griffiths, "Buddha and God: A Contrastive Study in Ideas of Maximal Greatness," in *Indian Philosophy: Philosophy of Religion*, ed. Roy W. Perrett (New York: Routledge, 2001), 132–159; 142; see also Roy Tzohar, *A Yogācāra Buddhist Theory of Metaphor* (New York: Oxford University Press, 2018), 179–180.
38. Tzohar, *A Yogācāra Buddhist Theory*, 180–188; Sthiramati's remarks are made on verse 22 of Vasubandhu's *Triṃśikā*, which says, as Sthiramati interprets it, that the reality of the mental must be seen before the causal characterization of the process may be rightly apprehended. Buescher, *Sthiramati's Triṃśikāvijñaptibhāṣya*, 126.
39. Gustav E. Mueller, "The Hegel Legend of 'Thesis-Antithesis-Synthesis,'" *Journal of the History of Ideas* 19, no. 3 (June 1958): 411–414. The model is Johann Gottlieb Fichte's.
40. Plato offers such a hermeneutic model in *Republic* V, 476c6–7. (As do the *Brahmasūtras* 3.2.3, a foundational text for the Vedānta tradition, when it argues that dreaming is erroneous because its nature is not manifested in that state entire, as discussed in Arindam Chakrabarti, "Dream and Love at the Edge of Wisdom: A Contemporary Cross-Cultural Remapping of Vedānta," in *The Bloomsbury Research Handbook of Vedānta*, ed. Ayon Maharaj [London: Bloomsbury Academic,

2020], 445–472.) I have been particularly influenced by Jonathan Lear's account, underscoring Plato's emphasis on a lack of orientation in experience: "In dreams, we experience images without recognizing them as images and without understanding their deeper meanings. It is not quite correct to say that in dreams we think we are awake. Part of what it is to think that we are awake is to exercise the capacity to distinguish between waking and dream states, and it is this capacity that goes to sleep . . . so again there is disorientation: we lose the capacity to recognize our dream as a dream and thus to determine what it is about." See Jonathan Lear, *Wisdom Won from Illness: Essays in Philosophy and Psychoanalysis* (Cambridge, MA: Harvard University Press, 2017), 212. I think that the threefold structure of experience concerns orientation as well.

41. Édouard Huber, *Sūtrālamkāra, Traduit en Français sur la version Chinoise de Kumārajīva* (Paris: Leroux, 1908), 342–355.
42. For the connection between the use of frame stories and the idea of a dream within a dream, analogous to a play within a play, see Wendy Doniger O' Flaherty, "The Dream Narrative and the Indian Doctrine of Illusion," *Daedalus* 111, no. 3 (Summer 1982): 93–113; for a South Asian context in which the earlier analogues for the narrative technique appear to lie in ritual structure, see C. Z. Minkowski, "Ritual Structure," *Journal of the American Oriental Society* 109, no. 3 (1989): 401–420.
43. Jean Starobinski, *Montaigne in Motion* (Chicago: University of Chicago Press, 1985), 3.
44. Buddhism is associated with these features in Buddhist tales. See Andy Rotman, *Divine Stories*, 11.
45. Friedrich Nietzsche, "On Truth and Lies in a Nonmoral Sense," quoted in Paul Feyerabend, *Philosophy of Nature* (Cambridge: Polity, 2018), 78.
46. He is more careful elsewhere, though he does not allow for forms of order captured in descriptions of phenomena that do not so much violate causality as gesture at a system other than our own: "Indeed, it is only by means of the rigid and regular web of concepts that the waking man clearly sees that he is awake; and it is precisely because of this that he sometimes thinks that he must be dreaming when this web of concepts is torn by art . . . In fact, because of the way that myth takes it for granted that miracles are always happening, the waking life of a mythically inspired people—the ancient Greeks, for instance—more closely resembles a dream than it does the waking world of a scientifically disenchanted thinker." Nietzsche, "On Truth and Lies," quoted in Feyerabend, *Philosophy of Nature*, 78. Stories suggest that such an order is there, though these are orders that are not so much given as made, representing orders of belief and experience into which one has to be tutored. See Amber D. Carpenter, "Transformative Vision: Coming to See the Buddha's Reality," in *Buddhist Literature as Philosophy, Buddhist Philosophy as Literature*, ed. Rafal K. Stepien (Albany: State University of New York Press, 2020), 35–61.
47. Carpenter, "Transformative Vision," 42.
48. The way a concept of realism about truth entails something like a concept of omniscience for Michael Dummett. See Michael Dummett, "The Metaphysics of Time," in *Truth and the Past* (New York: Columbia University Press, 2004), 94–95. For the concepts of omniscience in connection with karma possibly in play here, see Prahlad Pradhan, *Abhidharmakośabhāṣya of Vasubandhu* (Patna: K. P. Jayaswal Research Institute, 1967), 478; 474. Kapstein, *Reason's Traces*,

375; 148. See Paul Griffiths, *On Being Buddha: The Classical Doctrine of Buddhahood* (Albany: State University of New York Press, 1994), 69; P. S. Jaini, "On the Sarvajñatva (Omniscience) of Mahāvīra and the Buddha," in *Buddhist Studies in Honor of I. B. Horner*, ed. Lance Cousins (Dordrecht: Reidel, 1974), 71–90; Sara McClintock, *Omniscience and the Rhetoric of Reason: Śāntarakṣita and Kamalaśīla on Rationality, Argumentation, and Religious Authority* (Somerville, MA: Wisdom Publications, 2010).

49. Verse 22d in Silk, *Materials*, 145. It explicitly goes on to mention omniscience.
50. For such an interpretation of Vasubandhu oriented by his oeuvre and not only *The Twenty Verses*, see Jonathan C. Gold, *Paving the Great Way: Vasubandhu's Unifying Buddhist Philosophy* (New York: Columbia University Press, 2015), 215.
51. Maria Heim, *Voice of the Buddha: Buddhaghosa on the Immeasurable Words* (New York: Oxford University Press, 2018), 36–43; though she would also recommend dropping all talk of meaning as providing truth conditions as well. The notion of analysis without end is also how the *Vibhāṣā* puts things, claiming with respect to the interpretation of the Buddha's utterances that as the meanings of his words are limitless, explication and analysis must continue without end. See Collett Cox, "The Unbroken Treatise: Scripture and Argument in Early Buddhist Scholasticism," in *Innovations in Religious Traditions: Essays in the Interpretation of Religious Change*, ed. Michael A. Williams, Collett Cox, and Martin Jaffee (Berlin: Mouton De Gruyter, 1992), 143–190. For the claim that "reality" is a vacuous concept in Yogācāra, see Gold, *Paving the Great Way*, 274n30.
52. Labor that was undertaken by generations of Buddhist scholars as well. If I understand Roy Tzohar's account correctly, Sthiramati's overarching philosophical project may well have been to try to secure the meaningfulness of crediting characteristic Yogācāra claims with a distinctively metaphysical status notwithstanding the pressures of the above variety of contextualism. See Tzohar, *A Yogācāra Buddhist Theory*, 178–205.
53. I found helpful here Mark A. Wrathall's comments on the conditions of truth as discussed by Heidegger and Davidson in *Unconcealment: Truth, Language, and History* (Cambridge: Cambridge University Press, 2011), 47.
54. Verse 27 in Buescher, *Sthiramati's Triṃśikāvijñaptibhāṣya*, 134.
55. G. E. M. Anscombe, *An Introduction to Wittgenstein's Tractatus* (New York: Harper and Row, 1959), 19.
56. In 25ab, and in comments thereon, Buescher, *Sthiramati's Triṃśikāvijñaptibhāṣya*, 128–130.
57. Verse 22c in Buescher, *Sthiramati's Triṃśikāvijñaptibhāṣya*, 126. More particularly, the concrete particulars are specified in terms of their being "conditioning factors" (*saṃskāras*).
58. 25a–c and commentary thereon, Buescher, *Sthiramati's Triṃśikāvijñaptibhāṣya*, 130.
59. Pruden, *Abhidharmakosabhasyam of Vasubandhu*, 3:813; Shastri, *Abhidharmakośa and Bhāṣya of Ācārya Vasubandhu*, 811; Gold, *Paving the Great Way*, 38. The issue concerns the *svabhāva* or nature of something.
60. Comment to 25c, Buescher, *Sthiramati's Triṃśikāvijñaptibhāṣya*, 130.
61. Verse 25d in Buescher, *Sthiramati's Triṃśikāvijñaptibhāṣya*, 130.
62. Buescher, *Sthiramati's Triṃśikāvijñaptibhāṣya*, 134.
63. As Sthiramati recognizes in his commentary introducing verse 22 of the *Triṃśikā*: "If all this is simply presentation of content, how is it not in contradiction with scripture? That there

are three natures—the constructed, the causally dependent, and the perfected—is stated in scripture, and because of that there is no contradiction: on account of the fact that it is only given that there is just presentation that the three natures can be established." Buescher, *Sthiramati's Triṃśikāvijñaptibhāṣya*, 122.

64. The claim is made clearest in *Triṃśikā* 17b–c: "Insofar as something is constructed it does not exist" (*yad vikalpyate tena tan nāsti*). On *vikalpa* as process, Vasubandhu is explicit in the *Triṃśikā* 21ab: "But the dependent nature is construction, which occurs in reliance on conditions" ("paratantrasvabhāvas tu vikalpaḥ pratyayodbhavaḥ"). Buescher, *Sthiramati's Triṃśikāvijñaptibhāṣya*, 122. As Sthiramati explicitly says in his comments on *Triṃśikā* 20: "A thing, that is to say, a cognitive object that has been constructed, does not exist, on account of its not being an existing particular. Therefore, that thing is precisely something whose nature is constructed, *and not something whose nature involves being directly subject to causes and conditions.*" Buescher, *Sthiramati's Triṃśikāvijñaptibhāṣya*, 122 (my emphasis).
65. David Lasar Friedmann, *Madhyāntavibhāgaṭīkā: Analysis of the Middle Path and the Extremes* (Utrecht: 1937), 14.
66. Glossing verse 21cd, Buescher, *Sthiramati's Triṃśikāvijñaptibhāṣya*, 124.
67. Buescher, *Sthiramati's Triṃśikāvijñaptibhāṣya*, 132.
68. Buescher, *Sthiramati's Triṃśikāvijñaptibhāṣya*, 134.
69. Buescher, *Sthiramati's Triṃśikāvijñaptibhāṣya*, 139.
70. Buescher, *Sthiramati's Triṃśikāvijñaptibhāṣya*, 139.
71. Buescher, *Sthiramati's Triṃśikāvijñaptibhāṣya*, 139.
72. Buescher, *Sthiramati's Triṃśikāvijñaptibhāṣya*, 134.
73. See Matthew T. Kapstein, "Buddhist Idealists and Their Jain Critics on Our Knowledge of External Objects," *Royal Institute of Philosophy Supplement* 74 (2014): 123–147; Gold, "No Outside, No Inside." I hope to take up elsewhere the connection between the practice intimated here by Sthiramati and the attentional practice of nonapprehension—the yoga of *anupalamba*—expressed (and, I am tempted to say, exemplified and enacted) in the *Perfection of Wisdom* literature.
74. See Natalie D. Gummer, "Sacrificial Sūtras: Mahāyāna Literature and the South Asian Ritual Cosmos," *Journal of the American Academy of Religion* 82, no. 4 (December 2014): 1091–1126; 1102–1103.
75. Bertrand Russell, *A Critical Exposition of the Philosophy of Leibniz* (London: Allen and Unwin, 1937), xiii.
76. Nicholas Rescher, *G. W. Leibniz's Monadology: An Edition for Students* (Pittsburgh, PA: University of Pittsburgh Press, 1991), 11.

CONCLUSION: THE FUTURE OF PAST SYSTEMS OF POSSIBILITY

1. Andy Rotman, *Divine Stories: Divyāvadāna, Part 2* (Somerville, MA: Wisdom Publications, 2018), 95.
2. J. J. Jones, *The Mahāvastu* (London: Luzac, 1949), 1:6.

3. Jones, *The Mahāvastu*, 1:23–24.
4. C. D. C. Reeve, *Action, Contemplation and Happiness: An Essay on Aristotle* (Cambridge, MA: Harvard University Press, 2012), 1.
5. Brian O'Shaughnessy, *The Will: A Dual Aspect Theory, Volume 2* (Cambridge: Cambridge University Press, 2008), 319–326; Peter Godfrey-Smith, *Other Minds: The Octopus, the Sea, and the Deep Origins of Consciousness* (New York: Farrar, Straus and Giroux, 2017), 24.
6. See Tyler Burge, "Individualism and Self-Knowledge," *Journal of Philosophy* 85, no. 11 (November 1988): 649–663; 650. See also Burge, "Individualism and the Mental," *Midwest Studies in Philosophy* 4, no. 1 (September 1979): 73–121.
7. I ask the reader here to allow me the use of this word "constraint" in a manner at once consistent with Vasubandhu's sense of *naiyamya*—the fact of having constraints, constitutive in part of what we mean to gesture at in speaking of worlds—and the use of *niyama* on the part of Vasubandhu's interlocutor, thought to be an essential feature of our experiences being about some stretch of "the" world.
8. The story is included in Leszek Kolakowski, *Is God Happy? Selected Essays* (New York: Penguin, 2012), 307–313; 311.
9. Edwin Curley, "Dialogues with the Dead," *Synthese* 67, no. 1 (April, 1986): 33–49.
10. Robert Irwin, *Night and Horses and the Desert: An Anthology of Classical Arabic Literature* (Woodstock, NY: Overlook Press, 2002), 86.
11. Lauren M. Bausch, "Kosalan Philosophy in the Kāṇva Śatapatha Brāhmaṇa and the Suttanipāta" (PhD diss., University of California, Berkeley, 2015), 166, 171; 3.
12. Karl Marx, *Economic and Philosophical Manuscripts of 1884* (Mineola, NY: Dover, 2007), 156.
13. Leszek Kolakowski, *Main Currents of Marxism* (New York: W. W. Norton, 2005), 111.
14. Kolakowski, *Main Currents*, 111.
15. As it would, should one wish to connect Vasubandhu's commitment to the twofold constraint provided by being a life-form and one's cosmological past with, say, Hegel's account of action as reconstructed by Charles Taylor. Taylor's Hegel also asks us to make two recontextualizations: we must recontextualize the activity of an individual within a community, and the community within the work of spirit. See Charles Taylor, "Hegel and the Philosophy of Action," in *Hegel on Action*, ed. Arto Laitinen and Constantine Sandis (New York: Palgrave-Macmillan, 2010), 22–41. While they are formally similar, much will depend on the exact way of motivating each of the concepts involved.
16. Marx, *Economic and Philosophical Manuscripts*, 75.
17. Vasubandhu has two accounts from which to choose. In *Against Selves* he offers a demanding version according to which what is done is not only caused but rendered intelligible by rationalizing pro-attitudes such as desires (wanting this-and-that), beliefs, and even deliberation. Matthew T. Kapstein, *Reason's Traces: Identity and Interpretation in Indian and Tibetan Buddhist Thought* (Somerville, MA: Wisdom Publications, 2001), 373. But there is also a less stringent account on which action as intending is really "shaping of consciousness in relation to that which is good, bad, or neither." See Artemus B. Engle, *The Inner Science of Buddhist Practice: Vasubandhu's Summary of the Five Heaps with Commentary by Sthiramati* (Ithaca, NY: Snow Lion, 2009), 232.

18. Prahlad Pradhan, *Abhidharmakośabhāṣya of Vasubandhu* (Patna: K. P. Jayaswal Research Institute, 1967), 126; see Sonam Kachru, "Things You Wouldn't Think to Look for in One Place: A Note on an All-Too-Brief Example on Life and Matter in Abhidharmakośabhāṣyam ad 3.14c," *Journal of the American Oriental Society* 137, no. 4 (2017), 677.
19. From *Genjokoan*, quoted in Bret W. Davis, "The Philosophy of Zen Master Dōgen: Egoless Perspectivism," in *The Oxford Handbook of World Philosophy*, ed. William Edelglass and Jay L. Garfield (Oxford: Oxford University Press, 2011), 348–361; 357.
20. Vincent Eltschinger, *Caste and Buddhist Philosophy: Continuity of Some Buddhist Arguments Against the Realist Interpretation of Social Denominations* (Delhi: Motilal Banarsidass, 2012), 113. See Bryce Huebner, "The Interdependence and Emptiness of Whiteness," in *Buddhism and Whiteness: Critical Reflections*, ed. George Yancy and Emily McRae (Lanham, MD: Lexington Books, 2019), 231.
21. "For experience," says Dharmakīrti, "generates convictions of certainty according to the repetition of thoughts. For example, even though there is no difference in the seeing of visible properties, there are ideas of a corpse, an object of desire and something to be eaten." Translation in Richard P. Hayes, "Whose Experience Validates What for Dharmakīrti?" in *Relativism, Suffering and Beyond: Essays in Memory of Bimal K. Matilal*, ed. Purushottama Bilimoria and J. N. Mohanty (Delhi: Oxford University Press, 1997), 105–118. For background to the verse, see Étienne Lamotte, *Le Traité de la Grande Vertu de Sagesse de Nāgārjuna (Mahāprajñāpāramitāśāstra)*, vol. 2, *Chapitres 16–30* (Louvain: Publications de l'Institut Orientaliste de Louvain, 1981), 733.
22. John D. Dunne, *Foundations of Dharmakīrti's Philosophy* (Somerville, MA: Wisdom Publications, 2004), 184–186.
23. Catherine Prueitt, "Karmic Imprints, Exclusion, and the Creation of the Worlds of Conventional Experience in Dharmakīrti's Thought," *Sophia* 57, no. 2 (2018): 313–335.
24. I am quoting here from Carl Bielefeldt's translation, which I have found online: https://zmm.org/wp-content/uploads/2020/02/Mountains-and-Rivers-Sutra-Bielefeldt-Translation.pdf, 6–7. See also Dōgen, "Mountains and Waters Sūtra," in *Moon in a Dewdrop: Writings of Zen Master Dōgen*, ed. Kazuaki Tanahashi (New York: North Point Press, 1985), 97–107; 104.
25. This is indebted to John Haugeland's interpretation of Heidegger's sense of Dasein. See John Haugeland, *Dasein Disclosed: John Haugeland's Heidegger* (Cambridge, MA, Harvard University Press, 2013), 182. Unlike Haugeland's Heidegger, Dōgen does not believe we already know whether or not we may extend such a form of understanding to animals.
26. Quoted in Davis, "The Philosophy of Zen Master Dōgen," 358. In *Mountains and Waters Sutra*, Dōgen says: "Do not foolishly assume that all kinds of beings must use as water what we understand as water. When those who study Buddhism seek to learn about water, they should not stick to (the water of) humans"; Bielefeldt, "The Mountains and Rivers Sutra," 7. See also Tanahashi, *Moon in a Dewdrop*, 106.
27. Quoted in Davis, "The Philosophy of Zen Master Dōgen," 357. Dōgen embeds his discussion of the image within the following frame: "In general, then, the way of seeing mountains and rivers differs according to the type of being that sees them . . . and these different ways of seeing are the conditions under which water is killed or given life." Bielefeldt, "The

Mountains and Rivers Sutra," 4; Tanahashi, *Moon in a Dewdrop*, 102. See also the discussion of "It is like a palace for fish, a jeweled ornament for gods," in the *Genjokoan*, discussed in Davis, "The Philosophy of Zen Master Dōgen," 358.

28. Bielefeldt, "The Mountains and Rivers Sutra," 4–5; Tanahashi, *Moon in a Dewdrop*, 102.
29. Bielefeldt, "The Mountains and Rivers Sutra," 4; Tanahashi, *Moon in a Dewdrop*, 102.
30. Quoted in Haugeland, *Dasein Disclosed*, 253.
31. Haugeland, *Dasein Disclosed*, 253–254.
32. See Ian Hacking, *Historical Ontology* (Cambridge, MA: Harvard University Press, 2002), 97. A finer specification would also speak of variable attitudes that can be associated with different moves that could possibly be made within a style of reasoning.
33. As Feyerabend once put it, "There seems to exist strong *prima facie* evidence *against* the existence of insuperable conceptual schemes." Paul Feyerabend, *Philosophy of Nature* (Cambridge: Polity, 2018), 211–213. See also Michael Forster, "On the Very Idea of Denying the Existence of Radically Different Conceptual Schemes," *Inquiry* 41 (1998): 133–185; Michael Forster, *Wittgenstein on the Arbitrariness of Grammar* (Princeton, NJ: Princeton University Press, 2004), 28–30.
34. Peter Brown, *The Body and Society: Men, Women and Sexual Renunciation in Early Christianity* (New York: Columbia University Press, 2008), xlv.
35. Brown, *The Body and Society*, xlv.
36. Steven Collins, *Nirvana and Other Buddhist Felicities: Utopias of the Pali Imaginaire* (Cambridge: Cambridge University Press, 1998), 81.
37. Sheldon Pollock, "Pretextures of Time," *History and Theory* 46, no. 3 (2007): 366–383.
38. In an interview with Samuel Loncar and in conversation with Peter Adamson for the *Los Angeles Review of Books*, Carlos Fraenkel sounded a similar note of caution: "Again: it seems to me that being a philosopher and pursuing the truth in a Platonic or Aristotelian universe isn't the same as being a philosopher and pursuing the truth in our post-metaphysical universe." Loncar, "Decolonizing Philosophy: Samuel Loncar Interviews Carlos Fraenkel and Peter Adamson About Islam, Reason, and Religion," *Marginalia*, December 21, 2018, https://marginalia.lareviewofbooks.org/decolonizing-philosophy-samuel-loncar-interviews-carlos-fraenkel-peter-adamson-islam-reason-religion/. The debate may be fruitfully connected to the work of Pierre Hadot and Michel Foucault. On the one hand, Hadot wished for Foucault to have seen the significance of cosmology and the need to situate care of the self within such a cosmic dimension. See Pierre Hadot, *Philosophy as a Way of Life*, ed. Arnold I. Davidson (Oxford: Blackwell, 1995), 26; on the other hand, Hadot could maintain that "modern man can practice the spiritual exercises of antiquity, at the same time separating them from the philosophical or mythic discourse which comes along with them." See *Philosophy as a Way of Life*, 212. The question is not whether they can be separated. The question is the change in meaning consequent to any such separation.
39. I should say that I have been inspired in this work by two compelling attempts to capture something of the experience of being an intellectual in a medieval Buddhist world. See Malcolm David Eckel, *To See the Buddha: A Philosopher's Quest for the Meaning of Emptiness* (Princeton, NJ: Princeton University Press, 1992); see also Maria Heim, *Voice of the Buddha: Buddhaghosa on the Immeasurable Words* (New York: Oxford University Press, 2018).

40. Premodern traditions typically answer a generalized version of such a question quite explicitly, though scholars and contemporary philosophers have been slower to thematize what is at issue here: a variety of faith, or confidence in one's orientation to the moral and rational intelligibility of the world and the sense it makes to pursue certain projects of self-transformation within it. One may point to the role of *śraddhā* in Indian traditions, quite distinct from attitudes directed at propositions beyond what we have evidence for, as it is in Christian traditions, and Christian-influenced traditions. See Matthew T. Kapstein, "Stoics and Bodhisattvas: Spiritual Exercise and Faith in Two Philosophical Traditions," in *Philosophy as a Way of Life, Ancients and Moderns: Essays in Honor of Pierre Hadot*, ed. M. Chase, S. R. L. Clark, and M. McGhee (Oxford: Wiley-Blackwell, 2013), 99–115; especially 107–113.
41. Robert Musil, *The Man Without Qualities* (New York: Vintage International, 1996), 1:10–11.
42. Pradhan, *Abhidharmakośabhāṣya of Vasubandhu*, 121. As Robert Kritzer notes, later in the discussion (in connection with the apparently spontaneous generation of maggots in rotting meat), Vasubandhu brings an inconclusive discussion of the possible explanations and causal antecedents for this phenomenon to an end by saying (in my gloss): "This is precisely why the Buddha said that 'the actions and results of beings are inconceivable'" (*ata eva coktaṃ bhagavata acintya sattvānāṃ karmavipāka iti*). See Robert Kritzer, "Rūpa in the Antarābhava," *Journal of Indian Philosophy* 28 (2000): 235–272; 263n50. Any future study of such a norm of inconceivability in *The Cutting Edge of Buddhist Thought* must begin with Robert Kritzer, "Unthinkable Matters: The Term *acintya* in the Abhidharmakośabhāṣya," in *Early Buddhism and Abhidharma Thought: In Honor of Doctor Hajime Sakurabe on His Seventy-Seventh Birthday*, ed. Sakurabe Ronshu Committee (Kyoto: Heirakuji Shoten, 2002), 65–86.
43. See II.121 in S. K. Belvalkar, *Kāvyādarśa of Daṇḍin* (Poona: Oriental Book-Supplying Agency, 1924), 24.
44. For this translation, and for helpful remarks contextualizing it as an argument with Tu Fu on the comparative longevity of the environment and works of civilization, see Donald Keene, *A History of Japanese Literature: World Within Walls, Japanese Literature of the Pre-Modern Era, 1600–1867* (New York: Columbia University Press, 1999), 105.
45. See Mencius, *Mencius*, trans. D. C. Lau (New York: Penguin Classics, 2004), 248; for Ye Xie's "On the Origins of Poetry," see Stephen Owen, *Readings in Chinese Literary Thought* (Cambridge, MA: Harvard University Press, 1992), 577. I owe the citations to Mencius and to Ye Xie, to Karl-Heinz Pohl, "Continuities and Discontinuities in Chinese Literary Criticism—From the Premodern to the Modern Periods," in *Is a History of Chinese Literature Possible? Towards the Birth of Chinese Literary Criticism*, ed. Wolfgang Kubin (Munich: Edition Global, 2013), 1–24; 5.

APPENDIX: *THE TWENTY VERSES* OF VASUBANDHU IN TRANSLATION

1. Matthew T. Kapstein, *Reason's Traces: Identity and Interpretation in Indian and Tibetan Buddhist Thought* (Somerville, MA: Wisdom Publications, 2001), 349.
2. See Richard Nance, *Models of Teaching and the Teaching of Models: Contextualizing Indian Buddhist Commentary* (New York: Columbia University Press, 2012), 100–120.

3. See Birgit Kellner and John Taber, "Studies in Yogācāra-Vijñānavāda Idealism I: The Interpretation of Vasubandhu's *Viṃśikā*," *Asiatische Studien* 68, no. 3 (2014): 709–756.
4. J. A. Silk, *Materials Towards the Study of Vasubandhu's Viṃśikā (I): Sanskrit and Tibetan Critical Editions of the Verses and Autocommentary; An English Translation and Annotations* (Cambridge, MA: Harvard University Department of South Asian Studies, 2016).
5. Fernando Tola and Carmen Dragonetti, *Being as Consciousness: Yogācāra Philosophy of Buddhism* (New Delhi: Motilal Banarsidass, 2004), 167n44; Kellner and Taber, "Studies in Yogācāra-Vijñānavāda Idealism."
6. See Paul J. Griffiths, "Buddhist Hybrid English: Some Notes on Philology and Hermeneutics for Buddhologists," *Journal of the International Association of Buddhist Studies* 4, no. 2 (1981): 17–33.
7. Lawrence J. McCrea and Parimal G. Patil, *Buddhist Philosophy of Language in India: Jñānaśrīmitra on Exclusion* (New York: Columbia University Press, 2010), 35–40.
8. See "Mahāyāna" in Robert E. Buswell Jr. and Donald S. Lopez Jr., *The Princeton Dictionary of Buddhism* (Princeton, NJ: Princeton University Press, 2014).
9. José Ignacio Cabezón, "Vasubandhu's *Vyākhyāyukti* on the Authenticity of the Mahāyāna Sūtras," in *Texts in Context: Traditional Hermeneutics in South Asia*, ed. Jeffrey R. Timm (Albany: State University of New York Press, 1992), 221–243.
10. See Silk, *Materials*, 151.
11. At the time of writing this, I could not get access to my papers or books. The relevant discussion may be found on pp. 302–303 of Gelongma Karma Migme Chodron's translation into English of Étienne Lamotte's French translation of the *Mahāprajñāpāramitāśāstra*, available online: https://archive.org/details/mahaprajnaparamitasastraofnagarjunavol1etiennelamotte_357_g.
12. Sylvain Lévi, "Notes Indiennes. I: Deux notes sur la Viṃśatikā de Vasubandhu: 1. La défaite de Vemacitra; 2. Un fragment de l'Upāli sutra en Sanscrit," *Journal Asiatique* 206 (1925): 17–35. One may consult the Pāli version of the narrative of Upāli as well: http://www.themindingcentre.org/dharmafarer/wp-content/uploads/2009/12/27.1-Upali-S-m56-piya.pdf.

BIBLIOGRAPHY

Ackerman, Jennifer. *Notes from the Shore*. New York, Penguin, 1996.

Agostini, Giulio. "Buddhist Sources on Feticide as Distinct from Homicide." *Journal of the International Association of Buddhist Studies* 27, no. 1 (2004): 63–97.

Akins, Kathleen. "Of Sensory Systems and the 'Aboutness' of Mental States." *Journal of Philosophy* 93, no. 7 (July 1996): 337–372.

Alanen, Lilli. "Descartes's Dualism and the Philosophy of Mind." *Revue de Métaphysique et de Morale* 94, no. 3 (1989): 391–413.

Ambrose, Alice. "Wittgenstein on Mathematical Proof." *Mind* 91 (1982): 264–272.

Anscombe, G. E. M. *An Introduction to Wittgenstein's Tractatus*. New York: Harper and Row, 1959.

Arsić, Branka. *On Leaving: A Reading in Emerson*. Cambridge, MA: Harvard University Press, 2010.

Augustine. *Concerning the City of God Against the Pagans*, trans. Henry Bettenson. London: Penguin Books, 2003.

Aung, Shwe Zan, and Rhys Davids, trans. *Points of Controversy, or Subjects of Discourse*. London: Pali Text Society, 1979.

Aurelius, Marcus. *Marcus Aurelius: Meditations*, trans. Gregory Hays. New York: Modern Library, 2003.

Austin, J. L. *Sense and Sensibilia*. Oxford: Oxford University Press, 1962.

Bapat, P. V., and A. Hirakawa. *Shan-chien-P'i-P'o-Sha: A Chinese Version by Saṁghabhadra of Samantapāsādikā*. Poona: Bhandarkar Oriental Institute, 1970.

Barnes, Elizabeth. *The Minority Body: A Theory of Disability*. Oxford: Oxford University Press, 2016.

Barwich, Ann-Sophie. "A Critique of Olfactory Objects." *Frontiers in Psychology* 10, no. 1337 (2019): https://doi.org/10.3389/fpsyg.2019.01337.

Bateson, Gregory. *Naven: A Survey of the Problems Suggested by a Composite Picture of the Culture of a New Guinea Tribe Drawn from Three Points of View*. Stanford, CA: Stanford University Press, 1958.

Bausch, Lauren M. "Kosalan Philosophy in the Kāṇva Śatapatha Brāhmaṇa and the Suttanipāta." PhD diss., University of California, Berkeley, 2015.

Beal, Samuel. *Si-Yu-Ki, Buddhist Records of the Western World: Translated from the Chinese of Hiuen Tsiang (A.D. 629)*. 2 vols. London: Kegan and Paul, 1906.

Beckett, Samuel. *Proust and Three Dialogues with Georges Duthuit*. London: J. Calder, 1965.

Belvalkar, S. K. *Kāvyādarśa of Daṇḍin*. Poona: Oriental Book-Supplying Agency, 1924.

Bennett, Jonathan. "Leibniz's Two Realms." In *Leibniz: Nature and Freedom*, ed. Donald Rutherford and J. A. Cover, 135–156. Oxford: Oxford University Press, 2005.

Bhattacharya, Vidushekhara. *The Āgamaśāstra of Gauḍapāda*. Delhi: Motilal Banarsidass, 1989 [1943].

Biderman, Shlomo. *Crossing Horizons: World, Self, and Language in Indian and Western Thought*. New York: Columbia University Press, 2008.

Birch, Jonathan, Alexandra K. Schnell, and Nicola S. Clayton. "Dimensions of Animal Consciousness." *Trends in Cognitive Sciences* 24, no. 10 (October 2020): https://doi.org/10.1016/j.tics.2020.07.007.

Black, Max. *A Companion to Wittgenstein's Tractatus*. Cambridge: Cambridge University Press, 1971.

Block, Ned. "On a Confusion About a Function of Consciousness." *Behavioral and Brain Sciences* 18 (1995): 227–247.

Blumenberg, Hans. *Lebenszeit und Weltzeit*. Frankfurt: Suhrkamp, 1986.

Bodewitz, H. W. *Jaiminīya Brāhmana 1.1–65: Translation and Commentary, with a Study of Agnihotra and Prāṇāgnihotra*. Leiden: E. J. Brill, 1973.

Born, Max. *The Born-Einstein Letters*. New York: Walker, 1971.

Brakke, David. "The Problematization of Nocturnal Emissions in Early Christian Syria, Egypt, and Gaul." *Journal of Early Christian Studies* 3, no. 4 (1995): 419–460.

Brandom, Robert B. *A Spirit of Trust: A Reading of Hegel's Phenomenology*. Cambridge, MA: Harvard University Press, 2019.

Brewster, Ernest Billings. "The Yoga of Dying: Xuanzang on the Nature of Death." PhD diss., Harvard University, 2018.

Bronkhorst, Johannes. *Buddhist Teaching in India*. Somerville, MA: Wisdom Publications, 2009.

——. *Karma and Teleology: A Problem and Its Solutions in Indian Philosophy*. Tokyo: International Institute for Buddhist Studies, 2000.

——. "On the Nature of pradhāna." In *Expanding and Merging Horizons: Contributions to South Asian and Cross-Cultural Studies in Commemoration of Wilhelm Halbfass*, ed. Karin Preisendanz, 373–381. Vienna: Austrian Academy of Sciences Press, 2007.

Brown, Peter. *The Body and Society: Men, Women and Sexual Renunciation in Early Christianity*. New York: Columbia University Press, 2008.

Brunnhölzl, Karl. *A Compendium of the Mahāyāna: Asaṅga's Mahāyānasaṃgraha and Its Indian Commentaries*. 3 vols. Boulder, CO: Snow Lion, 2018.

Buescher, H. "Distinguishing the Two Vasubandhus, the Bhāṣyakāra and the Kośakāra, as Vijñānavāda-Yogācāra Authors." In *The Foundation for Yoga Practitioners*, ed. U. T. Kragh, 368–396. Cambridge, MA: Harvard University Department of South Asian Studies, 2013.

——. *Sthiramati's Triṃśikāvijñaptibhāṣya: Critical Editions of the Sanskrit Text and Its Tibetan Translation*. Vienna: Verlag der Österreichischen Akademie der Wissenschaften, 2007.

Burge, Tyler. "Individualism and Self-Knowledge." *Journal of Philosophy* 85, no. 11 (November 1988): 649–663.

——. "Individualism and the Mental." *Midwest Studies in Philosophy* 4, no. 1 (September 1979): 73–121.

Burnyeat, Myles. "Idealism and Greek Philosophy: What Descartes Saw and Berkeley Missed." *Philosophical Review* 91, no. 1 (January 1982): 3–40.

——. *The Theaetetus of Plato*. Indianapolis, IN: Hackett, 1990.

Buswell Jr., Robert E., and Donald S. Lopez Jr. *The Princeton Dictionary of Buddhism*. Princeton, NJ: Princeton University Press, 2014.

Cabezón, José Ignacio. *Dose of Emptiness: An Annotated Translation of the "Stong Thun Chen Mo" of Mkhas Grub Dge Legs Dpal Bzang.* New York: State University of New York Press, 1998.

—. *Sexuality in Classical South Asian Buddhism.* Somerville, MA: Wisdom Publications, 2017.

—. "Vasubandhu's *Vyākhyāyukti* on the Authenticity of the Mahāyāna Sūtras." In *Texts in Context: Traditional Hermeneutics in South Asia*, ed. Jeffrey R. Timm, 221–243. Albany, NY: State University of New York, 1992.

Campany, Robert Ford. *The Chinese Dreamscape: 300 BCE–800 CE.* Harvard-Yenching Institute Monograph Series 122. Cambridge, MA: Harvard University Asia Center, 2020.

Carpenter, Amber D. "Persons Keeping Their Karma Together: The Reasons for the Pudgalavāda in Early Buddhism." In *The Moon Points Back*, ed. Koji Tanaka, Yasuo Deguchi, Jay L. Garfield, and Graham Priest, 1–45. New York: Oxford University Press, 2015.

—. "Transformative Vision: Coming to See the Buddha's Reality." In *Buddhist Literature as Philosophy, Buddhist Philosophy as Literature*, ed. Rafal K. Stepien, 35–61. Albany: State University of New York Press, 2020.

Chakrabarti, Arindam. "Dream and Love at the Edge of Wisdom: A Contemporary Cross-Cultural Remapping of Vedānta." In *The Bloomsbury Research Handbook of Vedānta*, ed. Ayon Maharaj, 445–472. London: Bloomsbury Academic, 2020.

Chalmers, David. "The Virtual and the Real." *Disputatio* 9, no. 46 (2017): 309–352.

Chapple, Christopher Key, and Arindam Chakrabarti, eds. *Mind, Morals, and Make-Believe in the Mokṣopāya (Yogavāsiṣṭha).* Albany: State University of New York Press, 2015.

Chatterji, A. K. *The Yogācāra Idealism.* Varanasi: Banaras Hindu University, 1962.

Chu, Junjie. "A Study of Satimira in Dignāga's Definition of Pseudo-Perception (PS 1.7cd–8ab)." *Wiener Zeitschrift für die Kunde Südasiens* 48 (2004): 113–149.

Clark, Andy. *Being There: Putting Brain, Body, and World Together Again.* Cambridge, MA: MIT Press, 1997.

Cleary, Thomas, trans. *The Flower Ornament of Scripture: A Translation of the Avatamsaka Sutra.* Boulder, CO: Shambhala, 1993.

Collins, Steven. "The Body in Theravāda Monasticism." In *Religion and the Body*, ed. Sara Coakley, 185–204. Cambridge: Cambridge University Press, 1997.

—. *Nirvana and Other Buddhist Felicities: Utopias of the Pali Imaginaire.* Cambridge: Cambridge University Press, 1998.

—. *Self and Society: Essays on Pali Literature and Social Theory: 1988–2010.* Chiang Mai: Silkworm Books, 2013.

Conze, Edward. *The Large Sutra on Perfect Wisdom with the Divisions of the Abhisamayālaṅkāra.* Delhi: Motilal Banarsidass, 1979.

Corless, Roger, Takahiko Kameyama, and Richard K. Payne. "A Commentary on *The Upadeśa on the Sutras of Limitless Life with Gāthās on the Resolution to be Born* Composed by the Bodhisattva Vasubandhu." *Pacific World* 17 (2015): 69–235.

Cox, Collett. *Disputed Dharmas: Early Buddhist Theories of Existence: An Annotated Translation of the Section on Factors Dissociated from Thought from Saṅghabhadra's* Nyāyānusāra. Tokyo: International Institute for Buddhist Studies, 1995.

—. "On the Possibility of a Non-Existent Object of Consciousness: Sārvāstivādin and Dārṣṭāntika Theorie." *Journal of the International Association of Buddhist Studies* 11, no. 1 (1988): 31–89.

——. "The Unbroken Treatise: Scripture and Argument in Early Buddhist Scholasticism." In *Innovations in Religious Traditions: Essays in the Interpretation of Religious Change*, ed. Michael A. Williams, Collett Cox, and Martin Jaffee, 143–190. Berlin: Mouton De Gruyter, 1992.

Cozort, Daniel. *Unique Tenets of the Middle Way Consequence School.* Ithaca, NY: Snow Lion, 1998.

Curley, Edwin. "Dialogues with the Dead." *Synthese* 67, no. 1 (1986): 33–49.

Darwin, Charles. *Darwin.*, ed. Philip Appleman. New York: W. W. Norton, 1970.

Davids, Rhys. *The Questions of King Milinda, Part I.* Oxford: Clarendon Press, 1890.

Davis, Bret W. "The Philosophy of Zen Master Dōgen: Egoless Perspectivism." In *The Oxford Handbook of World Philosophy*, ed. William Edelglass and Jay L. Garfield, 348–361. Oxford: Oxford University Press, 2011.

Declos, Alexandre. "Goodman's Many Worlds." *Journal for the History of Analytical Philosophy* 7, no. 6 (2019): https://doi.org/10.15173/jhap.v7i6.3827.

Descartes, René. *Meditations on First Philosophy: With Selections from the Objections and Replies*, ed. John Cottingham. Cambridge: Cambridge University Press, 1996.

Des Chene, Dennis. *Physiologia: Natural Philosophy in Late Aristotelian and Cartesian Thought.* Ithaca, NY: Cornell University Press, 1996.

Dessein, Bart. "Of Tempted Arhats and Supermundane Buddhas: Abhidharma in the Krishna Region." In *Buddhism in the Krishna River Valley of Andhra*, ed. Sree Padma Holt and A. W. Barber, 41–80. Albany: State University of New York Press, 2008.

Dhammajoti, K. L. *Abhidharma Doctrines and Controversies on Perception.* Hong Kong: Centre of Buddhist Studies, University of Hong Kong, 2007.

——. "Ākāra and Direct Perception (pratyakṣa)." *Pacific World Journal* 3 (2007): 245–272.

——. *Entrance into the Supreme Doctrine: Skandhila's Abhidharmāvatāra*. Hong Kong: University of Hong Kong, 2008.

Dodds, E. R. *The Greeks and the Irrational.* Berkeley: University of California Press, 1951.

Dōgen. *Moon in a Dewdrop: Writings of Zen Master Dōgen*, ed. Kazuaki Tanahashi. New York: North Point Press, 1985.

——. "The Mountains and Rivers Sutra," trans. Carl Bielefeldt. https://zmm.org/wp-content/uploads/2020/02/Mountains-and-Rivers-Sutra-Bielefeldt-Translation.pdf.

Doniger O'Flaherty, Wendy. "The Dream Narrative and the Indian Doctrine of Illusion." *Daedalus* 111, no. 3 (Summer 1982): 93–113.

——. *Dreams, Illusions and Other Realities.* Chicago: University of Chicago Press, 1984.

——. *The Hindus: An Alternative History.* New York: Penguin, 2009.

——, ed. *Karma and Rebirth in Classical Indian Traditions.* Berkeley: University of California Press, 1980.

Dowling, Thomas Lee. "Vasubandhu on the Avijñapti-Rūpa: A Study in Fifth-Century Abhidharma Buddhism." PhD diss., Columbia University, 1976.

Dreyfus, Hubert L. "Intelligence Without Representation—Merleau-Ponty's Critique of Mental Representation: The Relevance of Phenomenology to Scientific Explanation." *Phenomenology and the Cognitive Sciences* 1 (2002): 367–383.

Dreyfus, Hubert, and Charles Taylor. *Retrieving Realism.* Cambridge, MA: Harvard University Press, 2015.

D'Sa, Francis X. *Śabdapramāṇyam in Śabara and Kumārila: Towards a Study of the Mīmāṃsā Experience of Language*. Vienna: Indologisches Institut der Universität Wien, 1980.

Dummett, Michael. *Truth and the Past*. New York: Columbia University Press, 2004.

Dunne, John D. *Foundations of Dharmakīrti's Philosophy*. Somerville, MA: Wisdom Publications, 2004.

Dupré, John. "The Lure of the Simplistic." *Philosophy of Science* 69, no. S3 (September 2002): https://doi.org/10.1086/341852.

Eckel, Malcolm David. *Bhāviveka and His Buddhist Opponents*. Harvard Oriental Series 70. Cambridge, MA: Harvard University Department of South Asian Studies, 2009.

——. "Bhavaviveka's Critique of Yogācāra Philosophy in Chapter XXV of the *Prajñapradīpa*." In *Miscellanea Buddhica*, ed. C. Lindtner, 25–75. Copenhagen: Akademisk Forlag, 1985.

——. *To See the Buddha: A Philosopher's Quest for the Meaning of Emptiness*. Princeton, NJ: Princeton University Press, 1992.

Eggen, Nora S. "A Multiverse of Knowledge: The Epistemology and Hermeneutics of the *'ālam* in Medieval Islamic Thought." In *Conceptualizing the World: An Exploration Across Disciplines*, ed. Helge Jordheim and Erling Sandmo, 40–53. New York: Berghahn Books, 2019.

Eltschinger, Vincent. *Caste and Buddhist Philosophy: Continuity of Some Buddhist Arguments Against the Realist Interpretation of Social Denominations*. Delhi: Motilal Banarsidass, 2012.

——. "Turning Hermeneutics into Apologetics—Reasoning and Rationality Under Changing Historical Circumstances." In *Scriptural Authority, Reason and Action*, ed. Vincent Eltschinger and Helmut Krasser. Vienna: Österreichischen Akademie der Wissenschaften, 2013.

Engle, Artemus B. *The Bodhisattva Path to Unsurpassed Enlightenment: A Complete Translation of the Bodhisattvabhūmi*. Boulder, CO: Snow Lion, 2016.

——. *The Inner Science of Buddhist Practice: Vasubandhu's Summary of the Five Heaps with Commentary by Sthiramati*. Ithaca, NY: Snow Lion, 2009.

Epicurus. *Epicurus: The Art of Happiness*, trans. George K. Strodach, foreword by Daniel Klein. New York: Penguin, 2012.

Feldman, Joel. "Vasubandhu's Illusion Argument and Parasitism of Illusion upon Veridical Experience." *Philosophy East and West* 55, no. 4 (October 2005): 529–541.

Ferris, Timothy. *The Whole Shebang: A State-of-the-Universe(s) Report*. New York: Simon and Schuster, 1997.

Feyerabend, Paul. *Philosophy of Nature*. Cambridge: Polity, 2018.

Fine, Kit. "Guide to Ground." In *Metaphysical Grounding*, ed. Fabrice Correia and Benjamin Schneider, 37–80. Cambridge: Cambridge University Press, 2012.

——. "The Question of Realism." *Philosophers' Imprint* 1 (2001): 1–30.

Forster, Michael. "On the Very Idea of Denying the Existence of Radically Different Conceptual Schemes." *Inquiry* 41 (1998): 133–185.

——. *Wittgenstein on the Arbitrariness of Grammar*. Princeton, NJ: Princeton University Press, 2004.

Frauwallner, Erich. "Dignāga's Ālambanaparīkṣā." In *Kleine Schriften*, 340–358. Wiesbaden: Franz Steiner Verlag, 1982.

——. "Vasubandhu's Vādavidhiḥ." *Wiener Zeitschrift für die Kunde Süd-Und Ostasiens und Archiv Für Indische Philosophie* 1 (1957): 104–147.

Freschi, Elisa. "Veṅkaṭanātha's Engagement with Buddhist Opponents in the Buddhist Texts He Reused." *Buddhist Studies Review* 33, no. 1–2 (2016): 65–99.

Friedmann, David Lasar. *Madhyāntavibhāgaṭīkā: Analysis of the Middle Path and the Extremes*. Utrecht: 1937.

Ganeri, Jonardon. *Attention, Not Self.* Oxford: Oxford University Press, 2017.

——. *The Concealed Art of the Soul: Theories of Self and Practices of Truth in Indian Ethics and Epistemology.* Oxford: Oxford University Press, 2012.

——. "Emergentisms, Ancient and Modern." *Mind* 120, no. 479 (July 2011): 671–703.

——. *The Self: Naturalism, Consciousness, and the First-Person Stance.* Oxford: Oxford University Press, 2012.

——. "Subjectivity, Selfhood and the Use of the Word 'I.'" In *Self, No Self? Perspectives from Analytical, Phenomenological, and Indian Traditions*, ed. Mark Siderits, Evan Thompson, and Dan Zahavi, 176–192. Oxford: Oxford University Press, 2010.

Gethin, Rupert. "Cosmology and Meditation: From the Āgañña-sutta to the Mahāyāna." *History of Religions* 36, no. 3 (1997): 183–217.

Giác, Thích Mãn. *The Philosophy of Vasubandhu.* Los Angeles: College of Buddhist Studies, 1989.

Gibson, J. J. *The Ecological Approach to Visual Perception.* Boston: Houghton Mifflin, 1986.

——. "A Preliminary Description and Classification of Affordances." In *Reasons for Realism*, ed. E. S. Reed and R. Jones, 403–406. Hillsdale, NJ: Lawrence Erlbaum Associates, 1982.

Godfrey-Smith, Peter. *Other Minds: The Octopus, the Sea, and the Deep Origins of Consciousness.* New York: Farrar, Straus and Giroux, 2017.

Gold, Jonathan C. "No Outside, No Inside: Duality, Reality and Vasubandhu's Illusory Elephant." *Asian Philosophy* 16 (2006): 1–38.

——. *Paving the Great Way: Vasubandhu's Unifying Buddhist Philosophy.* New York: Columbia University Press, 2015.

Gōmez, Luis O. *The Land of Bliss: The Paradise of the Buddha of Measureless Light: Sanskrit and Chinese Versions of the Sukhāvatīvyūha Sutras.* Delhi: Motilal Banarsidas, 2002.

Goodman, Nelson. *The Structure of Appearance.* Cambridge, MA: Harvard University Press, 1951.

Gould, Stephen Jay. "Challenges to Neo-Darwinism and Their Meaning for a Revised View of Human Consciousness." Tanner Lectures on Human Values, Clare Hall, Cambridge, April 30 and May 1, 1984. www.tannerlectures.utah.edu.

——. *Ever Since Darwin: Reflections in Natural History.* New York: W. W. Norton, 1979.

Griffiths, Paul J. "Buddha and God: A Contrastive Study in Ideas of Maximal Greatness." In *Indian Philosophy: Philosophy of Religion*, ed. Roy W. Perrett, 132–159. New York: Routledge, 2001.

——. "Buddhist Hybrid English: Some Notes on Philology and Hermeneutics for Buddhologists." *Journal of the International Association of Buddhist Studies* 4, no. 2 (1981): 17–33.

——. "Notes Towards a Critique of Buddhist Karmic Theory." *Religious Studies* 18, no. 3 (1982): 277–291.

——. *On Being Buddha: The Classical Doctrine of Buddhahood.* Albany: State University of New York Press, 1994.

——. *On Being Mindless: Buddhist Meditation and the Mind-Body Problem.* LaSalle, IL: Open Court Press, 1991.

Gummer, Natalie D. "Sacrificial Sūtras: Mahāyāna Literature and the South Asian Ritual Cosmos." *Journal of the American Academy of Religion* 82, no. 4 (December 2014): 1091–1126.

Hacking, Ian. *Historical Ontology.* Cambridge, MA: Harvard University Press, 2002.

Hadot, Pierre. *Philosophy as a Way of Life*, ed. Arnold I. Davidson. Oxford: Blackwell, 1995.

Hahn, Michael. *Invitation to Enlightenment*. Berkeley, CA: Dharma Publishing, 1998.

Hall, Bruce Cameron. "The Meaning of Vijñapti in Vasubandhu's Concept of Mind." *Journal of the International Association of Buddhist Studies* 9, no. 1 (1986): 7–23.

——. "Vasubandhu on Aggregates, Spheres, and Components: Being Chapter One of the Abhidharmakośa." PhD diss., Harvard University, 1983.

Hanneder, Jürgen. "Vasubandhus Viṃśaikā 1–2 anhand der Sanskrit-und tibetischen Fassungen." In *Indica et Tibetica: Festschrift für Michael Hahn*, ed. Konrad Klaus and Jens-Uwe Hartmann, 207–215. Vienna: Wiener Studien Zur Tibetologie und Buddhismuskunde, 2007.

Harper, Kyle. *From Shame to Sin: The Christian Transformation of Sexual Morality in Late Antiquity*. Cambridge, MA: Harvard University Press, 2013.

Harrison, Paul. "Mediums and Messages: Reflections on the Production of Mahāyāna Sūtras." *Eastern Buddhist* 35, no. 1/2 (2003): 115–161.

Harrison, Timothy M. *Coming To: Consciousness and Natality in Early Modern England*. Chicago: University of Chicago Press, 2020.

Hartfield, Gary. "Transparency of Mind: The Contributions of Descartes, Leibniz, and Berkeley to the Genesis of the Modern Subject." In *Departure for Modern Europe: A Handbook of Early Modern Philosophy (1400–1700)*, ed. Hubertus Busche, 361–375. Leipzig: Felix Meiner Verlag, 2011.

Haslanger, Sally. "What Is a (Social) Structural Explanation?" *Philosophical Studies* 173 (2016): 113–130.

Hattori, Masaaki. "*Bāhyārthasiddhi* of Śubhagupta." *Journal of Indian and Buddhist Studies* 8, no.1 (1960): 395–400.

——. *Dignāga, On Perception: Being the Pratyakṣapariccheda of Dignāga's Pramāṇasamuccaya*. Cambridge, MA: Harvard University Press, 1968.

——. "The Dream Simile in Vijñānavāda Treatises." In *Indological and Buddhist Studies: Volume in Honor of Professor J. W. de Jong on His Sixtieth Birthday*, ed. A. L. Hercus et al., 235–241. Canberra: Australian National University, Faculty of Asian Studies, 1982.

Haugeland, John. *Dasein Disclosed: John Haugeland's Heidegger*. Cambridge, MA: Harvard University Press, 2013.

Hayashi, Keijin. "The Term 'True Dream (Satyasvapna)' in the Buddhist Epistemological Tradition." *Journal of Indian Philosophy* 29 (2001): 559–574.

Hayes, Richard P. "Principled Atheism in the Buddhist Scholastic Tradition." *Journal of Indian Philosophy* 16 (1988): 5–28.

——. "Whose Experience Validates What for Dharmakīrti?" In *Relativism, Suffering and Beyond: Essays in Memory of Bimal K. Matilal*, ed. Purushottama Bilimoria and J. N. Mohanty, 105–118. Delhi: Oxford University Press, 1997.

Heidegger, Martin. *Being and Time*, trans. John Macquarrie and Edward Robinson. New York: Harper Perennial, 2008.

Heim, Maria. *Voice of the Buddha: Buddhaghosa on the Immeasurable Words*. New York: Oxford University Press, 2018.

Heim, Michael. *Virtual Realism*. New York: Oxford University Press, 1998.

Hilbert, David. "Hallucination, Sense Data and Direct Realism." *Philosophical Studies* 120 (2004): 185–191.

Hobbes, Thomas. *Leviathan*, ed. J. C. A. Gaskin. New York: Oxford University Press, 1998.

Huebner, Bryce. "The Interdependence and Emptiness of Whiteness." In *Buddhism and Whiteness: Critical Reflections*, eds. George Yancy and Emily McRae, 229–251. Lanham, MD: Lexington Books, 2019.

Huber, Édouard. *Sūtrālamkāra, Traduit en Français sur la version Chinoise de Kumārajīva*. Paris: Leroux, 1908.

Huntington, Eric. *Creating the Universe: Depictions of the Cosmos in Himalayan Buddhism*. Seattle: University of Washington Press, 2019.

Inami, M. "Nondual Cognition." In *Religion and Logic in Buddhist Philosophical Analysis*, ed. H. Lasic, E. Franco, and B. Kellner, 177–196. Vienna: Verlag der Österreichischen Akademie der Wissenschaften, 2011.

Inwood, Michael. *Heidegger: A Very Short Introduction*. Oxford: Oxford University Press, 2000.

Irwin, Robert. *Night and Horses and the Desert: An Anthology of Classical Arabic Literature*. Woodstock, NY: Overlook Press, 2002.

Jackson, A. V. Williams. *Vāsavadattā: A Sanskrit Romance*. New York: Columbia University, 1913.

Jacobi, Hermann. *Jaina Sūtras*, trans. Hermann Jacobi. 2 vols. Delhi: Motilal Banarsidass, 1964.

Jaini, P. S. "On the Sarvajñatva (Omniscience) of Mahāvīra and the Buddha." In *Buddhist Studies in Honor of I. B. Horner*, ed. Lance Cousins, 71–90. Dordrecht: Reidel, 1974.

Jha, Ganganath. *Gautama's Nyāyasūtras (With Vātsyāyana-Bhāṣya)*. Poona: Oriental Book Agency, 1939.

——. *Slokavarttika: Translated from the Sanskrit with Extracts from the Commentaries Kasika of Sucarita Misra and Nyayaratnakara of Partha Sarthi Misra*. Delhi: Sri Satguru Publications, 1983.

Johnston, Mark. "The Authority of Affect." *Philosophy and Phenomenological Research* 63, no.1 (July 2001): 181–214.

——. *Saving God: Religion After Idolatry*. Princeton, NJ: Princeton University Press, 2009.

Jones, Ernest. *Sigmund Freud: Life and Work*. 3 vols. London: Hogarth, 1953–1957.

Jones, J. J. *The Mahāvastu*. 3 vols. London: Luzac, 1949.

Kachru, Sonam. "As If a Stage: Towards an Ecological Concept of Thought in Indian Buddhist Philosophy." *Journal of World Philosophies* 5, no. 1 (2020): 1–29.

——. "Dream Argument." In *The Encyclopedia of Philosophy of Religion*, ed. Stewart Goetz and Charles Taliaferro. New York: John Wiley, forthcoming.

——. "The Mind in Pain: The View from Buddhist Systematic and Narrative Thought." In *The Bloomsbury Research Handbook of Emotions in Classical Indian Philosophy*, ed. Maria Heim, Chakravarthi Ram-Prasad, and Roy Tzohar. London: Bloomsbury Academic, forthcoming.

——. "Minds and Worlds: A Philosophical Commentary on Vasubandhu's Twenty Verses." PhD diss., University of Chicago, 2015.

——. "Ratnakīrti and the Extent of Inner Space: An Essay on Yogācāra and the Threat of Genuine Solipsism." *Sophia* 58, no. 1 (2019): 61–83.

——. "Things You Wouldn't Think to Look for in One Place: A Note on an All-Too-Brief Example on Life and Matter in Abhidharmakośabhāṣyam ad 3.14c." *Journal of the American Oriental Society* 137, no. 4 (2017): 669–678.

——. "The Traces of the World in the Tracks of the Philosophers." In *Reasons and Lives in Buddhist Traditions: Studies in Honor of Matthew Kapstein*, ed. Dan Arnold, Cécile Ducher, and Pierre-Julien Harter, 323–338. Somerville, MA: Wisdom Publications, 2019.

Kagan, Shelly. *How to Count Animals, More or Less*. Oxford: Oxford University Press, 2019.

Kant, Immanuel. "What Does It Mean to Orient Oneself in Thinking?" In *Religion Within the Boundaries of Mere Reason, and Other Writings*, ed. Allen Wood and George di Giovanni, 1–15. Cambridge: Cambridge University Press, 1998.

Kapstein, Matthew T. "Buddhist Idealists and Their Jain Critics on Our Knowledge of External Objects." *Royal Institute of Philosophy Supplement* 74 (2014): 123–147.

——. *Reason's Traces: Identity and Interpretation in Indian and Tibetan Buddhist Thought*. Somerville, MA: Wisdom Publications, 2001.

——. "Stoics and Bodhisattvas: Spiritual Exercise and Faith in Two Philosophical Traditions." In *Philosophy as a Way of Life, Ancients and Moderns: Essays in Honor of Pierre Hadot*, ed. M. Chase, S. R. L. Clark, and M. McGhee, 99–115. Oxford: Wiley-Blackwell, 2013.

——. "Who Wrote the Trisvabhāvanirdeśa? Reflections on an Enigmatic Text and Its Place in the History of Buddhist Philosophy." *Journal of Indian Philosophy* 46, no. 1 (2018): 1–30.

Keenan, John P. *The Summary of the Great Vehicle*. Berkeley, CA: Numata Center for Buddhist Translation and Research, 2003.

Keene, Donald. *A History of Japanese Literature: World Within Walls, Japanese Literature of the Pre-Modern Era, 1600–1867*. New York: Columbia University Press, 1999.

Kellner, Birgit. "Changing Frames in Buddhist Thought: The Concept of Ākāra in Abhidharma and in Buddhist Epistemological Analysis." *Journal of Indian Philosophy* 42 (2014): 275–295.

Kellner, Birgit, and John Taber. "Studies in Yogācāra-Vijñānavāda Idealism I: The Interpretation of Vasubandhu's *Viṃśikā*." *Asiatische Studien* 68, no. 3 (2014): 709–756.

Kimhi, Irad. "Causation and Non-Reductionism." PhD diss., University of Pittsburgh, 1993.

Kinga, Elselijn. "Were You a Part of Your Mother?" *Mind* 128, no. 511 (July 2019): 609–646.

Kobayashi, Hisayasu. "On the Development of the Argument to Prove Vijñaptimātratā." In *Religion and Logic in Buddhist Philosophical Analysis: Proceedings of the Fourth International Dharmakīrti Conference*, ed. Helmut Krasser, Horst Lasic, Eli Franco, and Birgit Kellner, 299–308. Vienna: Verlag der Österreichischen Akademie der Wissenschaften, 2011.

——. "Prajñākaragupta on the Two Truths and Argumentation." *Journal of Indian Philosophy* 39 (2011): 427–439.

Kolakowski, Leszek. *Is God Happy? Selected Essays*. New York: Penguin, 2012.

——. *Main Currents of Marxism*. New York: W. W. Norton, 2005.

——. *Metaphysical Horror*. Chicago: University of Chicago Press, 2001.

——. *The Presence of Myth*, trans. Adam Czerniawski. Chicago: University of Chicago Press, 1989.

Kramer, Jowita. "Descriptions of 'Feeling' (*vedanā*), 'Ideation' (*saṃjñā*), and 'the Unconditioned' (*asaṃskṛta*) in Vasubandhu's *Pañcaskandhaka* and Sthiramati's *Pañcaskandhakavibhāṣā*." *Rocznik Orientalistyczny* 65, no. 1 (2012): 120–139.

——. "Some Remarks on the Proofs of the Store Mind (*Ālayavijñāna*) and the Development of the Concept of *Manas*." In *Text, History, and Philosophy*, ed. Bart Dessein and Weijen Teng, 146–169. Leiden: Brill, 2016.

Kritzer, Robert. "Rūpa and the Antarābhava." *Journal of Indian Philosophy* 28 (2000): 235–272.

——. "Semen, Blood and the Intermediate Existence." *Journal of Indian and Buddhist Studies* 46, no. 2 (March 1988): 30–36.

——. "Unthinkable Matters: The Term *acintya* in the Abhidharmakośabhāṣya," in *Early Buddhism and Abhidharma Thought: In Honor of Doctor Hajime Sakurabe on His Seventy-Seventh Birthday*, ed. Sakurabe Ronshu Committee, 65–86. Kyoto: Heirakuji Shoten, 2002.

Kuhn, Thomas S. "A Function for Thought Experiments." In *The Essential Tension: Selected Studies in Scientific Tradition and Change*, 240–265. Chicago: University of Chicago Press, 1964.

——. *The Structure of Scientific Revolutions*. 2nd ed. Chicago: University of Chicago Press, 1970.

Lamotte, Étienne. *Le Traité de la Grande Vertu de Sagesse de Nāgārjuna* (*Mahāprajñāpāramitāśāstra*). Vol. 2, *Chapitres 16–30*. Louvain: Publications de l'Institut Orientaliste de Louvain, 1981 [1949].

——. *Mahāyānasaṃgraha, La Somme du Grand Véhicule d'Asaṅga, Volume II: Translation and Commentary*. Louvain: Bureaux du Muséon, 1938–1939.

Langenberg, Amy Paris. *Birth in Buddhism: The Suffering Fetus and Female Freedom*. London: Routledge, 2017.

——. "Love, Unknowing, and Female Filth: The Buddhist Discourse of Birth as a Vector of Social Change for Monastic Women in Premodern South Asia." In *Primary Sources and Asian Pasts*, ed. Peter C. Bishop and Elizabeth A. Cecil, 308–340. Berlin: Walter de Gruyter, 2020.

La Vallée Poussin, Louis de. "The Five Points of Mahādeva and the Kathāvatthu." *Journal of the Royal Asiatic Society* 1, no. 42 (1910): 413–423.

Lawrence, Bruce B. *Shahrastani on the Indian Religions*. The Hague: De Gruyter Mouton, 2012.

Lear, Jonathan. "Leaving the World Alone." *Journal of Philosophy* 79 (1982): 382–403.

——. *Wisdom Won from Illness: Essays in Philosophy and Psychoanalysis* (Cambridge, MA: Harvard University Press, 2017.

Lennon, Thomas M. "Locke on Ideas and Representation." In *The Cambridge Companion to Locke's "Essay Concerning Human Understanding,"* ed. L. Newman, 231–257. Cambridge: Cambridge University Press, 2007.

Lévi, Sylvain. "Notes Indiennes. I: Deux notes sur la Viṃśatikā de Vasubandhu: 1. La défaite de Vemacitra; 2. Un fragment de l'Upāli sutra en Sanscrit." *Journal Asiatique* 206 (1925): 17–35.

——. *Un système de philosophie bouddhique: Matériaux pour l'étude du système Vijñāptimātra*. Paris: Honoré Champion, 1932.

Lin, Qian. "Mind in Dispute: The Section on Mind in Harivarman's *Tattvasiddhi." PhD diss. University of Washington, 2015.

Lincoln, Bruce. "'The Earth Becomes Flat': A Study of Apocalyptic Imagery." *Comparative Studies in Society and History* 25, no. 1 (January 1983): 136–153.

Locke, John. *An Essay Concerning Human Understanding*, ed. Peter H. Nidditch. Oxford: Clarendon Press, 1979.

Loncar, Samuel. "Decolonizing Philosophy: Samuel Loncar Interviews Carlos Fraenkel and Peter Adamson About Islam, Reason, and Religion." *Marginalia*, December 21, 2018, https://marginalia.lareviewofbooks.org/decolonizing-philosophy-samuel-loncar-interviews-carlos-fraenkel-peter-adamson-islam-reason-religion/.

Lusthaus, Dan. *Buddhist Phenomenology: A Philosophical Investigation of Yogācāra Buddhism and the Ch'eng Wei-Shih Lun*. London: Routledge, 2002.

Mabbett, I. W. "The Symbolism of Mount Meru." *History of Religions* 23, no. 1 (August 1983): 64–83.

Macdonald, Margaret. "Sleeping and Waking." In *Journey into Philosophy: An Introduction with Classic and Contemporary Readings*, ed. Stan Baronett, 80–90. New York: Routledge, 2017.

MacKenzie, Matthew. "Enacting Selves, Enacting Worlds: On the Buddhist Theory of Karma." *Philosophy East and West* 63, no. 2 (April 2013), 194–212.

——. "Enacting the Self: Buddhist and Enactivist Approaches to the Emergence of the Self." *Phenomenology and the Cognitive Sciences* 9, no. 1 (2010): 75–99.

Mair, Victor H. *Wandering on the Way: Early Taoist Tales and Parables of Chuang Tzu*. Honolulu: University of Hawai'i Press, 1998.

Marx, Karl. *Economic and Philosophical Manuscripts of 1884*. Mineola, NY: Dover, 2007.

Matilal, B. K. *Perception: An Essay on Classical Indian Theories of Knowledge*. Oxford: Clarendon Press, 1986.

McClintock, Sara L. "Ethical Reading and the Ethics of Forgetting and Remembering." In *A Mirror Is for Reflection: Understanding Buddhist Ethics*, ed. Jake H. Davis, 185–202. New York: Oxford University Press, 2017.

——. *Omniscience and the Rhetoric of Reason, Śāntarakṣita and Kamalaśīla on Rationality, Argumentation, and Religious Authority*. Somerville, MA: Wisdom Publications, 2010.

McCrea, Lawrence J., and Parimal G. Patil. *Buddhist Philosophy of Language in India: Jñānaśrīmitra on Exclusion*. New York: Columbia University Press, 2010.

McGinn, Colin. *Consciousness and Its Objects*. Oxford: Clarendon Press, 2004.

McGovern, William Montgomery. *A Manual of Buddhist Philosophy*. Vol. 1, *Cosmology*. London: Kegan Paul, Trench and Trubner, 1923.

McLaughlin, Brian, and Karen Bennett. "Supervenience." In *Stanford Encyclopedia of Philosophy*, ed. Edward N. Zalta. Stanford University, Winter 2018 edition. https://plato.stanford.edu/archives/win2018/entries/supervenience/.

McNicholl, Adeana S. "Celestial Seductresses and Hungry Ghosts: Preta Narratives in Early Indian Buddhism." PhD diss., Stanford University, 2019.

Mencius. *Mencius*, trans. D. C. Lau. New York: Penguin Classics, 2004.

Menn, Stephen. *Descartes and Augustine*. Cambridge: Cambridge University Press, 1998.

Merleau-Ponty, M. *Phenomenology of Perception*, trans. Colin Smith. London: Routledge and Kegan Paul, 1962.

Meyers, Karin. "The Dynamics of Intention, Freedom, and Habituation According to Vasubandhu's *Abhidharmakośabhāṣya*." In *A Mirror Is for Reflection: Understanding Buddhist Ethics*, ed. Jake H. Davis, 239–257. New York: Oxford University Press, 2017.

Mills, Ethan. "External-World Skepticism in Classical India: The Case of Vasubandhu." *International Journal for the Study of Skepticism* 7, no. 3 (2017): 147–172.

Minkowski, C. Z. "Ritual Structure." *Journal of the American Oriental Society* 109, no. 3 (1989): 401–420.

Mueller, Gustav E. "The Hegel Legend of 'Thesis-Antithesis-Synthesis.'" *Journal of the History of Ideas* 19, no. 3 (June 1958): 411–414.

Musil, Robert. *The Man Without Qualities*. 2 vols. New York: Vintage International, 1996.

Nabokov, Vladimir. *Transparent Things*. New York: Vintage International, 1989.

Nance, Richard. *Models of Teaching and the Teaching of Models: Contextualizing Indian Buddhist Commentary.* New York: Columbia University Press, 2012.

——. "On What Do We Rely When We Rely on Reasoning?" *Journal of Indian Philosophy* 35, no. 2 (April 2007): 149–167.

Nuttall, A. D. *Dead from the Waist Down: Scholars and Scholarship in Literature and the Popular Imagination.* New Haven, CT: Yale University Press, 2003.

Nyāyavārttika, ed. Vindhyesvariprasad. Benares: Kashi Sanskrit Series, 1916.

Olivelle, Patrick. *The Early Upanisads: Annotated Text and Translation.* New York: Oxford University Press, 1998.

O'Shaughnessy, Brian. *The Will: A Dual Aspect Theory, Volume 2.* Cambridge: Cambridge University Press, 2008.

Owen, Stephen. *Readings in Chinese Literary Thought.* Cambridge, MA: Harvard University Press, 1992.

Park, Changhwan. "The Sautrantika Theory of Seeds (bija) Revisited: With Special Reference to the Ideological Continuity Between Vasubandhu's Theory of Seeds and Its Srilata/Darstantika Precedent." PhD diss., University of California, Berkeley, 2007.

Peterman, Alison. Review of *The Well-Ordered Universe: The Philosophy of Margaret Cavendish*, by Deborah Boyle. *Notre Dame Philosophical Reviews*, March 4, 2019, https://ndpr.nd.edu/news/the-well-ordered-universe-the-philosophy-of-margaret-cavendish/.

Plutarch. "Superstition." In *Moralia*. Vol. 2, trans. Frank Cole Babbit, 452–495. Loeb Classical Library 222. Cambridge, MA: Harvard University Press, 1928.

Pohl, Karl-Heinz. "Continuities and Discontinuities in Chinese Literary Criticism—From the Premodern to the Modern Periods." In *Is a History of Chinese Literature Possible? Towards the Birth of Chinese Literary Criticism*, ed. Wolfgang Kubin, 1–24. Munich: Edition Global, 2013.

Pollock, Sheldon. "Pretextures of Time." *History and Theory* 46, no. 3 (2007): 366–383.

Pradhan, Prahlad. *Abhidharmakośabhāṣya of Vasubandhu.* Patna: K. P. Jayaswal Research Institute, 1967.

Pruden, Leo M., trans. *Abhidharmakosabhasyam of Vasubandhu.* 4 vols. Berkeley, CA: Asian Humanities Press, 1988–1990.

Prueitt, Catherine. "Karmic Imprints, Exclusion, and the Creation of the Worlds of Conventional Experience in Dharmakīrti's Thought." *Sophia* 57, no. 2 (2018): 313–335.

——. "Shifting Concepts: The Realignment of Dharmakīrti on Concepts and the Error of Subject/Object Duality in Pratyabhijñā Śaiva Thought." *Journal of Indian Philosophy* 45 (2017): 21–47.

Putnam, Hilary. *The Threefold Cord: Mind, Body, and World.* New York, Columbia University Press, 1999.

Ram-Prasad, Chakravarthi. "Dreams and Reality: The Śaṅkarite Critique of Vijñānavāda." *Philosophy East and West* 43, no. 3 (July 1993): 405–455.

——. "Dreams and the Coherence of Experience: An Anti-idealist Critique from Classical Indian Philosophy." *American Philosophical Quarterly* 32, no. 3 (1995): 225–239.

Rancière, Jacques. *The Politics of Aesthetics*, trans. Gabriel Rockhill. New York: Continuum, 2004.

Ratié, Isabelle. "The Dreamer and the Yogin: On the Relationship Between Buddhist and Śaiva Idealisms." *Bulletin of the School of Oriental and African Studies* 73, no. 3 (2010): 437–478.

Reeve, C. D. C. *Action, Contemplation and Happiness: An Essay on Aristotle.* Cambridge, MA: Harvard University Press, 2012.

Reiss, John O. *Not by Design: Retiring Darwin's Watchmaker*. Berkeley: University of California Press, 2009.

Rescher, Nicholas. *G. W. Leibniz's Monadology: An Edition for Students*. Pittsburgh, PA: University of Pittsburgh Press, 1991.

Ridley, Mark. *How to Read Darwin*. New York: W. W. Norton, 2005.

Rieff, Philip. *Freud: The Mind of the Moralist*. New York: Viking Press, 1959.

Rinpoché, Kalu. *Jamgön Kongtrul: The Treasury of Knowledge: Book Six, Part Three: Frameworks of Buddhist Philosophy*. Boulder, CO: Snow Lion, 2007.

Rotman, Andy. *Divine Stories: Divyāvadāna, Part 2*. Somerville, MA: Wisdom Publications, 2018.

——. *Hungry Ghosts*. New York: Simon and Schuster, forthcoming.

Russell, Bertrand. *A Critical Exposition of the Philosophy of Leibniz*. London: Allen and Unwin, 1937.

Ryose, Wataru S. "A Study of the *Abhidharmahṛdaya*: The Historical Development of the Concept of Karma in the Sarvāstivāda Thought." PhD diss., University of Wisconsin, 1987.

Sanderson, Alexis. "The Sarvāstivāda and Its Critics: Anātmavāda and the Theory of Karma." In *Buddhism into the Year 2000*, ed. Dhammakaya Foundation, 33–48. Bangkok: Dhammakaya Foundation, 1994.

Sangpo, Gelong Lodrö. *Annotated Translation of Louis de La Vallee Poussin, Abhidharmakośabhāṣya: The Treasury of the Abhidharma and Its (Auto)commentary*. 4 vols. Delhi: Motilal Banarsidass Publishers, 2012.

Sāṅkṛtyāyana, Rāhula. *Pramāṇavārttikabhāṣyam*. Patna: Tibetan Works Series, 1953.

Sartre, Jean-Paul. *No Exit and Three Other Plays*. New York: Vintage International, 1989.

Scharfstein, Ben-Ami. *A Comparative History of World Philosophy from the Upanisads to Kant*. Albany: State University of New York Press, 1998.

Schmithausen, Lambert. "Aspects of Spiritual Practice in Early Yogācāra." *Journal of the International College for Postgraduate Buddhist Studies* 11 (2007): 213–244.

——. *Plants in Early Buddhism and the Far Eastern Idea of the Buddha-Nature of Grasses and Trees*. Lumbini: Lumbini International Research Institute, 2009.

Scholem, Gershom. *Major Trends in Jewish Mysticism*. New York: Shocken Books, 1974.

Sharf, Robert. "Is Nirvāṇa the Same as Insentience? Chinese Struggles with an Indian Buddhist Ideal." In *India in the Chinese Imagination: Myth, Religion, and Thought*, ed. John Kieschnick and Meir Shahar, 141–171. Philadelphia: University of Pennsylvania Press, 2014.

——. "Knowing Blue: Early Buddhist Accounts of Non-Conceptual Sense Perception." *Philosophy East and West* 68, no. 3 (July 2018): 826–870.

Shastri, D. N. *Critique of Indian Realism: The Philosophy of Nyāya-Vaiśeṣika and Its Conflict with the Buddhist Dignāga School*. Delhi: Motilal Banarsidass, 1997.

Shastri, Dvarikadas. *Abhidharmakośa and Bhāṣya of Ācārya Vasubandhu with Sphūtārthā Commentary of Ācārya Yaśomitra*. Varanasi: Bauddha Bharati Press, 1987.

Shea, Nicholas. *Representation in Cognitive Science*. Oxford: Oxford University Press, 2018.

Shulman, David. *More Than Real: A History of the Imagination in South Asia*. Cambridge, MA: Harvard University Press, 2012.

——. "The Scent of Memory in Hindu South India." In *The Smell Culture Reader*, ed. Jim Drobnick, 411–427. Oxford: Berg, 2006.

Shulman, Eviatar. *Rethinking the Buddha: Early Buddhist Philosophy as Meditative Perception.* Cambridge: Cambridge University Press, 2017.

Siderits, Mark. *Buddhism as Philosophy: An Introduction.* London: Ashgate, 2007.

Silk, J. A. *Materials Toward the Study of Vasubandhu's Viṁśikā (I): Sanskrit and Tibetan Critical Editions of the Verses and Autocommentary; An English Translation and Annotations.* Cambridge, MA: Harvard University Department of South Asian Studies, 2016.

Simonsson, N. "Reflections on the Grammatical Tradition in Tibet." In *Indological and Buddhist Studies, Volume in Honour of Professor J. W. de Jong on His Sixtieth Birthday*, ed. L. A. Hercus et al., 531–544. Canberra: Australian National University, Faculty of Asian Studies, 1982.

Smith, Justin E. H. *Divine Machines: Leibniz and the Sciences of Life.* Princeton, NJ: Princeton University Press, 2011.

Smith, Sean M. "A Buddhist Analysis of Affective Bias." *Journal of Indian Philosophy* 1 (2019): 1–31.

Sober, Elliott. "What Is the Problem of Simplicity?" In *Simplicity, Inference, and Modelling*, ed. Arnold Zellner, Hugo A. Keuzenkamp, and Michael McAleer, 13–32. Cambridge: Cambridge University Press, 2002.

Sprigge, Timothy. *James and Bradley: American Truth and British Reality.* Chicago: Open Court, 1993.

Starobinski, Jean. *Montaigne in Motion.* Chicago: University of Chicago Press, 1985.

Strawson, Galen. *Real Materialism and Other Essays.* Oxford: Clarendon Press, 2008.

——. *Selves: An Essay in Revisionary Metaphysics.* Oxford: Oxford University Press, 2011.

Strong, John S. *The Legend and Cult of Upagupta: Sanskrit Buddhism in North India and South East Asia.* Princeton, NJ: Princeton University Press, 1992.

——. *Relics of the Buddha.* Delhi: Motilal Banarsidass Press, 2007.

Stuart, Daniel M. "Becoming Animal: Karma and the Animal Realm Envisioned Through an Early Yogācāra Lens." *Religions* 10, no. 6, (2019): 363, https://doi.org/10.3390/rel10060363.

——. "A Less Traveled Path: Meditation and Textual Practice in the *Saddharmasmrtyupasthana(su tra).*" PhD diss., University of California, Berkeley, 2012.

Sugden, Robert. "Credible Worlds: The Status of Theoretical Models in Economics." *Journal of Economic Methodology* 7, no. 1 (2000): https://doi.org/10.1080/135017800362220.

Sullivan, Peter M. "The Totality of Facts." *Proceedings of the Aristotelian Society* 100 (2000): 175–192.

Swanson, Paul L. *T'ien-T'ai Chih-I's Mo-Ho Chih-Kuan: Clear Serenity, Quiet Insight.* 3 vols. Honolulu: University of Hawai'i Press, 2018.

Taber, John. "Kumārila's Refutation of the Dreaming Argument: The *Nirālambanavāda-adhikaraṇa.*" In *Studies in Mīmāṃsā*, ed. R. C. Dwivedi, 27–52. Delhi: Motilal Banarsidass, 1994.

Tanaka, Kenneth K. "Simultaneous Relation (Sahbhū-hetu): A Study in Buddhist Theory of Causation." *Journal of the International Association of Buddhist Studies* 8, no. 1 (1985): 91–111.

Tat, Wei. *Ch'eng Wei-Shih Lun: Doctrine of Mere Consciousness.* Hong Kong: Ch'eng Wei-Shih Lun Publication Committee, 1973.

Tātparya-ṭīkā, ed. R. S. Dravid. Varanasi: Chowkhamba, 1925.

Taylor, Charle. "Hegel and the Philosophy of Action." In *Hegel on Action*, ed. Arto Laitinen and Constantine Sandis, 22–41. New York: Palgrave-Macmillan, 2010.

Tendzin, Padma. *Suhridlekha.* Varanasi: Central Institute of High Tibetan Studies, 2002.

That, Le Manh. "The Philosophy of Vasubandhu." PhD diss., University of Wisconsin, 1974.

Thompson, Evan. "Jonardon Ganeri's Transcultural Philosophy of Attention." *Philosophy and Phenomenological Research* 101, no. 2 (September 2020): 489–494.

——. *Waking, Dreaming, Being: Self and Consciousness in Neuroscience, Meditation, and Philosophy.* New York: Columbia University Press, 2017.

——. "What's in a Concept: Conceptualizing the Non-Conceptual in Buddhist Philosophy." In *Reasons and Empty Persons: Mind, Metaphysics, and Morality: Essays in Honor of Mark Siderits*, ed. Christian Coseru. London: Springer, forthcoming.

——. *Why I Am Not a Buddhist.* New Haven, CT: Yale University Press, 2020.

Thompson, Michael. "Forms of Nature: 'First,' 'Second,' 'Living,' 'Rational' and 'Phronetic.'" In *Freiheit: Stuttgarter Hegel-Kongress 2011*, ed. Gunnar Hindrichs and Axel Honneth, 701–735. Frankfurt: Vittorio Klostermann, 2013.

——. *Life and Action: Elementary Structures of Practice and Practical Thought.* Cambridge, MA: Harvard University Press, 2012.

Tola, Fernando, and Carmen Dragonetti. *Being as Consciousness: Yogācāra Philosophy of Buddhism.* New Delhi: Motilal Banarsidass, 2004.

Tzohar, Roy. "Imagine Being a Preta: Early Indian Yogācāra Approaches to Intersubjectivity." *Sophia* 56, no. 2 (2017): 337–354.

——. *A Yogācāra Buddhist Theory of Metaphor.* New York: Oxford University Press, 2018.

Ueda, Yoshifumi. "Two Main Streams of Thought in Yogācāra Philosophy." *Philosophy East and West* 17 (1967): 155–165.

Urban, Hugh B., and Paul J. Griffiths. "What Else Remains in Śūnyatā? An Investigation of Terms for Mental Imagery in the Madhyāntavibhāga-Corpus." *Journal of the International Association of Buddhist Studies* 17, no. 1 (1994): 1–26.

Valberg, J. J. *Dream, Death and the Self.* Princeton, NJ: Princeton University Press, 2007.

Van Fraassen, Bas C. "'World' Is Not a Count Noun." *Noûs* 29 (1995): 139–157.

Veber, Michael. "A Different Kind of Dream-Based Skepticism." *Synthese* (2018): https://doi.org/10.1007/s11229-018-01910-2.

Venkatesananda, Swami. *Vasiṣṭha's Yoga.* Albany: State University of New York Press, 1993.

Vintiadis, Elly, and Constantinos Mekios. *Brute Facts.* Oxford: Oxford University Press, 2018.

Von Leyden, W. "Descartes and Hobbes on Waking and Dreaming." *Revue Internationale de Philosophie* 10, no. 1 (1956): 95–101.

Von Rospatt, Alexander. *The Buddhist Doctrine of Momentariness: A Survey of the Origins and Early Phase of This Doctrine Up to Vasubandhu.* Stuttgart: Franz Steiner Verlag, 1995.

Waldron, William S. *The Buddhist Unconscious: The* Ālaya-vijñāna *in the Context of Indian Buddhist Thought.* New York: RoutledgeCurzon, 2003.

——. "How Innovative Is the Ālayavijñāna? The Ālayavijñāna in the Context of Canonical and Abhidharma VijñaanaTheory Part II." *Journal of Indian Philosophy* 23, no. 1 (March 1995): 9–51.

Ward, Dave, David Silverman, and Mario Villalobos. "Introduction: The Varieties of Enactivism." *Topoi* 36 (2017): 365–375.

Westerhoff, Jan. *Twelve Examples of Illusion.* Oxford: Oxford University Press, 2010.

Wezler, Albrecht, and Shujun Motegi. *Yuktidīpikā: The Most Significant Commentary on the Sāṃkhyakārikā.* Stuttgart: Franz Steiner Verlag, 1998.

White, David Gordon. "'Dakkhiṇa' and 'Agnicayana': An Extended Application of Paul Mus's Typology." *History of Religions* 26, no. 2 (November 1986): 188–213.

White, Hayden. "The Value of Narrativity in the Representation of Reality." *Critical Inquiry* 7, no. 1 (Autumn 1980): 5–27.

Whitely, Cecily M. K. "Aphantasia, Imagination and Dreaming." *Philosophical Studies* (September 2020): https://doi.org/10.1007/s11098-020-01526-8.

Wiggins, David. *Sameness and Substance Renewed.* Oxford: Oxford University Press, 2001.

Willemen, Charles, Bart Dessein, and Collett Cox. *Sarvāstivāda Buddhist Scholasticism.* Leiden: Brill, 1998.

Wilson, Catherine. "Vicariousness and Authenticity." In *The Robot in the Garden: Telerobotics and Telepistemology in the Age of the Internet*, ed. Ken Goldberg, 64–90. Cambridge, MA: MIT Press, 2001.

Windt, Jennifer M. *Dreaming: A Conceptual Framework for Philosophy of Mind and Empirical Research.* Cambridge, MA: MIT Press, 2015.

——. "The Immersive Spatiotemporal Hallucination Model of Dreaming." *Phenomenology and the Cognitive Sciences* 9 (2010): 295–316.

——. "Reporting Dream Experience: Why (Not) to Be Skeptical About Dream Reports." *Frontiers in Human Neuroscience* 7, no. 708 (November 2013): https://doi.org/10.3389/fnhum.2013.00708.

Wittgenstein, Ludwig. *The Blue and the Brown Books.* Oxford: Blackwell, 1958.

Wogihara, U., ed. *Sphuṭārthā Abhidharmakośavyākhyā.* Tokyo: Sankibo Buddhist Book Store, 1989.

Wrathall, Mark A. *Unconcealment: Truth, Language, and History.* Cambridge: Cambridge University Press, 2011.

Wright, Charles. *Negative Blue: Selected Later Poems.* New York: Farrar, Strauss and Giroux, 2000.

Yamabe, Noboyoshi. "On the School Affiliation of Aśvaghoṣa: 'Sautrāntika' or 'Yogācāra'?" *Journal of the International Association of Buddhist Studies* 26, no. 2 (2003): 225–255.

Yeh, Ah-Yueh. "The Characteristics of 'Vijñāna' and 'Vijñapti' on the Basis of Vasubandhu's *Pañcaskandhaprakaraṇa.*" *Annals of the Bhandarkar Oriental Research Institute* 60 (1979): 175–198.

Zhi, Li. *A Book to Burn and a Book to Keep (Hidden): Selected Writings*, ed. Rivi Handler-Spitz, Pauline C. Lee, and Haun Saussy. New York: Columbia University Press, 2016.

Zimmerman, Michael. *The Immorality of Punishment.* New York: Broadview Press, 2011.

——. "A Mahāyānist Criticism of *Arthaśāstra*: The Chapter on Royal Ethics in the *Bodhisattvagocaropāya-visaya-vikurvana-nirdeśa-sūtra.*" *Annual Report of the International Research Institute for Advanced Buddhology at Soka University for the Academic Year 1999* 3 (2000): 177–211.

——. "Only a Fool Becomes a King: Buddhist Stances on Punishment." In *Buddhism and Violence*, ed. Michael Zimmerman, 213–242. Lumbini: International Research Institute, 2006.

Zwilling, Leonard, and Michael J. Sweet. "Like a City Ablaze: The Third Sex and the Creation of Sexuality in Jain Religious Literature." *Journal for the History of Sexuality* 6, no. 3 (January 1996): 359–384.

INDEX

CPSIA information can be obtained
at www.ICGtesting.com
Printed in the USA
LVHW100318190622
721593LV00003B/278

9 780231 200011